Psychology

Theoretical–Historical Perspectives

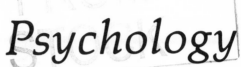

Psychology
Theoretical–Historical Perspectives

EDITED BY

R. W. RIEBER

John Jay College
City University of New York
New York, New York

College of Physicians and Surgeons
Columbia University
New York, New York

KURT SALZINGER

New York State Psychiatric Institute
New York, New York

Polytechnic Institute of New York
Brooklyn, New York

1980

ACADEMIC PRESS
A Subsidiary of Harcourt Brace Jovanovich, Publishers
New York   London   Toronto   Sydney   San Francisco

ACADEMIC PRESS, INC.
111 Fifth Avenue, New York, New York 10003

United Kingdom Edition published by
ACADEMIC PRESS, INC. (LONDON) LTD.
24/28 Oval Road, London NW1 7DX

Library of Congress Cataloging in Publication Data
Main entry under title:

Psychology, theoretical–historical perspectives.

Based on a conference held under the auspices of the
New York Academy of Sciences.
Includes bibliographies and index.
1. Psychology––History––United States––Congresses.
I. Rieber, Robert W. II. Salzinger, Kurt.
BF95.P77   150'.973   79–6790
ISBN 0–12–588265–3

PRINTED IN THE UNITED STATES OF AMERICA

80 81 82 83   9 8 7 6 5 4 3 2 1

Contents

Part I
Psychology Becomes a Science:
European and Nineteenth Century Influences

1

Part II
Socioeconomic and Political Factors
in the Development of Psychology

Part III
Psychological Systems:
Past, Present, and Future

12

The Assimilation of Psychoanalysis in America   *263*
MAURICE GREEN AND R. W. RIEBER

13

In Tribute to Piaget: A Look at His Scientific Impact
in the United States   *305*
GILBERT VOYAT

14

Genetic Epistemology and Developmental Psychology   *315*
BÄRBEL INHELDER

15

Some Recent Research and Its Link with a New Theory
of Groupings and Conservations Based on Commutability   *329*
JEAN PIAGET

Epilogue

16

List of Contributors

Numbers in parentheses indicate pages on which the author's contributions begin.

HELMUT E. ADLER (11), Department of Psychology, Yeshiva University, New York, New York 10033

DAVID BAKAN (125), Department of Psychology, York University, Downsview, Ontario, Canada M3J 1P3

ARTHUR L. BLUMENTHAL (25), Department of Psychology, University of Massachusetts at Boston, Boston, Massachusetts 02125

JOHN M. BROUGHTON (81), Department of Developmental Psychology, Teachers College, Columbia University, New York, New York 10027

WILLARD F. DAY, JR. (203), Department of Psychology, University of Nevada, Reno, Nevada 89557

SOLOMON DIAMOND (43), Department of Psychology, California State University, Los Angeles, California 90032

MAURICE GREEN (263), College of Physicians and Surgeons, Columbia University, New York, New York 10032

HOWARD E. GRUBER (145), Institute for Cognitive Studies, Rutgers University, Newark, New Jersey 07102

MARY HENLE (177), Department of Psychology, The New School for Social Research, New York, New York 10003

RICHARD P. HIGH (57), Department of Psychology, Lehigh University, Bethlehem, Pennsylvania 18015

BÄRBEL INHELDER (315), Center for Research in Genetic Epistemology, Geneva, Switzerland

JEAN PIAGET (329), Center for Research in Genetic Epistemology, Geneva, Switzerland

R. W. RIEBER (1, 103, 263), Department of Psychology, John Jay College, City University of New York, New York, New York 10019; College of Physicians and Surgeons, Columbia University, New York, New York 10032

KURT SALZINGER* (1, 337), New York State Psychiatric Institute, New York, New York 10032; Polytechnic Institute of New York, Brooklyn, New York 11201

B. F. SKINNER (191), Department of Psychology, Harvard University, Cambridge, Massachusetts 02138

GILBERT VOYAT (305), Department of Psychology, City College, City University of New York, New York, New York 10031

WILLIAM R. WOODWARD (57), Department of Psychology, University of New Hampshire, Durham, New Hampshire 03824

* Presently on leave in the Division of Applied Research, National Science Foundation, Washington, D.C. 20550

Preface

The study of the history of psychology has come into its own at last. Increasing numbers of students as well as professionals in all fields of psychology have begun to study seriously the "roots" of the discipline—the places and times from which it arose. This book is an analysis of these places and times, furnished by the foremost students of the history and by two of the major figures in that history: Skinner and Piaget.

The contributors offer analyses of the three major theoretical currents in psychology, the Geneva school, behaviorism, and psychoanalysis, as well as a description of the oldest part of experimental psychology, psychophysics. Not forgotten is Gestalt psychology, an older theory, the major effect of which can be seen in some of the more recent ferment in cognitive psychology. Furthermore, the authors do not avoid discussion of some of the political ramifications of the field, in the context of its history. Finally, we offer what will no doubt be for many years a significant analysis of the place of Charles Darwin in our current psychological thinking.

It seems unlikely that this book will evoke complete agreement as to the validity of its analyses; in fact, many of the statements will undoubtedly elicit argument. What is important in such controversy, however, is not the particular view expounded by a particular author, although the views are well reasoned, but rather that the chapter raises a problem to be thought about, argued about, and, most important, further investigated. This book constitutes no simple listing of facts, telling us once more when such and such a laboratory was established. It goes far beyond that in supplying us with theories and systematic conceptualizations within which to give meaning to the facts as we know them.

Who should read a book such as this? We believe that both students and scholars in the history of psychology will profit from perusing this book. As we continue on the road of specialization, the need for understanding that we work in a context that influences what we do and what we believe we should do is ever greater. The context can be the scientific one, as evidenced, for example, in the relay switches and their relationship to early behavioristic theories, and the computer and its relationship to cognitive theories of today. The context is also larger than that, however; and we must realize that as academic positions dry up and work in psychology becomes applied, we will change our research, the context in which we work, and, therefore, our history.

This book was inspired by a conference held under the auspices of the New York Academy of Sciences and organized by R. W. Rieber, Kurt Salzinger, and Thom Verhave. The proceedings of that conference were published in the *Annals of the New York Academy of Sciences*, Volume 291, under the title: *The roots of American psychology: Historical influences and implications for the future*, edited by R. W. Rieber and Kurt Salzinger. Earlier versions of a number of the chapters originally appeared in that volume of the *Annals* and some chapters are being printed in this book for the first time.

The editors wish to thank the New York Academy of Sciences for cooperating with us in the further dissemination of papers presented under their auspices, and we are particularly grateful to Dr. Sidney Borowitz, Executive Director of the Academy.

Psychology

Theoretical–Historical Perspectives

R. W. RIEBER

KURT SALZINGER

An Overview of the Theories and History of Psychology

When psychologists finally admitted that psychology, like other sciences, has a past, and that knowing it will help to understand the present and to plan for the future, they began the field of the history of psychology. The American Psychological Association now has a Division of the History of Psychology with some 500 members as of 1978; and a number of journals regularly publish articles on the history of psychology. Serious work is being produced by these people and we felt that the time had come for some synthesis to be presented within the confines of one book. The New York Academy of Sciences Conference served as an unplanned "pilot" for the project, thus making this book more soundly based than would otherwise have been possible.

Part I, "Psychology Becomes a Science: European and Nineteenth Century Influences," begins with Helmut E. Adler's discussion of Fechner's influence on the development of American psychology. It is ironic that Fechner, the most mystical of psychologists, enabled psychologists to move away from mental to materialistic philosophy, because the latter was the world that he wanted most to escape. Viewing this giant of psychology, one is tempted to make such extreme statements as "without his contribution we should have had quantification much later, if at all," but extreme statements are seldom correct. After all, quantification in psychology had to be—and still must be—continuously reinvented. Nevertheless, his logarithmic law not only showed that sensation could be measured, but also, and probably more importantly, provided the methods of obtaining the relevant data. Methods like

PSYCHOLOGY:
THEORETICAL-HISTORICAL PERSPECTIVES

ISBN 0-12-588265-3

these often remain long after the theories or concepts that gave rise to them have vanished.

Adler shows how Fechner was attacked early on by such notables as William James for producing a psychology that was "basically boring" and "contributed nothing." Yet Fechner's philosophy was much closer to James's than were his contributions in experimental method and quantification. Later attacks on Fechner's law came from Stevens, who sought to substitute the power law for Fechner's, and from Swets and Green, who insisted that the concept of threshold (another of Fechner's contributions) is not useful. Nevertheless, Fechner, who is no longer given a central place in American introductory psychology texts, made a contribution to American psychology that continues to show itself in current developments.

Arthur L. Blumenthal presents a revised view of Wundt's place in psychology, taking care to avoid the traps encountered in determining the correct version of history. The psychologist is interested, of course, in the underlying reasons for historical distortion such as the trap of "presentism," the tendency to read the past in terms of the present particularly when the path from one historical moment to another is not obvious. It must be noted that such distortion need not be obvious even to the person responsible. Distortions that occur in historical writings are cumulative and depend on such factors as quality of translation, personal animosities, and even general political climates. In Wundt's case, the distortion relates in the end to a war between the countries of which the battling theoreticians are citizens. In this chapter, the reader should be alert not only to the new substantive information, but also to the methodological information on gathering historical information and the importance of reevaluating it at various times.

Solomon Diamond admits the greater recognition given to Wundt, but considers the influence of Galton to have been greater in the long run. Diamond makes it clear that the essence of Galtonism is the conviction that any significant problem in human behavior can be stated in terms that allow quantitative study. It was this conviction that made American psychology the leading psychology of the times. It was mainly Cattell and later Jastrow that helped bring this about. Moreover it was Galton's methods that American psychologists were interested in most. These methods included test batteries, word association, the questionnaire, twin comparison, classification based on the normal distribution, and especially correlation and regression techniques. In essence, Diamond makes it clear that Galton's influence has been more lasting than that of Wundt. Diamond's major reasons for Galton's lack of recognition are: (a) his work lacked the allure of a "system"; (b) his contributions arose from a problem which, though central to his thought, was and remains peripheral to that of most psychologists; and (c) quantitative method arouses enthusiasm in only a minority of psychologists.

Richard P. High and William R. Woodward provide a historical review that traces the changing conceptions of self and personality from William James to

Gordon Allport. It is argued that two persistent and apparently contradictory ideas have guided the nature of personality theory during the period 1875–1961. On one hand, the "humanist" attempts to do full justice to the richness, complexity, and uniqueness of the farthest reaches of human nature. On the other hand, the "learning theorist" attempts to articulate the particular mechanisms responsible for the development of personality. Finally, neither a strict behaviorism nor a rigid humanism serves the interests of the psychology of personality. Perhaps the best compromise according to these authors, found in the early functional theorists and the later Allport, is a methodologically diverse, cognitive approach to the study of the development of personality.

Part I concludes with John M. Broughton's picture of the development of the concept of the self in psychology. He demonstrates how this concept remains very much a problem for psychologists today although it is concealed by the increasing influence of empiricism and positivism in psychological thinking. According to these two perspectives, there is no "self" as such. At best there is only a phenomenal "self-concept" that is empirically derived from self-experience or attributions made by others. However, this Humean view presents two problems: It fails to overcome the difficulties inherent in Descartes's notion of a substantial soul, and it is based on an incoherent set of assumptions about the mind, the person, and objectivity. A more recent view, dependent upon organismic metaphors, also dismisses the self as a reification, arguing that subjectivity is nothing but a functional process. This approach also suffers from explanatory inadequacies and internal incoherence. A third theory, structuralism, offers some improvements over the alternatives, but in its more radical attempt at eliminating the self has met with no greater success.

A return to the forgotten insights of Kant's critical rationalism clarifies the real problem of subjectivity. Through an examination of the relation of theoretical reason to practical reason, Kant demonstrated the need for a transcendental notion of the self. However, Kant's emphasis on the individual, formal, cognitive and conscious aspects of self and rationality creates further problems. Society, culture, and history are largely ignored, and the issues of desire and freedom therefore receive too narrow an interpretation. The concept of self calls for a critical integration of these vital concerns.

Part II, Socioeconomic and Political Factors in the Development of Psychology, is introduced by R. W. Rieber's discussion of the groundwork for psychology before the Civil War. In his analysis, Thomas C. Upham represents the culmination of the Puritan tradition in the field of mental and moral philosophy, and appears in retrospect as a principal founder of a truly indigenous American system of psychology. The selection of Upham has its basis in the fact that his system was the single most compatible with the prevailing American social image, created as it was to help mold that image.

Upham was one in a line of natural successors to Jonathan Edwards, whose ideas in turn stem from the tradition of natural religion founded in England by Baxter, Wilkins, Watts, Doddridge, Mason, and others. His work synthesized the opposition to Kant and the rising transcendentalist schools. Upham's entire system is based on the still current notion that the study of the normal will aid in understanding the abnormal, and vice versa. The principal method associated with this doctrine, in its pursuit of salvation and self-knowledge, is the teaching of proper moral action and the "cure of the soul." The latter is in some measure an eighteenth century version of "mental hygiene" and psychotherapy.

Rieber's study is a "blend of living and dead history" that is "not altogether irrelevant to, or markedly different from, current discussions of free will and related problems." Upham's system, rather than its content, was new and different because it contained the essence of the American dream as it is known even now. Although this dream may not have been fulfilled, it has not been replaced, possibly because we still subscribe to its premises. A view of this dream in a formative stage may help us achieve a better understanding of psychology and more particularly of the psychosocial distress of our time.

David Bakan's inquiry into the political factors that have influenced the development of American psychology addresses the advisability of abandoning prediction and control as formulated in the past. The definition of psychology as the study of behavior should be replaced, says Bakan, with the classical definition of the past, namely, the study of thinking, feeling, and willing. The establishment in scientific psychology fostered a parametric theory of human nature articulated with a fact module method. The goal of parametric theory was the identification of "controlling" variables and their separation from interfering variables. Pursuing this goal helped psychology gain acceptance as a legitimate science in the larger community of the basic sciences. After World War II, a professionalization in psychology took place outside the colleges and universities. The political and economic factors of this process were important in making psychology what it is today. Bakan would rather see psychology emphasize the human aspect of the organism in its total complexity than use the parametric model. It is fair to say that Bakan's views of psychology are controversial.

In the next chapter, Howard Gruber considers the influence of Darwin's evolutionary theories on psychology. He maintains that a scientific theory is a much denser structure than is generally recognized. Almost every component idea is itself an intricate structure, and the whole is a complex of interacting parts. In the process of theory construction, therefore, as one theory is assimilated by another, the earlier is necessarily distorted and only partially represented in the latter. One consequence of this complexity is that although some Darwinian ideas have been assimilated into psychological theories, the basic conception has been neglected. There is only one diagram in *On the Origin of Species*, and that illustrates Darwin's notion that according to

Gruber "in the panorama of nature organized beings represent a tree irregularly branched,' " as Darwin wrote in 1837, prior to formulating his theory of evolution. Gruber writes "Darwin used this metaphor in many theoretically productive ways. Yet this conception of fundamental irregularity in nature remains foreign to psychology and other social sciences, fields still dominated by a largely Newtonian world view. Some potentially useful implications of Darwin's metaphor are discussed, bearing on the role of the individual in history and on the virtues of 'weak theory.' " Gruber also relates the role of the individual to the social context of history.

In the opening article of Part III, "Psychological Systems: Past, Present, and Future," Mary Henle discusses the question: "Why wasn't the influence of Gestalt psychology in America greater than it has been?" Aspects of the social and intellectual scene following the rise of Gestalt psychology must be considered in her attempt to answer this question. In America, certain misunderstandings of Gestalt psychology have arisen and have continued even up to the present. Henle clearly points out that Gestalt psychology has had a significant influence in American psychology despite its relative isolation. It helped reshape the field of perception and inspired research in many related areas. There is convincing evidence to demonstrate that the more fashionable new directions in psychology today, such as developmental cognition, the contextual study of memory, and the new interpersonal social psychology, are greatly indebted to Gestalt psychology.

From Gestalt psychology in America attention shifts to operant behavior as discussed by its outstanding proponent, B. F. Skinner. This chapter addresses the experimental analysis of behavior, the name by which Skinner's kind of psychology has become known and is still prospering under, although with a greater emphasis on applied problems than before. Skinner points out how his behavior in doing experiments was molded by the observations he was making. He stresses how his plans were modified with the accidental discovery of orderly changes in the animal's behavior. He had planned to determine how an animal responded to a distracting noise as it traversed an eight-foot-long runway. From the beginning, Skinner tried to make his apparatus do much of his work, including some automatic recording, but he could not help but notice that the rat was behaving lawfully in ways other than he expected the apparatus to reveal. These ways could be best described by measuring the delay to the next response. That was enough, as he said, to change the direction of his research. The point that Skinner has often maintained and that his students also hold to is that the experimenter must be sensitive to the changes to behavior of the organism being worked with. The experimental analysis of behavior, like the behavior that it seeks to describe, is controlled by its consequences.

In recounting his progress from studying the reflex à la Pavlov and Sherrington to looking at operant behavior, Skinner goes from being a psychologist interested in studying reflexes, that is, being a stimulus–response psychologist to being a radical behaviorist. This is an important change often forgotten by those who cavalierly categorize Skinner among the stimulus–response psychologists. Thus he is not concerned with the stimulus that elicits the response, but rather with the stimuli that control the response; and even more important, he is concerned with the reinforcement contingencies that control behavior. Finally, the reader is directed to what Skinner writes about his book on verbal behavior—a book he believes is his most important work and yet a book that has received less than its share of attention by both linguists and psycho-linguists. This is an important chapter because we have possibly the most significant living psychologist telling us about his view of behavior and of psychology itself.

To the exposition of what the leading living behaviorist himself thinks of behaviorism, we have added a chapter from Willard Day on the historical antecedents of behaviorism. It is important to lay out the facts so that we know where present-day radical and methodological forms of behaviorism come from (and that at least these two different forms coexist) and where radical behaviorism differs from Watsonian behaviorism. The man entrusted with this formidable task is particularly well suited to it, because he not only works in this area experimentally but also is the editor of *Behaviorism*, a journal that discusses the epistemology of behaviorism.

In this chapter on behaviorism, the reader is directed to consider the fact that current psychology has changed its ways of making theories. The days of grand theories are gone. Instead, experimental psychologists caught in the rigor of their experimental procedures construct complicated models of behavior requiring pages of complex flow charts with continuous and interrupted lines showing the direction of flow of information from one hypothetical part of the "mind" to another, and all they describe are the processes involved in the subject's uttering the word "old" or "new" in a memory recognition task in which the most important measure is reaction time. By contrast, behaviorism is still concerned with all behavior and does not shrink from the task of explaining all kinds of behavior, including even language, and viewing each in the same way. At the very least since such an approach presents a challenge that still exists today, we should all learn to understand, if not respond to, it.

The theme of psychology in America is furthered in the chapter by R. W. Rieber and Maurice Green. Although, the Freudian and psychoanalytic terms are household words to most psychologists and every text in historical systems covers the basis of that school of thought, Green and Rieber present the story of the Americanization of psychoanalysis, providing details of the many circumstances that made this possible. Puritan Calvinist tradition started the process by emphasizing the inner life of the person and the importance of emotions or "affections." The new thought movement, or mind cure movement as William James called it, added to this as did the Emmanuel movement, particularly with the influence of I. Coriat following Freud's visit to the United States. After World War II, the Americanization of psychoanalysis was complete as economic and political reasons made it important to enable psychoanalysis to infiltrate the popular culture. The movement gradually gave way to "psychoanalytically oriented" approaches and finally to the new biological psychiatry. The reasons for its rise and fall are given and discussed at length in this paper.

It is important for the reader to note that the material in this section was prepared by writers who are for the most part advocates of certain theoretical positions, not merely chroniclers of what happened or even interpreters of what is going on today. As a result, their statements dealing with conflicting theories tell us more about their own theories than about the conflicting ones. Gilbert Voyat attacks behaviorism in his chapter, using experimental psychology, clinical psychology, and educational psychology. He makes an attempt to separate the different approaches taken by behaviorism and by the Geneva school but it is fair to say that his characterization of behaviorism would not be acceptable to all behaviorists. He correctly points out that Piaget's influence is greatest in the field of education, less in clinical psychology, but effectively nonexistent in traditional experimental psychology. Presumably that is fair enough, since Piaget was hardly influenced by the latter—as is pointed out by Bärbel Inhelder in her chapter.

Unashamedly talking of the workings of the mind, Inhelder describes Piaget's interest in how that mind grows (a concept that came naturally to Piaget from his zoology background) through the various stages of cognitive development. Part of Piaget's originality is to be attributed to his interest in problems with which traditional experimental psychology simply did not concern itself.

Furthermore, Piaget's interest in the unfolding of the successive stages of thought is directed not only at the development of cognition in the child but also at the development of the course of scientific thought over time. Inhelder reviews Piaget's work on sensorimotor development which ultimately gives way to the operations of thought. Children, according to Piaget, make things consistent in their own minds and also match their models of what happens to the reality outside; the latter brings us to thoughts about causality. Other concepts taken up by Inhelder are "reflexive abstractions" and "constructive generalization" to explain later stages of the child's development. She concludes her chapter by returning to a discussion of the parallel paths traveled by the child's development of thought and the scientist's development of theories.

Finally, Jean Piaget's brief contribution to this book provides an interesting example of the way in which he and his students work. Somehow the basis of work in this group seems to be neither the logical derivation of one concept from another, although some of that does indeed take place, nor that the new concepts seem to derive so much from empirical experiments, although some no doubt do. Instead it seems to come from contemplating how the child deals with various problems. The idea of "generating new possibilities" probably stems more from consideration of the way the scientist solves problems than from any other factor. As such it provides Piaget with a rather great degree of freedom in deciding how to investigate this phenomenon and it is done by a rather simple series of techniques that provide the child with the opportunity to show how he or she would decide on the number of different ways in which one can accomplish a certain task. Even if one disagrees with the theoretical conceptualizations of the Geneva school, one cannot help but admire this approach. All of this then stimulates Piaget to examine "correspondences" among objects, the operations that the child presumably uses to extract common forms from the objects for comparison and for the later important psychological operation of "grouping" objects.

We decided to end the book on a light note, hence the epilogue. Enough time has passed that we can laugh at the history of psychology instead of becoming upset. There is a moral to the epilogue; we leave it to the reader to figure it out.

Part I

Psychology Becomes a Science: European and Nineteenth Century Influences

HELMUT E. ADLER   **1**

Vicissitudes of Fechnerian Psychophysics in America

*Parallelismus strictus existet inter animam
et corpus, ita ut ex uno, rite cognito, alterum
construi possit.*
FECHNER, 1823[1]

ELEMENTE

DER

PSYCHOPHYSIK

VON

GUSTAV THEODOR FECHNER.

ERSTER THEIL.

LEIPZIG,
DRUCK UND VERLAG VON BREITKOPF UND HARTEL.
1860.

[1]A strict parallelism exists between mind and body in such a way that from one, properly understood, the other can be constructed.

PSYCHOLOGY:
THEORETICAL-HISTORICAL PERSPECTIVES

ISBN 0-12-588265-3

At the beginning of scientific psychology stands the figure of Gustav Theodor Fechner (1801–1887), the romantic mystic, who almost inadvertently shaped the future course of psychology by being the first to successfully apply quantitative thinking to the study of sensations. As the above quotation from Fechner's "Premises" (his *Habitilationsschrift* in 1823) indicates, the problem of the relationship of body and mind had occupied his thinking for many years prior to the "proper understanding" that came to him in the morning of 22 October, 1850 and that resulted in the publication of his *Elemente der Psychophysik* (1860) 10 years later.

Fechner's nature combined two contradictory elements. On the one hand, he was a romantic idealist, given to wide-ranging speculative thinking, under the influence of the nature philosophy of Oken (1809) and the idealism of Fichte (Everett, 1892), Schelling (Robinson, 1976), and Hegel (Stace, 1924/1955). On the other hand, he was careful, painstaking, if somewhat plodding, scientist, in the tradition of E. H. Weber and L. H. F. von Helmholtz. Stimulated by Herbart's (1816/1891) attempt at a mathematical psychology, but vigorously rejecting Herbart's approach, he formulated his own solution, founded on "the basis of material phenomena that underlie the psychical, because they allow a direct mathematical approach and definite measurement, as is not true with respect to the psychical [Fechner, 1851, p. 373]."

In his search for a quantitative solution to the "functionally dependent relations of body and soul or, more generally, of the material and the mental, of the physical and the psychological worlds [Fechner, 1860/1966, p. 7]," he provided the basis of a new psychology, which was able to move away from mental philosophy, much as the physical sciences had earlier separated from natural philosophy. Quantification made it possible to apply the scientific method, with its emphasis on meaurement and experimentation, to mental phenomena (Zupan, 1976). Fechner was the first to clarify the nature of such measurement and to standardize the methods by which such measurements were to be made.

Fechner did not attain his ultimate goal, the refutation of a materialistic world view, but his psychophysics carried the seeds of an entirely new approach to what was then called the study of the mind. As Boring (1961) has put it: "That had to happen before anything else could take place in respect to scales and measurement in the psychological sphere [p. 8]." Although there had been a great deal of psychological thinking prior to this innovation, it had not led to a scientific psychology. Eighteenth-century mental philosophers had recognized the need for mental measurement but had lacked the methods to translate their convictions into practice (Ramul, 1960; Zupan, 1976). Sensory phenomena had been studied by physiologists and physicists, but that alone would not have led to an independent science. One does not classify E. H. Weber, Helmholtz, Mach, or Aubert primarily among psychologists, even though they made highly significant contributions to psychology. The essential idea that the mind—consciousness—could be measured was missing. As a consequence of Fechner's contribution, psychology advanced from prescience to a science. This change was such an important landmark that it is proper to divide the history of psychology into a pre-Fechnerian and a post-Fechnerian period, just as biology can be divided into a pre-Darwinian and a post-Darwinian phase and physics has its pre-Einsteinian and post-Einsteinian conception of the physical world.

Fechner's methods were quickly accepted by leading European scientists. Wundt taught the first course on "psychology as a natural science" at Heidelberg in 1862, while still a *Privatdozent* (Bringmann, Balance, & Evans, 1975). Mach lectured on psychophysics in Vienna in 1863, although he already considered "Fechner's theory of formulae of measurement . . . erroneous [Mach, 1886/1959, p. 370]." American psychologists also picked up the new psychophysical methods and began experimentation. Charles S. Peirce (Cadwallader, 1974), best known as the founder of pragmatism but also accomplished in chemistry, physics, and astronomy as well as psychology, called for American scientists to follow the lead of Fechner and Wundt. He published, in 1877, what was probably the first psychophysical experiment carried out in this country (Peirce, 1877). It independently reported the discovery of what is now called the Bezold–Brücke effect, the change of apparent hue as a function of luminance of light from a monochromatic source, after Bezold but before Brücke. The first American textbook incorporating a full account of psychophysics was published by G. T. Ladd in 1887. Ladd had never had any formal instruction in psychology. His independent discovery of these new quantitative methods was an exciting personal experience for him and well worth the six years he invested in the compilation of *Elements of Physiological Psychology* (Mills, 1974). The efforts of these self-starters were soon augmented by the arrival of the first generation of European-trained psychologists. It was the age of the founding of laboratories at American universities: G. S. Hall (Wundt's first American student) at Johns Hopkins in 1884, James McK. Cattell at Pennsylvania in 1887, E. B. Titchener at Cornell in 1892. They brought with them not only the laboratory skills of the "new" psychology but also knowledge of the controversies that had developed with regard to Fechner's philosophy and the interpretation of his measurements. Fechnerian psychophysics began to undergo the first of its many transformations. It was its fate to undergo many more changes. Because of this fact, it has frequently been the case that writers have lost sight of Fechner's lasting achievement, the successful introduction of measurement that irreversibly set the future course of psychology in the direction of a quantitative science.

Quantitative Psychology

In its wider sense, psychophysics was to be concerned not only with sense perception but also with the "intensity of attention, clearness of consciousness, and so forth" (Fechner, 1860/1966, p. 48), in fact, any psychological process. The means of measurement and the operations of measuring were to be found in procedures setting up an equivalence between physical magnitude and a psychological unit of measurement (Fechner, 1860). As Fechner pointed out, even physical measurement in its "most general and ultimate sense" is derived from "the fact that an equal number of equally strong psychical impressions are due to an equal number of equally large physical causes [1860/1966, p. 51]."

Fechner understood the essential nature of measurement as "the assignment of numerals to objects or events according to rule—any rule" (Stevens, 1959, p. 18). The manipulation of numbers thus obtained, according to the formal model of mathematics, leads directly to the specification of relationships that cannot be directly observed. It is widely believed, for example, that the origins of geometry were connected with the need to fix land boundaries in Egypt after the annual Nile floods and that mathematical analysis began with the need to predict astronomical events connected with the seasonal changes of the sun and the planets.

It was Fechner's goal to set up the proper operations by which numerical values could be assigned to psychological variables. He accomplished this task by first defining the concept of sensitivity, deriving from it the notion of the threshold, and devising or standardizing the procedures by which the threshold was to be found. He ended by constructing his famous psychological scale:

> The magnitude of the sensation is not proportional to the absolute value of the stimulus, but rather to the logarithm of the stimulus magnitude, when the latter is expressed in terms of its threshold value, i.e., that magnitude considered as a unit at which the sensation appears and disappears. In short, it is proportional to the logarithm of the fundamental stimulus value [Fechner, 1860, Vol. II p. 13].

Early Critics of Psychophysics

If, as has been claimed (Estes, Koch, MacCorquodale, Meehl, Mueller, Schoenfeld, & Verplanck, 1954), the success of a theory should be judged by the number of fruitful inquiries to which it gives rise, psychophysics has achieved a very high rank on any scale. But when it first came upon the scene, it met some determined opposition. The foremost American critic also happened to be the most highly regarded American psychologist, William James. He was well acquainted with Fechner's work, but he was not impressed, as we may gather from a letter to G. Stanley Hall written in 1880, in which James comments regarding Fechner: "I have always thought his psychophysics as moonshiny as any of his other writings [H. James, 1920, Vol. 2, pp. 18–19]." A decade later, in his *Principles of Psychology*, James expressed his opinion publicly that this "dreadful literature" of psychophysics, the outcome of which was "just *nothing*," could hardly "have arisen in a country whose natives could be *bored* [W. James, 1890, Vol. 1, p. 192ff]."And in perhaps the best-known passage he praises Fechner, "that dear old man," and dismisses his work that he feared "could saddle our Science forever with his patient whimseys, and, in a world so full of more nutritious objects of attention, compel all future students to plough through the difficulties, not only of his own works, but of the still drier ones written in his refutation [W. James, 1890, Vol. 1, p. 549]."

As Boring (1942) has pointed out, James could not appreciate Fechner's psychophysics, because James approached psychology as a phenomenalist and was thus a forerunner of those present trends in psychology that stress richness, wholeness, and understanding at the expense of precision and quantitative relationships. But interestingly enough, Fechner's own philosophy was essentially in agreement with James's point of view. Wertheimer (1972) cites Fechner's attempts at relating mind and body as a synthesis between richness and precision in the handling of psychological issues. And James himself, as Marylin Marshall (1974) points out, eventually discovered a close elective affinity with Fechner's philosophy, albeit not with his psychophysics.

Other critical voices were raised with respect to Fechner's fundamental assumptions, while his methods were seen as needing modifications. Joseph Jastrow, a student of Peirce and the first American Ph.D. in psychology, published his critique in 1888. James McK. Cattell, in collaboration with G. S. Fullerton, a philosopher, published a revision of psychophysical methodology that introduced a functional point of view in 1892. Instead of accepting the threshold as a fact to be described, they saw it in terms of a subject's success or failure to discriminate a given stimulus difference. Also in 1892, at the First Annual Meeting of the American Psychological Association (at a time when annual dues were $3), Hugo Münsterberg, then on his first visit to join James at Harvard, decried the tendency of experimental psychology merely to accumulate figures (Sokal, 1973).

E. B. Titchener (1905) provided an unparalleled thorough and erudite review and a searching critique of the whole field in his *Experimental Psychology*, summarizing a literature that had already become unwieldy. Who cannot sympathize when we read: "There has been a strong tendency in the past few years toward the multiplication of psychological journals. Indeed, the number of serial publications is now so large and specialized, that they will hardly be found all together in a single institutional library,—to say nothing of a private library [Vol. 2, Pt. 2, p. 418]." After declining to accept the contention that sensations had a measurable magnitude, the so-called quantity objection; admitting the equality of just noticeable differences only in a modified way; and rejecting the psychophysical interpretation of Weber's law, what did Titchener find was left of Fechner's system? In the first place, Fechner "paved the way for experimental psychology [Vol. 2, Pt. 2, p. cviii]." Second, we owe him the comprehensive development of the methods of just noticeable differences, the method of right and wrong cases (constant stimuli), and the method of average error. Third, Fechner developed the concept of the difference threshold. Fourth, Fechner collected valuable data under the guidance of his own theory and by the methods that he had developed. Finally, he should receive sole credit for the concept of mental measurement. Titchener's evaluation closes what might be called the classical period of psychophysics, but further changes were to come as innovative ideas permeated psychology.

Psychophysics Adapts to New Trends

The new trends influencing psychophysics were probability theory and behaviorism. Fechner himself had made use of the normal probability integral, or Gaussian distribution, as he called it, in developing the method of right and wrong cases. Cattell in 1893 had attempted a statistical approach to discrimination. But it remained for L. L. Thurstone (1927) to develop fully the potentialities of a probability approach to psychological scaling. His law of comparative judgment was constructed on the assumption that a given stimulus did not correspond to a single point on a psychological dimension but instead corresponded to a distribution centered around a point. Distances between points on a continuum could be scaled in terms of the probability of the differences between the two distributions. He distinguished five cases, of which Case V, assuming equal dispersions, has been found to be the most useful. Thurstone's scaling has been applied to physical stimuli only to a limited extent but found its widest application in attitude scaling.

Another attempt to incorporate probability principles was due to Crozier (1940). It centered on the neural correlates of sensory stimulation. His basic assumption was that the population of excitatory neurons varied in threshold according to a normal probability distribution. The importance of his theory lay in the fact that the resulting functions became independent of the particular sense organ being stimulated.

The impact of behaviorism is best exemplified by the writings of G. Bergmann and K. W. Spence (1944) and of C. H. Graham (1950, 1958). According to the former, the process of psychophysical measurement becomes the verbal discrimination of human observers or their motor responses in accordance with verbal instructions. Observers may use numerals in their response, but these are not the same as physical measurements. Psychophysical measurement becomes a technique in its own right that cannot be subsumed under any customary classifications of physical measurement.

According to Graham, one seeks to establish specific, explicitly stated relations between a stimulus, a response, and whatever hypothesized variables became logically necessary. On the one hand, there are the physical changes in the environment, on the other hand, the behavioral manifestations of the organism as a function of these stimuli. Responses are often restricted to such statements as "Yes," "No," or "Equal."

> From such a relation it is possible to obtain a new datum, a value of the stimulus variable that corresponds to a particular probability of response occurence—for example the 50% value . . . and so derive . . . perceptual functions . . . functions obtained from a sequence of experiments concerned with finding thresholds under many different conditions [Graham, 1958, pp. 67–68].

Under this approach, the threshold becomes a dependent variable of behavior, unlike the classical sensory concept with its intervening variable connotation. Another consequence of this interpretation is the evaporation of any differences between "sensory" and "perceptual" phenomena.

The Nature of the Psychophysical Law

Fechnerian scaling was based on indirect methods, ultimately on discrimination. Fechner's famous logarithmic law depended on integration of just noticeable differences (JNDs). It assumed that all JNDs are equal in subjective magnitude. In contrast to this approach, there have come into prominence the so-called direct methods of scaling that result, in many cases, in a different kind of mathematical function, the power law.

Direct scaling has a respectable history. It goes back to Plateau's attempt, in 1852, to equate intervals of lightness. This blind Belgian physicist had asked eight artists to paint a gray that appeared half-way between a white and a black surface (Plateau, 1872). This is the method of bisection. Other well-known direct methods are the category rating scale, where subjects are given some number of categories prior to the experiment and instructed to assign the stimuli, one at a time, to one of the categories. A third type of direct scaling involves the setting of one stimulus so that it stands in direct ratio to another stimulus. Merkel in 1888 asked subjects to set a variable stimulus so that the sensation it produced was judged as twice as great as the comparison stimulus. Fullerton and Cattell (1892) had used a similar procedure, asking their subjects for both multiples and fractions of a standard. Richardson and Ross (1930) were the first to use direct assignment of numerals to classify the loudness of tones, a method now designated as magnitude estimation and figuring prominently in recent psychophysical scaling.

S. S. Stevens and his collaborators, determined the shape of many sensory functions by this method, leading him to propose the power law as the general psychophysical function (Stevens, 1957) and to advocate the repeal of Fechner's law (Stevens, 1961). Briefly stated, the power law describes the relationship

or
$$\log \Psi = \beta \log \Phi + k'$$
$$\Psi = k\Phi^{\beta},$$

where Ψ is equal to psychological magnitude, Φ is equal to stimulus intensity, $\log k = k'$ is equal to a constant, and the exponent β is specific to a particular sense modality. Expressed in words, it states that "equal stimulus ratios produce equal sensation ratios." This law holds for prothetic continua, such as loudness, that have purely quantitative changes, but not for metathetic continua that undergo qualitative as well as quantitative changes, such as pitch. Contrast this function with Fechner's logarithmic law, the *Massformel*,

$$\Psi = k \log(\Phi/b),$$

where Ψ is equal to sensation magnitude, Φ is equal to stimulus magnitude, b is equal to threshold stimulus magnitude, and k is equal to a constant. Fechner's law can be expressed in words as "equal stimulus ratios produce equal sensation intervals."

The internal consistency of Stevens's sensory scales has been supported by cross-modality matching. In this procedure, stimuli in one dimension, for example luminance, are adjusted by a subject so that their magnitudes appear to match those in another continuum, such as loudness. Predictions can now be made of the slope of one of the functions from knowledge of the slope of the other.

Stevens's law as a statement of empirical relationships has been widely accepted, but Stevens's assumption that he was measuring sensations directly has been questioned (e.g., by Mackay, 1963; Savage, 1966; Treisman, 1964). The application of his methods to the study of sensory processes has been very productive (cf. Marks, 1974). Direct scaling also has been generalized successfully to such social variables as status, the seriousness of offenses, and the severity of recommended punishment (Ekman & Sjöberg, 1965; Stevens, 1966, 1972). It might be added that Fechner (1860) had anticipated the usefulness of measurement and scaling in this area and cited as his example the logarithmic relation between *"fortune physique" and "fortune morale,"* of money and its subjective value, that Bernoulli had put forward in 1738 (Bernoulli, 1738/1954).

Stevens's is by no means the only alternative method of scaling that has been advanced in recent years. Norman Anderson's (1970, 1975) theory of functional measurement proposes two laws. A number of physical stimuli *S* impinge on the organism and are converted by a valuation operation or psychophysical law into psychological stimuli *s*. The psychological stimuli are combined according to an integration function or psychological law to yield an implicit response *r*, which is then transformed into the overt, observable response *R*. The psychophysical law therefore becomes the function that relates the physical stimulus to its subjective counterpart, while the psychological law relates the subjective stimulus values to the response via the nonobservable covert response. To a Fechnerian, there are strong echoes of outer and inner psychophysics in this theory. Compare Fechner's formulation: "By its nature, psychophysics may be divided into an outer and an inner part, depending on whether consideration is focused on the relation of the psychical to the body's external aspects, or on those internal functions with which the psychic are closely related [1860/1966, p. 9]."

Recent Developments

At first glance, animal psychophysics seems a paradox. Animals (apart from a few chimpanzees and a gorilla) cannot tell us about their sensations. To an objective psychologist, this fact may be an advantage, of course. But does a mind–body problem exist for animals? Fechner would have smiled. He was sure that not only animals but even plants and the whole of nature shared in the world soul (Woodward, 1972).

Ratliff and Blough's adaptation of the tracking technique to obtain sensory thresholds (Blough, 1958; Ratliff & Blough, 1954) has been applied to a wide variety of psychophysical measurements in animals. Adler (1963), for example, measured dark adaptation and spectral sensitivity of starlings and robins in order to define the limits of their sensory capacity for the purpose of evaluating the validity of theories of animal navigation. Herrnstein and van Sommers (1962) have tested a procedure that yielded magnitude estimation scales for pigeon's judgment of luminance. Signal detection theory has been applied to pigeon data by Wright (1974).

The same theory of signal detection has done away with the concept of the threshold, so dear to Fechner (Green & Swets, 1966; Swets, 1961). This theory treats separately the measure of sensitivity and the decision criterion of the observer. It assumes a continuum of sensory excitation and derives its quantitative data from judgments generated under the control of such factors as instructions, values and costs, or the observer's motivation. Since these conditions may vary, there is no fixed threshold. The threshold also has not fared well in the hands of the neural quantum theorists (Corso, 1956, 1963). Whereas the previously described theory took account of noise—that is, stimulation extraneous to the particular stimulus value being tested—the theory of the neural quantum attempts to do away with noise entirely. Under these conditions momentary, random fluctuations in neural sensitivity affect the stimulus magnitude necessary to activate a given neural unit, resulting in a discontinuous psychophysical function. No threshold in Fechner's sense exists. It is of historical interest that attacks on the threshold concept can already be found in Jastrow's critique of 1888. In a different vein, the extension of the ideas of relativistic physics to psychophysics has led to the suggestion that the notion of an unchanging physical world may also have to be replaced by one in which reality itself depends, at least in part, on the observer, according to Rosen (1976). Acceptance of this position would help to account for deviations from Weber's law, as Rosen argues, and by extension could also be applied to deviations from the logarithmic law and the power law.

All of the theories of scaling and psychological measurement so far discussed have shared the notion of some unit of measurement that was applied to the data. In a reversal of this position, Coombs (1950, 1960) has advocated an approach by which data define the measurement scale. It is an axiomatic theory, placing mathematical terms, such as the real numbers, in correspondence with properties of empirical observations. (For a detailed exposition, see Baird & Noma, 1978; Krantz, Atkinson, Luce, & Suppes, 1974; Krantz, Luce, Suppes, & Tversky, 1971; for an application to psychophysical measurement see Falmagne, 1976.) There are no a priori assumptions about the nature of the measurement scale, which may, in fact, frequently have more than one dimension. The focus of analysis is shifted to the response. The raw data are the decisions of the subjects, for example, their preferences or the order they impose on an array of stimuli. But it should be noted that instead of treating these responses as pure data, they are now seen as reflecting some internal, subjective choice mechanism. Fechnerian judgments originally conceived as sensory distances now become conscious choices under the influence of motivational factors. As Galanter (1974) points out, however, while these new developments have served to augment our understanding of motivational variables and decision-making mechanisms, they have not altered the general form nor the approximate magnitude of the perceptual functions that were first observed late in the nineteenth century. Fechner undoubtedly would have subsumed them under the topic of inner psychophysics.

Conclusions

Where then do these developments leave Fechner? They leave his contributions undiminished. He still deserves the credit for being the first to introduce measurement into psychology and thereby radically changing its direction. The exact nature of the functions is immaterial in this context, as far as the judgment of history is concerned.

Yet Fechner is not cited frequently in today's psychological literature. His name appears rarely in our introductory textbooks. There is a reason for this lack of interest and relative neglect outside of the realm of the specialist. It was James who made the distinction between the tough- and the tender-minded. The tender-minded are in the majority at the present time. It looks as if William James will have the last laugh. Most Americans did not put up with an old man's patient whimseys. But for the minority of America's psychologists who seriously try to advance psychology as a science, there remains a great debt. Fechner's insights had fallen on fertile soil. A viable and lively branch of psychology had taken root in America. Psychology had become an experimental science.

References

Adler, H. E. Psychophysical limits of celestial navigation hypotheses. *Ergebnisse der Biologie,* 1963, *26,* 235–252.

Anderson, N. H. Functional measurement and psychophysical judgment. *Psychological Review,* 1970, *77,* 153–170.

Anderson, N. H. On the role of context effects in psychophysical judgment. *Psychological Review,* 1975, *82,* 462–482.

Baird, J. C., & Noma, E. *Fundamentals of scaling and psychophysics.* New York: Wiley, 1978.

Bergmann, G., & Spence, K. W. The logic of psychophysical measurement. *Psychological Review,* 1944, *51,* 1–24.

Bernoulli, D. Exposition of a new theory on the measurement of risk. *Econometrica,* 1954, *22,* 23–25. (Originally published, 1738.)

Blough, D. S. A method for obtaining psychophysical thresholds from the pigeon. *Journal of the Experimental Analysis of Behavior,* 1958, *1,* 31–43.

Boring, E. G. Human nature vs. sensation: William James and the psychology of the present. *American Journal of Psychology,* 1942, *55,* 310–327. (Reprinted in E. G. Boring, *Psychologist at large.* New York: Basic Books, 1961.)

Boring, E. G. Fechner: Inadvertent founder of psychophysics. *Psychometrika,* 1961, *26,* 3–8. (Reprinted in E. G. Boring, *History, psychology and science: Selected papers* [R. I. Watson & D. T. Campbell, Eds.]. New York: Wiley, 1963.)

Bringmann, W. G., Balance, W. D. G., & Evans, R. B. Wilhelm Wundt 1832–1920: A brief biographical sketch. *Journal of the History of the Behavioral Sciences,* 1975, *11,* 287–297.

Cadwallader, T. C. Charles S. Peirce (1839–1914): The first American experimental psychologist. *Journal of the History of the Behavioral Sciences,* 1974, *10,* 291–298.

Cattell, J. McK. On errors of observation. *American Journal of Psychology,* 1893, *5,* 285–293.

Coombs, C. H. Psychological scaling without a unit of measurement. *Psychological Review,* 1950, *57,* 145–158.

Coombs, C. H. A theory of data. *Psychological Review,* 1960, *67,* 143–159.

Corso, J. F. The neural quantum theory of sensory discrimination. *Psychological Bulletin,* 1956, *53,* 371–393.

Corso, J. F. A theoretico-historical review of the threshold concept. *Psychological Bulletin,* 1963, *60,* 356–370.

Crozier, W. J. On the law of minimal discrimination of intensities: IV. Δ I as a function of intensity. *Proceedings of the National Academy of Sciences,* 1940, *26,* 382–389.

Ekman, G., & Sjöberg, L. Scaling. *Annual Review of Psychology,* 1965, *16,* 451–474.

Estes, W. K., Koch, S., MacCorquodale, K., Meehl, P. E., Mueller, C. G., Schoenfeld, W. N., & Verplanck, W. S. *Modern learning theory.* New York: Appleton-Century-Crofts, 1954.

Everett, C. C. *Fichte's science of knowledge.* Chicago: S. C. Griggs, 1892.

Falmange, J.-C. Random conjoint measurement and loudness summation. *Psychological Review,* 1976, *83,* 65–79.

Fechner, G. T. *Premissae ad theoriam organismi generalem.* Leipzig, 1823. (Quoted by M. E. Marshall, G. T. Fechner: Premises toward a general theory of organisms (1823). *Journal of the History of the Behavioral Sciences,* 1974, *10,* 438–447.)

Fechner, G. T. *Zend-Avesta, oder über die Dinge des Himmels und des Jenseits, vom Standpunkt der Naturbetrachtung.* Leipzig: L. Voss, 1851.

Fechner, G. T. *Elemente der Psychophysik* (2 vols.). Leipzig: Breitkopf & Härtel, 1860. (Reprinted Amsterdam; E. J. Bonset, 1964.)

Fechner, G. T. *Elements of Psychophysics* (Vol. 1). (H. E. Adler, Trans., D. H. Howes, & E. G. Boring, Eds.). New York: Holt, Rinehart & Winston, 1966. (Originally published, 1860.)

Fullerton, G. S., & Cattell, J. McK. On the perception of small differences. *University of Pennsylvania Philosophical Series,* 1892, *2.*

Galanter, E. Psychological decision mechanisms. In E. C. Carterette & M. P. Friedman (Eds.). *Handbook of perception* (Vol. 2, chap. 4, Psychophysical judgment and measurement.) New York: Academic Press, 1974.

Graham, C. H. Behavior, perception and the psychophysical methods. *Psychological Review,* 1950, *57,* 108–120.

Graham, C. H. Sensation and perception in an objective psychology. *Psychological Review,* 1958, *65,* 65–76.

Green, D. M., & Swets, J. A. *Signal detection theory and psychophysics.* New York; Wiley, 1966.

Herbart, J. F. *A text-book in psychology: An attempt to found the science of psychology in experience, metaphysics, and mathematics* (M. K. Smith, Trans.). New York: Appleton, 1891. (Originally published, 1816) (Excerpted in W. Sahakian [Ed.] *History of psychology: A source book in systematic psychology.* Itasca, Ill.: F. E. Peacock, 1968.)

Herrnstein, R. J., & van Sommers, P. Method for sensory scaling with animals. *Science,* 1962, *135,* 40–41.

James, H. (Ed.). *The letters of William James* (Vol. 2). Boston: The Atlantic Monthly Press, 1920.

James, W. *The principles of psychology* (2 vols.). New York: Holt, 1890.

Jastrow, J. Critique of psychophysic methods. *American Journal of Psychology,* 1888, *1,* 271–309.

Krantz, D. H., Atkinson, R. C., Luce, R. D., & Suppes, P. *Contemporary developments in mathematical psychology.* San Francisco: Freeman, 1974.

Krantz, D. H., Luce, R. D., Suppes, P., & Tversky, A. *Foundations of measurement.* New York: Academic Press, 1971.

Ladd, G. T. *Elements of physiological psychology.* New York: Charles Scribner's Sons, 1887.

Mach, E. *The analysis of sensations.* (C. M. Williams, Trans.) New York: Dover, 1959. (Originally published, 1886.)

Mackay, D. M. Psychophysics of perceived intensity: A theoretical basis for Fechner's and Stevens' laws. *Science,* 1963, *139,* 1213–1216.

Marks, L. E. *Sensory processes.* New York: Academic Press, 1974.

Marshall, M. E. William James, Gustav Fechner, and the question of dogs and cats in the library. *Journal of the History of the Behavioral Sciences,* 1974, *10,* 304–312.

Merkel, J. Die Abhängigkeit zwischen Reiz und Empfindung. *Philosophische Studien,* 1888, *4,* 541–594.

Mills, E. S. George Trumbull Ladd: The great textbook writer. *Journal of the History of the Behavioral Sciences,* 1974, *10,* 299–303.

Oken, L. *Lehrbuch der Naturphilosophie.* Jena, Germany: F. Frommann, 1809.

Peirce, C. S. Note on the sensation of color. *American Journal of Science,* 3rd series, 1877, *13,* 247–251.

Plateau, J. A. F. Sur la mesure des sensations physiques, et sur la loi qui lie l'intensité de ces sensations a l'intensité de la cause excitante. *Bulletin de l'académie Royale de Belgique,* 1872, *33,* 376–388.

Ramul, K. The problem of measurement in the psychology of the eighteenth century. *American Psychologist*, 1960, *15*, 256-265.

Ratliff, F., & Blough, D. S. *Behavioral studies of visual processes in the pigeon*. USN, Office of Naval Research, Tech. Rep., Project NR 140-072, 1954.

Richardson, L. F., & Ross, J. S. Loudness and telephone currents. *Journal of General Psychology*, 1930, *2*, 288-306.

Robinson, D. N. *An intellectual history of psychology*. New York: Macmillan, 1976.

Rosen, S. M. Toward relativization of psychophysical "relativity." *Perceptual and Motor Skills*, 1976, *42*, 843-850.

Savage, C. W. Introspectionist and behaviorist interpretations of ratio scales of perceptual magnitudes. *Psychological Monographs*, 1966, *80*, (19, Whole No. 627).

Sokal, M. M. APA's first publication: Proc. Amer. Psychol. Ass. 1892-1893. *American Psychologist*, 1973, *28*, 277-292.

Stace, W. T. *The philosophy of Hegel: A systematic exposition*. New York: Dover, 1955. (Originally published, 1924.)

Stevens, S. S. On the psychophysical law. *Psychological Review*, 1957, *64*, 153-181.

Stevens, S. S. Measurement, psychophysics, and utility. In C. W. Churchman & P. Ratoosh (Eds.). *Measurement: Definitions and theories*. New York: Wiley, 1959.

Stevens, S. S. To honor Fechner and repeal his law. *Science*, 1961, *133*, 80-86.

Stevens, S. S. A metric for social consensus. *Science*, 1966, *151*, 530-541.

Stevens, S. S. *Psychophysics and social scaling*. Morristown, N.J.: General Learning Press, 1972.

Swets, J. A. Detection theory and psychophysics: A review. *Psychometrika*, 1961, *26*, 49-63.

Thurstone, L. L. A law of comparative judgment. *Psychological Review*, 1927, *34*, 273-286.

Titchener, E. B. *Experimental psychology* (Vol. 2, Pt. 2). New York: Macmillan, 1905.

Treisman, M. Sensory scaling and the psychophysical law. *Quarterly Journal of Experimental Psychology*, 1964, *16*, 11-22.

Wertheimer, M. *Fundamental issues in psychology*. New York: Holt, Rinehart & Winston, 1972.

Woodward, W. R. Fechner's panpsychism: A scientific solution to the mind–body problem. *Journal of the History of the Behavioral Sciences*, 1972, *8*, 367-386.

Wright, A. A. Psychometric and psychophysical theory within a framework of response bias. *Psychological Review*, 1974, *81*, 322-347.

Zupan, M. L. The conceptual development of quantification in experimental psychology. *Journal of the History of the Behavioral Sciences*, 1976, *12*, 145-158.

Recommended Readings

Coren, S., Porac, C., & Ward, L. M. *Sensation and perception*. New York: Academic Press, 1979.

Falmagne, J.-C. Foundations of Fechnerian psychophysics. In D. Krantz, R. C. Atkinson, R. D. Luce, & P. Suppes (Eds.) *Contemporary developments in mathematical psychology*. Vol. 2. San Francisco: Freeman, 1974. Pp. 121-159.

Fechner, G. T. *Elements of Psychophysics* (Vol 1.) Trans. H.E. Adler, D.H. Howes, and E.G. Boring, Eds. New York: Holt, Rinehart & Winston, 1966.

Galanter, E. Contemporary Psychophysics. In R. Brown, E.H. Hess, & G. Mandler (Eds.), *New directions in psychology*. New York: Holt, Rinehart & Winston, 1962.

Marks, L.E. *Sensory Processes*. New York: Academic Press, 1974.

Woodward, W.R. Fechner's panpsychism: A scientific solution to the mind-body problem. *Journal of the History of the Behavioral Sciences*, 1972, *8*, 367-386.

ARTHUR L. BLUMENTHAL **2**

Wilhelm Wundt and Early American Psychology: A Clash of Cultures

GRUNDZÜGE

DER

PHYSIOLOGISCHEN PSYCHOLOGIE.

VON

WILHELM WUNDT,
PROFESSOR AN DER UNIVERSITÄT ZU LEIPZIG.

ZWEITE VÖLLIG UMGEARBEITETE AUFLAGE.

MIT 180 HOLZSCHNITTEN.

ERSTER BAND.

LEIPZIG.
VERLAG VON WILHELM ENGELMANN
1880

PSYCHOLOGY:
THEORETICAL-HISTORICAL PERSPECTIVES

ISBN 0-12-588265-3

Attempts to subsume mental processes under the types of laws found in the physical sciences will never by successful. Volitional activities are the type in terms of which all other psychological phenomena are to be construed.
WILHELM WUNDT, 1866, 1908

I must confess that to my mind there is something hideous in the glib Herbartian jargon about Vorstellungmassen and their Hemmungen and Hemmungssummen, and sinken and erheben and schweben, and Verschmelzungen and Complexionen.
WILLIAM JAMES, 1890

There are many psychologists who have a predilection for the cortex; my own leaning is towards the sense organ.
EDWARD B. TITCHENER, 1908

We need a psychology that is usable, that is dietetic, efficient for thinking, living and working, and although Wundtian thoughts are now so successfully cultivated in academic gardens, they can never be acclimated here, as they are antipathetic to the American spirit and temper.
G. STANLEY HALL, 1912

Historiography

Long after the prominence of Wilhelm Wundt as a psychological theorist had faded from the collective consciousness (or collective verbal behavior) of American psychologists, the most successful historian of psychology at mid-twentieth century, E. G. Boring (1929, 1942, 1950), summarized Wundt's work with the following dozen or so points: Wundt's psychology began as physiological psychology (1950, p. 317); Wundt claimed psychology as one of the natural sciences (p. 319); to Wundt "scientific" meant experimental (p. 320); Wundt made introspection the primary method of his laboratory (p. 328); Wundt borrowed British associationism and was an elementalist (in the sense of mental chemistry) (p. 329); Wundt was a mind–body dualist (p. 333); Wundt opposed the implication of an active agent (p. 339); Wundt's psychology was exceptional for its narrowness (p. 343); and Wundt's life was withdrawn from the world of the affairs of common men (p. 344).

For some time afterward, psychologists in English-speaking (and many other) countries paraphrased Boring whenever writing about Wundt. Eventually, however, a later generation of scholars gradually came to the reexamination of the original historical documents in the original language, and they have shown Boring's preceding statements to be questionable. Wundt's views were either the opposite of or were fundamentally different from each of the above descriptions (Blumenthal, 1970, 1975, 1979; Bringmann, Balance, & Evans, 1975; Danziger, 1979, 1980; Klein, 1970; Leahey, 1979; Mischel, 1970; Rappard, 1979; Sabat, 1979).

Understandably, initial reactions to this revisionist history have included disbelief. Psychologists untrained in the problems of historiography certainly might ask if the reporting of such history was not a rather straightforward task; and so how could such error possibly arise?

One answer has come from Samelson (1974), who has described how social scientists have the habit of creating "myths of origins" that evolve, consciously or unconsciously, in such ways as to serve the function of justifying their present position in the course of history. This may even result, I might add, in serious distortions in the translation of a body of literature from one language into another.

As students of history soon learn, this is an age-old problem in historiography in general, whether it be political history, intellectual history, or the history of psychology. So allow me to illustrate the problem further with a neutral example from another discipline—that of the history of British royalty—and then perhaps the parallel situation in psychology will seem more in the realm of possibilities.

For centuries in Great Britain, children learned from folk tale and nursery rhyme of the succession of English kings. One dramatic moment in those tales is when the reign of the Plantagenet kings comes to an end and the reign of the Tudors begins. Richard III, last of the Plantagenets and considered a villain, is slain by the conquering forces of Henry VII, first of the Tudors. The death of Richard was rarely thought of as much of a loss, it seems, because he was described as both physically deformed and mentally deranged, and worse, a psychopath who had assassinated two nephews to fend off their threat to his rule. Such ugly recollections trace back to accounts written by the great Sir Thomas More, who came along too late ever to have known Richard, but who did, nevertheless, receive firsthand accounts from Henry, the conquering Tudor king.

Thomas More was a man of such respect and authority that it was considered bad manners to contradict him. And yet the occasional historian working here and there in dusty corners of old monasteries, publishing in obscure academic journals, was able to show that Richard's nephews had, in fact, outlived him. Hence, he could not have been their assassin. Also, it was shown that Richard was not deformed in the ways shown in later caricatures and, further, that in his deeds as king he was a noteworthy humanitarian admired by his subjects.

The old legends of Richard's villainy, however, had developed a robust life of their own, and they survived admirably. They became the subject of one of Shakespeare's plays and were reported as fact in early editions of the *Encyclopedia Britannica*. In a word, these legends now served a cultural function in making one part of British history more intelligible. In particular, they made the succession of kings from Plantagenet to Tudor appear as an upward move in the advance of British civilization.

The lesson of this example is that history is often written by the momentary victors when the defeated are not around to argue their case.

Now let us return to the history of psychology. Today everyone could agree, I should think, that the traditionally received history of Wundtian psychology was not written by Wundtians. And in some quarters of American psychology, there arose such severe hostilities toward Wundt that it may well have been felt that a history of the Wundtian era written by a Wundtian would be prima facie inappropriate. In any case, the history of the Wundtian era in psychology has often been cast in the form of legends about Wundt that, whether true or false, appear in textbooks largely as pedagogical devices for illustrating psychology's later progress in the American twentieth century. To the degree that is true, the curiosity of the historical scholar might well be aroused. One might thus suspect that it could possibly be interesting to search out some summaries and interpretations of Wundt written by, say, German, Italian, Danish, Russian, or even English-speaking intellectual historians who were either quite close to, or sympathetic to, Wundt and who were not prompted by the later presentist motives (e.g., Goldenweiser, 1932; Höffding, 1915; Hoffmann, 1924; Kiesow, 1929; Passkönig, 1912; Petersen, 1925; Sganzini, 1913; or Villa, 1903). Or if truly ambitious, one might even turn to the serious study of Wundt's own writings in the original language.

There is, it is true, relatively little serious study of Wundtian thought that appears in English. Many more of Wundt's books, in fact, were translated into Russian—even into Spanish—than were ever translated into English. Moreover, the scattered English translations have, in most cases, a serious problem, which is indicated well by the statement of two influential translators themselves (Creighton and Titchener) in their preface to a brief edition of Wundt's *Vorlesungen* (1894): "We have aimed to furnish a literal, as distinguished from a verbal rendering of the German text," and "have attempted a precise use of words even at the cost of literary effect [p. iii]." That decision—a sad one indeed since the "precision" now appears doubtful—seems to have been the model for most of the few other translations. Although a dedicated reader might disentangle the awkward syntax of these translations, still the liberties that were taken to reshape Wundt's thoughts is another matter. Those distortions made it easier to give out-of-context quotations that were to help form some extreme misreadings on the part of later historians. This is not the place to go into the technical details of translation errors. (For a few examples, see Blumenthal, 1977, 1979.)

The remainder of this chapter will, for the most part, be concerned with the sources, direct and indirect, of the distortions and subsequent erasure of Wundtian psychology from the consciousness of the twentieth century. But first, we must reflect on the essence of that psychology.

Wundt's Psychology

The dominant school of psychological thought in mid-nineteenth-century Germany was that of J. F. Herbart whose theories were fundamentally mechanistic and associationistic though tempered with some native German rationalism. Herbart's work was decidedly nonexperimental, for at heart he was a mathematician and a model-builder in his approach to psychology. It was in those days around midcentury, however, that the experimental method began to receive wide notice because of its successes in the hands of physiologists. The idea then came about quite naturally, and was frequently suggested in Germany, that these new methods—involving measurement, replicability, public data, and controlled tests—might be usefully applied to any and all problems of human knowledge. And in this way, the adjective "physiological" (*physiologischen*) came to mean "experimental." Thus, there was talk of "physiological pedagogy," "physiological aesthetics," "physiological linguistics," and "physiological psychology."

The young Wilhelm Wundt—then a laboratory assistant at Heidelberg—took up the challenge of these proposals. And in so doing, his 60-year career as a scientific psychologist began one day in one of those moments of propitious insight. It happened at a time in his life when friends described him as an absent-minded, daydreaming young scholar of Heidelberg. One of the notions that was then occupying the wandering thoughts of young Wundt was the "personal equation" problem found in astronomers' research. If you do not remember, there had been systematic differences between astronomers in their measures of the passage of stars across grid lines in telescopes. These slight differences in measured star transits depended on whether the astronomer first focused his attention on the star or on his timing device. Around 1860, after setting up some crude apparatus to simulate this situation and to make measurements, Wundt realized that he was measuring the speed of a central mental process—that for the first time, he thought, a self-conscious experimental psychology was taking place. The time it takes to switch attention voluntarily from one stimulus to another had been measured—it varied around a tenth of a second.

At this moment, the unfolding of Wundt's theoretical system begins. For it was not the simple fact of the measured speed of selective attention that impressed him as much as it was the demonstration of a central, voluntary control process. From then on, a prominent theme in Wundtian psychology was the distinction between voluntary and involuntary actions. This seems clearly related to classical German philosophical traditions that were strongly present in Wundt's thoughts—that is, the philosophies of Leibniz, Kant, Tetens, Fichte, and Schopenhauer. In Wundt's work, the central control process is represented by the term "apperception," which is a term that abounds in the German philosophical literature though rarely incorporated into Anglo-American thought.

Wundt was so elated by his measurement of the central control process that he went immediately to Speyer, Germany, to an annual convention of scientists. And standing there before a skeptical audience, the unknown young Wundt proudly announced the death of Herbartian psychology and the beginning of a new experimental psychology founded on his measurement of the central mental control process. He argued against Herbart's mental mechanics with the counter claim of the essential unity of consciousness, which was shown by the simple demonstration (Wundt's experiment) that we can apprehend only one thing at a time. We can only switch attention from single item to single item and at a rate no faster than approximately .1 sec per item.

The criticism of Herbart was to be extended to all of classical associationism. It is not correct to conceive of laws of association as operating directly or automatically, because, as Wundt claims in his *Grundzüge*, they are always subject to the accommodation of the central control. Wundt promises, in his early writings, that complex and often ad hoc associationist explanations of psychological phenomena will be replaced or augmented by more powerful laws of attention (or "apperception").

Among his philosophical predecessors, it was those "philosophers of the will" that impressed Wundt the most. It was apparently from Schopenhauer that he derived his central theoretical tenet that "volition is the type of phenomenon in terms of which all other psychological phenomena should be construed [1908, p. 162]." At about the same time he arrived in his new professorship at Leipzig and began organizing the psychological laboratory there, Wundt chose the word "voluntarism" (*Voluntarismus*) as the designation for his school of psychology. That word was actually suggested to him by a colleague at Leipzig, the historian Paulsen. It was not at all strange that Wundt should maintain close contact with historians, because before he ever lectured on psychology, he had lectured on history and cultural anthropology in his early years at Heidelberg (E. Wundt, 1927), where he had earned his living, however, as a physiologist and physician.

Schopenhauer's studies of volition were, of course, highly metaphysical. In that Wundt was vigorously antimetaphysical, he did not follow Schopenhauer in that approach and so described himself as "the first empirical voluntarist." Nevertheless, whenever a voluntarist philosophy appears, its immediate corollaries are purposivism and motivation. In Wundtian thought, this shows up in the view that psychological processes are understandable only in terms of their goal orientations or consequences, which is not the case for the events of physics (Wundt, 1866). Thus, Wundt came to the fateful separation of physical and psychological causality—a trend in his thinking that was raised to the level of a "principle" in the early 1890s. It was this principle that kept Wundt entangled in debate with the positivist movement. That movement, in opposition to Wundt, called for the "unity of the sciences" and hence opposed this distinction of types of causality. And it at times also called for the reduction of all sciences to physics. (See Danziger, 1979, in regard to the debates between the Wundtians and the positivists.)

"Physical causality" in Wundt's accounts is classical mechanics. In "psychological causality," as Wundt claims, new terms are introduced that are not found in physics; these are "purpose," "value," and "anticipations of the future." The central mechanism of psychological causality was, of course, apperception, which in modern terms translates roughly as "selective attention."

For Wundt, however, attention was more than mere selectivity; it was more fundamentally constructive and creative. And with that capacity in mind, Wundt derived his first principle for the description of elemental psychological processes—"the principle of creative synthesis." It is the statement that all experiences are constructed internally under the control of the central volitional process. The mental constructions produce new qualities, forms, or values that cannot be wholly attributed to external stimuli or to more elemental events. The synthesis ensures that the events of immediate experience will be organized into coherent wholes.

A number of corollaries followed this first principle of synthesis. A second principle, "the principle of psychic relations," states that the significance of any mental event is dependent upon its context. Each experience depends not only on integration and construction but also on the comparison and relation of that experience to its context. A third principle of "psychological contrasts" concerned related opponent-process effects. Simply stated, antithetical experiences intensify each other. After a period of pain, a slight pleasure will loom large; a sweet substance tastes much sweeter if eaten after a sour substance; and so on.

A parallel set of three principles concerned the extended development of psychological processes, whereas the above three are primarily concerned with the briefer development of immediate perceptions, cognitions, or memories. These further generalizations begin with "the principle of mental growth," which refers to the progressive integration or summation of experiences over longer intervals of time. Concept formation is the best example. Such formations are the basic mechanism of the continuity of experience and action. Without them, individual creative syntheses would remain separated from each other so that life would be disorganized and chaotic.

The second developmental principle is "the principle of heterogeneity of ends." It says that sequences of voluntary activity can be understood only in terms of the ends or goals toward which they are directed, but when those goals are attained, new and unforeseen results are always produced. That is, although we may be propelled by purposes and goals, we can never fully anticipate what the consequences of our actions will be.

The last of these Wundtian generalizations, "the principle of development toward opposites," is an extension of the above principle of contrasts. It states that people's emotions, behaviors, and experiences, when viewed developmentally, fluctuate between opposing tendencies. A long period of one type of activity or experience builds up a pressure to seek some opposite form of experience or action. These fluctuations, Wundt observed, are found not only in the life and experience of the individual but also in the pattern of human history. Moods, styles, and social systems all reflect such cyclic patterns.

It was characteristic of Wundt's writing that he amassed so much material, ostensibly illustrating these six generalizations, that it seems few have ever been able to read through it all. Let me summarize by quoting Charles Hubbard Judd, who may have read it all and who was, I believe, one of the more dedicated and consistent of Wundt's American students. Judd (1932) concludes that Wundt's psychology was "functional and synthetic, never atomistic and structural [p. 219]."

On the last page and last paragraph of his *Lectures on Human and Animal Psychology*, Wundt summarizes the essence of his psychology, so I will present that statement here. The following is taken from the 1892 edition, which appeared at the midpoint of his career:

> Physical causality and psychological causality are polar opposites. The former always implies the postulate of a material substance; the latter never transcends the limits of what is immediately given in mental experience. "Substance" is a surplus metaphysical notion for which psychology has no use. And this accords with the fundamental character of mental life, which I would always have you keep in mind: It does not consist in the connection of unalterable objects and various states. In all its phases it is *process*; an *active*, not a passive, existence; *development*, not fixation. The understanding of the basic laws of this development is the primary goal of psychology [p. 495].

Let us now return to the historical issues that form the primary focus of the present chapter.

The Leibnizian versus the Lockean Tradition

G. S. Brett, once considered the most erudite among historians of psychology, employed a productive historical distinction between two contesting views of man (Brett, 1912). One view is identified largely with German philosophical traditions that received a strong impulse from Gottfried Leibniz at the beginning of the eighteenth century. This impulse underwent various transformations through German rationalism and romanticism. The other viewpoint, associated most often with English philosophy, may be linked with the name of John Locke, who held a position in the English-speaking world analogous to that of Leibniz in the German world. The names of Locke and Leibniz stand as symbols of two often opposed cultural trends that we must observe if we are to understand the history of psychology. In recent times, it was Gordon Allport who in his influential book *Becoming* (1955) brought home to American students the importance of this distinction.

Wundt viewed his psychology as the modern representative of the Leibnizian tradition, including the works of Spinoza, Wolff, Tetens, Kant, Humboldt, Mendelsohn, Hegel, Schelling, Fichte, and Schopenhauer. These influences included Leibniz's notions of volition, levels of consciousness, and holistic orientations; Spinoza's assertion that volition, or desiring and striving, is the supreme human faculty; Wolff's analyses of the distinctions between empiricist and rationalist psychology; Mendelsohn's notions of feelings and emotions; Kant's notion of volitional apperception; Hegel's use of developmental laws; Schelling's and Teten's writings on emotion and volition; and finally Fichte and Schopenhauer as more direct sources of Wundt's voluntarism. To say the least, Wundt was not unmindful of these historical antecedents. Most of his texts begin with a history-of-philosophy orientation.

Recall, now, the Lockean tradition. For those readers in the Anglo-American (and French) worlds, we have because of our history and cultural forms been most comfortable, or at least most instructed, in this tradition. Among the English thinkers, we regard Adam Smith, Hartley, Hume, and the Mills as our own. They are so familiar as to need little introduction. They, of course, showed many variations in their empiricist and materialist formulations. Closely related to this tradition were similar streams of thought in France carried forward by such thinkers as Diderot, Montesquieu, Condillac, or Condorcet.

Locke had taught that there is nothing in our mental processes but the product of sensation. This had prompted Leibniz to reply that there is nothing, of course, except the mental processes themselves. Leibniz thereby charged Locke with overlooking those central processes which, as Leibniz felt, are directive in the formation of experience. Among the intellectual descendants of these two philosophers, this difference of view has continued down to the present day.

Both Locke and Leibniz stood on the threshold of the burst of eighteenth-century intellectual activity known as the Enlightenment. The Anglo–French Enlightenment was, in particular, especially concerned with making a break with the mysticism and hermetic thought that had been strong in the previous intellectual epoch (see Robinson, 1975). Inspired by Newton's physics, the English and French thinkers that followed consistently attempted to reorient philosophy on a basis of physical science. For psychology in the Lockean tradition, this often meant a picture of man as under strict environmental control, or it meant models of man based on machines or on analogies to Newtonian mechanics. While rejecting the past, there was a spirited futurism found among many of these thinkers, and it shows in their many programs and projects for utopian societies (see Becker, 1932). In contrast to that Enlightenment spirit, the German *Aufklarung* generally retained a strong historical orientation. Thus, when considering a better or more perfect world, the German thinker would be more likely to describe a return to some golden or classical age in the past.

The American Temper

Early American thought is an offshoot of the Anglo-French Enlightenment. Locke's philosophy had spread rapidly throughout the colonies and had become a gospel in American academic institutions and eventually in

American politics (Roback, 1964). Locke's political philosophy spelled out the argument that should a king's rule become tyrannical and inimical to the welfare of his subjects, then those subjects would be justified in rebellion.

American society at its outset, however, was guided more by the practical necessities of survival. As a new society without a unique intellectual tradition of its own and remote from European educational centers, there is little wonder that this society would quite generally celebrate the yeoman's life and become suspicious of the obscurities of foreign philosophical systems. The pioneer's glorification of the ordinary man gave him special faculties that pedantic philosophers were thought to lack.

But there is one other exceptional example (besides that of Locke) of the acceptance of a European philosopher in America that is rather striking. The case I have in mind occurs later in the nineteenth century—that of Herbert Spencer, the self-made, self-educated, civil engineer turned philosopher. Some have described Spencer's work as having a rather home-spun, cracker-barrel quality. But it was more than his particular style that brought him success in America. According to the historian Hofstadter (1944), of all nineteenth-century philosophers, Spencer was closest to the spirit of the earlier Anglo-French Enlightenment of the eighteenth century. Yet, Spencer was also armed with visions for the *practical* application of the Darwinian theory of evolution.

Like his intellectual ancestors, Spencer had futurist utopian visions. He saw evolution marching forward toward the greatest perfection and the most complete happiness. But then we find that this final reward was offered in return for an acceptance of the miserable social and political conditions of the industrial society in which Spencer lived in England. Spencer's sociological writings give arguments against all state aid to the poor, sanitary supervision, regulations on housing, and protection from medical quacks. As he explained, "The whole effort of nature is to get rid of the poor and unfit, to clear the world of them, and make room for the better [Spencer, 1864, p. 415]."

Spencer made one celebrated visit to America in 1882, and it is likely that no other foreign intellectual has received a more welcoming reception here. No less than Andrew Carnegie promoted Spencer and entertained him lavishly. And some of Spencer's writings, which had not sold well in Europe, were serialized in popular American magazines.

Hofstadter (1944) described this period in American history, a time of rapid expansion and industrialization, as "a vast human caricature of the Darwinian struggle for existence and the survival of the fittest [p. 44]." Spencer furnished that society with its rationalizations in the form of social Darwinism. But as Hofstadter recounts, Spencer fell from American popularity as suddenly as he had arrived when it became obvious to influential Americans that a free social evolution was not proceeding in the desired directions. After Spencer's appeal had faded, in its place came *pragmatism*, a wholly American prescription that allows that men should manipulate and reorient the environment according to their needs and desires. The psychological viewpoints that were then emerging from James, Dewey, Hall, Cattell, Thorndike, and many of their compatriots were in Hall's (1912) words, "dietetic, efficient for living, working and thinking [p. 414]."

One trend, of perhaps special interest to the intellectual historian, was the Englishman Titchener's (Figure 2.1) influence in recasting Wundtian thought to render Wundt more compatible with British (Lockean) philosophical traditions (see Danziger, 1979). While at Cornell, Titchener cast himself successfully in the role of the primary representative of Wundtian psychology in

FIGURE 2.1 *Edward B. Titchener (1867–1927). One of Wundt's most influential students.*

America. (At the time, there was considerable competition for that role.) Yet in Titchener's hands, Wundt's principles of apperception, voluntarism, and purposivism, and Wundt's dominant interests in history are extremely muted or even fundamentally changed. Titchener's treatment of Wundt may be analogous in some respects to the British distortions of the viewpoints of the Viennese philosopher Wittgenstein, who had been transplanted to the British intellectual community early in this century (see Janik & Toulmin, 1973).

The Clash Of Cultures

In the late nineteenth century, practical necessities of American life included increasing needs for higher education. The German universities had, in that century, grown more rapidly than those elsewhere, and one could then find certain types of medical and scientific training only in Germany. Between mid-nineteenth century and World War I, approximately 50,000 Americans sought higher degrees in German (and Austrian) universities. The medical degree was most often sought, for a German medical degree would allow one to charge higher fees after the return to an American medical practice. At one point, American medical students were so numerous in Vienna that they were able to take over classes and demand that instruction be given in English. In spite of such linguistic reactions, American curiosity about things German was now growing. In the case of psychology, at that time, this meant curiosity about Wilhelm Wundt, the one professor who had done more than anyone else to put that discipline on a scientific foundation.

William James was an early follower, and indeed avid admirer, of Wundt (James, 1875). But alas, scholarly relations between Wundt and James apparently had no chance of success, and the sarcastic comments they soon directed toward each other are still quoted in textbooks. It may have started with Wundt, who did not reciprocate James's early admiration. Wundt only acknowledged that James was a talented writer but apparently felt that James never bore any sophisticated or original views on psychology.

The antagonism, however, ran much deeper than this, and it ran much beyond these two men. There was clearly, as is reflected in James's writings, a bewilderment on the part of many Americans for the intricate and painstaking laboratory methods of German science. (For a description of James's appeal to anti-German prejudices in his rejections of German experimental science, see Littman, 1979.) It was the same or a similar spirit that separated the two even more deeply in the realm of philosophy, where the intricacies and subtleties of language are so critical—the German linguistic forms seldom translating in any simple way into English. To James, the German-style scientific laboratory was a confusing "three-ring circus." To him, the language of German philosophy was simply "hideous." These and many similar comments by the highly influential James and several of his American contemporaries appealed to the native American xenophobia noted in the previous section.

Later, it was mostly James's polemics against Wundt that would be frequently remembered and quoted, but those statements were only a part of James's larger reaction. For example, James had acted as chairman for an international psychological congress in Paris in 1889. Upon his return, he described Herbert Spencer as "an ignoramus," G. E. Müller as "brutal," and Gustav Fechner as a man whose careful work in psychophysics would produce "just nothing."

Many American students who went to study in Wundt's laboratory had difficulties not unlike those suffered by James. The problems they faced are easy to understand. Imagine the 22-year-old American, with only a year or two of college German and an introductory philosophy course to prepare him, struggling to understand Wundt's lectures. Many of them survived, it seems, because although Wundt did not speak English, he understood it well enough so that the Americans were not compelled to answer in German. But at one point, according to Tawney (1921), Wundt had been on the verge of banning American students from his program because so many had lacked sufficient facility in German.

Indeed, despite all the American students who went abroad to attend Wundt's lectures, very little of Wundt's psychological system survived the return passage. It may be that it was seldom well understood. It is extremely clear that what did come back with these young Americans was the laboratory apparatus and the floor plan of Wundt's Leipzig laboratory. These were the things, from Wundt, which seemed to have the greatest impact on early American psychology. Viewed superficially, the early laboratories at Johns Hopkins, Harvard, Cornell, Chicago, Clark, Berkeley, Stanford, and other places would have appeared to be a great monument to Wundt. The instrumentation from the Leipzig laboratory proliferated in its American setting. But then when one reads the early American journals of psychology, one quickly realizes that Wundt was not truly honored in all this carpentry and shop work. That is, the tachistoscopes, timers, guages, and so on were not used for the study of volition but were soon measuring the habits, sensations, and associations of the Lockean tradition.

Wundt's first American student, G. Stanley Hall, dropped out of Wundt's lectures after one semester to turn to more understandable lectures that concerned physiology. Many years later, Hall brought out a book titled *Founders of Modern Psychology* (1912), which was widely read and which contained a 150–page chapter on Wundt. It is largely an intellectual biography of Wundt, yet it contains a large amount of fabricated information about Wundt's life and work, and like several other American writers of the time, Hall reveals conflicting feelings toward Wundt. In Leipzig, the German translation of Hall's text was received with disappointment, and Wundt (1915) immediately published a notice in a German literary magazine in which he said that Hall's account of his personal history "is a fictitious biography which was invented from beginning to end [p. 1080]." Several later American textbooks cited Hall's chapter as a source and accepted uncritically its description of Wundt. And up to and including the present day, Hall's chapter remains the longest and most detailed study of Wundt available in English.

Among the other early American students of Wundt, there was the highly energetic James McKeen Cattell, who unlike Hall, stuck it out in Leipzig and eventually, after some interruptions, received a Ph.D. from Wundt. But Cattell characterized himself as having no taste for philosophy, as being an apparatus man, and as having no interest in theorizing (Roback, 1964). It was Cattell whom Wundt singled out with that phrase so tirelessly repeated in American historical accounts, "ganz Amerikanisch," or "typically American."

Recognizing certain obvious scientific accomplishments in Wundt's formative psychological laboratory, many early American psychologists reflected ambiguous feelings toward Wundt. For example, Knight Dunlap, an early American behaviorist who once failed an attempt to learn German and who professed a dislike of German philosophy, included the following comment in his autobiography of 1932:

> The astonishing thing clearly seen in retrospect is that where we apparently have made our greatest breaks with the past, we have actually honored historical consistency the most. In casting overboard the most confusing accumulations of theory and interpretation (for which we may hold the Germans largely responsible), we have based our progress more solidly upon the methods and practical aims of the German laboratories. If we consider the long line of researches upon reaction-times, perception of space and time, memory and learning, and all the other studies of performance initiated a generation ago, we realize that our reconstructions and reformulations are but preparation for the more vigorous attack on these problems . . . we are but the more honoring the sturdy pioneers who filed the claims on the territories we now occupy [p. 58].

Another strong feature of the activities of that early generation of Wundt-trained American psychologists was their immediate turn, in so many cases, to applied and commercial interests. Even the most application-oriented of the German psychologists, Hugo Münsterberg, ended up pursuing his career in America. And Cattell, Judd, Hall, Witmer, Scripture, and many others were all soon engaged in commercializing psychology in one form or another. Contrary to superficial accounts, Wundt did not oppose applied psychology as such. He did oppose the use of the graduate schools of science and philosophy and of the Ph.D. degree as the route to applied technologies. There were, in Germany, numerous technological institutes that could ostensibly serve this function. Moreover, Wundt felt that a loss of sensitivity to the distinction between pure and applied science could be harmful to both areas (Wundt, 1910).

With the approach of World War I, the schism between Wundt and many of his American counterparts grew to a hopeless breach. His former students in America were now embarrassed by Wundt's political actions. In 1914, along with 92 other German professors, Wundt signed a manifesto appealing to the international community for understanding of the German position. Then came his book *Nations and Their Philosophies* (1914a), in which English and, by implication, American commercialism and morality is examined unfavorably. And finally, there appeared a pamphlet by Wundt titled *Concerning True War* (1914b), containing similar sentiments.

Let us look briefly at what Wundt said in these writings. The English and Americans, he felt, view the existence of man as a sum of commercial transactions that everyone makes as favorable for himself as possible. And so material values are wholly dominant in those societies, with all other aspects of life subordinate. The primary goals of British and American sciences is, he claimed, useful inventions and physical comforts, rather than the deepening of man's understanding of himself and of nature.

In describing what he found to be a shallowness of British ethical theories (particularly Spencer's), and what he found to be a simplistic, naive realism in British and American philosophy, he used as epithets the words "egotistic utilitarianism," "materialism," "positivism," and "pragmatism." In regard to political freedom, he claimed that the Anglo-American societies had little to do with true individualism. Rather, they led only to a leveling of life and a lack of diversity, where small but powerful economic interests are the chief agents in the formation of public opinion.

Wundt, it seems, feared the trends in the mass democratic civilization of the West. But it was not the fear of a defender of an old aristocracy (indeed Wundt had been involved in reform movements that went against the old German aristocracy). It was, rather, the fear of an intellectual fighting for a cultural heritage that he had dedicated his life to preserving and extending and that was now slipping away. His Leibnizian tradition, which he felt offered a higher view of man because of its emphasis on volition and intellect (Wundt, 1917), was now under severe threat from foreign forces and ideologies (cf. Ringer, 1969).

Among the reactions in Germany that followed upon the loss of the war there was a public clamor to abandon the older professors and to convert German universities into centers for applied subjects and practical training. The German psychological laboratories then went into decline under the pressure of this and other social-economic upheavals, although German psychology was not without some significant accomplishments during the period between the world wars. After Wundt's death, the old Leipzig laboratory became heavily concerned with "psychotechnics." Wundt was rarely ever read again in the English-speaking world.

It is one of the ironies of recent history that the anti-German attitudes of the American public were much greater during World War I than they were during World War II. The emotional rejections of German psychology (and science) that one reads in the literature of the World War I period may be interpreted in that light. At about the time of Wundt's death in 1920, caricatured accounts of him and of his psychology were beginning to appear, some from those writers in Germany who were eager to supersede him, some from those in America who were seeking additional justifications for divergent trends that were occupying the newer psychology in this country. These descriptions of Wundt were often motivated not out of serious or sympathetic interest in accurate historical portrayal but rather out of the usual presentist motives of elevating the status of one's own present-day work.

The particular descriptions of Wundt that became the accepted and ritual descriptions through the influence of E. G. Boring's 1950 history text may be seen today as the result of the many historical forces reviewed in this chapter. This is not to discredit Boring or his monumental work, for, at the time of its writing, Boring's description of Wundt was probably the most intelligible and most acceptable one for the great majority of American psychologists. For them, it served to crystalize a then coherent explanation of the history of psychology that had evolved in a way that was satisfying, that justified the course of psychology's progress in the first half of the twentieth century.

References

Allport, G. *Becoming: Basic considerations for a psychology of personality.* New Haven: Yale University Press, 1955.

Becker, C. L. *The heavenly city of the eighteenth-century philosophers.* New Haven: Yale University Press, 1932.

Blumenthal, A. L. *Language and psychology: Historical aspects of psycholinguistics.* New York: John Wiley, 1970.

Blumenthal, A. L. A reappraisal of Wilhelm Wundt. *American Psychologist*, 1975, *30*, 1081–1086.

Blumenthal, A. L. The founding father we never knew. *Contemporary Psychology*, 1979, *24*, 449–453.

Boring, E. G. *A history of experimental psychology.* New York: Century, 1929. (2nd ed., 1950.)

Boring, E. G. *Sensation and perception in the history of experimental psychology.* New York: Appleton-Century-Crofts, 1942.

Brett, G. S. *A history of psychology* (Vol. 2). London: Allen, 1912.

Bringmann, W., Balance, W., & Evans, R. Wilhelm Wundt 1832–1920: A brief biographical sketch. *Journal of the History of the Behavioral Sciences*, 1975, *11*, 287–397.

Danziger, K. The positivist repudiation of Wundt. *Journal of the History of the Behavioral Sciences*, 1979, *15*, 205–230.

Danziger, K. The history of introspection reconsidered. *Journal of the History of the Behavioral Sciences*, (in press).

Dunlap, K. Autobiography. In C. Murchison (Ed.), *A history of psychology in autobiography* (Vol. 2). Worcester, Mass,: Clark University Press, 1932.

Goldenweiser, A. *History, psychology, and culture.* New York: Knopf, 1932.

Hall, G. S. *Founders of modern psychology.* New York: Appleton, 1912.

Höffding, H. *Modern philosophers.* London: Macmillan, 1915

Hoffmann, A. (Ed.). *Wilhelm Wundt, Eine Würdigung.* Erfurt: Stenger, 1924.

Hofstadter, R. *Social Darwinism in American thought.* Philadelphia: University of Pennsylvania Press, 1944.

James, W. Review of *Grundzüge der physiologischen Psychologie* by W. Wundt. *North American Review*, 1875, *121*, 195–201.

James, W. *Principles of psychology*, Vol. I. New York: Holt, 1890.

Janik, A., & Toulmin, S. *Wittgenstein's Vienna*. New York: Simon and Schuster, 1973.

Judd, C. Autobiography. In C. Murchison (Ed.), *History of psychology in autobiography*. Worcester, Mass.: Clark University Press, 1932.

Kiesow, F. Il principio della sintesi creatrice di G. Wundt e la teoria della forma. *Archivo italiano di Psicologia*, 1929, *7*, 61–79.

Klein, D. B. *A history of scientific psychology*. New York: Basic Books, 1970.

Leahey, T. Something old, something new: Attention in Wundt and modern cognitive psychology. *Journal of the History of the Behavioral Sciences*. 1979, *15*, 242–252.

Littman, R. Social and intellectual origins of experimental psychology. In E. Hearst (Ed.) *The first century of experimental psychology*. Hillsdale, N.J.: Erlbaum, 1979.

Mischel, T. Wundt and the conceptual foundations of psychology. *Philosophical and Phenomenological Research*, 1970, *31*, 1–26.

Passkönig, O. *Die Psychologie W. Wundts*. Leipzig: Siegismund and Volkening, 1912.

Petersen, P. *Wilhelm Wundt und seine Zeit*. Stuttgart: Frommanns, 1925.

Rappard, H. *Psychology as self-knowledge: The development of the concept of the mind in German rationalistic psychology and its relevance today*. Assen, The Netherlands: Van Gorcum, 1979.

Roback, A. *A history of American psychology* (2nd ed.). New York: Colliers, 1964.

Robinson, D. *An intellectual history of psychology*. New York: Macmillan, 1975.

Ringer, R. *The decline of the German madarins*. Cambridge, Mass.: Harvard University Press, 1969.

Sabat, S. Wundt's physiological psychology in retrospect. *American Psychologist*, 1979, *34*, 635–638.

Samelson, F. History, origin myth and ideology: "Discovery" of social psychology. *Journal for the Theory of Social Behavior*, 1974, *4*, 217–231.

Sganzini, C. *Die Fortschritte der Völkerpsychologie von Lazarus bis Wundt*. Berne: Francke, 1913.

Spencer, H. *Social statics*. New York: Appleton, 1864.

Tawney, G. In memory of Wilhelm Wundt. *Psychological Review*. 1921, *28*, 178–181.

Villa, G. *Contemporary psychology* . (H. Manacorda, Trans.). London: Swan Sonnenschein, 1903. (Originally published, 1899.)

Wundt, E. *Wilhelm Wundts Werke*. Munich: Beck, 1927.

Wundt, W. *Die physicalischen Axiome und ihre Beziehung zum Causalprinzip*. Erlangen, Enke, 1866.

Wundt, W. *Grundzüge der physiologischen Psychologie*. Leipzig: Engelmann, 1874.

Wundt, W. *Vorlesungen über die Menschen- und Theirseele*. Hamburg: Voss, 1892. (Translated by J. Creighton and E. Titchener as *Lectures on human and animal psychology*. New York: Macmillan, 1894.)

Wundt, W. *Logik*, Vol. III. Stuttgart: Enke, 1908.

Wundt, W. Über reine und angewandte Psychologie. *Psychologische Studien*. 1910, *5*, 1–47.

Wundt, W. *Die Nationen und ihre Philosophie*. Leipzig: Kröner, 1914. (a)

Wundt, W. *Über den wahrhaften Krieg*. Leipzig: Kröner, 1914. (b)

Wundt, W. Eine Berichtigung. (Gegen das Buch von Stanley Hall, Die Begrunder der modernen Psychologie.) *Literarisches Zentralblatt für Deutschland*, 1915 (84), 1080.

Wundt, W. *Leibnitz*. Leipzig: Kröner, 1917.

Recommended Readings

Blumenthal, A. L., Language and psychology. *Historical aspects of psycholinguistics*. New York: John Wiley, 1970.

Klein, D. B., *A History of scientific psychology: Its origins and philosophical backgrounds*. New York: Basic Books, Inc., 1970. (Especially Chapter 23.)

Mischel, T. Wundt and the conceptual foundations of psychology. *Philosophy and Phenomenological Research*, 1970, *31*, 1–26.

Rieber, R. W., *et al.*, (Ed.). *Wilhelm Wundt and the making of scientific psychology.* New York: Plenum Publishing Co., 1980.

Rychlak, J. F. *The psychology of rigorous humanism.* New York: John Wiley & Sons, 1977. (Especially Chapter 3.)

Vanderplas, J. M. *Controversial issues in psychology.* Boston: Houghton Mifflin Company, 1966. (Especially Sections 2 and 4.)

Francis Galton
and American Psychology

ANTHROPOMETRIC
LABORATORY

For the measurement in various
ways of **Human Form and Faculty**.

Entered from the Science Collection of the S. Kensington Museum.

This laboratory is established by Mr. Francis Galton for
the following purposes:—

1. For the use of those who desire to be accurate-
ly measured in many ways, either to obtain timely
warning of remediable faults in development, or to
learn their powers.

2. For keeping a methodical register of the principal measurements of each person, of which he
may at any future time obtain a copy under reasonable restrictions. His initials and date of birth will
be entered in the register, but not his name. The
names are indexed in a separate book.

3. For supplying information on the methods,
practice, and uses of human measurement.

4. For anthropometric experiment and research,
and for obtaining data for statistical discussion.

Charges for making the principal measurements:
THREEPENCE each, to those who are already on the Register.
FOURPENCE each, to those who are not:— one page of the
Register will thenceforward be assigned to them, and a few extra
measurements will be made, chiefly for future identification.

The Superintendent is charged with the control of the laboratory
and with determining in each case, which, if any, of the extra measurements may be made, and under what conditions.

H & W Brown, Printers, 20 Fulham Road, S W

PSYCHOLOGY:
THEORETICAL-HISTORICAL PERSPECTIVES

ISBN 0-12-588265-3

Karl Pearson (1924, p. 340) has told us that Francis Galton's motto was *"Whenever you can, count."* He followed it with extraordinary persistence. For example, having had his portrait painted at age 60 and again at 81, Galton (1905) could report that each artist had touched the brush to canvas about 20,000 times, although the first used slow, methodical strokes and the second (in the impressionist era) made flurries of quick dabs. The habit of counting repetitive acts is also a conspicuous behavior of many American psychologists. One of the most distinguished of these, while taking part in a conference in a high-level government office, skillfully increased the rate of finger wagging by a long-winded participant by reinforcing each such gesture with a nod of his head. This is not in itself proof of Galton's enduring influence, but it does illustrate the fact that American psychology is largely imbued with the essence of Galtonism: the conviction that any significant problem can be stated in terms that make it accessible to quantitative study.

That conviction was the foundation for each of Galton's many important contributions. Some that had very wide application in the work of other psychologists are these:

1. The method of word association (Galton, 1879), which first opened the way to quantitative analysis of the higher thought processes and individual dynamics.
2. The introduction of test batteries (Galton, 1885a) to arrive at a many-sided assessment of abilities for a given person.
3. Systematic use of the questionnaire (Galton, 1880), out of which all inventory-type tests were developed.
4. Use of the normal distribution for purposes of classification (Galton, 1869), which has been a boon to the sophisticated, as well as devising the system of scoring by centile ranks (Galton, 1885b), which has made it possible for us to communicate with the unsophisticated.
5. The method of twin comparison, which, aside from its special application to the problem of nature versus nurture, is notable as the first use of a control group in psychological research, since Galton (1876) compared results based on pairs of identical twins with those based on fraternal twins.
6. Finally, and most important in this abbreviated list, the concepts of regression (Galton, 1885c) and correlation (1888), which opened up new possibilities for the analysis of complex phenomena that, like heredity, are dependent on multiple influences.

In early textbooks and manuals of experimental psychology, Galton's name is cited most often in connection with Galton's whistle, Galton's bar, or Galton's weights. These products of his anthropometric research were to be found in almost every laboratory in which students were trained in the psychophysical methods. His more important innovations in experimental design and statistical analysis of data were assimilated more slowly, but without them, it would have been a far more difficult task to give psychology its new direction, that is, to change it from a normative science, which had been conceived as the propaedeutic basis for philosophy, into a functional science of behavior, independent of philosophy.

James McKeen Cattell was the most important conduit of Galton's influence on American psychology (Figure 3.1). Early in this century, Cattell's rank among American psychologists, as judged by his peers, was second only to that of William James (Cattell, 1903 and 1929). When Galton died, only five months after the passing of James, Cattell (1911) wrote that these were the two greatest men he had known. In later years, he said flatly that Galton was

FIGURE 3.1 *James McKeen Cattell. One of Galton's most influential students.*

the greatest man he had ever known (Cattell, 1928, 1929). Rating scientists for distinction was a serious matter to Cattell, who would not have made such a judgment without due deliberation.

Since Cattell had both G. Stanley Hall and Wundt as his formal teachers, we cannot assess his relationship to Galton without reviewing the full course of his university students. In 1880, Cattell, not yet 20, heard Lotze at Göttingen (Sokal, 1971). After an interlude of study at Paris and Geneva, he spent a semester at Leipzig, where he heard both Wundt and Heinze. After this double exposure to the new psychology, he planned to continue his work under Lotze (Note 1), but this plan was upset by Lotze's sudden death. In 1882 Cattell enrolled at Johns Hopkins University and won a scholarship with an essay on Lotze's philosophy. There were no psychology courses during the first semester, and his principal interests then were team sports and personal experimentation with drugs. Then Hall was brought in, and Cattell enrolled in his laboratory course along with John Dewey, Joseph Jastrow, and E. M. Hartwell. Except for Cattell, they were all to complete doctorates at Johns Hopkins. In Hall's laboratory, Cattell performed the pioneer experiment on the time required to recognize letters. The next year, Cattell left Johns Hopkins because of what he perceived as double-dealing when, despite private assurances to the contrary, Hall recommended Dewey more strongly for the scholarship that Cattell had been holding (Ross, 1972). He returned to Leipzig and Wundt faute de mieux.

The results of the experiments performed at Johns Hopkins are included in Cattell's first article in the *Philosophische Studien* (1885). The clue to the fact that it was not performed at Leipzig is in the initials of the observers who participated. They include J.D. for Dewey, E.H. for Hartwell, and G.H. for Hall. One can only speculate as to what extent Cattell's resentment toward Hall, and to what extent Wundt's jealousy of other laboratories, contributed to the failure to mention where the experiment had been performed.

Cattell was justly proud of this experiment, but he is not strictly accurate in the claim that it was the first to be concerned with individual differences and to make no appeal to introspection. This point is not trivial, because it is so often said that interest in individual differences was an autochthonous development of American soil. Obersteiner (1879), a collaborator of Exner at Vienna, published an account of reaction-time experiments in which he emphasized the importance of differences among individuals. He found no sex difference in maximum speed of reaction, but said that persons of the serving class are less consistent in performance and that extremely long times are an indication of mental derangement. Since this article appeared in English, it might well have been known to Cattell, and was almost certainly known to Hall, before Cattell did his experiment. Furthermore, Galton's friend Romanes (1883) reported an experiment in which the subjects were allowed 20 seconds to read a short printed paragraph and were then required to write down all they could remember. Although the subjects were "accustomed to read much" they showed "a positively astonishing difference . . . with respect to the rate at which they were able to read [p. 136]." Romanes also remarked that the swifter readers generally retained more of the content than the slow readers. Even at this early date, therefore, Cattell and America had no monopoly on psychological research in individual differences, or on using objective criteria of performance.

At Leipzig, Cattell broke precedent by rejecting the introspective problem that Wundt assigned to him, and he was permitted to continue work on his own problem. This time, he used far more elegant apparatus of his own design—the gravity tachistoscope and the voice-key (Cattell, 1886)—and the work was carried on in his own rooms rather than in Wundt's laboratory, in part because of "Wundt's refusal to admit any subject to the laboratory except a psychologist who could use the results introspectively [Cattell, 1928, p. 430]."

After leaving Leipzig, Cattell spent the greater part of 2 years in England. He participated in a stillborn effort to establish a psychological laboratory at Cambridge (Sokal, 1972) but worked chiefly at Galton's laboratory, which had originally been established at the International Health Exhibition. Cattell (1928) states that he helped set it up in its new quarters at the South Kensington Museum of Science and that he and Galton "began in cooperation the preparation of a book of instructions for a laboratory course in psychology [p. 432]." It was an ideal learning situation. The famous article "Mental Tests and Measurements" (Cattell, 1890) was one outgrowth of this experience, and the recommendation in it that all students should take a battery of anthropometric tests followed a line of thought that Galton (1874) had initiated much earlier. Its most important outcome was that, as Walker (1929) points out, Cattell's psychology courses were the first "to make consistent and systematic use of statistical methods [p. 157]." It was a sharp turn from the Leipzig orientation, for, as Walker also states, "It does not appear that Wundt himself was committed to a belief in the statistical treatment of the results of experimentation [p. 165]." It was from Galton that Cattell acquired that faith that caused it to be said, supposedly first by Titchener, that "Cattell's god is Probable Error" (Wells, 1944).

Galton was a figure with whom Cattell could readily identify. Both men had a flair for mechanical invention, and they also shared an obvious pride of membership in that natural aristocracy of talent that even Thomas Jefferson (1818/1925) recognized as deserving of recognition. By calling Galton the greatest man he ever met, Cattell, who was probably conscious of the many points of resemblance, was not lowering his own stature. His career might have been quite different had it not happened that, as Lyman Wells (1944) put it, his "formative years brought him into contact with another exceptional man through whom his interests were fixed upon the quantitative properties of the human mind [p. 274]." It is clear that Cattell profited from his contact with Galton immeasurably more than from his contact with Wundt, and American psychology profited as a result.

Joseph Jastrow was another conduit of Galton's influence. He inherited no silver spoon and had no opportunity to study abroad. While still a student, he began earning money by writing papers of a popular scientific character (Jastrow, 1930). Thus, he was launched on his career as a popularizer of scientific psychology, whose own contributions were of secondary importance. The titles of some of Jastrow's early papers show the Galton influence already at work: "Some Peculiarities in the Age Statistics of the United States" (1885a); "Composite Portraiture" (1885b); "The Longevity of Great Men" (1886); "The Dreams of the Blind" (1888a); "Eye-Mindedness and Ear-Mindedness" (1888b).

In 1888 Cattell returned from England to a chair at the University of Pennsylvania, Jastrow received an appointment at Wisconsin, and Hall and Sanford went from Johns Hopkins to newly founded Clark University. Almost overnight, America had four active psychology laboratories in place of one.

With a means of livelihood at last assured, Jastrow took leave the following spring for his first trip abroad. On his return, ever the popularizer, he published a series of articles on "Aspects of Modern Psychology" (Jastrow, 1890). He said of Galton's work that it "could not readily be classified in the psychological activity of any country [p. 96]," but formed "a unique chapter of science, interesting no one more deeply than the students of scientific psychology [p. 96f]." He described American psychology as characterized by "a readiness to introduce innovations whenever circumstances will allow, and . . . utilizing the freedom . . . of intellectual and educational youthfulness [p. 98]." With hindsight, we may read these statements to mean that Galton was laying down new lines for psychology, and only the Americans were free enough from the restraints of traditional university disciplines to follow in the path he indicated.

Jastrow was active in the American Association for the Advancement of Science, and he was asked to organize the psychology exhibit for the World's Columbian Exposition, which opened in Chicago in 1893. Galton's influence was dominant in shaping the result, which Jastrow (1930) later described as "the first attempt to introduce tests to the American public [p. 142]." All visitors were informed that "any one who wishes can have, by the payment of a small fee, various tests applied and can be measured and recorded upon cards which are given to the person, while the record is made upon the charts and tables hanging on the walls of the laboratory [World's Columbian Exposition, 1893, p. 1092]." It was as if Galton's anthropometric laboratory had been transported to Chicago. Popplestone (Note 2) points out that the lack of any historical record of the public response compels us to wonder if the affair may not have been a dud, perhaps because it was located in a remote corner of the vast exposition grounds. Whatever the public response may have been, this mobilization of all the current techniques of testing surely stimulated additional interest among psychologists themselves.

Even before the exposition opened, Titchener (1893) deplored the manner in which the exhibit confused anthropometrics with psychology, using the very argument that had driven Cattell to experiment in his own rooms: that a psychological experiment presupposes introspectively practiced observers. "It is one of the commonest errors," he wrote, "that since we are all using our minds, in some way or another, everyone is qualified to take part in psychological experimentation. As well maintain, that because we all eat bread, we are all qualified to bake it [p. 190]." His protest was futile. Soon most of the new psychology laboratories, though they might be headed by Wundt's former students, were busy with anthropometrics. Titchener (Note 3) in desperation wrote to Galton to solicit aid to repulse the invasion. "You would speak with authority," he wrote, "as you could not be suspected of wanting to undervalue Anthropometry. Unless some sort of protest is made, the American laboratories will all run over into anthropometrical statistics: which are, of course, valuable—but not psychology." The appeal is testimony to the high prestige that Galton enjoyed, but he must have been amused to be thus solicited to assist in throttling his own creation to defend the purity of experimental psychology.

Madison Bentley (1936), then a student at Cornell, later said of this period that among the "adventitious" factors that shaped the careers of young psychologists might be the "worship of a Wundt or a Galton [p. 56]." Among the partisans of Galton, we must count Terman and Thorndike. Terman (1932) wrote in his autobiography: "Of the founders of modern psychology, my greatest admiration is for Galton [p. 331]." Thorndike (1936) wrote: "Excellent work can surely be done by men with widely different notions of what psychology should be, the best work of all perhaps being done by men like Galton, who gave little or no thought to what it is or should be [p. 270]."

The case of Robert S. Woodworth (1932) is most interesting. If we say with Boring (1950b) that "it is almost true that American psychology was personified in the person of Cattell [p. 163]," we may add that it is equally true that his student Woodworth personified the shift of orientation without which such a statement could not approach validity. Woodworth's undergraduate teacher in philosophy directed him to study science as a preparation for philosophy; when later he abandoned philosophy in favor of a career in psychology, he spent more than 5 years of apprenticeship as a physiologist, to complete the preparation. Yet he found in Cattell, whose attention went to the probable error and not to the brain, "The chief of all [his] teachers in giving shape to [his] psychological thought and work [Woodworth, 1932, p. 367]." This epitomizes the development of American psychology during the last quarter of the nineteenth century. Having begun as a propaedeutic to philosophy, it was soon caught up in the fascination of research on the physiology of brain, nerves, sense organs, and muscle, but then transferred its principal energies to the study of behavior, including especially the quantitative study of competence in all its manifestations. Psychology was able to pass through the two earlier phases because of the fluidity of the new universities, one consequence of which was that instruction in "mental science" passed from the hands of the college presidents, who almost invariably had theological training, into the hands of specialists. If we wish to claim the third phase as distinctively American, we shall have to give Galton a posthumous grant of American citizenship. We must ask whether the swift progress of individual psychology in the United States is not to be explained by the absence of the restraints on such development that were imposed by the more rigid university structure in Europe, at least as much as by the presence of stronger motivating forces in that direction.

In 1904, when the world met at St. Louis, psychology had another chance to speak to the nation. On that occasion, Cattell (1904) not only rejected mentalism, in his statement that "it is usually no more necessary for the subject to be a psychologist than it is for the vivisected frog to be a physiologist [p. 180]," but also rejected all limiting definitions for the new science, declaring that psychology consists of "what the psychologist is interested in *qua* psychologist [p. 179]." It was the first time that psychology had been defined broadly enough to include Cattell's true mentor, Galton.

By the time of the entry of the United States into World War I, the study of individual differences accounted for well over half of all work reported at meetings of the American Psychological Association, other than papers of historical and philosophical nature, which had meanwhile declined from the largest to the smallest category (Cattell, 1917). American psychologists had developed the skills that they put to work in the war effort.

In 1929 Cattell presided over the Ninth International Congress at New Haven. It was neither in his nature nor in the American character to acknowledge the full extent of our indebtedness to foreign mentors. "Wundt and Galton," he said, "are the foreign psychologists whom we most honor, but it may be that if neither of them had lived psychology in America would be much what it is [1929, p. 3]." Boring (1929) concurred in part, writing that "it is an open question as to how much [Galton] influenced Cattell and the American tradition of individual psychology and the mental tests [p. 428]." In the revised edition of his history (1950a), this passage is omitted, and we read instead: "Perhaps it is true that America, while giving homage to Wundt, has overlooked Galton, to whom it owes a greater debt [p. 488]." Let us now consider some of the reasons why we have been so much more ready to give homage to one than to the other.

The rise of American psychology was linked with the reform of American higher education, which was signaled in 1869 by the election of a chemist, Charles Eliot, as president of Harvard University. The theological domination of the colleges was to give way to an industrial–scientific orientation. The German universities were taken as models. Their strength was in their laboratories, which had originated with Liebig's chemical laboratory at Giessen in 1824, and had subsequently provided the basis for Germany's world leadership in physiology. For a young man seeking a job in the expanding system of American universities, experience in a German university was like money in the bank. Students of chemistry and physiology flocked to Germany. Psychologists were by comparison a miniscule group, but when they heard of a psychology laboratory at Leipzig, it became their Mecca. Even those who disliked what they found there were often victims of the cognitive dissonance effect. After a young man spends several years of effort to earn a degree in a foreign country, all the while yearning for a sweetheart back home, and then returns triumphantly to a prestigious job and chances of advancement, he is unlikely to say that another course of study might have been more satisfying. Wundt was more than a prophet: He really led his American students into the promised land. Galton, on the other hand, was a man who lacked university status in a country that lacked a psychology laboratory and where the leading universities were still primarily devoted to educating country divines who might make a hobby of science. Americans might read his books and articles with excitement, but there was no economic inducement to acclaim him as a leader.

It is universally agreed that all Galton's work in psychology radiated from one dominant concern: to learn how we might best manipulate the forces of evolution to mankind's advantage. While philosophers battled over the ethical implications of natural selection, or attempted to subordinate it to a cosmic drive toward higher forms of existence, Galton the pragmatist turned his attention to the phenomenon of variation, as providing the means by which we might accelerate the process. The anthropometric laboratory he set up at great personal expense was a device to tease the public into providing the data he needed for his research. His interest in individual differences was therefore derivative, but the resulting anthropometric work attracted the interest of psychologists. His ideas about evolution were more correct than Spencer's, and his ideas on the mechanism of heredity were more correct than Darwin's, but they had little following. It was Spencer who was almost universally regarded as the grand theorist of evolution. The American historian Fiske (1874) had ranked Spencer's achievement with that of Newton, and the British zoologist Mitchell (1910) compared him to Descartes and declared that his writings "may be regarded as the *Principes de la Philosophie* of the 19th century [p. 32]."

Galton's influence derived wholly from his genius in quantitative investigation. He arrived at the concepts of regression and correlation because they were peculiarly appropriate to the study of heredity and thus also to the study of any complex phenomenon that is influenced in its quantitative manifestation by a large number of causal factors. Indeed, it has proved even more valuable for econometrics than for anthropometrics. No rival claims of priority, no record of independent discovery by others, dims the brilliance of this discovery. For Cattell to have said that American psychology might have been much the same without Galton is an understandable expression of vanity, but it is difficult to see how a historian can concur in that judgment. As we have seen, Boring did retreat from it.

The principal focus of this chapter has been on Galton's positive contributions. There was also a negative aspect that should not go unmentioned. He was not free from the almost universal prejudice of his time that saw white Europeans as of greater worth than other races. Galton's advocacy of eugenics provided racists with a rationale for genocide that has been extensively exploited in the United States. When, however, we assess the degree of his culpability on this issue, we should not attribute to him opinions that were not his own. His views, as he himself remarked (1903), were often misrepresented. I shall discuss briefly some aspects of his thinking that are usually overlooked.

1. It was not in Galton's manner of thinking to condemn a whole race as inferior. Once, after hearing a paper about the "dealings of colonists with aborigines," he said in discussion (which was reported in the third person) that "ethnologists were apt to look upon race as something more definite than it really was. He presumed it meant no more than the average of the characteristics of all the persons who were supposed to belong to the race, and this average was continually varying [Galton, 1882, p. 352]." He went on to indicate his regret that Englishmen did not, like the ancient Romans, live more closely with the populations of the subject colonies and make them more welcome in England. The notion of racial "purity" had no place in Galton's scheme of eugenics.

2. Galton was always more interested (as Pearson, 1930, p. 233, points out with obvious regret) in raising high intelligence than in eliminating low intelligence, which he was much more willing to leave to the slow processes of natural selection. He never subscribed to the theory of degeneration, which was so popular late in the nineteenth century and which was the basis of the direction that the eugenics movement took after Galton's death.

3. He always insisted that the great need was for research, to acquire a knowledge of heredity that would be a sufficient basis for wise eugenic practices (or, as we would now say, for informed genetic counseling). He fully recognized the danger of even well-intentioned programs based on inadequate knowledge. He wrote, for example: "Our present ignorance of the conditions by which the level of humanity may be raised is so gross, that I believe if we had some dictator of the Spartan type, who exercised absolute power over marriages . . . and who acted with the best intentions, he might perhaps do even more harm than good to the race [1884, p. 3]."

4. Finally, Galton was fully aware of the need for attention to environmental influences, both in research on heredity and in efforts to improve society. The conclusion of his study of twins, in which he defined the nature–nurture issue, was stated thus: "Nature prevails enormously over nurture when the differences in nurture do not exceed what is commonly to be found among persons of the same rank of society and in the same country [1876, p. 404]." He perfectly appreciated the statistical fact that more genetic gold can be mined

from the great masses of the disadvantaged than from the thin stratum of those who have risen to distinction (1885b). That is why he could claim that "the sterling values of nurture, including all kinds of sanitary improvements" were "powerful auxiliaries" to his cause (1873, p. 116). He also emphasized that "it cannot be too strongly hammered into popular recognition that a well-developed human being, capable in body and mind, is an expensive animal to rear [Galton, 1903, as quoted in Pearson, 1930, p. 253]." To rear, be it noted, not to breed.

It is especially fitting for American psychologists to recall one more expression of Galton's recognition of the power of environment: "The most likely nest . . . for self-reliant natures is to be found in States founded and maintained by emigrants [1883, p. 82]." Surely, this is one reason why American psychology displayed what Jastrow called "a readiness to introduce innovations [1890, p. 98]." Galton's innovative methods for the study of human capacities were accepted as a part of psychology, and they helped to give American psychology its distinctive character. It seems quite unlikely that the same development could have taken place in anything like the same time span without Galton's influence.

Reference Notes

1. Sokal, M. M. *Influences on a young psychologist: James McKeen Cattell, 1880–1890.* Paper presented at the meeting of the History of Science Society, Washington, D.C., 1969.
2. Popplestone, J. A. *The psychological exhibit at the Chicago World's Fair of 1893.* Paper presented at the meeting of the Western Psychological Association, Los Angeles, 1976.
3. Titchener, E. B. Letter to Francis Galton, dated 18 April 1898. (Copy in Archives of the History of American Psychology, The University of Akron, Akron, Ohio.)

References

Bentley, M. Autobiography. In C. Murchison (Ed.), *History of psychology in autobiography* (Vol. 3). Worcester, Mass.: Clark University Press, 1936.

Boring, E. G. *History of experimental psychology.* New York: Appleton-Century, 1929.

Boring, E. G. *History of experimental psychology* (2nd ed.). New York: Appleton-Century, 1950. (a)

Boring, E. G. The influence of evolutionary theory upon American psychological thought. In S. Persons (Ed.), *Evolutionary thought in America.* New Haven: Yale University Press, 1950. (b)

Cattell, J. McK. Ueber die Zeit der Erkennung und Nennung von Schriftzeichen, Bildern und Farben. *Philosophische Studien,* 1885, *2,* 635–650.

Cattell, J. McK. Psychometrische Untersuchungen. I. Apparate und Methoden. *Philosophische Studien,* 1886, *3,* 305–335.

Cattell, J. McK. Mental tests and measurements. *Mind,* 1890, *15,* 373–380.

Cattell, J. McK. Statistics of American psychologists. *American Journal of Psychology,* 1903, *14,* 310–328.

Cattell, J. McK. The conceptions and methods of psychology. *Popular Science Monthly,* 1904, *66,* 176–186.

Cattell, J. McK. Francis Galton. *Popular Science Monthly*, 1911, *78*, 309–311.

Cattell, J. McK. Our psychological association and research. *Science*, 1917, *45*, 275–284.

Cattell, J. McK. Early psychological laboratories. In M. L. Reymert (Ed.), *Feelings and emotions; the Wittenberg Symposium*. Worcester, Mass.: Clark University Press, 1928.

Cattell, J. McK. *Psychology in America. Address of the president of the Ninth International Congress of Psychology*. New York: Science Press, 1929.

Fiske, J. *Outlines of cosmic philosophy* (2 vols.). London: Macmillan, 1874.

Galton, F. *Hereditary genius*. London: Macmillan, 1869.

Galton, F. Hereditary improvement. *Fraser's Magazine*, 1873, *7* (NS), 116–130.

Galton, F. Proposal to apply for anthropological statistics from schools. *Journal of the Anthropological Institute*, 1874, *3*, 308–311.

Galton, F. The history of twins, as a criterion of the relative power of nature and nurture. *Journal of the Anthropological Institute*, 1876, *5*, 391–406.

Galton, F. Psychometric experiments. *Brain*, 1879, *2*, 149–162.

Galton, F. Statistics of mental imagery. *Mind*, 1880, *5*, 301–318.

Galton, F. Discussant. *Journal of the Anthropological Institute*, 1882, *11*, 352–353.

Galton, F. *Inquiries into human faculty and its development*. New York: Macmillan, 1883.

Galton, F. *Record of family faculties*. London: Macmillan, 1884.

Galton, F. On the anthropometric laboratory of the late International Health Exposition. *Journal of the Anthropological Institute*, 1885, *14*, 205–219. (a)

Galton, F. Some results of the anthropometric laboratory. *Journal of the Anthropological Institute*. 1885, *14*, 275–287. (b)

Galton, F. Types and their inheritance. *Science*, 1885, *6*, 268–274. (c)

Galton, F. Co-relations and their measurement, chiefly from anthropometric data. *Proceedings of the Royal Society*, 1888, *45*, 135–145.

Galton, F. In *The Daily Chronicle* (London), 29 July, 1903. (Excerpts in K. Pearson, *The life, letters and labours of Francis Galton* [Vol. 3a]. Cambridge, England: University Press, 1930.)

Galton, F. Number of strokes of the brush in a picture. *Nature*, 1905, *72*, 198.

Jastrow, J. Some Peculiarities of the Age Statistics of the United States. *Science*, 1885, *5*, 461–464. (a)

Jastrow, J. Composite Portraiture. *Science*, 1885, *6*, 165–168. (b)

Jastrow, J. The Longevity of Great Men. *Science*, 1886, *8*, 294–296.

Jastrow, J. The Dreams of the Blind. *New Princeton Review*, 1888, *5*, 18–24. (a)

Jastrow, J. Eye-mindedness and Ear-mindedness. *Popular Science Monthly*, 1888, *33*, 597–608. (b)

Jastrow, J. Aspects of modern psychology. In H. Oldenberg, J. Jastrow, & C. H. Cornill, (Eds). *Epitomes of three sciences*. Chicago: Open Court Publishing Company, 1890.

Jastrow, J. Autobiography. In C. Murchison (Ed.), *History of psychology in autobiography* (Vol. 1). Worcester, Mass.: Clark University Press, 1930.

Jefferson, T. Letter dated 28 October, 1818. In P. Wilstach (Ed.), *Correspondence of John Adams and Thomas Jefferson*. Indianapolis: Bobbs-Merrill, 1925.

M[itchell], P. C. Evolution. In *Encyclopaedia Britannica* (11th ed.). Cambridge, England: University Press, 1910.

Obersteiner, H. Experimental researches on attention. *Brain*, 1879, *1*, 439–453.

Pearson, K. *The life, letters and labours of Francis Galton* (3 vols. in 4). Cambridge, England: University Press, 1914, 1924, 1930.

Romanes, G. J. *Mental evolution in animals*. London: Kegan Paul & Co., 1883.

Ross, D. *G. Stanley Hall: The psychologist as prophet*. Chicago: University of Chicago Press, 1972.

Sokal, M. M. The unpublished autobiography of James McKeen Cattell. *American Psychologist*, 1971, *26*, 626–635.

Sokal, M. M. Psychology at Victorian Cambridge—The unofficial laboratory of 1887–1888. *Proceedings of the American Philosophical Society*, 1972, *116*, 145–147.

Terman, L. M. Autobiography. In C. Murchison (Ed.), *History of psychology in autobiography* (Vol. 2). Worcester, Mass.: Clark University Press, 1932.

Thorndike, E. L. Autobiography. In C. Murchison (Ed.), *History of psychology in autobiography* (Vol. 3). Worcester, Mass.: Clark University Press, 1936.

Titchener, E. B. Anthropometry and experimental psychology. *Philosophical Review*, 1893, 2, 187–192.

Walker, H. M. *Studies in the history of statistical Method*. Baltimore: Williams & Wilkins, 1929.

Wells, F. L. James McKeen Cattell: 1860–1944. *American Journal of Psychology*, 1944, 57, 270–275.

Woodworth, R. S. Autobiography. In C. Murchison (Ed.), *History of psychology in autobiography* (Vol. 2). Worcester, Mass.: Clark University Press, 1932.

World's Columbian Exposition. *Official Directory*. Chicago, Ill., 1893.

Recommended Readings

Cravens, H. *The triumph of evolution: American scientists and the heredity-environment controversy*. Philadelphia: University of Pennsylvania Press, 1978.

Forrest, D. W. *Francis Galton: The life and work of a Victorian genius*. New York: Taplinger Publishing Co., 1974.

Galton, F. *Memories of my life*. London: Methuen & Co., 1908.

Pearson, K. *The life, letters and labours of Francis Galton*. (3 vols. in 4.) Cambridge: The University Press, 1914, 1924, 1930.

Sokal, M. M. Psychology at Victorian Cambridge—the unofficial laboratory of 1887–1888. *Proceedings of the American Philosophical Society*, 1972, 116, 145–147.

Walker, H. *Studies in the history of statistical method*. Baltimore: Williams & Wilkins, 1927.

RICHARD P. HIGH
WILLIAM R. WOODWARD

4

William James and Gordon Allport: Parallels in Their Maturing Conceptions of Self and Personality

> No psychology, at any rate, can question
> the existence of personal selves. The worst
> a psychology can do is so to interpret these
> selves as to rob them of their worth.
> JAMES, 1890, Vol. 1, p. 220

> If you are working with animal
> drives—fine; but don't forget that you have
> bracketed human aspirations.
> ALLPORT, 1968, p. 23

AMERICAN SCIENCE SERIES—ADVANCED COURSE

THE PRINCIPLES

OF

PSYCHOLOGY

BY

WILLIAM JAMES
PROFESSOR OF PSYCHOLOGY IN HARVARD UNIVERSITY

IN TWO VOLUMES

VOL. I

NEW YORK
HENRY HOLT AND COMPANY
1890

The intuitively obvious, but scientifically precarious, status of the notion of the whole person stands in the not-too-distant background of the remarks by William James and Gordon Allport. In fact, the question of how to deal with the whole person—whether broached directly in terms of character, self, personality, or the ego or more obliquely as executive routines, habit, family hierarchies, or the past history of reinforcement—represents one of the most resilient and controversial issues in the history of psychology. After examining the modern era, for example, Hall and Lindzey (1970) commented that: "One of the striking phenomena of the past sixty years in psychology has been the demise and subsequent rebirth of self and ego concepts [p. 291]." The polemics surrounding this problem are also easy to document; one need only turn to the behaviorism-humanism controversy (e.g., Koch, 1961; May, 1967; Skinner, 1969; Wann, 1964). Happily, there are signs that this "controversy" is now evolving into a "dialogue" through which a more balanced synthesis may emerge (e.g., Arnold, 1976; Keen, 1975; Krasner, 1978; Giorgi, 1970). It is with this trend in mind that we shall reexamine the integration of mechanism and purpose in the psychological thought of James and Allport.

There are two related reasons for returning to Allport and James. First, each is a member, in a nontrivial sense, of *both* the scientific and humanist traditions. Of course, scientific psychologists pay lip service to the "fundamental problems of human experience" and humanists tip their proverbial caps to the "progress of science." But the fact is that most of us do our studying and writing—our work—as scientists or humanists, and we cannot be considered, in more than a trivial sense, members of both traditions. In James and Allport, however, we find psychologists who made significant contributions to both the humanist and scientific traditions—they continually confronted the complex particulars of the human condition in their work as scientific psychologists. The second reason is really a continuation of the first. That is, as one reads James and Allport it becomes clear that their fundamental goal as psychologists was to integrate the scientific and humanist traditions—to create a psychology that could do justice to the farthest reaches of human experience. Each met experience as it appeared in all its richness and complexity, and neither allowed methodological presuppositions to dictate de jure the contents of their systems. As such, their systems stand as lonely monuments for a unified personality psychology of the future.

The body of this chapter is divided into two broad sections, devoted to James and Allport, respectively. In both, we follow a rough chronology of the thinker's development, with the aim of articulating how each sought to in-

FIGURE 4.1 *Gordon Allport (1897-1967).*

tegrate mechanism and purpose by means of a superordinate construct that deals with the whole person. The first section begins with an examination of the humanist and scientific strains of James's thought between 1870 and 1890. It is then argued that James sought to integrate these traditions by embedding his notion of the whole person into his theory of action in the *Principles*. The second section follows up with an investigation of these same two strains in the development of Allport's conceptions of common traits and functional autonomy. Then we argue that both find a concrete application in the notion of ego-involvement in the service of a higher ideal than self. Our conclusion is that there is a lesson here for personality theory, that it must use science but not ape it, if it is to do justice to the humanity of the whole person.

The Ambivalent Legacy of William James

JAMES'S EARLY COMMITMENT TO THE WHOLE PERSON: THE HUMANIST TRADITION

Put perhaps too simply, the humanist is concerned with the life experiences of the whole person. The reflective, philosophical lineage of this tradition calls forth, at least to us moderns, the somewhat derisive epitaph "armchair"—but such connotations are misleading in at least one important respect. That is, the humanist's primary data are real-life experiences of wide-awake, passionately striving human beings, which are a far cry from either the armchair or the psychological laboratory! The humanist tends to view the experimental

laboratory as the breeding ground for a reductionism that systematically excludes the real-life concerns of the whole person. This approach to human experience has a long, rich, and to the scientist notoriously vague heritage.

William James's humanism appears in his earliest writings, and like the
commitment of so many humanists, his commitment to this approach is
rooted in his own life (1842–1910). His long struggle with free will has been
well documented (Perry, 1935, Chap. 19). Educated as a scientist in an era
shaken by Darwin's evolutionary theory, he feared the moral implications of
an entirely mechanistic universe. This conflict reached its crescendo in the late
1860s, when he was harassed by psychosomatic problems and bouts of severe
depression. Then, in 1870, he made the following entry in his diary:

> I think yesterday was a crisis in my life. I finished reading . . . Renouvier's second
> "*Essais*" and see no reason why his definition of Free Will—"the sustaining of a
> thought because I choose to when I might have other thoughts"—need be the defini-
> tion of an illusion. . . . My first act of free will shall be to believe in free will [H.
> James, 1920, Vol. 1, p. 147].

In a very important sense, James's determined effort *to believe* in his freedom
set the foundation for his early thought. What we find in the early James is a
continuous attempt to go beyond the abstractions of science and philosophy
and do full justice to the particulars of human experience. Specifically, two
related themes reappear—a formulation of an essentially *active self* whose
ideals are *fulfilled in concrete action*.

The early fruits of this approach appeared in a French journal in 1878, in
the form of a defense of the belief in human freedom (James, 1878/1969b).
The distinctive characteristic of his argument was that it sought to answer a
metaphysical question in terms of the practical effects of that belief in concrete
action. His justification for this mode of argument was that freedom only
becomes a problem when it is experienced in real-life situations. To treat this
question at an entirely abstract level necessarily involves taking it out of the
concrete particulars that create the problem! Thus, in spite of the irrational
implications of his position, he argued that a person becomes free by choosing
to believe in his freedom and acting on that belief. For James, the belief in
human freedom energizes a person and thereby creates results in action that
would not appear without that belief. In a sense, he argued that a person
chooses to feel helpless or in control and that that decision affects his
behavior. At the same time, he offered a process account of freedom, in which
individual freedom is an effort-filled achievement rather than a faculty of
mind.

From freedom, James turned to an analysis of the motives underlying
philosophical belief. This might sound like a strange transition until one examines the intellectual climate of the time. On one hand, the empiricists were
setting the foundation for a thoroughly objective study of *Homo sapiens*. On
the other hand, the neo-Hegelians were weaving an entirely rational view of

human nature and the universe. Somewhere in the middle was a struggling William James, hemmed in by contradictory emotional tendencies that neither of the dominant philosophies recognized as real! His solution was to write a series of essays (1879/1969c; 1881/1956; 1882) that sought to make clear that any conception of human nature, however abstract it might appear on paper, is rooted in the subjective interests of the thinker. Within James's analysis of philosophical belief, the diversity of philosophies is to be understood in terms of the diversity of human temperaments.

> Pretend as we may, the *whole man* within us is at work when we form philosophical opinions. Intellect, will, taste and passion co-operate just as they do in practical affairs. . . . It is almost impossible that men who are themselves working philosophers should pretend that any philosophy can be, or ever has been, constructed without the help of personal preference, beliefs or divination [1882, p. 74, italics added].

Thus, James conceived of all philosophical activity, including science, as a sort of Rorschach test for intellectuals. Motivated by the contradictory ideals of abstract unity and the desire to do justice to the particulars of experience, he saw philosophers of his time offering interpretations of human nature that did violence to neither the facts nor their most cherished ideals.

One implication of his analysis of philosophical belief is that it portrays mind as thoroughly teleological—the ultimate goals of the whole person affect the structure and contents of his philosophical system. Thus, for example, the determinist's belief in determinism is, within James's analysis, just as much a subjective act of faith as his own belief in freedom. Both such affirmations are rooted in the ideals of the believer. James examined the question of teleology at some length in his critique of Spencer in 1878 (1878/1969d). Spencer's psychology was an attempt to integrate evolutionary theory and traditional empiricism, to show that association and its physiological correlate could account for all levels of experience. In his own *The Principles of Psychology*, for example, Spencer (1855/1892) wrote that mind could be viewed as "the continuous adjustment of internal relations to external relations [Vol. 1, p. 239]." James was critical of this definition of mind because it concealed the teleological character of human experience. Thus, he wrote that "we are all fated to be, *a priori, teleologists*, whether we will or no[t]. *Interests* which we bring with us, and simply posit or take our stand upon, are the very flour out of which our mental dough is kneaded [1878/1969d, p. 61, italics added]." That is, for James, humans do not simply stand by and passively record the relations that the world offers. We select particular aspects of experience while ignoring numerous other aspects, and our selections are guided by our subjective interests. This active, dynamic aspect of mind is what Spencer ignored and James emphasized at every opportunity. Like Spencer, James was working within the reflex action theory of mind—in which stimuli are operated upon by the brain and give rise to responses—but he interpreted this process in teleological terms. That is, the interests of the whole person direct his attention to particular aspects of stimuli and thereby guide his responses in the world.

This background leads us to James's conception of the whole person in the *Principles*, to a formulation of self that imputes meaning and value to the objects of experience on the basis of its own standards. This dynamic, action-oriented formulation of the whole person appears in his "Consciousness of Self" chapter (e.g., 1890, Vol. 1, pp. 297–298). But, on the whole, this chapter is a philosophical description of the *experience of self* rather than a psychological analysis of the *function of self or the whole person* in our daily activities, what would be called a theory of personality today. The closest James comes to offering such an analysis is his much-neglected chapter on "The Perception of Reality." In this chapter, he is concerned with articulating the varieties of human belief, and to accomplish this task, he delineates seven "sub-universes of reality" (1890, Vol. 2, p. 291). The subuniverses—for example, the world of ethical relations, the world of physical things, the world of science, the worlds of madness—are the variety of self-contained belief systems that confer reality on what is given in experience. Things become real or unreal, meaningful or meaningless, within the context of these subuniverses. Taken abstractly, they are different cognitive frames of reference. But as a humanist, James goes beyond such a description in two important respects. First, he takes pains to make clear that each subuniverse, as a complex of subjective interests, is rooted in a person's emotional nature. *"The world of living realities . . . is . . . thus anchored in the Ego, considered as an active and emotional term. . . .* Whatever things have intimate and continuous connection with my *life* are things whose reality I cannot doubt [1890, Vol. 2, pp. 297–298, italics added]." It is, then, the functioning of complexes of interests (values, purposes) in the *lives* of individual human beings that James was trying to give voice to in his treatment of the subuniverses.

His analysis is crude in a number of respects, but his intent is unmistakable. He is trying to develop a level of explanation that distinguishes between different types of people on the basis of their fundamental interests and ideals. At this level of the progress of individual lives, people differ in what might be called their Life Plan—that superordinate system of values (interests, purposes) that gives meaning and structure to their particular activities. This is the second sense in which James went beyond a merely abstract description of the subuniverses. He stated that the subuniverses come to be hierarchically organized within individuals and that this superordinate scheme of values creates that person's reality. It is within this context that he wrote that

> Each thinker . . . has dominant habits of attention; and these *practically elect from among the various worlds some one to be for him the world of ultimate realities.* From this world's objects he does not appeal. Whatever positively contradicts them must get into another world or die [1890, Vol. 2, pp. 293–293].

Thus, beyond the moment-to-moment teleology (interests) that directs particular activities, there is for James a fundamental teleology—a more or less stable Life Plan that persists through time and gives a unified meaning to diverse activities.

There is, then, an essential unity to James's humanism that began with his declaration of freedom and culminated, in some sense, in his formulation of the subuniverses. The unifying theme can be viewed as a continuing examination of the foundations of human belief, and, in working out this problem, he articulated his notion of the whole person. It began as a young intellectual's attempt to justify his belief in human freedom. In exploring this question, however, he discovered an unarticulated region of value-laden assumptions and subjective interests, which philosophers of his time were unwilling to acknowledge. He then expanded his focus to human belief in general and found the same region of the only vaguely felt but definitely structured system of values that puts intensity and time-spanning unity on the bare bones of human action. At this point, he was addressing the function of self in action, what would today be called a theory of personality.

JAMES'S MECHANISM FOR VOLUNTARY ACTION: THE SCIENTIFIC TRADITION

James never developed his formulation of the subuniverses but he did offer a mechanism for voluntary action in the *Principles* that is intimately related to his notion of the whole person. In turning to his mechanism for voluntary action, we are taking up the other "half" of the Jamesian legacy—the scientific tradition. In marked contrast to the humanist's concern for the emergent value of the particulars of experience, the scientist seeks to subsume the particulars under general laws—to reduce the passionate to the lawful play of physical mechanisms. The strengths of this tradition are, of course, its clarity, precision and control, but its critics have always argued that the whole person gets lost in a morass of muscle twitches, experimental hypercontrol, and physicalistic analogies. Let us now turn to the mechanistic side of James's psychology.

The year 1878 was a momentous one in James's life, for Henry Holt asked him to write a textbook in psychology for the prestigious American Science Series. Beyond being a family friend, James was selected because he was educated as a medical doctor, had read widely in the European experimental psychology, and was teaching the "new" psychology at Harvard. After 12 years of work, he submitted a 1400-page manuscript that solidified his position as a pioneer in American scientific psychology. The manuscript was published in 1890 as *The Principles of Psychology*. We could choose any number of scientific themes in the *Principles*, but, with the topics of self and personality in mind, we shall opt for his theory of voluntary action.

Like too few humanists since his time, James took science seriously. He recognized full well, for example, that a person's beliefs must be corroborated by the world of objects. Our ability to create our worlds is thus subject to severe limitations. He even entertained the notion, common in his time, that people are really complex machines reacting to stimuli on the basis of past experience. As a scientist, then, he was rightfully impressed with Hughlings Jackson's isolation of the sensory and motor areas of the cortex. And although he rejected the Meynert scheme of the nervous system, which rigidly divided the cortex and subcortical regions into the physical mediators of habits and instincts, respectively, he did so on empirical rather than philosophical grounds (1890, Vol. 1, p. 64; pp. 72–78). This is the side of James that one sees on reading his "Habit" chapter, which seems like a manifesto of mechanistic materialism, or his "Association" chapter, which contains an outright reduction of associational laws to "the physical fact that nerve-currents propagate themselves easiest through those [brain] tracts . . . which have already been most in use [1890, Vol. 1, p. 563]." This is nothing more than the law of least resistance, the central pillar of Spencer's evolutionary psychology. We shall attempt to show, however, that his concessions to a mechanistic psychology were tactical rather than doctrinaire, a preparation for his theory of voluntary action.

Most importantly, James's treatment of habit and association saved him from the untenable position that a person can accomplish an act through willful effort that had not already been learned. In other words, he wanted to make clear that voluntary actions are secondary or previously learned: "We learn all our *possibilities* by way of experience [1890, Vol. 2, p. 487]." The essence of James's theory then became the effortful attention to one of the possibilities given by experience. With the dual processes of attention (selection based on interests) and habit (associations of objects), he offered a conception of experience in which there is a continuous reciprocal transaction between the knower and the known. The world offers a multitude of relations between objects, and the thinker, by selecting those relations that are compatible with the thinker's interests, acts to change the world of objects.

James first approached volition in an 1880 essay, where he challenged the then prevalent theory that the feeling of willful effort is actually the discharge of neural energy from the motor cortex to the muscles. The details of his arguments are complex and need not concern us here (Note 1). What is important is the alternative he offered, which can be divided into four parts. At its foundation is a behavioral conception of ideas, what he called the doctrine of *ideomotor action*. According to this doctrine, an idea—a sensory process—automatically expresses its motor effects unless it is inhibited by an antagonistic idea. Thus, for example, the idea of moving my hand results in that movement unless that idea is contradicted. For James, ideas are correlates of neural processes on their way to becoming manifest in action.

The second component of James's theory of voluntary action is the notion of *afferent or kinesthetic feedback*. That is, once a sensory process discharges into a motor process resulting in muscle movements, these movements give rise to kinesthetic feelings of the effects of the movements. Thus the fundamental unit of voluntary action is neither S–R nor S–O–R; instead it is a feedback loop, which might be schematized as S–O–R–S^k. The importance of S^k, the kinesthetic feeling of the effects of movements, can be seen when we turn to the third feature of his theory, which deals with the distinction between voluntary and involuntary actions. For James, this distinction is a matter of physiology. Voluntary movements are those in which S^k, now called an "idea" of the effects of the movement, can come to be *associated* with the original sensory process, S, so that when S is excited, S^k arises before the response occurs. As he wrote in the *Principles*, "when a sensation has once produced a movement in us, the next time we have the sensation, it tends to suggest the idea of the movement, even before the movement occurs [1890, Vol. 2, p. 585]." In experiential terms, voluntary actions are purposive, goal-directed actions that are preceded by an idea. Physiologically speaking, they are actions in which an association between an idea and its motor effects can be established. In contrast, involuntary actions are simply those in which such an association cannot be formed. Thus, for example, I can voluntarily move my hand but I cannot sneeze at will.

Thus far, James's theory of voluntary action can be characterized as cognitive, dynamic, molar, and action oriented. Its cognitive flavor comes through most clearly when it is recognized that James conceived of volition as the process of effortfully attending to an idea until its motor effects become manifest. Its dynamic character appears when it is recognized, as we have noted, that attention is directed by a person's subjective interests. Lastly, James's theory is molar and action oriented in the sense that it is less concerned with the physiological correlates of ideas than it is with ideas as meaningful plans of action.

FIAT, WHOLE PERSON, AND ACTION: JAMES'S INTEGRATION OF THE MECHANISTIC AND TELEOLOGICAL ASPECTS OF SELF

When contemporary experimental psychologists have returned to James's theory of action (e.g., Kimble & Perlmuter, 1970), they have dealt with his notions of ideomotor action, feedback, and association. We must now turn, however, to the fourth and most radical feature of James's theory—the *fiat of will*. He introduced this notion in trying to do justice to the familiar experience of a crisis of will—when a conscious decision between alternative modes of action is filled with painful hesitation and emotional turmoil. This state of turmoil is actually experienced, and James, ever true to experience, sought to understand it with reference to the fiat. He used a number of phrases to communicate the full meaning of this notion. In his 1880 essay, he called it the "mental 'click' of resolve" (1880/1969a, p. 196). In a later article, he described it as a "genuine and sincere mental consent" (1888, p. 247). And in the *Principles*, he called it simply the "act of mental consent" (1890, Vol. 2, p. 526). It may involve the steadfast attention to, or inhibition of, an idea, but in either case, the fiat is experienced as a process by which we "keep affirming and adopting a state of mind of which disagreeableness is an integral factor" (James, 1969a, p. 199). Is the fiat free? For James, it seemed to be in some cases, but before we get seduced by this metaphysical question, however important it may be, we must turn to the role of the fiat in James's theory of voluntary action.

At first glance, the fiat may appear to be a thinly disguised manifestation of the Victorian era's obsession with "will power," the last remnant of a faculty psychology (May, 1969). But we have already seen that James was entirely unsympathetic with this approach. The fiat is neither a faculty nor the mere discharge of a discrete sensory process into an isolated response. Instead, the fiat is best viewed within the context of James's attempt to integrate the humanist and scientific strains of the *Principles* (Note 2). More specifically, we see the fiat as the essence of his attempt to incorporate his formulation of self as the whole person with his mechanism for voluntary action. As such, it is the crux of James's psychology, his formal reconciliation of teleology and mechanism.

James discusses "the more *intimate* nature of the volitional process" in an important section of his "Will" chapter entitled "Will is a Relation between the Mind and its 'ideas' " (1890, Vol. 2, p. 559). It is essential to understand what he means by this rather ambiguous heading, for it stands at the foundation of his integration of mechanism and purpose. What he is reacting against is the notion that will is the process that transforms ideas (mental happenings) into movements (physical happenings). He wanted no part of this formulation; his doctrine of ideomotor action stated that ideas automatically express their motor effects *without* volitional mediation. At the same time, James argued that volition is an entirely mental (i,e., cognitive–emotive) process that is completed when we consent to the reality of an idea. When this act of consent occurs, the intended idea fills our experience and automatically results in motor effects. The movements themselves, however, are a matter of physiology rather than volition. In summarizing this section, James wrote that: "I want more than anything to emphasize the fact that *volition* is primarily *a relation* . . . between *our Self* and our own *states of mind* [1890, Vol. 2, pp. 567–568, italics added]." What he means when he refers to "the Mind" in the title of this section, then, is "our Self," what we have called the whole person. Volition can then be understood as an entirely cognitive–emotive process, a dynamic relation between an organized, valuing self and an idea, construed as a plan of action. There is a reciprocity between self and action here that is characteristic of James's psychology. Ideas are viewed in terms of concrete plans of action, but the actions themselves are not the whole of the story. Taken within the context of a self-as-life-plan, actions are an expression of, and perhaps the fulfillment of, the ideals of a whole person.

As James wrote:

When an idea stings us in a certain way, makes as it were a certain electric connection with our Self, we believe it *is* a reality. When it stings us in another way, makes
another connection with our Self, we say, let it be a reality. . . . It [the "quality of
reality"] means *our* adoption of things, *our* caring for them, *our* standing by them
[1890, Vol. 2, pp. 568–569].

For James, then, volition is like belief, in that it is rooted in our emotional
nature. It is connected with our lives. Volition differs from belief, however, in
that it deals with those aspects of experience in which the decisions of individual selves play an essential part in making a mere possibility into a reality. In saying "let it be" to a particular idea, we both create a reality and express our selves in concrete action.

James's integration of the humanist and scientific traditions might be summarized in the following manner. As a scientist, he sought to place a theory of
voluntary action on solid ground. In doing this, however, it became clear that
human action is irrevocably tied to the ideals, motives, or values of the actor.
As he wrote in the *Principles*, "we reach the heart of our inquiry into volition
when we ask by what process it is that the thought of any given object comes
to prevail in the mind [1890, Vol. 2, p. 561]." Going a step further, he realized
that motivational questions, whether posed in terms of drives, needs,
motives, or subjective interests, can only be answered within the context of a
frightfully complex Life Plan that places a higher value on some things than
on others. It is for this reason that terms like "pleasure" and "pain" beg the
motivational question rather than answer it, for only by knowing a person's
Life Plan can we define those terms. With this realization, James saw no other
alternative than to embed his teleological conception of the whole person into
the center of his mechanism for voluntary action. Mechanistic habits are fully
acknowledged, but they are viewed as serving the interests (purposes, ideals,
needs) of the whole person.

Gordon Allport's Reconstruction of James's Legacy

For all its richness and suggestiveness, James's integration of the humanistic
and scientific traditions was clearly somewhat unstable. By 1920, his conception of the self had splintered. On the one hand, the behaviorists John B. Watson (1919) and Edward L. Thorndike (Note 3) were enlarging his theory of
voluntary action to the neglect of cognitive interests. On the other hand,
Mary Calkins (1910) was promoting a humanistic investigation called "self
psychology" founded upon "basal attitudes" to the neglect of volitional
mechanisms. Meanwhile, a young graduate student at Harvard, Gordon
Allport, wrote a review article on "Personality and Character" in 1921 that
signaled the beginning of a reintegration of the two Jamesian themes.

ALLPORT AGAINST THE SPECIFICITY TRADITION:
COMMON TRAITS

Gordon Allport (1897–1967) is remembered in personality theory today largely for his trait theory (Fig. 4.1). It may strike the modern reader as confusing, therefore, to open our portrayal of Gordon Allport's theory of personality with the claim that he actually *opposed* specific traits. But this was certainly as much the case as with James's criticism of habits. For instance, in his review article in 1921, Allport criticized John B. Watson's theory that our laryngeal, motor, and visceral habits are organized into a "reaction mass" of responses to the environment (Watson, 1919). His doctoral thesis in 1922 went beyond this mechanistic theory in two respects (Note 4). In the first place, it was statistical as well as experimental. Allport measured the errors of overestimation and underestimation by subjects who were asked to move their hand a certain specified distance on a horizontal board. He found that manic persons consistently overestimated and that depressive ones consistently underestimated. The use of more than one subject was an improvement upon the method of his own teacher, Hugo Münsterberg (1892), who had devised a slide-rule apparatus to measure his own emotions at various times during the day. In addition, he employed the latest statistical techniques to discover the three "common traits" (areal, centrifugal, emphasis) in the scores on a battery of 18 psychomotor tasks. A third respect in which Allport's theory went beyond its competitors, therefore, was that it made use of more than one test to identify each common trait. The particular scientist whom he criticized in his *Studies in Expressive Movement* (Allport & Vernon, 1933) was Edward Lee Thorndike (1906, 1932), who relied upon single transfer of training experiments to determine the "identical elements" in personalities. Allport (1937b) was also critical of factor analytic investigations of personality traits, and he warned that "technical aids should never be allowed to lower the basic requirement of psychological intelligibility [p. 301]."

The distinguishing feature of Allport's concept of traits is that it never lost contact with the whole person. He drew upon two empirical concepts—consistency and congruence—to pin down this unity. Consistency was generated through reliability coefficients of the impressions of judges with the scores on personality tests (Note 5). Congruence was less tractable to measurement, being the familiar problem of validity, and Allport here invoked Harry Murray's method of multiple diagnosis. He frankly compared it to the European structural methods of intuition, empathy, and *Verstehen* as employed in the understanding of works of art.

Allport's contact with the various German and Austrian schools of Gestalt psychology during his postgraduate year abroad in 1922–1923 had taught him to be suspicious of the narrowness of the analytic and experimental traditions (Allport, 1923). The school of Wilhelm Dilthey, for instance, emphasized that higher-level concepts should take precedence over reductionistic ones in the "human studies" (Hodges, 1969). In *The Study of Values* with Philip Vernon in 1931, Allport adopted the six fundamental ways of looking at life that

Dilthey's student Eduard Spranger had proposed: theoretic, economic, aesthetic, social, political, and religious. How similar to James's seven subuniverses of reality! This a priori list of common traits was given external validation through testing the degree to which individuals subscribe to each of them. The test revealed "inclusive values" (cf. Newcomb, Turner, & Converse, 1965) such that business persons, for example, are more "economic" and "political" but less "social," while nurses are more "religious" and "social" (in the philanthropic sense). Thus, certain values tended to covary, since a high score on one value required a person to slight other values. Over the years, this test has proven to have predictive power for occupational choice and to reveal the fundamental unity in personalities.

It is helpful to compare Allport's schematic representation of the unity of personality with the teaching of William James. In his book *Personality: A Psychological Interpretation,* Allport (1937b), depicted traits as lying midway between conditioned reflexes and the total personality. James, too, recognized the essence of personality as including both habits and selves. He was, as we have seen in the preceding discussion, justifiably critical of both the empiricistic and the rationalistic definitions of these concepts, preferring to introduce the middle term "interests." Clearly, interests resemble traits in being derived from habits, yet they are oriented toward purposes of the whole person. Indeed, Allport (1943b) himself recognized the self, free will, and individuality as "the productive paradoxes of William James." He was perfectly aware of the tension between habits and interests in the Jamesian conception: "Effort and interest are here made the guides of conduct. The ball and chain logic of habit, for all its dramatic appeal, really plays only an isolated and eccentric role in James' thought [1943b/1968, p. 308]." Yet like James, he also saw this as a necessary tension.

It is this guiding role of interests or human purposes that typified the flexible trait theory of Allport. Of over 17,000 trait names, he found clusters of between 5 and 10 in most individuals (Allport & Odbert, 1936). The classic case, one from which he taught for many years, was described in *Letters from Jenny* (1965). The death of Jenny's husband, the care she bestowed upon her only child Ross, in addition to her "lone wolf" temperament, produced a personality structure aptly described by 36 judges in terms of the trait clusters quarrelsome–suspicious, self-centered, independent–autonomous, dramatic–intense, aesthetic–artistic, aggressive, cynical–morbid, and sentimental. Since each of these trait clusters included many specific traits, and since there was basic agreement among the judges, this diagnosis confirmed Allport in his conclusion that there is a basic structure of natural "cleavages" in personality.

ALLPORT AGAINST THE GENERAL MOTIVE TRADITIONS: FUNCTIONAL AUTONOMY

William James, as has been indicated, took science seriously. Science in James's day included two general principles: association and hedonism. His theory of voluntary action accounted for the origin of new habits and their direction by interests in a way which subsumed both principles. Pleasure and pain are among the causes of action, but the selection among ideas in volition may include much else besides feelings. Implicit in this mechanism whereby kinesthetic cues come to be associated with the effects of a previous reflex were the individual choices of the whole person as based upon his Life Plan.

Similarly for Gordon Allport, science was of paramount importance. He constructed his trait theory in response to a vast mental testing literature. Yet, he knew that any theory of personality would ultimately have to deal with the learning tradition as well, for structures do have to be acquired. He was again dissatisfied with Thorndike and Watson. Thorndike offered "stimulus response elements" (Allport, 1937a, p. 248), while Watson "gave man less than his due by depicting him as a bundle of unrelated reaction tendencies" (Allport, 1967, p. 15). Allport (1967) confessed in his autobiography that he had actually sought more than a science of personality: "I wanted to fashion an experimental science, so far as appropriate, but chiefly I wanted an image of man that would allow us to test in full whatever democratic and humane potentialities that he might possess [p. 15]." The realization of this image is seen in Allport's constant concern with concrete life issues, such as the psychology of radio, and later with the social issues that came to light during World War II. These will be discussed in the subsequent section.

The centerpiece of both of Allport's chief works, *Personality: A Psychological Interpretation* (1937b) and *Pattern and Growth in Personality* (1961), was the theory of functional autonomy, or the transformation of motives into "self-sustaining *contemporary* systems, growing out of antecedent systems, but functionally independent of them [1937a, p. 143]." The sailor who continues to yearn for the sea after he has retired, the workman who feels compelled to keep high standards even though his security no longer depends upon it, the mother who learns to love her children despite their imperfections—each exemplifies (a) the discontinuity of the present motivational state from the past, and (b) the uniqueness of each individual's choice of goals. In both respects, the theory was new, and it was directed against the prevailing general drive theories—psychoanalytic and hormic (as McDougall's instinct theory was called)—as well as against the general reflexes and rewards implicit in the learning theories of John B. Watson (1919) and Edward Lee Thorndike (1932). Characteristically for Allport, the theory was based upon a review of the experimental literature. His case rested on the following research topics: (a) the circular reflex, as a baby throwing a spoon to the floor; (b) conative perseveration, when incompleted tasks are better remembered; (c) conditioned reflexes, for example, phobias, not requiring reinforcement; (d) counterparts in animal behavior, such as the rat continuing to perform a task when satiated or the rat or mollusc persisting in a rhythm when removed to an artificial environment; (e) neuroses, for example, stammering, tics, or other symptoms of anxiety; (f) acquired interests, such as college courses sometimes engendered; (g) acquired sentiments of curiosity of motherhood; and (h) the dynamic character of personal values, reflected in word-association studies (Cantril, 1932; Cantril & Allport, 1933), which showed that "people respond more quickly to words with . . . interest than to words relating to interests they lack [Allport, 1937a, p. 151]."

Allport's principle of functional autonomy attracted a good deal of notoriety in the decade following its appearance in 1937. Although much of the criticism was negative, the principle has survived in textbooks up to the present. This is reminiscent in a way of the fate of James's program, which splintered into Life Plans and habits, existential choices, and mechanisms of purposive behavior. Without taking the time to review all of the criticisms, we shall attempt to classify them briefly into instinctivist and environmental and to state the thrust of their content. Then we shall note how Allport answered them and what influence they had on subsequent formulations of his personality theory. In the final section of this discussion of Allport, the replacement of both trait theory and functional autonomy by an ego psychology will be addressed.

The purposivist critique came from the hormic perspective of William McDougall (1907), and it was made by Peter A. Bertocci in 1940, following the death of McDougall. It is necessary to appreciate that McDougall was a very strong force in American psychology up through the 1930s. His position, in brief, was that "to be a human being is to be limited (though plastic) to certain basic motives and generic directive urges" (Bertocci, 1940, p. 511). In today's terminology, psychoanalytic instincts or ethological fixed-action patterns would represent the purposivist camp. From such native processes as hunger, sex, fear, and anger, the learned propensities of mastery, recognition, curiosity, and the like may be derived. This criticism evoked the following concession from Allport:

> I did not stress sufficiently my belief that not all motives are to be viewed as functionally autonomous . . . to my mind the most incomplete aspect of my theory consists in my failure to give criteria whereby one might distinguish functionally autonomous from unchanged motives. I can simply say that I believe the problem to be soluble [Bertocci, 1940, pp. 526a, 528, cf. Allport, 1940].

In 1961, therefore, Allport specified two kinds of functional autonomy: (a) perseverative, in which basic neurological principles are involved and which include the research topics a–e listed earlier; and (b) propriate, which "reach beyond present knowledge of the way the nervous system operates [p. 230]" and include topics f–h. These latter motives include, for example, the abilities of Galileo, Mendel, Schubert, and Van Gogh that turned into passionate interests; the selective proficiency of subjects tested in a task they valued; and the self-image and life-style by which lives are directed.

The opposite critique from the mechanist perspective was provided by David McClelland in 1942, Dorothy Rethlingshafer in 1943, and Neal Miller in 1951. It addressed the fundamental question of how functional autonomy is supposed to occur. Each of these papers was cogently argued on the basis of extensive empirical evidence, in contrast to the purely logical arguments of Bertocci. McClelland (1942), then a student of Robert R. Sears at Yale, argued as follows: "Learning may produce changes in any aspect of the motivational sequence. New instigators, new instrumental acts, and new goal responses may be acquired [p. 273]." To account for the autonomy of certain behaviors, McClelland and later Miller mentioned delay of extinction due to failure to notice stimulus removal in avoidance conditioning, differential reinforcement in the case of the sailor who continued to love the sea, and secondary rewards and generalization of reinforcement. The factor of delay of extinction, otherwise known as the time during which a behavior persists, was addressed from a Lewinian point of view by Dorothy Rethlingshafer (1943), whose research on the "tendency to continue" indicated wide individual differences in the so-called Zeigarnik effect, the memory for incompleted tasks.

Replying on the basis of new evidence in 1961, Allport characteristically absorbed these criticisms into his argument. He cited traumatic avoidance learning (Solomon & Wynn, 1954), partial reinforcement (Ferster & Skinner, 1957), reverberating activity (Hebb, 1949), higher-order schemata (Piaget, 1947/1950), and homeostasis (Stagner, 1951) as "quasi-mechanical" explanations for functional autonomy. He noted that $S-R$ explanations such as Neal Miller's grow exceedingly vague in reference to "complex human situations" (Allport, 1961, p. 245), while he lauded Kurt Lewin for "special clarity on the contemporaneousness of all motivation" (Allport, 1961, p. 221). In sum, Allport accepted all of these arguments but relegated them to explanations of perseverative functional autonomy; his defense of propriate functional autonomy was rooted in different soil. This brings us to the final phase of his theoretical development.

EGO-INVOLVEMENT, THE LAW OF EFFECT AND THE LIVED PHILOSOPHY OF LIFE: ALLPORT'S INTEGRATION OF THE NOMOTHETIC AND IDIOGRAPHIC ASPECTS OF PERSONALITY

The crux of William James's conception of self was the effortful act of consenting to an idea, for this act more than anything else was the true expression of the person. This consent was a moral act in that it represented a relation, a human relation, between our self and our world. It is significant that James did not fully articulate this root idea until 1890, when he was 48 years old. The belief in human freedom was the first step in 1870, followed in 1880 by the mechanism of volition; but the full conception of self as a structured pattern of beliefs or values that he called the subuniverses of reality was not described until 1889. Finally, in 1890 he enlarged the "Will" chapter with five types of practical decisions, of which only the last—the "dead heave of the will" (1890, Vol. 2, p. 534)—was the fulfillment of self through realizing a human potentiality. Thus, he brought together the motivational and cognitive components of his conception of human nature, which has come down to us almost intact in the existential and phenomenological literature of the present day (e.g., Linschoten, 1968; May, 1958).

One is tempted to postulate that a certain fund of life experience is requisite for a mature personality theory. This seems to hold true of the biographical development of Sigmund Freud, Alfred Adler, Abraham Maslow, and Carl Rogers in relation to their guiding ideas. When we turn to Gordon Allport, the postulate is clearly confirmed. He formulated his trait theory of cognitive structure in the 1920s and his motivational theory of functional autonomy in the 1930s. Both theories were based upon negative critiques of prevailing traditions—specific traits and common drives. Not until 1943, however, when Allport was 46 years old, did he actually propose the concept of ego-involvement as a positive foundation for the study of personality.

In 1943 Allport published an important essay, "The Ego in Contemporary Psychology," which has been credited by some people with reintroducing the self to psychology. From our perspective, the essay was pivotal in crystalliz-ing the issue of specificity and generality in human action that we see as the key to Allport's theory of personality. Allport acknowledged as much him-self:

A few years ago I found myself involved in a controversy in the field of personality. Certain experimenters claimed that their findings demonstrated a situational specificity in human conduct. For example, a child honest in one situation would not be found honest in another, a person confident in one judgment would not be confi-dent in another. Whole books were written in defense of specificity. Other in-vestigators, by other methods, found a person honest in one situation to be honest in another, a person confident in one judgment to be confident in another, and whole books were written in defense of generality. It was a pleasant battle while it lasted. An arbitrator arose, a peacemaker by temperament—Gardner Murphy was his name—and he proposed a compromise. "Honesty," he suggested, "is either a general characteristic or a set of specific habits, depending on your interest and your emphasis" (Murphy and Jensen, 1932, p. 385). Murphy was right, but it was not un-til recently that the deciding interest and critical emphasis became clear, at least to me. For my own belated insight I am indebted to an experiment by Klein and Schoenfeld (1941) [1934b].

The Klein and Schoenfeld experiment had two conditions for subjects taking six mental tests: non-ego-involved and ego-involved. To involve the subjects, they were told that the scores would count on their college record. Confidence ratings administered afterward with regard to the accuracy of their perfor-mances were inconsistent in the first condition and consistent in the second. The conclusion was that a general trait of confidence was shown, but only when the subjects were ego-involved.

In his characteristic manner, Allport deftly assembled the experimental and clinical evidence for ego-involvement. Hadley Cantril had found that people's political judgments differed when they were questioned face-to-face versus when they put their answers in a box. Other evidence included Else Frenkel-Brunswik's (1930) selective memory, Muzafer Sherif's (1936) social norms, Carl Rogers's (1942) client-centered therapy, and level of aspiration studies inspired by Kurt Lewin (Hoppe, 1930). But it was Allport's claim that the law of effect in learning applied more to non-ego-involved than to ego-involved behavior that generated an important debate. In a symposium on "The Ego and the Law of Effect" in 1945, this claim was challenged by two proponents of learning theory. Philip Blair Rice (1946) questioned Allport's assertion that "a student who makes an A record in a course in college shows no tendency to repeat that course [Allport, 1943/1960, p. 84]." Rice argued that the reinforcement in the law of effect depends upon what is conceived as satisfied: for example, the specific choice of the course, and the general "system of interests" such as acquiring credits, the mastery of a new subject, or the novel problem solving itself. Concluded Rice: "the Law of Effect, so applied, is also compatible with what Allport has said about the functional autonomy of motives [Rice, 1946, p. 314]." O. Hobert Mowrer went further by reducing ego-involvement to interests, and interests to "emotional arousal." Through this derived drive, as well as its mediation through symbolic processes, Mowrer (1946) argued that:

> We do not need a whole new set of terms and concepts to understand and explain the motivational and consummatory processes which occur in the case of "ego-involved behavior." Allport agrees that the Law of Effect works well enough in the latter case, and I submit that it also works very well in the former case [p. 323].

Elsewhere, Mowrer and Ullmann (1945) had demonstrated that the single factor learning theory, by admitting conflict of rewards and punishments as well as the factor of time, could account for both nonintegrative, or neurotic, and integrative, or normal, behavior.

Allport (1946) replied in his own defense that the ego processes are irreducible and that effect is a secondary principle of learning. He accepted the term "interests" but refused to admit their derivation from satisfaction and dissatisfaction; rather, a person's interests comprise "the combined influence of his motives, the present requirements of the situation, active participation, and a knowledge of relevant facts, including a memory of his previous success and failure [p. 345]." Allport was supported in this defense by his student Leo Postman, who concluded an extensive review article on "The History and Present Status of the Law of Effect" in 1947 by agreeing that "the capacity to relate environmental events to one's interest system, to discriminate between relevant and irrelevant means, far transcends the operation of effect, however broadly conceived [p. 549]." The meaning of this statement is perhaps best appreciated, however, by noting the kinds of "interest systems" with which Allport was primarily concerned in his own research from World War II through his death in 1967.

During the war years, Allport learned firsthand about the potential of humankind for evil and good, for prejudice and altruistic actions. He responded by involving himself in the Society for the Psychological Study of Social Issues in 1936, by assisting countless refugee scientists in finding positions in the United States, and by writing on such topics as morale, participation, peace, international cooperation, rumor, love and hate, tensions that cause wars, reduction of group prejudice, social service, public health, religion, and social encounter. Just as James in his later years had lived out his experiential theory of self by taking it to the people in public lectures and inspirational books, Allport strove to apply his psychological understanding to real-life issues. Midway through this epoch in his career, Allport composed *Becoming: Basic Considerations for a Psychology of Personality* (1955). In this book he redefined the ego as "propriate striving" and characterized it in terms of the life histories he had come to know. Earlier, he had translated the doctrine of ideal types, which he had learned from the *Verstehendepsychologie* of Dilthey, Spranger, Jaspers, and other German authors, into the concept of "the unifying philosophy of life" (Allport, 1937, pp. 225–231; 1961, pp. 294–304). The "proprium" was henceforth his name for "the special aspects of personality that have to do with warmth, with unity, with a sense of personal importance" (1955, in Maddi, 1971, p. 318). He drew the comparison with the taxonomic scheme of William James for the knowing self and the three types of empirical me, noting that here too "the ego *qua* knower is somehow contained within the ego *qua* known" (1955, in Maddi, 1971, p. 317). Here it should be noted that both men sought to return the study of the person to real-life experiences—to common sense made rigorous.

It is fitting to close by mentioning two features of Allport's own mature personality that illuminate his conception of the person. One is his generous concern for the problems of others, which is only sketchily represented in his principle of "the enlargement of interests" (1960, p. 172) and "ego extension" (1960, p. 162). Social encounter for him was a lived philosophy of life. The other is his sensitivity to the limits as well as the strengths of human character. In this aspect, he went beyond the ideal types of the German school to the actual types of American pragmatic psychology. His respect for the nomothetic and lawlike was qualified by his appreciation of the idiographic and particular, and the latter extended from the ridiculous of rumor to the sublime of social participation.

Conclusion

It can truly be said that an empirical science of personality was born in the twentieth century. But the question deserves to be raised once again whether the scientific is the truest picture of human beings. What we have found in the nineteenth-century theories of self, of which James's was one of the most highly developed, is the conceptual framework for the empirical quandary to come. James's psychological formulation of self as the whole person, a hierarchically organized system of values and interests, is a clarification, an explication of common sense. For James, self is rooted in a person's emotional and aesthetic nature, which is, to some degree, a function of past experience; but it is also forever pointed toward the future with interests guiding the selection of objects and goals. Joining the scientific conception of a volitional act with the humanistic conception of the Life Plan was the decisive creation of self through the fiat. In it, the sum total of a person's life experience—if properly attuned—could guide his choice among the subuniverses of reality.

How different the twentieth-century approach, so much less in touch with real-life experiences, so much more nomothetic! For Allport, as for James, the scientific tradition was guilty of excessive reductionism and sheer rampant "methodolatry." Personality for Allport was from the first a human study. As such, the discipline ought to incorporate the differential and behavioristic traditions of specific traits and learned habits, and ought also to also address the psychoanalytic and hormic conceptions of general instincts and sentiments in the past. But beyond this, personality psychology might as well admit that traits are sometimes discontinuous with the past and motives are often contemporaneous. Combining common traits and functional autonomy, then, was the ego-involved decision, the striving that made a difference not only to the self but to the self-in-relation-to-society. Through a lifetime of human concerns, Allport came to describe the unifying philosophy of life more and more in terms of lived experiences of an altruistic nature.

Standing back for a final look at these two grand systems of personhood, we find a fundamental covergence. Formulated vis-à-vis the mechanistic philosophies of Spencer and Thorndike, they were far more individualized in their Life Plan and unifying philosophy of life. Articulated against the merely purposive philosophies of the Kantians and McDougall, they were far more circumspect in their claims as to the origin of the volitional act in the motives of the present. While hospitable to the scientific model, in other words, neither was beholden to it. In Allport's words (1943b/1968)

> Narrow consistency can neither bring salvation to your science nor help mankind. Let your approaches be diverse, but let them in aggregate do full justice to the heroic qualities of man. If you find yourselves tangled in paradoxes, what of that? Who can say that the universe shall not contain paradoxes simply because he himself finds them unpalatable? To accommodate the whole of human experience keep layers of space and air and vision in your scientific formulations [pp. 126–127].

This, perhaps, is the lesson learned from James and Allport for theories of personality to come. To be a psychologist is to be a scientist seeking nomothetic laws, but it is also to be a humanist appreciative of idiographic uniqueness, as exemplified by William James and Gordon Allport.

Acknowledgments

Richard High wrote the first part and William Woodward the second; however, the chapter was developed and reworked together. We wish to thank the listeners at invited colloquia at the University of New Hampshire (29 September 1978) and Wellesley College (28 October 1978) for their helpful critical comments. This study is an outgrowth of a previous but entirely separate paper, William Woodward, "Lotze, the Self, and American Psychology," *Annals of the New York Academy of Sciences*, 1977, *291*, 168–180. The authors wish especially to thank Professor Amedeo P. Giorgi for his thoughtful criticisms.

Reference Notes

1. Woodward, W. R. William James' theory of volition: The historical origin of the law of effect. Unpublished manuscript, University of New Hampshire.
2. High, R. P. Shadworth Hodgson and the psychology of William James: Experience, teleology and realism. Unpublished doctoral dissertation, University of New Hampshire, 1978.
3. Woodward, W. R. *The moral foundation of the New Psychology: From the feeling of effort to the law of effect.* Paper presented at Cheiron, the International Society for the History of the Behavioral and Social Sciences, Wellesley, Mass., 2 June 1978.
4. Allport, G. W. An experimental study of the traits of personality. Unpublished doctoral dissertation, Harvard College Library, Harvard University, 1922.
5. Bender, I. E. A study in integrations of personalities by prediction and matching. Syracuse University Library, 1935.

References

Allport, G. W. Personality and character. *Psychological Bulletin*, 1921, *18*, 441–455.
Allport, G. W. The Leipzig Congress of Psychology. *American Journal of Psychology*, 1923, *34*, 612–615.
Allport, G. W. The functional autonomy of motives. *American Journal of Psychology*, 1937, *50*, 141–156. (a)
Allport, G. W. *Personality: A psychological interpretation.* New York: Henry Holt, 1937. (b)
Allport, G. W. Motivation in personality: Reply to Mr. Bertoci. *Psychological Review*, 1940, *37*, 533–554.
Allport, G. W. The ego in contemporary psychology. *Psychological Review*, 1943, *50*, 451–478. (a)
Allport, G. W. The productive paradoxes of William James. *Psychological Review*, 1943, *50*, 95–120. (b)
Allport, G. W. Effect: A secondary principle of learning. *Psychological Review*, 1946, *53*, 335–347.
Allport, G. W. *Becoming: Basic considerations for a psychology of personality.* New Haven: Yale Univ. Press, 1955.
Allport, G. W. *Personality and social encounter. Selected essays.* Boston: Beacon Press, 1960.
Allport, G. W. *Pattern and growth in personality.* New York: Holt, Rinehart & Winston, 1961.
Allport, G. W. *Letters from Jenny.* New York: Harcourt, Brace & World, 1965.
Allport, G. W. Gordon W. Allport. In E. G. Boring & G. Lindzey (Eds.), *A history of psychology in autobiography* (Vol. 5). New York: Appleton-Century-Crofts, 1967.
Allport, G. W. *The person in psychology. Selected essays.* Boston: Beacon Press, 1968.
Allport, G. W., & Odbert, H. S. Trait-names: a psycho-lexical study. *Psychological Monographs*, 1936, *47*, 1–171.

Allport, G. W., & Vernon, P. E. *The study of values.* Boston: Houghton Mifflin, 1931.
Allport, G. W., & Vernon, P. E. *Studies in expressive movement.* New York: Macmillan, 1933.
Arnold, W. J., *Nebraska Symposium on Motivation: Conceptual foundations of psychology.*
    Lincoln: University of Nebraska Press, 1976.
Bertocci, P. A. A critique of G. W. Allport's theory of motivation. *Psychological Review*, 1940,
    47, 501–532.
Calkins, M. W. *A first book in psychology.* 1910.
Cantril, H. General and specific attitudes. *Psychological Monographs*, 1932, 42, 1–109.
Cantril, H., & Allport, G. W. Recent applications of the study of values. *Journal of Abnormal
    and Social Psychology*, 1933, 28, 259–273.
Ferster, C. B., & Skinner, B. F. *Schedules of reinforcement.* New York: Appleton-Century-Crofts,
    1957.
Frenkel-Brunswik, E. Mechanisms of self-deception. *Journal of Social Psychology*, 1930, 10,
    409–420.
Giorgi, A. *Psychology as a human science.* New York: Harper and Row, 1970.
Hall, C. S., & Lindzey, G. *Theories of personality* (2nd ed.). New York: Wiley, 1970.
Hebb, D. O. *The organization of behavior.* New York: Wiley, 1949.
Hodges, H. A. *Wilhelm Dilthey: An introduction.* New York: Howard Fertig, 1969. (Originally
    published, 1944.)
Hoppe, F. Erfolg und Miserfolg. *Psychologische Forschung*, 1930, 14, 1–62.
James, H. *The letters of William James* (2 vols.). Boston: Atlantic Monthly Press, 1920.
James, W. Rationality, activity and faith. *Princeton Review*, 1882, 2, 58–86.
James, W. What the will effects. *Scribner's Magazine*, 1888, 3, 240–250.
James, W. The psychology of belief. *Mind*, 1889, 14, 321–352.
James, W. *The principles of psychology* (2 vols.). New York: Henry Holt, 1890.
James, W. Reflex action and theism. In W. James, *The will to believe.* New York: Dover, 1956.
    (Originally published, 1881.)
James, W. The feeling of effort. In R. B. Perry (Ed.), *Collected essays and reviews.* New York:
    Russell and Russell, 1969. (Article originally published, 1880.) (a)
James, W. Quelque considerations sur la methode subjective. In R. B. Perry (Ed.), *Collected
    essays and Reviews.* New York: Russell and Russell, 1969. (Article originally published,
    1878.) (b)
James, W. The sentiment of rationality. In R. B. Perry (Ed.), *Collected essays and reviews.* New
    York: Russell and Russell, 1969. (Article originally published, 1879.) (c)
James, W. Some remarks on Spencer's definition of mind as correspondence. In R. B. Perry (Ed.),
    Collected essays and reviews. New York: Russell and Russell, 1969. (Article originally pub-
    lished, 1878.) (d)
Keen, E. *A Primer in Phenomenological Psychology.* New York: Holt, Rinehart, & Winston, Inc.,
    1975.
Kimble, G. A., & Perlmuter, L. C. The problem of volition. *Psychological Review*, 1970, 77,
    361–384.
Klein, G. S., & Schoenfeld, N. The influence of ego-involvement on confidence. *Journal of Ab-
    normal and Social Psychology*, 1941, 36, 249–258.
Koch, S. Psychological science versus the science–humanism antinomy: Intimations of a signifi-
    cant science of man. *American Psychologist*, 1961, 16, 629–639.
Krasner, L. The future and the past in the behaviorism–humanism dialogue. *American
    Psychologist*, 1978, 33, 799–804.
Linschoten, H. *On the way toward a phenomenological psychology.* Pittsburgh, Pa.: Duquesne
    University Press, 1968.
Maddi, S. (Ed.). *Perspectives on personality. A comparative approach.* Boston: Little, Brown,
    1971.
McClelland, D. Functional autonomy of motives as an extinction phenomenon. *Psychological
    Review*, 1942, 49, 272–283.

McDougall, W. *An introduction to social psychology.* Boston: John W. Luce, 1907.
May, R. *Existence: A new dimension in psychiatry and psychology.* New York: Basic Books, 1958.
May, R. *Psychology and the human dilemma.* Princeton: D. Van Nostrand, 1967.
May, R. *Love and will.* New York: Norton, 1969.
Miller, N. E. Learnable drives and rewards. In S. S. Stevens (Ed.), *Handbook of experimental psychology.* New York: Wiley, 1951.
Mischel, W. *Personality and assessment.* New York: Wiley, 1968.
Mischel, W. *Introduction to personality* (2nd ed.). New York: Holt, Rinehart & Winston, 1976.
Mowrer, O. H. The law of effect and ego psychology. *Psychological Review,* 1946, *53,* 321–334.
Mowrer, O. H., & Ullman, A. D. Time as a determinant in integrative learning. *Psychological Review,* 1945, *52,* 61–90.
Münsterberg, H. Die psychophysische Grundlage der Gefühle. *Proceedings of the 2nd International Congress of Experimental Psychology.* London: Williams and Norgate, 1892.
Murphy, G., & Jensen, G. *Approaches to personality.* New York: Coward-McCann, 1932.
Newcomb, T. M., Turner, H. H., & Converse, P. E. *Social psychology: The study of human interaction.* New York: Holt, Rinehart & Winston, 1965.
Perry, R. B. The thought and character of William James (2 vols.). Boston: Little, Brown, 1935.
Piaget, J. *The psychology of intelligence* (M. Piercy & D. E. Berlyne, Trans.). London: Routledge & Kegan Paul, 1950. (Originally published, 1947.)
Postman, L. The history and present status of the law of effect. *Psychological Bulletin,* 1947, *44,* 489–563.
Rethlingshafer, D. Experimental evidence for functional autonomy of motives. *Psychological Review,* 1943, *50,* 397–407.
Rice, P. B. The ego and the law of effect. *Psychological Review,* 1946, *53,* 307–347.
Rogers, C. R. *Counseling and psychotherapy.* Boston: Houghton Mifflin, 1942.
Sherif, M. *The psychology of social norms.* New York: Harper, 1936.
Skinner, B. F. *Contingencies of reinforcement.* New York: Appleton-Century-Crofts, 1969.
Solomon, R. L., & Wynn, L. C. Traumatic avoidance learning: The principles of anxiety conservation and partial irreversibility. *Psychological Review,* 1954, *61,* 353–385.
Spencer, H. *The principles of psychology* (2nd ed., 2 vols.). New York: Appleton, 1892. (Originally published, 1855.)
Stagner, R. Homeostasis as a unifying concept in personality theory. *Psychological Review,* 1951, *58,* 5–17.
Thorndike, E. L. *The principles of teaching.* New York: A. G. Seiler, 1906.
Thorndike, E. L. *The fundamentals of learning.* New York: Columbia University, 1932.
Wann, T. W. (Ed.). *Behaviorism and phenomenology.* Chicago: University of Chicago Press, 1964.
Watson, J. B. *Psychology from the standpoint of a behaviorist.* New York: J. B. Lippincott, 1919.

Recommended Readings

Allport, G. W., *Personality: A psychological interpretation.* New York: Holt, 1937.
Allport, G. W. William James and the behavioral sciences. *Journal of the History of the Behavioral Sciences,* 1966, *2,* 145–147.
Perry, R. B. The philosophy of William James. *Philosophical Review,* 1911, *20,*
Perry, R. B. *The thought and character of William James: as revealed in unpublished correspondence and notes, together with his published writings.* Vol. 1, *Inheritance and vocation;* Vol. 2, *Philosophy and psychology.* Boston: Little, Brown, 1935.
Rychlak, J. F. *The psychology of rigorous humanism.* New York: Wiley 1977. (Especially Chap. 4.)

JOHN M. BROUGHTON **5**

Psychology and the History of the Self: From Substance to Function

PSYCHOLOGY:
THEORETICAL-HISTORICAL PERSPECTIVES

ISBN 0-12-588265-3

What is the self? Should we believe many contemporary analytic philosophers who delight in pointing out how simpleminded we are to make such quaint linguistic blunders? According to this view, it is simply a case of misplaced concreteness, a confusion of the reflexive "myself" with the substantive "my self." Case closed.

Let us suppose instead that when Descartes sat up rather sharply in his bath one evening and enunciated "I think therefore I am,"[1] he crystallized a problematic of the self that has yet to be satisfactorily resolved. The soul represents a key problem of the modern philosophy to which Descartes gave birth. As this problem has not met with resolution, even atheistic, anti-Cartesian thinkers as divergent as Horkheimer (1974) and Wittgenstein (Dilman, 1974) have been unwilling to let it be concealed.

Nevertheless, what can the preoccupations of philosophers have to do with psychology? We are now entering the fourth generation of "psychologists" proper. This has been enough time for the profession to produce, according to the best Darwinian principles of selective breeding, the first pure strains of graduates totally devoid of philosophic contamination. Positivistic science, having won the day, now prides itself on its purely objective approach to brain and behavior and feels well rid of the self and other reifications that so weighed down its forebears, the philosophical psychologists of the last century. Even before John Dewey was old enough to start using a stick, Gordon Allport (1943) had announced with relief the demise of the self at the hands of positivistic rigor and plain common sense. Even earlier, J. B. Watson (1924) had asserted with confidence, "No one has ever touched the soul, or seen one in a test tube, or has in any way come into relationship with it as he has with other objects of his daily experience [p. 3]."

Despite the solidarity of the profession, and its confidence in the progressive victory of science over philosophy and religion, it will be argued here that the self is alive and well, and present even in the hardest-nosed psychologist. There is an old southern admonition that goes: "If you don't look out where you're going, you'll finish up where you're headed." "Scientific" psychologists would do well to pay heed, unless they want to walk many a long mile only to find themselves in front of the mirror in Descartes's bathroom again. Noam Chomsky, admitting the Cartesian nature of his linguistics (1966), and by implication of cognitive psychology (Jones, 1975),

[1] Professor Sogito (1978) has suggested that the original pronouncement was in fact the context-dependent "I sink therefore I am," in the verification of which deep thought, Cartesian philosophy almost suffered an untimely demise.

has perhaps acknowledged more than anyone that the ideology of progress will not wash: Major problems of human thought are not simply dissolved by the passage of years. Perhaps Descartes was right after all and his soul was immortal. At any rate, we need to return to the early philosophical working out of the concept of self, in the conviction that we are still caught up in it.[2]

The Cartesian Heritage

An *homme* of his time, Descartes focuses on the puzzle of how the world is to be rationally known. His conclusion is that only those things that can be interpreted in terms of a mathematical system of formal proof are substantial, and only the substantial is real. Applying this model to the self, he conceptualizes it as a nonmaterial substance. It is differentiated from the material kind of substance by the manner in which it is known, by its inherent cognitive reflexivity. It needs only itself in order to exist. This reflexive quality allows mind to judge rationally. The very decisiveness of this differentiation of mind makes the body over entirely to the material world, of which it is now but an inanimate part. Sensation and feeling are located in this material body and are thus exiled from the self. In this manner, the mind is "purified" so that it can become capable of grasping those abstract truths that transcend the sensory world (Bakan, 1980). The subjective personal body[3] therefore vanishes, leaving a chasm between the self of pure consciousness and the world, a world in which subjectivity can no longer have any impact.

Along with the mind–body dualism, Descartes introduces the epistemological dualism of subject and object,[4] which divides the self into subject–self and object–self. It is in fact the reflexivity of the cognitive faculty that makes possible the interpretation of experience in terms of mind and body substances. In a way, cognitive reflexivity replaces the subjectivity of the personal body. Two consequences follow. First, cognitive reflexivity cannot know the self as embodied and hence cannot know the self as acting. Second, subjectivity cannot include the object–self of reflection, because that half is systematically organized. This means that subjectivity is confined to the subject–self. However, since order and regularity are the qualities of the material

[2] It should be noted that the following analysis is a rather abstract and professionally oriented history of ideas, meaning one that concentrates on the evolution of concepts *internal* to philosophic and psychological disciplines. The examination of the crucial determining conditions in the sociohistorical context or the forms of intellectual discourse has been attempted in another paper, where some of the political and ideological consequences of "self theories" are considered (Broughton, in press [d]).

[3] On the personal body, see Baldwin (1906). On the more recent "philosophy of embodiment," see Spicker (1970). Phenomenology and existentialism, while central to an understanding of the self, have been omitted from the following discussion on account of their almost negligible impact on American concepts of self.

[4] A detailed analysis of these two dualisms and their influence has been given by Lovejoy (1955).

world, the subject–self can be no more than idiosyncratic, creative spontaneity. Such spontaneity is indeterminate and therefore can be nothing other than simple error. It should be noted that this conclusion is by no means a necessary result of any subject–object distinction. It is the peculiar consequence of the particular fact that Cartesian metaphysics objectifies subjectivity and objectivity in terms of mind and body substances.

The Critique of the Soul

There is a strong tradition of nonegological ("without a self") theories of consciousness (Henrich, 1969), which can be traced from Hume through James to Watson and Allport, the basic philosophical principles being fairly continuous despite the crossing of disciplinary boundaries. These theories originate in a reaction against the substantiality of the Cartesian self (Frondizi, 1953). Descartes, a doubting Thomas if ever there was one, had concluded in his famous "cogito" that all I can assert with confidence is *that* I am, something that is real and thinks (and doubts). But in its critical skepticism, reflection is unable to further specify *what* I am with a comparable degree of certainty.

Locke went about undermining the concept of substance applied to the material world. Hume, and after him Lotze and James, transposed the force of this critique into the inner world. They queried the inference that thought had to be the attribute of some *thing*. Hume had, in some ways, the same attitude that we have already seen in Watson. The self, like any other aspect of the world, is never given to us as a whole. All we know are the individual data of sense experience,[5] a bundle of states of consciousness. The soul is therefore an illusion. The self is nothing more than an experience-of-myself. The subject is just another object of knowledge. A similar emphasis on the empirical self is evident in James (1890, pp. 291–401), who confined self to the present, passing thought. "The thoughts themselves are the thinker," said he.

Hume's empiricism and James's dynamic development of its psychological component placed the self, as "me," entirely within experience, making possible a purely psychological approach to the self as *self-concept*.[6] In contemporary psychology, the self-concept is thought of as constructed by the individual. It is the product of a cognitive induction performed on the regularly recurring features of self-experience. The product is not a substantial thing but is an "abstraction" or "inference" (Schafer, 1972).

In order to understand the peculiar properties and problems of the notion of self-concept, we first have to take a look at the Kantian philosophy of self, developed partly in reaction against Hume's.

---

[5] "When I enter most intimately into what I call myself, I always stumble on some particular perception or other [Hume, 1740/1928. p. 252]."

[6] On the self-concept, see Wylie (1961) and Gergen (1971).

The Kantian Transcendental Self

Contemporary psychology, including self-concept theory, is dominated by a metatheoretical form or school of thought called "positivism." Engendered by Hume, it has nevertheless undergone a considerable historical development since then (Kolakowski, 1972).[7] Positivism has selectively employed some Kantian as well as pre-Kantian concepts. But in the main, it has had to achieve its present form by suppressing some of the most crucial features of Kantian philosophy, since Kant certainly aimed to nip in the bud those tendencies of thought that positivism has potentiated (Habermas, 1971). Looking at Kant's view of the self can therefore help one to understand the problems with positivistic accounts of the empirical self.

Hume had been aware (Frondizi, 1953, pp. 121ff) that the issue of personal identity discussed by Locke, Condillac, and others presented certain problems for his interpretation of the self. How can I remain myself despite change? How are the self-experiences held together over time? Indeed, how can they comprise "a bundle" at all, at any time? Hume appealed to a loosely conceived principle of psychological association. However, connections compromise the original assumption that sensory impressions are independent units, an assumption made to counter the "substance" notion. Furthermore,

> The substantiality of the soul is only apparently done away with; for it lives on in the substantiality of the sensuous impression. After all, as before, the conviction prevails that only that is truly "real" and the ground of the real, which stands for itself alone and is intelligible purely of itself as an isolated existence [Cassirer, 1923, p. 331].

As Merleau-Ponty (1962) has argued in detail, the notion of sensory impressions is extremely abstract. It is first a technical tool of psychologists and not a primary unit of our day-to-day experience.

Kant approaches the problem with a more radical concept. For him, it is the "bundling," in fact the unity of all consciousness, that necessitates the postulation of a "transcendental self." On the one hand, this self is a purely formal entity, not objectified in experience. It is a center of reference, like the "vanishing point" that exists virtually at the convergence of all lines in a perspective drawing. On the other hand, this formal unity of consciousness is the ground of the possibility of any and all experience. The world can only be understood as objective and unitary by being brought into relation with the transcendental subjective unity of the self.

Kant borrows from Cartesian thought the focus on the "cogito." Like

[7] While positivism is hardly a monolithic entity, five basic assumptions that most forms of positivism share are: (a) phenomenalism; (b) nominalism; (c) scientism; (d) objectivism; and (e) unitary method for all science (Kolakowski, 1972). For a thorough account of logical positivism, see G. Radnitzky (1968). For a good example of a modern positivist psychologist, see Brunswik (1950).

Hume, he sheds the excess baggage of substance. However, Kant refuses to accept Hume's equation of existence with essence (the same equation J. B. Watson made, as we saw earlier). Hume had assumed that by dismissing the substantial soul he had dismissed the self altogether. But Kant understood that this dismissal must lead to relativism (Cassirer, 1923; Marcuse, 1968). For Kant, the transcendental ego exists, even though it is not an essence or substance. It is the subject of knowledge, subtending the "unity of apperception," the unity of perception's structure, which comes about in the very process of experiencing.

This Kantian unity betokens a radical transformation in the concept of the subject–object relation. In Locke, Condillac, and Hume, impressions are made upon a receptive consciousness lying within the mind. For Kant, we know the world only because the spatiotemporal forms of our intuition are actively imposed upon it, generating a sensory manifold, out of which a combination of formal and empirical concepts constructs objects of thought (Lavine, 1950). This construction is carried out according to normative constraints, or rules, such that laws of nature and knowledge are constructed simultaneously and are therefore necessarily identical. The rules are provided to our understanding by "reason."[8] Thus, Kant departs from Hume in accepting that objects are only known in relation to our experience without leaping to the inference that therefore law, necessity, and science are nothing but psychological aspects of our experiential associations (Cassirer, 1923, pp. 387ff).

A different kind of *self-consciousness* is implied by this view of consciousness and knowledge. While Kant shares with Descartes the rationalist concern with the logically prior self-experience that tells me that I exist as something apart from the objects of knowledge, for Kant that experience is independent of introspection (Coplestone, 1964). Rather, the self is implicit in the form of actively experiencing and knowing the world. It is almost an "outgoing" self-consciousness rather than the "inward-looking" reflection it is for both Descartes and Locke. Self-consciousness is, in a new way, built into consciousness of the world. Thus, while we are aware of the self empirically, the self can be known in a manner that does not involve a self-concept. It can be known in and through the form-giving of thought, its unity, and the original productivity of consciousness. Kant's position is made persuasive by the fact that it is hard to see how, without such mental activity, Hume could account for the phenomena of perception and association, which he largely assumed as givens, much as without a subject, the subjective impressions could not have been subjective.

The Reaction of Positivist Psychology to Kant

Because the subject participates actively in the construction and interpretation of reality, Kant accepts as a matter of necessity what Hume seems only to

---

[8] The conception of normative rationality is continued in the modern structuralist study of universal cognitive competences.

lament: the fact that reality can never be known in itself, as something independent of our ways of apprehending it. It is only known to us by appearing to us, as "phenomena." However, the very fact that reality is unitary and that we experience appearances necessarily implies that it is the "noumenal" reality-in-itself whose appearance we apprehend. Correspondingly, the object–self—the self known to us through self-consciousness—is and must be the phenomenal appearance of the noumenal transcendental self. Otherwise, the manifest unity of the self would be inexplicable.

Modern science and analytic philosophy behave as though the concept of noumenal reality represents a lapse of sanity on Kant's part. As a result, they cling to the notion that reality is only given phenomenally, in "data," while vigorously eschewing any consideration of, or reference to, some reality lying behind or beyond. This is the ontological epistemology of positivism (Kolakowski, 1972; Phaskar, 1976), a sophisticated form of skepticism strongly influenced by Hume's. While Kant's own argument points out the futility of such a position, let us consider the consequences of positivism for our understanding of the self.

For modern positivism, knowledge exhausts our apprehension of reality, and science is the only way to knowledge. Positivism favors pragmatic scientific activity, and although engaged in profoundly metaphysical pronouncements itself, it claims to be opposed in principle to any metaphysical or epistemological speculations. Facts are reified as discrete, fixed, and publicly observable regularities in phenomena. They are made objective by the consensual elimination of individual idiosyncracies. In other words, the self is, as we saw in following out the consequences of Cartesian thought, a private and capricious source of error. It has to be brought under social regulation through a neutral public method of controlled observation and manipulation. Objectivity is achieved through the elimination of subjectivity.[9] This is a stark contrast to the fertile interpenetration in Kant's conception, where objective and subjective are entirely correlative. For Kant, the pure subjective form can only exist as the form of something objective, and only by taking on that form can its objects become part of objective reality (Adorno, 1978). For the positivist, the only way in which subjectivity is anything more than superfluous is as an object, as in the empirical "me" of the self-concept.[10]

However, the searchlight of Kant's critical philosophy illuminates many problems that not only are not solved by dispensing with the noumenal thing-in-itself, but are actually *created* by so doing.[11] First, converting the self en-

[9] "Kant's successors, by abolishing the thing-in-itself, endeavored to do away with this ambiguity. They endeavored to give the pure 'I think,' or unity of thought, a completely objective sense [Dewey, 1902, p. 608]."

[10] In the more "organic" positivists like Mead (1934), subjectivity is construed positively, as novelty, spontaneity, or creativity (the "I"), as Carveth (1976) has described. However, closer inspection reveals that this is still a vestigial category within Mead's theory, as in many types of humanistic functionalism, and amounts to only caprice, irregularity, and error given the benefit of the doubt (Zahaykevich, 1976).

[11] These problems are more carefully detailed in Broughton and Riegel (1977).

tirely into an object must, by the force of Kant's argument, set up another subject, since there cannot be a known without a knower.[12] Second, how is the unity of the self-concept and its relation to the conceiver's consciousness to be maintained? As in Hume's case, the self-experiences always threaten to either coalesce into a substantial self-concept or to become reified as separate substantial units. Third, why do we call this pattern of data a *self*-concept? If we interpret "self-concept" purely in the sense of a reflexive relation, between *what* and *what* is the relation to obtain? At some point, according to the precepts of positivism, the concept must be anchored in relation to the regular behaviors of a person, if it is to have any integrity at all. How is this to be done, and how would the conceiver know that the relation between himself or herself and this person is one of identity? Fourth, how can one observe one's own behavior in the first place?

These difficulties and contradictions of self-concept psychology are demonstrably framed within a Kantian perspective. However, one need not commit oneself to Kant's philosophy in order to see the redundancy, incoherence, and inadequacy of positivist psychology's reduction of the self. It is to Kant's credit that the issues he raised as needing explanation if thought were to be at all possible (e.g., the unity of experience, personal identity, the objectivity of knowledge), provide the framework for such a consistent and powerful critique, exposing the internal confusions of philosophies like positivism that came later and prided themselves in having transcended the Kantian problematics entirely.

The Organic Metaphor

Kant represents a kind of watershed between the ascendancy of the physical sciences with their concept of material substance and the ascendancy of the biological sciences with their concept of organic form (Collingwood, 1945; MacMurray, 1957). Romanticism established the *organism* as the new root metaphor. Thereby, a temporal dimension of progressive differentiation within a coherent whole is envisioned, leading to a synthetic equilibrium of functional units. Such an equilibrium constitutes the form of the real, of thought and of the self.

So far, we have confined our analysis of Kant to the theoretical self.

[12] "Apart from the interpretation of reflective self–consciousness, the empirical or object-self—called by James the 'me'—as opposed to the rational or subject-self—called by James the 'I'—has had full treatment by the psychologists, both as to its elements and to its genesis. Contemporary psychology has accepted the fact that the self-content is complex. The assertion of an absolutely simple and indecomposable self, revealed by intuition and made the object of knowledge, is now seldom heard, and when it is heard it is usually based upon a failure to distinguish between the 'me' and the 'I'; or, if not that, the reference is to the continuous subject, which, by the terms of the distinction, can only be analysed by first converting it into an object, and thereby setting up another subject—which again defeats analysis [Baldwin & Stout, 1902, p. 508]."

However, it is Kant's conclusion that theoretical activity is always secondary to the practical, especially in the case of the self. In accepting responsibility for our own actions, we assume that we are free, that is, have free will. Yet in the Kantian world of experience, everything conforms to the laws of the constructive mind and has a corresponding necessity or determinism. If the freedom of the self does not reside in the world of experience, then it must inhabit another world beyond experience. This is the reason that Kant gives for what we have already seen him doing: locating the self in the noumenal sphere of things-in-themselves, beyond direct knowledge. What Romanticism does is to combine this self-in-itself with the purely formal transcendental unity of apperception, conceiving the whole as a teleologically developing organism. This romantic self, in a new level of temporal self consciousness, not only looks forward to its purpose or ends, but also projects itself back into the past, giving itself a life history. Mead (1936) compares this self to the self of adolescents, a parallel developed later in an empirical direction by Kohlberg and Gilligan (1971; cf. Broughton, 1979).

As with Kant's self, the romantic self exists only in relation to a nonself, an other that is only possible in relation to the subject. However, subject and object are more closely identified. Reality is destined to be interpreted in terms of the self. Correspondingly, the self is projected into the world, so that the world can be identified with the self. The reflexive subject–object relation becomes a unity, the primary aspect of experience. Thus, self can be immediately experienced, rather than existing as nothing more than a postulate in a noumenal limbo. Indeed, it becomes the *most* real thing in experience. The world rotates around self-consciousness.

Modern psychology appears to have derived three notions of self, each from an aspect of the Romantic concept (Figure 5.1). First, there is the humanistic view that the subject–object relation is a false dualism, to be collapsed into a single metaphysical-cum-epistemological principle such as *experiencing.* For example, Gendlin (1962; Klein, Mathieu, Gendlin, & Kiesler, 1969) uses "experiencing" as his central concept, by which he intends a prelogical "felt meaning." His work is a good illustration of the possibility of making immediate awareness central to a psychology of self. It also illustrates the problems of "subjectivizing" the self. How can that self know anything, anyone, or even itself with any degree of objectivity? It was this very threat that Kant foresaw as a tendency in Romantic thought, that provoked his *Critique.* He was afraid that any possibility of objectivity would be lost, and all experience, including the scientific and moral, would come to be judged by purely aesthetic criteria of what satisfies the mind (MacMurray, 1957, Chap. 2).

A second thread drawn from the skein of the romantic self is the *dialectic of self-consciousness.* In Baldwin, Mead, and eventually Kohlberg and even Laing, Goffman, and Cicourel, the functional interplay and organic balancing of self as subject and object is developed into a "symbolic interactionism." The self becomes a perspective, and rationality in the scientific as well as the moral

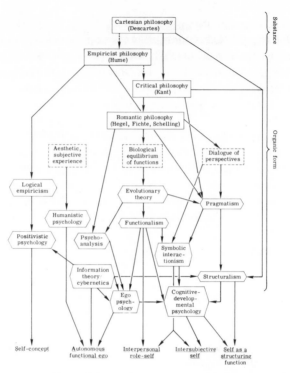

FIGURE 5.1 *Some conceptual lines of descent from Cartesian and Kantian philosophy to contemporary theories of the self.*

sphere comes to be based upon an interpersonal exchange, a complex reciprocation of perspectives at different levels. This symbolic interactionism and the interpersonal self it implies are dealt with elsewhere (Broughton & Freeman-Moir 1980; Broughton & Riegel, 1977).

The third thread, and the one to be considered in more detail at this point, is the idea of *functional activity* as the form of subjectivity.

The Functional Ego

As we shall see, there are several modern psychological theories, all influenced by biological metaphors, that conceptualize the self in terms of some kind of functional mental activity. Theorists as diverse as Piaget, Erikson, and Allport fall under this description. It is not enough, however, to simply attribute this twentieth-century predilection to the impact of evolutionary theory, or even to the organic metaphor of the Romantics. Nor can it be blamed on industrialization and the increasing prominence of "work" as a philosophical concept. We have to go back further, back to Hume and Kant again.

One of the more obvious fruits of Hume's critique of the soul is the suggestion that instead of postulating some thinking *thing*, the thinking *activity* itself is the self. One appeal of this alternative is that it appears compatible with the Kantian framework, requiring only that in place of "formal unity" we read "functional unity." Under this reading, the self would be identified with the constructive activity of mind.

It certainly seems that reason is primarily practical in Kant's account. Reason comprises practical *rules* for the appropriate use of the categories in the search for knowledge. This is why rational judgment carries a normative quality. We are *duty bound* to rational judgments of fact as much as to rational judgments of right. Neither moral nor scientific objectivity (justice or truth) is reducible to personal inclination.

Nevertheless, the fact that reason is practically oriented to the normative guidance and direction of epistemic processes does not imply that the self is a function. We might have begun to doubt that suggestion anyway, simply on the grounds that the psychological concept of function did not succeed the old biological concept of function until the nineteenth century (Young, 1966). But could we not argue that Kant simply needs updating? Could not the shift from substance to function (Cassirer, 1923) after Descartes be seen as an advance passing through Kant's self on the way from "I am a substance whose essential attribute is thinking" to "I am a thinking organism"?

The explicit supplanting of the Kantian self by a *functional self* is most clearly illustrated in Allport's work (1943, 1955). He dismissed the self-as-knower[13] and substituted the "proprium," a kind of dynamic self-concept. It comprises values, attitudes, and self-perceptions that are of persistent importance to the individual, some "warmer" than others (1955, p. 42). The dynamism comes from superimposing upon the positivist's simple empirical self the functionalist image of man as a thinking, goal-directed organism. Early psychology had appropriated this image from evolutionary theory and from social Darwinism. Man was to be seen as using and developing his intelligence in competing, adapting, and preserving his biological boundaries in order to survive and progress.

The time dimension of personal identity (Locke, Condillac, Hume) or life history (the Romantics) is dealt with by Allport in a typically functionalist manner. At the core of the proprium, the current self-percept is in constant tension with a future-oriented "ideal self" composed of a person's "aspirations for himself," or "what he would like to become" (1955, p. 47),[14] which provokes a goal-oriented "propriate striving" in the individual, the aim of which

---

[13] "For the most part, since the time of Brentano and James, psychologists have passed this problem by. For our purposes, we need only record this first usage, and note its relative rarity [Allport, 1943, pp. 453-454]."

[14] In Allport, and in later functionally oriented theories like Erikson's, there is a clear compatibility between the image of a striving self and the concept of what Habermas (1979) has called "occupation-centered identity." Self as social role has not been dealt with here, although the reader is recommended to Verhave and van Hoorn (1977) for a historical treatment of the subject.

is to remove the inner discrepancy between actual and ideal state, restoring consistency to the person. The logical extension of this "discrepancy model" in a mechanistic direction is the *cybernetic self* of Bateson (1971). This is stripped down to a feedback-controlled system, wh..t he calls a "total self-corrective unit." Bateson, like Allport, dismisses "self," "consciousness," and the like as reifications of purely objective system properties of biological information mechanisms.

Allport himself prefers to compare his homeostatic striving mechanism to the concept of "self-actualization" in the more humanistic psychologies of Goldstein (1939) and Maslow (1962). We could draw a close parallel as well to White's (1959, 1975) concept of "competence motivation." These four psychologists, along with others like McClelland (1951) and Rogers (1961), were central to the development of a post-Freudian American functionalist personality theory, which is now usually called "ego psychology" (Jacoby, 1975).

This tradition has directly influenced popular American theories of stage-structural development across the life span. Loevinger (1976; Broughton & Zahaykevich, 1977), for example, bases her theory on a traditional functionalist concept of the ego as a "synthetic function" maintaining personal consistency. Kohlberg (1969), while claiming in the style of Piagetian structuralism to eschew "motives," falls back on White's competence motivation in order to explain movement from one stage of moral development to another, and upon the ego-psychological concept of "ego strength" to explain consistencies and inconsistencies between moral judgment and action. Although they are post-Freudian, Loevinger and Kohlberg have in common with the ego psychologists an inability and/or unwillingness to deal with Freud's central contributions to the theory of the self, the unconscious, and the ego's defenses (Blasi, in press; Broughton & Zahaykevich, 1980; Döbert & Nunner-Winkler, 1977).

In summary, then, the functional ego spawned by the organic metaphor seems to be progressing in American psychology, winning friends and influencing people in its ongoing adaptation to modern life.

Does Piaget not escape the mechanistic reductionism of the functionalists' self? It is true that many features of Piaget's theory are compatible with the modern structuralist tradition that is more faithful than most to the Kantian conception of self and reality (Broughton, 1980; in press [a],). However, the tradition of structuralism is, as Ricoeur (1963) has pointed out, "a Kantianism without a transcendental ego [p. 639]." In Levi-Strauss, for example, mind thinks man, and, as in Romantics like Fichte and Hegel, the logical or individual self is absorbed in a universal World-Soul (Broughton, in press [c]). Piaget, on the other hand, gravitates toward the functionalists, replacing the transcendental knower with a "structuring function," composed of reciprocal acts of assimilation and accommodation (Broughton, in press [b].) In the end, he settles for the same confounding of the epistemological subject–object interactionism with organism–environment interactionism that is presupposed by any cybernetic model.

The Return of the Repressed

Concerning the self, Allport (1943) said, "Psychologists have passed this problem by [p. 454]," not realizing how precisely true this wording was. In the spirit of Darwin (Gruber, 1974, Chap. 10), the modern functionalists have reduced the organic metaphor to the single dimension of a monistic materialism. In preferring Darwin to the exclusion of Hegel and other romantics, they "have passed by" the issue of the subject–object relation.[15] Epistemology was drowned in teleology, and teleology was progressively stripped of all its meaning as a matter of *value*. Neither freedom nor morality enter into human interaction when it is construed as a purely strategic issue (Habermas, 1971, 1975).

The problem of teleology and ends posed by Aristotle and refined in Kant's third *Critique*, is confronted by biological psychology as though it could be reduced to the naturalistic study of processes, dynamic equilibria, and goal-directed action. But this will not wash, on account of two major stumbling blocks. First, replacing substance with process can be as insignificant as replacing constancy with change.[16] Substance was, after all, a relational concept, as much as process. The superiority of the dynamic to the static is illusory, since each implies the other. This difficulty is parallel to the one Hume was seen to encounter, when he sought to shatter the unity and simplicity of the soul into a myriad of particulars. Hume could not avoid making the particulars in turn substantial and self-subsisting. It was as if Hume tried to switch the light on very quickly so as to catch a glimpse of the dark. Thus, processes and functions that do nothing more than replace the static with the dynamic do nothing to avoid the presupposition of substance.

The second stumbling block is that action without intention is blind. Feedback cannot operate unless (a) one knows that afferent information fed back was originally efferent from the same agent to which it is now returning; (b) that this agent is separate and autonomous from the objects of action; and (c) the returning information is distinguishable from internal or reafferent feedback concerning the agent itself (cf. von Holst, 1954). Even given these condi-

---

[15] That it is not inherent in functionalism to ignore or obscure the epistemological dualism of subject and object is witnessed by Dewey (1938) and Baldwin (1915), whose functionalism does not distract them from such inevitable philosophical issues.

[16] The equivalence of substance and process, and the way in which processes may become almost substantial, can be seen from the fact that the "Is the self a substance or abstraction?" problem discussed earlier recurs in relation to process as well (see Bugental, 1971).

tions, feedback and feedforward systems do not *know* anything; they only convey information for purposes specified by some agent. Servomechanisms can at best mimic self-consciousness and cannot account for the phenomenon of either consciousness or self-consciousness. This has been argued by Blasi and Hoeffel (1974) and Broughton (1974, Chap. 2; 1977) in pointing out that Piaget's recursive system of formal operational thought cannot form the basis for self-reflection that he claims it does.

Functional and systems models attempt a pragmatic objectification of consciousness in terms of mechanisms that simply cannot eliminate the problem of pure and practical reason. A piecemeal exchange of a functional ego for Kant's formal one puts the self back squarely in the phenomenal or empirically experienced world. Such a shift creates as many problems as it solves, as our consideration of the self-concept demonstrated. Such a shift ignores the reason that Kant had to postulate in the first place a special kind of formal existence for the noumenal self-in-itself. Like the law of contradiction, freedom is a necessary precept of reason. Freely willed action, for which we take responsibility, differs from thought in that action conditions or alters objects. Therefore, the objects of action, unlike the objects of knowledge, must be indeterminate, that is, nonspatiotemporal. If a person acts as a member of the phenomenal world, he or she acts out of inclination, and the action can always be understood in terms of cause and effect. It is a means to some end that has (teleologically) motivated or caused the action. Only if the individual acts as a member of the noumenal world, out of rule-bound duty, is the action guided by reason alone and therefore free (not a means to some end). The fact that there is a constant struggle between duty and inclination in each individual implies that the individual inhabits both worlds and therefore has both a noumenal and phenomenal (or empirical) self. Only the combined conception of normative reason and transcendental self can hold together practical and theoretical experience in a single whole. Because all reason is oriented to law, the theoretical is integrated with the practical while being secondary to it (MacMurray, 1957). The point of the thing-in-itself is to enable us to think the unity of the same self in both the theoretical and practical domains. Without it, it seems that the self would fall apart into theoretical and practical segments.

There is a certain truth to the notion that activity and functional relation are basic; to form a whole is indeed to *act* like a whole. There is also a certain truth to materialism's belief in the primacy of the object over the subject, despite their correlativity (Adorno, 1978). However, if we are to take advantage of whatever strengths may inhere in the powerful materialism of evolutionary theory and the cybernetic understanding of instrumental action or control, then we must recuperate a functionalism that is not antistructural, which broadens the sphere of the practical to include issues of value and freedom, and which does not totally subordinate the entire domain of theoretical reason.

Conclusion

This is perhaps a strange place to stop. We have just arrived at a respectable beginning. Clearly, the problems with the Kantian notion of transcendental subject are enormous. Kant is to be commended for his attempt to arrive at an integration of theoretical and practical reason (a more fruitful dualism than either mind–body or subject–object). However, Kant contradicts this intent by assuming that the theoretical subject of the "cogito" affords a privileged base from which to start. The universality of thought is taken as primary. In this, Kant was insufficiently radical in his doubting of Descartes and insufficiently suspicious of the false exaltation of mind. There are three adverse consequences. First, the object is made too dependent on the mental activities of the subject for its existence and nature. Rational law alone guarantees only incompletely the contact of a subject with some reality different from itself. Second, the treatment of the conscious is at the expense of the unconscious. The only unconscious permitted existence is of the theoretical kind. This is what Piaget has called the "cognitive unconscious," that is, the psychological processes by which consciousness occurs, which themselves cannot reach the level of awareness. The third adverse consequence is that since the "I think" is inherently private, starting from that point of departure leads Kant into extreme logical individualism. The curse of modern metaphysics is this raising of the individual to the form of unity. It makes it formally impossible to conceive of people in relations of intersubjectivity with each other either theoretically (knowing each other) or practically (cooperating with each other). One can only think about another, or about another's interests, or about one's duty to the other. The cognitive replaces the communicative context within which human relation actually exists and its various scientific, moral, and aesthetic qualities are worked out. When the primacy of the practical is acknowledged, and both subjectivity and universality are admitted to the social sphere, it becomes possible to dispute the firmness and immutability of the forms of transcendental consciousness. Even man as constituter is constituted by man. Even individuality is a manmade phenomenon. But transcendental consciousness has amnesia for its own social formation. Much as a transcendental subject cannot have experience, because it is not to be equated with individual consciousness, it cannot admit of a historical experience. Cutting itself off from its past, it cuts itself off from a future and therefore from any transformation. It makes of its captivity in a fixed noumenal world a necessity, and then a virtue. Instead, it should be seen as a predicament that frames the question of freedom for future thought.

The appropriate response to Kant's transcendental ego is not to dismiss it, as modern psychology has tried to do in its antiphilosophical machismo. To dismiss it is to prevent a possible awareness of an unfreedom yet to be liberated. To ignore it is to ignore the question of universality. To "pass it by" is to reconcile ourselves to the present narrow and technical interpretation of human being. Neither can we simply put Descartes behind us on account of his abstract concept of the individual or because he *only* liberated thought. The word "soul" has not left our language because

Soul is becoming, in retrospect, as it were, a pregnant concept, expressing all that is opposed to the indifference of the subject who is ruled by technology and destined to be a mere client. Reason divorced from feeling is now becoming the opposite of *Anima* or soul. Moreover, the idea of the soul stands for something further. Concern with it is not directed, as is reason (now narrowed to preoccupation with objects), simply to finding an orientation in regard to career and success. Where men still seriously speak of the soul, they are concerned rather with that truth which theology can no longer provide and which science dismisses as belonging to other branches of culture. They are concerned, that is, with what lies under or behind the world which Kant regards as pure phenomenon, with the Absolute which transcends the reality whose existence depends on the mind. Man is told not to stray into such spheres. But if he obeys the prohibition (which Kant himself transgressed), he surrenders the very longing for lack of which he will, in the last analysis, lose his vaunted autonomy [from Horkheimer, M. *Critique of Instrumental Reason,* copyright © 1974 by Seabury Press, New York, pp 60–61].

Acknowledgments

This chapter is gratefully dedicated to the late Klaus Riegel, who encouraged me to pursue the topic and stimulated my thinking greatly during the years prior to his death in 1977. I am much indebted to him and like so many others miss him terribly. I would also like to thank Candice Leonard and the Department of Speech Pathology and Audiology, Teachers College, for help in the preparation of the manuscript.

References

Adorno, T. W. Subject and object. In A. Arato & E. Gebhardt (Eds.), *The essential Frankfurt School reader.* New York: Urizen Press, 1978.
Allport, G. W. The ego in contemporary psychology. *Psychological Review,* 1943, 50, 451–478.
Allport, G. W. *Becoming.* New Haven: Yale University Press, 1955.
Bakan, M. Mind as life and form. In R. W. Rieber (Ed.), *Body and mind.* New York: Academic Press, 1980.
Baldwin, J. M. *Thought and things.* Vol. 1. *Genetic logic.* London: Swann Sonnenschein, 1906.
Baldwin, J. M. *Genetic theory of reality.* New York: G.P. Putnam, 1915.
Baldwin, J. M., & Stout, G. F. 'Self.' In J. M. Baldwin (Ed.), *Dictionary of philosophy and psychology.* London: Macmillan & Co., 1902.
Bateson, G. The cybernetics of "self": A theory of alcoholism. *Psychiatry,* 1971, 34, 1–18.
Blasi, A. Bridging moral cognition and moral action: A review of the literature and a functional model. *Psychological Review,* in press.
Blasi, A., & Hoeffel, E. C. Adolescence and formal operations. *Human Development,* 1974, 17, 344–363.
Broughton, J. M. The development of natural epistemology in the years 10–26. Unpublished doctoral dissertation, Harvard University, 1974.

Broughton, J. M. "Beyond formal operations": Theoretical thought in adolescence. *Teachers College Record*, 1977, *71*, 9, 87–98.

Broughton, J. M. *The self in early and late adolescence*. Paper presented at the conference on Recent Approaches to the Self, Center for Psychosocial Studies, Chicago, April 1979.

Broughton, J. M. Structural developmentalism: Without self, without history. In H. K. Betz (Ed.), *Recent advances in the social sciences*. Winnipeg: Hignell Printing Co., 1980.

Broughton, J. M. Structuralism and developmental psychology: I. Structuralism and Piaget's theory. *Human Development*, in press (a).

Broughton, J. M. Structuralism and developmental psychology: III. The problem of explaining knowledge in Piagetian theory. *Human Development*, in press (b)

Broughton, J. M. Structuralism and developmental psychology: IV. Knowledge without a self and without history. *Human Development*, in press (c)

Broughton, J. M. Psychology and ideology of self. In K. Larsen (Ed.), *Psychology and ideology*, Monmouth, Oregon: Institute for Theoretical History, in press (d).

Broughton, J. M., & Freeman-Moir, D. J. *The foundations of cognitive developmental psychology*. Norwood, N. J. : Johnson-Ablex, 1980.

Broughton, J. M., & Riegel, K. F. Developmental psychology and the self. *Annals of the New York Academy of the Sciences*, 1977, *291*, 149–167.

Broughton, J. M., & Zahaykevich, M. K. Review of Jane Loevinger's "Ego development." *Telos*, 1977, *32*, 246–253.

Broughton, J. M., & Zahaykevich, M. K. Personality and ideology in ego development. In V. Trinh van Thao & J. Gabel (Eds.), *La dialectique dans les sciences sociales*. Paris: Anthropos, 1980.

Brunswik, E. *The conceptual framework of psychology*. Chicago: University of Chicago Press, 1950.

Bugental, J. F. T. The self . . . process or illusion? In T. C. Greening (Ed.), *Existential humanistic psychology*. Belmont, Cal.: Brooks-Cole, 1971.

Carveth, D. L. The Hobbesian microcosm: On the dialectics of self in social theory. *Sociological inquiry*, 1976, *47*, 1, 3–12.

Cassirer, E. *Substance and function*. Chicago: Open Court, 1923.

Chomsky, N. *Cartesian linguistics: A chapter in the history of rationalist thought*. New York: Harper & Row, 1966.

Collingwood, R. *The idea of nature*. Oxford: Oxford University Press, 1945.

Coplestone, F. *A history of philosophy* (Vol. 6. Pt. 2: Kant). New York: Image Press, 1964.

Dewey, J. 'Subject.' In J. M. Baldwin (Ed.), *Dictionary of philosophy and psychology*. London: Macmillan & Co., 1902.

Dewey, J. *Logic*. New York: Holt, Rinehart & Winston, 1938.

Dilman, I. Wittgenstein on the soul. In G. Vesey (Ed.), *Understanding Wittgenstein*. Ithaca: Cornell University Press, 1974.

Döbert, R., & Nunner-Winkler, G. Factors determining performance-level of moral consciousness. In G. Portele (Ed.), *Socialisation und Moral*. Beltz: Weinheim/Basel, 1977.

Frondizi, R. *The nature of the self*. Carbondale, Ill.: Southern Illinois University Press, 1953.

Gendlin, E. T. *Experiencing and the creation of meaning*. New York: Free Press of Glencoe, 1962.

Gergen, K. J. *The concept of self*. New York: Holt, Rinehart & Winston, 1971.

Goldstein, K. *The organism*. New York: American Book Co., 1939.

Gruber, H. *Darwin on man*. New York: Dutton, 1974.

Habermas, J. *Knowledge and human interests*. Boston: Beacon, 1971.

Habermas, J. *Legitimation crisis*. Boston: Beacon, 1975.

Habermas, J. *Communication and the evolution of society*. Boston: Beacon, 1979.

Henrich, D. Self consciousness. Unpublished paper, University of Michigan, 1969.

Horkheimer, M. The soul. In *Critique of instrumental reason*. New York: Seabury Press, 1974.

Hume, D. *On human nature*. Oxford: Clarendon Press, 1928. (Originally published, 1740.)

Jacoby, R. *Social amnesia*. Boston: Beacon, 1975.

James, W. *The principles of psychology* (Vol. 1). New York: Holt, 1890.

Jones, B. Cartesian preconceptions in the shift from behaviorism to cognitive psychology. Paper presented at 7th Annual Conference of Cheiron, Society for History of Behavioral Sciences, Carleton College, Ottawa, June 1975.

Klein, M. H., Mathieu, P. L., Gendlin, E. T., & Kiesler, D. J. *The experiencing scale: A research and training manual.* Madison: Wisconsin Psychiatric Institute, 1969.

Kohlberg, L. Stage and sequence. In D. Goslin (Ed.), *Handbook of socialization theory and research.* Chicago: Rand McNally, 1969.

Kohlberg, L. & Gilligan, C. The adolescent as philosopher: The discovery of the self in a post-conventional world. *Daedalus*, 1971, *100* (4), 1051-1086.

Kolakowski, L. *Positivist philosophy.* Harmondsworth, England: Penguin, 1972.

Lavine, T. Knowledge as interpretation: An historical survey. *Philosophy & Phenomenological Research*, 1950, *10*, 526-540.

Loevinger, J. *Ego development.* San Francisco: Jossey-Bass, 1976.

Lovejoy, A. O. *The revolt against dualism.* La Salle, Ill.: Open Court, 1955.

MacMurray, J. *Self as agent.* London: Faber and Faber, 1957.

Marcuse, H. The concept of essence. In *Negations: Essays in critical theory.* Boston: Beacon, 1968.

Maslow, A. *Toward a psychology of being.* New York: van Nostrand, 1962.

McClelland, D. C. *Personality.* New York: Holt, Rinehart & Winston, 1951.

Mead, G. H. *Mind, self and society.* Chicago: University of Chicago Press, 1934.

Mead, G. H. *Movements of thought in the nineteenth century.* Chicago: University of Chicago Press, 1936.

Merleau-Ponty, M. *Phenomenology of perception.* New York: Humanities Press, 1962.

Phaskar, R. Philosophies as ideologies of science: A contribution to a critique of positivism. Unpublished manuscript, University of Edinburgh, Scotland, 1976.

Radnitzky, G. *Contemporary schools of metascience.* Göteborg, Sweden: Akademivorlaget, 1968.

Ricoeur, P. 'Réponses.' *Esprit*, 1963, *31*, 628-53.

Rogers, C. *On becoming a person.* New York: Houghton-Mifflin, 1961.

Schafer, R. Internalization: Process or fantasy? *Psychoanalytic Study of the Child*, 1972, *27*, 411-438.

Sogito, I. M. Swim or *sum? Review of Aqueous Humor*, 1978, *1* (1), 1-13.

Spicker, S. E. *The philosophy of the body: Rejections of Cartesian dualism.* Chicago: Quadrangle, 1970.

Verhave, T., & van Hoorn W. The temporalization of ego and society in the nineteenth century. *Annals of the New York Academy of Sciences*, 1977, *291*, 140-148.

von Holst, E. Relations between the central nervous system and the peripheral organs. *Animal Behavior*, 1954, *2*, 89-94.

Watson, J. B. *Behaviorism.* New York: The People's Institute, 1924.

White, R. W. Motivation reconsidered: The concept of competence. *Psychological Review*, 1959, *66*, 297-333.

White, R. W. *Lives in progress.* New York: Holt, Rinehart & Winston, 1975.

Wylie, R. C. *The self concept.* Lincoln: University of Nebraska Press, 1961.

Young, R. M. Scholarship and the history of the behavioral sciences. *History of Science*, 1966, *5*, 1-51.

Zahaykevich, M. K. The ego and the self in developmental stage theories. Unpublished paper, Teachers College. Columbia University, 1976.

Recommended Readings

Baldwin, J. M. *History of psychology: A sketch and an interpretation* (2 vols.). London: Watts & Co., 1913.

Becker, E. *The structure of evil.* New York: Free Press, 1968.

Broughton, J. M., & Zahaykevich, M. K., Personality and ideology in ego development. In V. Trinh van Thao (Ed.). *La dialectique dans les sciences sociales.* Paris: Anthropos, 1980.
Copelstone, F., *A history of philosophy* (Vol. 6, Part 2, Kant). New York: Image Books, 1964.
MacMurray, J. *The self as agent.* London: Farber & Farber, 1957.
Rieber, R. W. (Ed.) *Body and mind.* New York: Academic Press, 1980.
Wood, E. M. *Mind and Politics.* Berkeley: Berkeley University Press, 1972.

Part II

Socioeconomic and Political Factors in the Development of Psychology

R. W. RIEBER

6

The Americanization of
Psychology before William James

The American Dream
(18ᵀᴴ – 19ᵀᴴ Century)

Hope, Faith & Charity

PSYCHOLOGY:
THEORETICAL-HISTORICAL PERSPECTIVES

ISBN 0-12-588265-3

Edna Heidbreder in discussing the function and significance of psychological systems makes the following observation in her famous textbook

It is something of a paradox that systems of psychology flourish as they do on American soil. Psychology, especially in the United States, has risked everything on being science; and science on principle refrains from speculation that is not permeated and stabilized by fact. Yet there is not enough fact in the whole science of psychology to make a single solid system [1933].

The wisdom of Heidbreder's opinion would be shared by most psychologists evaluating the status of psychology today.

The groundwork for making the science of psychology into a single solid system is to be found in the American Puritan tradition of mental and moral philosophy. Thomas C. Upham[1] appears in retrospect as one of the principal founders of a truly indigenous American system of psychology. Nineteenth-century America accepted Upham for this role because the system presented in his textbooks was the one most compatible with the prevailing American social image.[2] Additionally, in a negative sense, we can say that Upham's work synthesized the opposition to Kant and the rising transcendentalist schools, those bogeymen of the American intellectual establishment.

The seed of this *ganz Amerikanisch* psychology was planted by its adopted father, Jonathan Edwards, who like Upham was strongly motivated by

---

[1] Thomas Cogswell Upham was born in Deerfield, New Hampshire on 20 January 1799. His father was a congressional representative and a leading citizen of New Hampshire. Upham was educated at Exeter Academy and Dartmouth College, graduating from the latter in 1818. After attending three years of theological study at Andover Seminary he was selected by his teacher Professor Moses Stewart to assist him in Greek and Hebrew instruction at the seminary. Subsequently Upham became pastor of the Congregational Church at Rochester until 1824, at which time he was chosen for the professorship of Mental and Moral Philosophy at Bowdoin College in Maine. In 1825 Upham added to his duties at Bowdoin that of instructor in Hebrew.

The result of Upham's earliest lectures was the first edition (1827) of his textbook *Elements of Intellectual Philosophy*. In 1831 this was expanded into a more systematic work of two volumes, with the title changed to *Elements of Mental Philosophy*. He published a *Manual of Peace* for the Peace Society in 1836 and *Outlines of Imperfect and Disordered Mental Action* in 1840.

In addition, Upham was the author of numerous books on the Christian life, such as *Principles of the Interior or Hidden Life* (1844), *Religious Maxims* (1846), *The Life of Faith* (1857) and *Treatise on Divine Union* (1857). He retired from Bowdoin in 1867 after a career of over four decades, and died in New York City on the night of 21 March 1872 (Packard, 1873).

[2] We have not yet had the opportunity of examining the Upham papers, which are supposed to be in the possession of Bowdoin College. A superficial search for them was unsuccessful.

pragmatic social and political considerations. It had been imported "with tax" from its English guardians, such as Joseph Butler (1736), Richard Baxter (1670), John Wilkins (1675), Isaac Watts (1741), Philip Doddridge (1765), John Mason (1745), and others. This doctrine, seeking a "natural" method for the pursuit of salvation and self-knowledge, emphasized the teaching of proper moral action and the "cure of the soul." Although still couched in a theological framework, these can be seen as earlier versions of the twentieth-century concept of mental hygiene and psychotherapy.

The term "psychology" should be clear enough, but what exactly is meant when we say that Upham created one that was "indigenous" and "American?" Certainly we do *not* mean to imply that a completely original psychology was ever developed in America. What we do mean is that the unique combination of historical circumstances in this country had been gradually producing a characteristic systematization of the subject matter of psychology, with particular emphasis and omissions that were "different enough to make a difference." From the vantage point of the present, this process might be compared to a certain selection of flowers still in the bud, out of a large and varied garden, which, not yet in bloom, may be difficult for us to identify; yet on closer examination, we find that while none of the flowers are really new, the composition of the bouquet is unique and especially suited to the occasion. Throughout the present chapter, we shall be using the word "tradition" to delineate particular historical contexts and processes out of which the ideas of present-day psychology have emerged. However, while it may be interesting and even necessary to know Reid or Stewart or Hartley, it is not sufficient. We are interested in how these concepts have become assimilated over a period of time. We also want to know how they help us better to understand the theories and methods of present-day psychology, as well as how they help us to pose and answer the most fruitful questions. Yet at the same time, we do not want to go to the other extreme by advocating a presentist or "whig conception" of history—that the significance of ideas in history is determined by the ideas that currently dominate—for this necessarily distorts the real nature of historical context (Stocking, 1968).

Whatever indigenous psychology there was in America was at first eclectic and highly systematic in nature. This is particularly apparent at the point at which Upham's system emerged. It was a eclecticism perhaps best described by Morell (1846). "Modern eclecticism . . . is the summing up of the positive and negative results of all of the systems, and the complete separation of that which is valid truth in them all from that admixture of error in which it was before involved."

In this context, Upham's contribution might be fairly described as a link from "the cure of the soul through the hand of God," to "the cure of the mind through the hand of science."[3]

---

[3] The term science refers to mental science, that is, psychology.

As we have already suggested, the importance of Upham's mental philosophy comes not from any great originality or controversial ideas but rather from the fact that it represents the mainstream, dead-center nineteenth-century American Protestant academic thinking on the subject. It was the most comprehensive publication of a truly indigenous system of American psychology, even though built upon the work of numerous predecessors. Upham's system held this position because it was the one most compatible with the emerging American social image. Not in its content, then, but as a system, Upham's was new and different, containing the essence of the American dream as we know it even today. Tarnished though this dream may be, it has not yet been replaced, perhaps because nearly all belligerents in our psychosocial controversies still subscribe to its premises. A view of this dream at a formative stage may help to give us a better perspective on psychology today and more particularly on the psychosocial distress of our times.

The image upheld in Upham's system could be instituted through the four great institutional pillars of society: church, school, family, and government.

1. Upham's moral system has some compatibility with that of Paley[4] but is more eclectic and less utilitarian, in the Lockean-sensationalist meaning of the term. The most important task of the church is to inculcate morality; sectarian differences are not very important and must be tolerated in a spirit of mutual respect. Questions of time and cosmos have been partitioned off into two subdivisions, historical criticism and science, respectively. As long as the church can invest these three functions—morality, history, and science—with a certain degree of sanctity, while in addition supporting the state that makes possible its own survival and proliferation, doctrinal differences are mere frills.

2. In Upham's view, education should cultivate all parts of mind, reason, affections, imagination aesthetics, literary and scientific skills, and so on, in a unified scheme that is itself part of the natural order of things. The child's mind is to be institutionalized to the greatest extent, so that the child's life may follow the prescribed image.

[4] Paley (1830) advocated the Lockean notion of man's natural right to prosperity. Some of his ideas were quite critical of the monarchy. For instance, he asked his readers to imagine a field of corn in which a flock of pigeons had settled: "If (instead of each picking where and what it liked, taking just as much as it wanted, and no more) you should see ninety-nine of them gathering all they got, into a heap; reserving nothing for themselves, but the chaff and the refuse; keeping this heap for one, and that the weakest, perhaps worst, pigeon of the flock; sitting round, and looking on, all the winter, whilst this one was devouring, throwing about and wasting it; and if a pigeon more hardy or hungry than the rest, touched a grain of the hoard, all the others instantly flying upon it, tearing it to pieces; if you should see this, you would see nothing more than what is everyday practised and established among men. Among men, you see the ninety-and-nine toiling and scraping together a heap of superfluities for one (and this one too, oftentimes the feeblest and worst of the whole set, a child, a woman, a madman, or a fool); getting nothing for themselves all the while, but a little of the coarsest of the provision which their own industry produces; looking quietly on, while they see the fruits of all their labour spent or spoiled; and if one of the number take or touch a particle of the hoard, the others joining against him and hanging him for the theft."

3. The family could help in the task of creating a new society by giving emotional security, primary discipline, and moral training to the preschool child. One of Upham's earliest books, a collection of poems entitled *American Cottage Life* (1850), was specifically intended as family reading.
4. Upham believed in the importance of a government based on the interests of agrarian capitalism; he saw a great compatibility between democracy and the free enterprise system and encouraged public service, particularly in his *Manual of Peace*. Agrarian capitalism, as we now know, could survive only so long as it remained profitable; it was killed by the very financial system it supported. The type of morality, science, and history that Upham taught are the religious and intellectual counterparts of this financial system. The popularity of the self-made man in the nineteenth century would inevitably lead to a self-made American psychology.

Two aspects of this major trend in the Protestant tradition are especially important for the history of ideas and germane to the present discussion: natural religion and millennialism. According to the first, God could be known not only through revelation (the Scriptures) but also through the accurate study of nature or creation reflecting its Creator. It was this very emphasis on nature, amounting in some cases to its actual or virtual deification, that would eventually drive God out of the picture.[5] According to the second of these doctrines, millennialism, the will of God was expressed through the acts of man and would lead through a steady, rapid, and rational progress to man's perfection. The cutting edge of psychological history is politics, and thus the psychopolitical concepts of "manifest destiny" and "might makes right" soon became the de facto theology of large modern states, and patriotism replaced the God that the study of nature was undermining. But for an interim period, which included Upham's lifetime, the new deity could still be called "God" and could still be more or less associated with genuine religious tradition. This combined essence of natural religion and millennialism was expressed in the concept of "natural history," and there was a natural history approach to the study of man, as to any other part of nature.

The goal of applied psychology was "cure of the soul." Natural religion spurred the search for data: "the proper study of mankind is man." This new understanding, with all its theological overtones, was to be applied toward the gradual improvement, or redemption of mankind, in accordance with "God's plan of salvation." For in the light of the doctrine of original sin, "cure of the soul" takes on universal proportions, since *everyone* is in need of the "cure." Thus, humanity had come to be regarded primarily as "masses"—even individualism was becoming a mass individualism[6]—and the most effective

---

[5] The Darwinian revolution helped to achieve this in the latter part of the eighteenth century.

[6] As in the western rush for gold, equally in the phrenology movement, designed to foster individuality and self-improvement while at the same time appealing to the millions.

way to "cure" man was through the combined effort of perfected social and political institutions. Americans, and even many Europeans, believed that only America offered the possibility for the construction of such a perfected society, and this is why the American dream was being constructed, with nineteenth-century psychology as one of its foundations—rightly so, for how could such a dream materialize without applied knowledge of the faculties of the mind of man?

Upham's System of a Sound and Disordered Mind

Mental philosophy grew out of an extended theological–psychological critique of Jonathan Edwards's *Freedom of the Will*. This effort had two immediate effects: First, the proliferation of threefold divisions of mental phenomena (intellect–will–sentiment), which allowed for a distinction between desire (sentiment) and motives (will); and second, taking its cue from Anglo-Scottish sources (particularly Reid, 1788, 1795; Stewart, 1792, 1828), a new division between mental and moral philosophy.

Upham's synthesis can be seen in better perspective if we compare it with the systems of two of his key predecessors, James Beattie and Thomas Brown. Beattie, today generally considered inferior to the other Scottish philosophers from a strictly philosophical point of view, nevertheless exerted a crucial influence on all the early American psychologists–philosophers, including Benjamin Rush, James Dana, Samuel West, Jonathan Edwards, Jr., John Witherspoon, Samuel Stanhope Smith, Levi Hedge, and Asa Burton (see Fay, 1939, and Roback, 1964, for information regarding these individuals), by consolidating, epitomizing, and popularizing the views of James Reid. Beattie's *System of Moral Philosophy*, published in London in 1790–1793, was soon reprinted in Philadelphia (1792–1794). In this work of his later years, Beattie seems less concerned with polemics against Locke and Hartley and more willing to incorporate some elements of their systems.

Beattie divides his moral science into psychology (or the study of the nature of mental faculties) and natural theology. The matter of psychology is further divided into perception and active faculties (or powers), the former including speech and language; the five primary or external senses; consciousness, or the mind reflecting upon itself; memory and attention; imagination; dreaming; and the secondary or internal senses of feeling (emotion); and the latter, passions and affections (expressive emotions), and the will, as free agent. Under natural theology, Beattie treats the existence and attributes (natural, intellectual, and moral) of God.

Thomas Brown further emphasized those elements from Locke and Hartley, such as the association of ideas, which were not imcompatible with the Scottish tradition. He felt that his predecessors Reid, Beattie, and Stewart had made the mind into a collection of faculties that too often seem to be separate entities in and of themselves; no sooner were certain affections of the mind classed together as belonging to the will and certain others as belonging to the understanding, than the will and the understanding seemed to become two contending powers of the mind. Brown suggested, in contradistinction, that the phenomena of mind should not be regarded as anything other than mind itself in various states of thought and feeling. The will is not considered as a state of mind and is simply implied within the system.

Brown (1820) divides all mental phenomena into external states and internal states. The former include all variety of sensations, while the latter are of two kinds—intellectual, divided further into simple and relative "suggestion," and emotional, comprising passions and desires.[7]

Upham, in keeping with his Calvinistic background, makes much more of the will than Brown or any of the Scottish school. According to Upham, volition *is* a state of mind, and the evidence of consciousness assures him that it is distinct from desire.

In the earliest version of his psychology, *Elements of Intellectual Philosophy*, Upham (1827, 1828) is careful to avoid the construction of a dogmatic system, but the germ of his later system is present nevertheless. In the next version, *Elements of Mental Philosophy* (1831), the mental operations have been divided into two types, intellectual and sentient. Significantly Upham from the start included material on pathology, or what he called disordered mental action, showing the influence of Benjamin Rush's *Diseases of the Mind* (1812), the first American textbook in psychiatry. An inadequate explanation of erratic mental action was the Achilles' heel of common-sense philosophy, which these Americans aimed to remedy.

A third volume of Upham's system of psychology appeared in 1834 under the title *A Philosophical and Practical Treatise on the Will*. With this, acknowledging the strong influence of Asa Burton (whose division was understanding, *taste*, and will), Upham finally arrived at his threefold division of the mind.[8]

A separate treatment of language is found in every edition; in the *Elements of Mental Philosophy* of 1836 it is appended to the first volume, after the section on intellect, while in the final system of 1869 it appears at the end of the last volume. All this suggests a lack of certainty in Upham's mind as to its proper place. He seems to have regarded language as a ubiquitous component of all mental operations but not as a constituent of the mind itself.[9] "Every language," he writes, "is in some important sense a mirror of the mind.

---

[7] Levi Hedge edited an American edition of Brown's *Lectures* in 1827.

[8] Hence, it is clear that the statment (Packard, 1873, p. 9) to the effect that the tripartite division appeared to Upham in a flash of inspiration is erroneous. James Dana (1770) implied a three-part division to refute Edwards, and Asa Burton (1824), without engaging in a direct polemic against Edwards, professed taste, and not the will itself, to be the real moral agent.

[9] This provides an important contrat with Rush (1865), see Ostwald and Rieber (1980, pp. 105–119).

Something may be learned of the tendency of the mental operation not only from the form or structure of language in general, but even from the import of particular terms. There can be no hesitation in saying that every language has its distinct terms expressive of the three-fold view of the mind [Upham, 1869, Vol. 1, p. 53]."

By the last edition, the system, unchanged in its essentials, had undergone considerable expansion. Under intellectual states of external origin, Upham deals with the five senses, habits of sensation and perception, conception, simplicity and "complexness" of mental states, abstraction, attention, and dreaming. Intellectual states of internal origin include consciousness, judgment, association, memory, reasoning, and imagination. The section concludes with the disordered intellectual actions, divided into "excited conceptions," or apparitions, and insanity proper. Upham suggested various degrees of disturbance of the mind, from a very mild state, analagous to what we would now call a minor maladjustment or mild neurosis, all the way up to various stages approaching full-blown psychosis.

Natural sensibilities again are divided into emotions and desires. The former section containing discussion of beauty, sublimity, and the ludicrous; the latter including instincts, appetites, propensities, affections malevolent and benevolent, love of the supreme being, and habits of the sensibilities. Under moral sensibilities or conscience, Upham discusses emotions of moral approval and disapproval, relation of the moral nature to reasoning, feelings of moral obligation, and moral education. The section concludes with a treatment of the sensibilities in a disordered state. (We see a general drift toward making morality and sentimentality the principle supports of society and religion.)

The final division of Upham's system, the will, was eventually transformed into two additional works, *A Philosophical and Practical Treatise on the Will* (1834) and *Outlines of Imperfect and Disordered Mental Action* (1840). Under "volitional states of the mind," Upham relates the intellect and sensibilities to the will and distinguishes between desires and volitions. In another section, he discusses "laws of the will," relating them to moral government, and "natures" and kinds of motives. A discussion of freedom of the will, and power of the will, follow the latter, which concludes with constancy of character and discipline of the will. A concluding section on "disordered action" of the will is found in all editions except the last (1869), which refers the reader to the *Outlines of Imperfect and Disordered Mental Action*. We shall discuss this book in more detail further on.

It is noteworthy that Upham uses the term "disordered mental action," as opposed to "pathology" favored by some of his contemporaries such as Isaac Ray (who was, incidentally, a Bowdoin college graduate).[10] "Pathology" sug-

---

[10] Worthy of further investigation is the question why Ray and Upham never referred to one another in their published writings. Ray was a life-long student of insanity and published the first *Mental Hygiene* in 1863. Perhaps Ray did not want to make use of nonmedical materials? Upham's silence is no less curious.

gests a medical model, whereas Upham insists upon an integrated model that is not strictly medical, in order to avoid so much as a hint of materialism. He is of course aware of the importance of the mind–body connection and admits that under certain circumstances insanity may have a physiological origin. Nevertheless, insanity is not exclusively a physical disease; the mind and the brain are not the same thing. And the mind's "secret impulses" are not physically caused. Upham recognizes the contribution of Cabanis but warns against the latter's materialism and skepticism. A nice contrast might be made with Benjamin Rush's (1786) "Influences of Physical Causes upon the Moral Faculty." Rush's position is that although some moral problems may be treated through counseling and education, many are more properly treated by medical means. There is no real disagreement between the two, merely different areas of emphasis.

Upham's entire system is based upon the still current notion that the study of the normal will aid in the understanding of the abnormal, and likewise the study of the abnormal will aid in the understanding of the normal. Indeed, this symmetry is worked out with such obsessive thoroughness as to raise the question "Was there madness to his method, or method to his madness?" A little of both, we suspect. For the *Outlines* corresponds exactly to the structure of his total system. He simply lifted the "disordered" sections of the system worked out in the three previous volumes and elaborated upon them while incorporating them into the *Outlines*. Sometimes one feels that this organization is too pat; everything fits. The structure of madness proceeds relentlessly from the structure of sanity, according to the eternal principle "Whatever exists can go wrong." The study of insanity, Upham (1840) feels, "ought not to be limited to anything short of the length and breadth and depth of the whole mind [p. 55]."

The period following Upham saw the continuing integration of the findings of abnormal with those of general psychology; in other words, the ancient relationship between physiology and pathology was now being applied to the study of the mind.[11] This set the stage for the new "mental physiology" of the late nineteenth century. There is also a parallel with the phrenology of Spurtzheim and Combe, in which phrenology becomes the model for the normal as well as the abnormal (see Fig. 6.1). These systems amount to what we might call a "divorce of convenience" or methodological monism; they deny neither mind nor body but are centered on one or the other. Often pursued with lack

---

[11] Previous efforts along these lines, but without a system, were made by John Haslam. A closer counterpart is Benjamin Rush, whose *Lectures on the Mind* correspond to his *Diseases of the Mind* in this way. The *Lectures* have been largely lost to history because they were never published; an annotated edition is currently being prepared by E. T. Carlson, J. L. Wollock, and P. S. Noel. During the later part of the nineteenth century, Carpenter (1874) developed this trend with the concept of "unconscious cerebration." Maudsley had a similar approach in his *Physiology and Pathology of the Mind* (1867). Frederick Beasley of Philadelphia wrote a book in 1822 entitled *A Search for the Truth in the Science of the Human Mind.* In this book, Beasley had a small section entitled "Alienation of the Mind."

FIGURE 6.1 *A nineteenth century caricature of the phrenology of Gall and Spertzheim.*

of perspective, they prepared the way for the more radical monisms of extreme idealism and ultramaterialism.

It was no coincidence that the *Outlines* was published in the Harper's Family Library series (No. 100). The work was clearly intended as "mental hygiene" for the layman (though that term is from a later period). A similar work was *On Man's Power over Himself to Prevent or Control Insanity* by John Barlow (1846), directed to the English public in the series *Small Books on Great Subjects* and subsequently reprinted in the United States. These authors could not, of course, give detailed prescriptions; they make general statements, leaving the reader to discover the application for himself. Nevertheless, it was their belief that the simple recognition of a problem was preventative in itself, because the will could then be directed to control the disorder.

The present study is a blend of living and dead history; in other words, its contents are not altogether irrelevant to, or markedly different from, current discussions of free will and related problems (see, for example, Skinner, 1971). It was the opinion of Howard (1958) that Upham's *Treatise on the Will* represents a conservative, academic compromise, a halfway house between the iron-block theology of Jonathan Edwards and the pluralistic indeterminism of William James—conservative, in that Upham, like most of the educators and clergy of his time, tried to reconcile his mental philosophy of the free will with the prevailing Calvinistic theology; academic, in that it is the statement of free will par excellence, to which most pre-Civil War professors of mental and moral philosophy adhered; and moreover, a historical compromise, in that it tries to avoid the direct confrontation of absolute determinism and absolute indeterminsim, which both Edwards and James considered unavoidable.

That Upham defended the cause of orthodoxy in his religious works, and frequently in moral terms even in the *Elements*, is true. Howard, while admitting this, nevertheless strongly denies that the Elements was designed to refute the German metaphysics of Kant and his school. Further, he believes that the threefold division of mental powers is not an original discovery of Upham, as would seem to be implied in Packard's account, since a threefold division (although different in substance) is an important feature of Kant's *Critique of Pure Reason*. But Howard has perhaps delved too deeply into the philosophical aspects of the question, without paying sufficient attention to circumstantial or contextual matters that are more important from a historical standpoint. It may well be true that Upham offers us no real contradiction to Kant. Curtis (1906) demonstrated close links between Kant and the Puritan philosophy, concluding that, "If Edwards may be charged with making God selfish, the same count may be made against Kant in regard to man [p. 62]." The historic fact remains nevertheless that Upham was hired by Bowdoin for the express purpose of combating Kant's influence (Hatch, 1929, p. 58; Packard, 1873, p. 8). This is all the more striking when we consider that the new German philosophy was in 1824 as yet scarcely known in this country. Obviously, the academic establishment perceived a serious threat from that quarter. Whether they judged him rightly or wrongly, Kant spelled infidelity and atheism to the guardians of America's morality. Upham's teacher, Moses Stewart, had made himself an excellent German scholar in order to keep abreast of the voluminous German theological literature. The fear was such that Stewart himself, certainly no Kantian, had undergone investigation by the trustees of Andover College in 1825. The committee claimed that "the unrestrained cultivation of German studies has evidently tended to chill the ardor of piety, to impair belief in the fundamentals of revealed religion, and even to induce for the time an approach to universal skepticism [Wellek 1942]." Fay comes closer to the truth in judging that Upham was an eclectic, who borrowed freely from the ancient writers and from the British, French, Germans, and Americans in the field of mental philosophy.

In order to understand a philosopher's problems and to estimate his success in solving them, we need to know more than a little about the traditions that intersect in his work.

It became generally accepted among the defenders of free will and the threefold division that any question about mental phenomena is a question of experience that must be referred to the psychology of consciousness. This gave to much of their work the character of what we would now call empirical psychology. Thus, while the immediate goal of these critiques of Edwards may have been to free the will from Calvinistic predestination, their remote effect was a "new science" of the mind. By Upham's time, the 1830s and 1840s, this dispute over the will had already been well worked over and was by no means unique to mental philosophy. Upham was indeed an eclectic, a positive virtue under the circumstances, which grew from a wish to avoid mere speculation as much as possible, to concentrate upon simple facts and the general laws that these facts demonstrated. In Upham's time, of course, moral and theological facts of life were as fundamental as pure mental phenomena in the scientific process; hence, it was not uncommon to explain mental phenomena by demonstrating moral rules. Upham, for example, argues that laws of the will are implied in moral government and the foresight of the deity. This double attention to empirical truth and moral sentiment led to a special relationship between mental and moral philosophy, described by President Samuel Stanhope Smith of Princeton University. "Moral philosophy," Smith (1812) wrote, "is an investigation of the constitution and laws of the mind, especially as it is endued with the power of voluntary action, and its susceptibility of the sentiments of duty and obligation [p. 9]."

John Gros (1795) defined moral philosophy as "that science which gives rules for the direction of the will of man in his moral state or in his pursuit of happiness [p. 7]." A similar position was taken by Thomas Clap (1765), president of Yale College. Two things are reflected here: first, that moral philosophy consists mostly of a system of rules for the formation of ethical judgments, directly related to the values of the culture; and second, that questions relating to consciousness and moral sensibilities will fall equally within the provinces of mental and moral philosophy. These have a common domain in man's consciousness and will, as the two faculties that direct and establish a moral nature. Hence, it would be a mistake to consider Upham's system as belonging exclusively to either psychology or moral philosophy, even as those disciplines were then understood. In fact, its strength lies in its use of psychological evidence as well as philosophical argument to solve the perennial problem of freedom of the will versus determinism and, in so doing, to facilitate the moral execution of an American dream.

Upham was certainly not the last of the American psychologist–philosophers to tackle the free-will problem. But in those prebehaviorist days, the defenders of free will were able to find support in psychological evidence even though Edwards's purely speculative arguments against freedom had largely been granted. Introspective analysis revealed the difference between externally motivated will and internal spontaneous desire, whereas Edwards's refutation of free will rests on the denial of such distinction. In other words, it seemed to the mental philosophers that Edwards had overlooked certain facts about the mind and its operation that would reduce his argument to a philosophical fantasy.

The nature of Upham's compromise position will now be clear. While maintaining a version of Edwards's determinism of the will, he nevertheless supports the notion of mental freedom, by appealing first to the significance of the moral fact of responsibility and second to the evidence of consciousness. The evidence for free will is unique; it is empirical and need not imply a universe of chance. In addition, Upham presents the thesis that if there is equally compelling evidence in support of determinism, then freedom and determinism must be compatible. The argument from consciousness, says

Upham, is as decisive as it is plain and simple, and this may be why he does not discuss it in great detail.

Upham characteristically emphasizes the inductive (i.e., common sense) observational evidence for freedom. In this way he avoids any need to indicate a chance universe before accepting free will.

These are the most important features of Upham's compromise solution to the question of the freedom of the will. It is a fundamentally sentimental solution, resolving the conflict between intellect and will by raising sentiment to par with both.

Upham's Competitors

Prior to the time of Calvin, the free will–determinism problem had not played a major role in Christian philosophy, largely owing to the continued survival, in some measure at least, of a "negative theology." According to this approach, the determinism of the universe, which is God's free will, is of an entirely superior order and includes within it all the possibilities of a man's freedom. Man's freedom simply does not include the possibility of achieving a rational overview of this order as it is present to God, but only the signatures of its existence as revealed and as manifested to man. This negative theology was unsurped by the arrogance of a rationalism incommensurate with its object. The advent of Romanticism in the late eighteenth century brought with it numerous attempts to redress this imbalance, including those of Reid and Stewart as well as Kant and the German school. The psychologist is particularly attracted to Upham's version, because it turns from airy speculation to the empirical evidence of consciousness; the philosopher perceives that Upham is at least on the right track in recognizing the need to reinstate a balance between the two poles of freedom and necessity, neither of which could carry any real meaning without the other. If his philosophical arguments are "superficial and meager," as Orestes Brownson (1842) asserted, if he glosses over the real difficulties of important philosophical problems, as the *North American Review* (Review, 1840b, p. 240) charged, it is because, still trapped within the confines of Lockean individualism, Upham did not see the deeper philosophical implications of the very existence of human consciousness, with its essentially active nature, and that all human knowledge, even knowledge of God, is ultimately an analogy to man.

Far from lessening Upham's importance for the history of American psychology, these shortcomings actually deepen our understanding of that history. Upham's psychological works, after all, were conceived as textbooks for use in a country that was self-consciously engaged in the task of constructing its national image in that most nationalistic of times. Textbooks were of fundamental significance toward that end; ordinary spellers, readers, grammars, and geographies expressed it so agressively as, for example, to cause great consternation in Canada, where American textbooks were often the only ones available (Wilson, 1970). Upham's work expressed the national image in a far more sophisticated but no less deliberate manner. Like any philosopher, he formulated answers to universal questions according to the outlook of his time and place and, by thus linking those universals with that outlook, consolidated and intensified it further. It is of no concern to history whether his answers were correct or not; for Upham was clearly the choice of the establishment.

According to the *New York Review*, January 1840,

> Professor Upham has brought together the leading views of the best writers on the most important topics of mental science, and exhibited them, as well as the conclusions which he himself adopts, with great good judgment, candor, clearness, and method. Mr. Upham is a calm and cautious thinker and writer; and we find no reason to differ from the substance of his views on almost all the subjects he has treated . . . of all the systematic treatises in use, we consider the volumes of Mr. Upham by far the best that we have [*Review*, 1840a].

In the opinion of the *North American Review*, July 1840,

> Though we are not prepared to wish, that any [textbook] should take the place of Locke's "Essay," or Reid's "Inquiry" in the lecture room, we suppose that they who are of a different mind may have to wait long before another appears of equal merit, on the whole, to the ones before us. . . . The method and diction are, in general, good; the questions come up in their natural order, and are discussed with regular fairness of mind; and pains are obviously taken throughout to simplify the study, and recommend it to the young [*Review*, 1840b].

Finally George Peck, in a lengthy and enthusiastic article in the *Meth Jist Quarterly Review*, April 1841, saw as the outstanding advantages of Upham's system:

1. It embraces a view of the whole mind.
2. The arrangement and classification is natural.
3. Terms are skillfully used.
4. Its style is transparent and based upon clear reasoning and rich illustration.
5. Other authors are given kind and courteous treatment.
6. The author fortifies his opinions with a course of consecutive and accumulative evidence.
7. The distinction between desire and volition is clearly established.
8. The existence of the moral sense, or conscience, is clearly demonstrated, and distinguished from reason.
9. Moral distinctions are shown to be the immutable foundation of virtue and obligation.
10. Freedom of will is supported on the solid foundation of its subjection to law.
11. It sheds light on the business of education, by showing that all the intellectual, sentiment, and voluntary powers are susceptible of cultivation.
12. It lays a philosophical basis for several of the leading truths of Christianity [Peck, 1841].

It is quite apparent that Upham's text had sold more copies than any of the competitors'. Moreover, it is clear from the foregoing that Upham had competitors, but these competitors, chiefly Neo-Kantians and Hegelians (transcendentalists), never came near achieving an upper hand in the academic establishment, the lifeline of the country's intellectual future. Coleridge, with his *Aids to Reflection* and *Biographia Literaria*, was the most important link to Kant in the English language. In the late 1820s, James Marsh, president of the University of Vermont, wrote to Coleridge, "The German philosopher Kant and his followers are very little known in this country and our young men who have visited Germany have paid little attention to that department of study while there. . . . I am indebted to your writings for the ability to understand what I have read of [Kant's] works [Wellek, 1942, p. 655]." Marsh set himself the task of adapting Coleridge to American needs and brought out the *Aids to Reflection*, with his own introductory essay, at Burlington, Vermont, in 1829.

The arousal of this new interest however led to the introduction of Victor Cousin, through Caleb S. Henry, professor of philosophy at New York University, who brought the French philosopher's intuitive idealism to America in 1834 with his adaptation of *Elements of Psychology*, the first book in the English language to use the word psychology in its title. (Both Fay [1939] and Roback [1964] were apparently unaware of this fact, for they erroneously attributed this distinction to Frederick A. Rauch's *Psychology*, first published in 1840.)

Among the German group, we should mention Frederick A. Rauch (1840), S. S. Schmucker (1842), Laurence P. Hickok (1854), and Asa Mahan (1845).

Rauch was probably the first to bring Hegel's ideas to America. Emigrating to the United States from Heidelberg in the mid-1830s, he was well equipped to achieve the task he set out for himself. His textbook *Psychology, A View of the Human Soul, including Anthropology* was first published in 1840, only 1 year before his death. In spite of this, it was well read and went through at least four reprintings in the 1850s. Rauch's objective was to unite German and American psychology into a unified approach to the study of the individual as an intricate part of the cosmos.

On the other hand, Schmucker and Mahan had no such intention; they expressed disappointment with the existing systems both American and European and set out to "roll their own." Although Schmucker and Mahan experienced some success, with their texts both going through several editions and printings, their impact upon American intellectual thought was at best marginal.

Hickok was the author of two books, *Empirical Psychology* (1854) and *Rational Psychology* (1849). His work was squarely in the German tradition founded by Christian Wolff in the eighteenth century. Fay pointed out that Hickok coined the term *introspection*, which was to become later in the century a household word for most psychologists.

In reviewing this list of Upham's rivals, two facts chiefly emerge: They were too late, for Upham's reputation was already entrenched before anything else resembling a "system" appeared; and second, they were of distinctly foreign character, at a time when European immigration and consequently prejudices were on the rise in the United States. The reaction of the *New York Review* to Rauch's *Psychology*, though benevolent, is typical:

> In the preface, the author informs us, that it was his wish to combine into one new and systematic whole, adapted to the state of this country, whatever is best in German and English philosophy. We do not think he has perfectly succeeded. The character of his work, as to form, method, development, mode of thought, and language, has a predominantly German cast. [Review, 1840c].

The review found a lack of sufficient development in some places, insufficient explanation in others, complaining that the important points are "not synthetically expressed, with that systematic order and connection, and with that fulness, precision and clearness," which are the requirements of a student text. In other words, Rauch was found wanting in precisely the virtues for which that same journal had praised Upham just 6 months earlier.

No, America was too intent upon building its own image to accept foreign philosophies. *"What shall be the type of our philosophy,"* thundered George Peck, *"and whence shall we obtain it?"* Peck goes on to reject in turn the Anglo-Scottish schools, Cousin, Kant, Fichte, Hegel, and Coleridge, concluding, "It is daily becoming more evident that we cannot *import* a system of philosophy from the other side of the Atlantic which shall meet the necessities of American mind. . . . Systems in order adequately to meet our wants, must grow up and be matured among ourselves [Peck, 1841, p. 263]."

And Orestes Brownson (1842) concurred, if somewhat more thoughtfully:

> The American philosopher . . . must not attempt a *new* system of philosophy; but must seek to continue uninterruptedly, by improving it, the philosophy the race has always embraced, and as modified by the faith and practice of his own nation. In other words, the American philosopher cannot transplant into his own country the philosophy of France or Germany, nor will it answer for him to seek to construct a philosophy for his countrymen from the French or German point of view. He must construct it from the English point of view, and continue English philosophy, as modified . . . by Jonathan Edwards, our only American metaphysician, and by our peculiar civil, political, social, and religious institutions. Our philosophy must be English philosophy Americanized, like the great mass of our population [p. 358].

It should by now be apparent that Upham was the major force behind the creation of such a system, and its kinship with the parent tradition made it most acceptable to a nineteenth-century English reviewer such as Robert Vaughn (1847, p. 93), who praised Upham as a "profound thinker."

Despite this evidence, Blakey (1848) showed little appreciation for Upham's work. But Herbert W. Snyder (1963, p. 210) called Upham the first great American textbook writer in the field of mental philosophy, and J. W. Fay

(1939, p. 107) ascribed to Upham anticipation of many ideas commonly supposed to be more recent, such as the distinction between introversion and extroversion, the emergence of suppressed desires in perverted forms, rationalization, and the James–Lange theory of emotion.

There were many other books on mental philosophy published during this period. Next to Upham's *Elements*, the texts written by Francis Wayland (1854), Leicester A. Sawyer (1839), and Joseph Haven (1857) were the most influential. These texts, while they competed on the market with those of Upham, did not represent competing schools of thought. For the most part, they appeared in the late 1850s, a good 25 years after Upham's first edition. Haven's *Mental Philosophy* was the most widely read and perhaps the best of the lot.

Francis Wayland (1854) president of Brown University and one of the best-known educators of the early nineteenth century, made the following comment suggested by Upham's work,

> Locke compares the mind to a sheet of blank paper, Professor Upham to a stringed instrument which is silent until the hand of the artist sweeps over its chords. Both of these illustrations convey to us truth in respect to the relation existing between the mind and the material system which it inhabits. The mind is possessed of no innate ideas. Its first idea must come from without. In this respect it resembles a sheet of paper. In its present state it can originate no knowledge until called into action by impressions made by the senses. In this respect it resembles a stringed instrument. Here, however, the resemblance ceases. Were the paper capable not only of receiving the form of the letters written upon it, but also of combining at will into a drama of Shakespeare or the epic of Milton; or were the instrument capable not only of giving forth a scale of notes when it was struck, but also of combining them by its own power into the Messiah of Handel; then would they both more nearly resemble the spiritual essence which we call mind.
>
> It is in the power of combining, generalizing, and reasoning, that the great differences of intellectual character consist. All men open their eyes upon the same world, but all men do not look upon the world to the same purpose [p. 6].

Conclusion

Where does psychology stand at the present time? In a microscopic view, one may say that the remnants of a nineteenth-century political economy, as suggested at the opening of this chapter, are still with us. Much of academic and applied psychology have taken on a corporate structure, closely resembling that of the business world. The ivory tower days are clearly no more, and it is not hard to understand how psychology has participated in the transformation that is making the American dream into a social, political, and economic nightmare. Psychology is an intricate part of the academic community, and we psychologists are being manipulated into the problem whether we like it or not: that aspect of the problem that manifests itself in the disintegration of American higher education. Outside the formal academic situation, we see the problem expressed in the chaotic activities of various purveyors of mental hygiene and psychotherapy, competing in the marketplace today like salesmen of soapsuds or potato chips.

A popular article by Christopher Lasch (1976) beautifully exemplifies this situation by pointing out that psychotherapists and mental health workers exercise literally priestly functions in our society and that psychotherapy has become the modern man's substitute for religion. Though somewhat simplistic in its expression, this idea has a great deal of validity, even if we cannot go so far as to agree with Lasch's conclusion that this "psychiatric priesthood" is actually running our society. While psychotherapists do play a major role in hastening the onset of a nightmare, they are no different in this respect than any other professional group, all too eager to cooperate with those who really do run the society, namely, the politicians, corporate industry, and organized crime.

As to the assumption of a religious role by the mental health professions, to the extent that this is true, its origin can be clearly perceived in our exposition of the role that mental pathology played in the development of an indigenous American psychology, which had its origin in the Protestant religion.

Not the least of Upham's attractions was his ability to describe mental operations in a manner that was not esoteric, not abstract, but pragmatic. He thus gave America what it wanted, a means of applying knowledge of the faculties of the mind to the task of building the nation. Even today, the persistence of this attitude is seen in the innumerable forms of applied psychology that infiltrate every institution in American life. And, in the powerful and personal appeal of psychology to the American public, witness the popularity of subjects in any way connected with psychology, the mind of the criminal, of the animal, of the politician. Perhaps this is because everyone seeks self-knowledge. And if someone packages it and puts it up for sale, the American public will buy it. From phrenology to psychoanalysis, it has experienced its most dramatic successes, and its most overwhelming influences, in the marketplace of the mind.

What is happening today is not exactly what happened in the past. But just as the important events in the development of the human infant manifest themselves throughout the rest of a person's life, so does the infancy of American psychology leave its vestiges, dressed though they may be in the most sophisticated technological trappings and disguised in the latest professional jargon. But this may have its brighter side as well. Here are just four current examples, although many more might be given: Donald Campbell (1975), president of the American Psychological Association (APA), wrote that present-day psychology and psychiatry are more hostile to religious morality than is scientifically justified. "I am indeed asserting a social functionality and psychological validity to concepts such as temptation and original sin due to human, carnal animal nature [pp. 1103, 1116]." This statement, though considerably weaker than the traditional doctrine of temptation and original sin as revealed Truth, is unquestionably a remnant of Jonathan Edwards's old Puritan psychology.

We have a second example in O. H. Mowrer (1967), past president of the APA, who wrote, "For twenty years I've had a growing conviction that the main reason mental illness has been such a mystery in our time is that we have so assiduously separated it from the realm of personal morality and immorality [p. 7]," a position quite compatible to that of the nineteenth-century mental and moral philosophers.

Jacob Bronowski, with a naive optimism that might be ludicrous were it not so serious, gives us our third example. In his popular book and television series, *The Ascent of Man*, Bronowski predicted that the future science would be a science of morality, and only a science of morality would enable man to prevail. This is of course merely a variation on the theme of our nineteenth-century moral science professors, though we do not know whether Bronowski was aware of the fact.

Our final example is taken from Erich Fromm (1955). In his book *The Sane Society*, Fromm comes to the conclusion that neurosis, in the final analysis, is moral failure and that mental illness is primarily due to the failure of the development of a humanistic value system based upon love.

In concluding this chapter, we may well ask the question, "What can psychologists do about the problems mentioned here?" The answer to this question is of course not easy. One is reminded of what Huxley said in his preface to *Brave New World*, "You pays your money and you takes your choice." It would appear that there are at least two possible choices today. The first is the highly materialistic dehumanizing trend to keep Western man adjusted to an increasingly irresponsible life-style, discouraging all notion of personal accountablity. We would reject this in favor of a psychology of humanistic interdependence based on sincerity, respect, and responsibility. Surely the life of the mind should be our prime concern as autonomous individuals if we are to play our role in developing a society in which humanity may prevail.

References

Baxter, R. *The life of faith*. London: Nevde Simmons, 1670

Beattie, J. *Elements of moral science* (Vols. 1, 2). Philadelphia: Matthew Carey, 1792, 1794.

Blakey, R. *History of the philosophy of mind*. (Vol. 4). London: Trelawney, Saunders, 1848.

Brown, T. *Lectures on the philosophy of the human mind*. (London: 1820) Philadelphia: John Grigg, 1824.

Brownson, A. O. Schmucker's psychology. *United States Magazine and Democratic Review*, 1842, 11, 358.

Burton, A. *Essays on some of the first principles of metaphysics, ethics, and theology*. Portland, Me.: Mirror Office, 1824.

Butler, J. *The analogy of religion*. London: Simmon, 1736.

Campbell, D. On the conflicts between bilogical and social evolution and between psychology and moral tradition. *American psychologist*, 1975, *30*, 1103–1126.

Carpenter, W. B. *Mental physiology*. London: Kegan Paul, 1874.

Clap, T. *An essay on the nature and foundation of moral virtue and obligation*. New Haven: Mecom, 1765.

Cousins, V. *Elements of psychology* (with Introduction and notes by C. S. Henry, Trans.). Hartford: Cooke, 1834.

Curtis, M. M. Kantean Elements in Jonathan Edwards. *In Philosophische Abhandlungen, Max Heinze . . . gewidmet*. Berlin: 1906.

Dana, J. *An examination of . . . Edwards's enquiry on freedom of will*. Boston: Kneeland, 1770.

Doddridge P. *A course of lectures*, London: Rivington, 1765.

Fay, J. W. *American psychology before William James*. New Brunswick, N.J.: Rutgers University Press, 1939.

Fromm, E. *The sane society*. New York: Holt, Rhinehart, Winston, 1955.

Gros, J. D. *Natural principles of rectitude*. New York: T. and J. Swords, 1795.

Hatch, L. C. *The history of Bowdoin College*. Portland, Me.: Loring, Short, and Harmon, 1929.

Haven, J. *Mental philosophy*. Boston: Gould and Lincoln, 1857; new ed. 1883.

Heidbreder, E. *Seven psychologies* New York: Appleton-Century-Crofts, 1933.

Hickok, L. P. *Rational Psychology*. Auburn, N.Y.: Derby, Miller, 1849.

Hickok, L. P. *Empirical psychology*. New York: Ivison, Blakeman, Taylor, 1854.

Howard, V. A. *The academic compromise on free will in nineteenth-century American philosophy: A study of Thomas C. Upham's "A philosophical and practical treatise on the will*. Doctoral dissertation, University of Indiana, 1958.

Lasch, C. Sacrificing Freud. *New York Times Magazine*, 22 February 1976.

Mahan, A. *A system of intellectual philosophy*. New York: Sexton and Miles, 1845 (2nd ed., 1854).

Mason, J. *A treatise on self knowledge*. London: Pike, 1745.

Morell, J. D. *Historical and critical view of speculative philosophy in the nineteenth century*. London: Pickering, 1846.

Mowrer, O. H. *Morality and mental health*. Chicago: Rand, McNally, 1967.

Ostwald, P. & Rieber, R. W. James Rush and the theory of voice and language. In R. W. Rieber, (Ed.), *Psychology of language and thought*. New York: Plenum, 1980.

Packard, A. S. *Address on the life and character of Thomas C. Upham*. Brunswick, Me.: Joseph Griffin, 1873.

Paley, E. (Ed.), *The works of William Paley*. London: Pickering, 1830.

Peck, G. Upham's mental philosophy. *Methodist Quarterly Review*, 1841, *23*, 276–281.

Rauch, F. A. *Psychology*. New York: Dodd, 1840.

Reid, T. *Essays on the active powers of the human mind*. London: Creek, 1788.

Reid, T. *Essays on the intellectual powers of man*. Dobson: London, 1795.

Review of *Elements of mental philosophy* By Thomas C. Upham. *New York Review*, 1840, 51, 240. (a)

Review of *Elements of mental philosophy* By Thomas C. Upham. *North American Review*, 1840, 51, 240. (b)

Roback, A. A. *History of American psychology* (New rev. ed.). New York: Collier, 1964.

Rush, B. *An oration delivered before the American Philosophical Society containing an enquiry into the influences of physical causes upon the moral faculty*. Philadelphia: Charles Cisp, 1786.

Rush, J. *Brief outline of an analysis of the human intellect*. Philadelphia: J. B. Lippincott, 1865.

Sawyer, L. A. *Mental philosophy*. New Haven: Durrie and Peck, 1839.

Schmucker, S. S. *Psychology*. New York: Harper, 1842 (2nd ed., 1855).

Skinner, B. F. *Beyond freedom and dignity*. New York: Alfred A. Knopf, 1971.

Smith, S. S. *Lectures on moral and political philosophy*. Trenton: Fenton, 1812.

Smith, W. *Professors and public ethics*. Ithaca: Cornell University Press, 1956.

Snyder, H. W. *History of American philosophy*. New York: Columbia University Press, 1963.

Stewart, D. *Elements of the philosophy of the human mind.* London: Crutch, 1792.

Stewart, D. *The active moral powers.* Boston: Wells & Lilly, 1828.

Stocking, G. W. *Race culture & evolution.* New York: Free Press, 1968.

Upham, T. C. *Elements of intellectual philosophy.* Portland, Me.: Shirley and Hyde, 1827 (2nd ed., 1828).

Upham T. C. *Outlines of imperfect and disordered mental action.* New York: Harper, 1840.

Upham T. C. *Elements of mental philosophy.* New York: Harper, 1869. (Originally published, 1831.)

Vaughn, R. American philosophy. *British Quarterly Review,* 1847, 88–119.

Watts, I. *The improvement of the mind.* London: Blackstone, 1741.

Wayland, F. *Elements of intellectual philosophy.* Boston: Phillips, Sampson, 1854.

Wellek, R. *Immanuel Kant in England, 1793–1838.* Princeton: Princeton University Press, 1931.

Wellek, R. The minor transcendentalists and German philosophy. *New England Quarterly,* 1942, *15,* 652–680.

Wilkins, J. *Principles and duties of natural religion.* London: Chiswell, 1675.

Wilson, J. D. Common school texts in use in Canada prior to 1845. *Papers of the Bibliographical Society of Canada,* 1970, *9,* 36–53.

Recommended Readings

Blau, J. *Men and movements in American philosophy.* New York: Prentice-Hall, 1952.

Easton, L. D. *Hegel's first American followers. The Ohio Hegelians: J. B. Stallo, Peter Kaufmann, Moncure Conway, August Willich.* Athens: Ohio University Press, 1966.

Flower, E., & Murphey, M. G. A history of philosophy in America (Vol 1). New York: G. P. Putnam's Sons, 1977.

Hovenkamp, J. *Science and religion in America: 1800–1860.* Philadelphia: University of Pennsylvania Press, 1978.

Riley, I. W. *American philosophy: The early schools.* New York: Dodd, Mead, & Co., 1907.

Schneider, H. W. *A history of American philosophy.* New York: Columbia University Press, 1963.

DAVID BAKAN

7

Politics and American Psychology

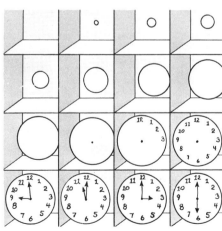

PSYCHOLOGY:
THEORETICAL-HISTORICAL PERSPECTIVES

ISBN 0-12-588265-3

Modern academic psychology claims almost direct descent from the German university of the late nineteenth century, from the period in which sensitivity in Germany to the question of academic freedom and infringements upon academic freedom was unusually high. And psychology in America is generally under the impression that it, especially with its emphasis upon experimentation, is truly free from political and religious influences, or the like.

Psychologists have a vision of the development of science. They imagine it to be quite autonomous. The view is that the development of a science proceeds by each piece of research giving rise to the next piece of research; in turn, generating the next piece of research giving rise to the next piece of research; in turn, generating the next piece of research, and so on. The elaboration of this view would focus attention on the presumptive interplay of theory and data, how new data challenge theory, how theory gets modified, how new theory suggests what new data to collect, how the data are collected, and how the new data thus collected challenge theory—and the renewal of the cycle.

When this view is incorporated into some history of science, where somehow the human identity of the major investigators presses upon one as important, that human identity is frequently squeezed into some narrow mold under rubrics such as "forerunner," "founder," "father of," or "follower of," whereas all of the other questions concerning the interactions of science and the two triads—thought-feeling-willi·   on the one hand, and social–political–economic, on the other—are generally given only minor attention.

There is certain good reason for this autonomous vision of science, a reason that is particularly important when we consider the science of psychology. That good reason for maintaining the view of science as autonomous results from the gnawing underthought that if a science is not thus autonomous it must necessarily be qualified in its authenticity. For characteristically, science is viewed as having its authenticity at some level outside the reach of the unique thoughts, feelings, and wishes, on the one hand, and the social, political, and economic context, on the other hand, associated with its investigators. For presumably, the "truth" of a scientific proposition inheres in its match with that which it speaks of and not its articulation with the psychological, social, political, or economic conditions of its investigators.

Indeed, there is often a kind of uncouthness and embarrassment associated with social science investigation. Social science investigation tends to indicate reasons for conduct other than those which participants would present to themselves or to others. We see this kind of seeming impropriety in writers as remote from each other as Jonathan Edwards, who argued that mean motives lurked behind seemingly altruistic motives, to Freud, who argued that the reasons for behavior were unconscious and/or lodged in childhood experiences, to Durkheim, who argued that human behavior was determined by "social facts" that only very sophisticated statistical demographic analysis might uncover. There is no way around it. An effort to understand the history of science in terms of reasons that may not have been apparent to investigators (or that they would not have wanted others to know about) is somehow less than polite.

It may be of some value for me to state my notion of science as simply as I can. For me, the major aim of science is to ascertain the nature of the circumstances that generate propositions. And the method of science is to study the propositions so generated.

I like this notion of science for several reasons. It allows the very study of science as an authentic part of the scientific enterprise, for certainly the scientific enterprise generates propositions. It allows that the circumstances studied by science have their own nature, as well as allowing that knowledge is contingent on the knowledge-getting process. It allows a place for the human sciences equal to that of the natural sciences. Although allowing for error, it does not fall into the quagmire of a total relativism. Finally, it allows the possibility that there are circumstances that do not or have not yet generated propositions, leaving the possibility that there is ultimate mystery in the universe.

Let me than enter upon this uncouth and impolite activity with respect to the development of American psychology. I will attempt to identify what appear to me to be some major contextual factors which have had an effect on the development of that science. My purpose is the same as the purpose of all intellectual enterprises: to contribute to emancipation. For, as I hope to indicate, the science of psychology has been under the influence of these factors in ways that are restrictive of development, and I hope, by offering such consideration, to work toward the removal of such influences.

American psychology developed largely within the academy, the colleges and universities. Up to, and for most of, the nineteenth century, the American academy was modest in size and was largely under the influence of the Protestant churches. Such psychology as was promoted under these auspices was closely related to the philosophy and the moral imperatives that the churches promoted. The explicit aim of the curriculum in psychology, where psychology was taught, was the development of such an understanding of psychological functions as would serve the promotion of moral virtues. It was a psychology of human conduct.

Things began to change drastically, however, from around the middle of the nineteenth century. Science came to be a significant presence in the academy. And the vocation of "scientist" came into being. It is a little hard now to imagine a world without scientists. Yet the word "scientist" did not even exist until it was coined by William Whewell in 1840. Science as a career, scientist-as-vocation, came into being as options for ambitious young men only very recently. Before that, science was largely avocational, as it was in the lives of Thomas Jefferson, Benjamin Franklin, and the like. Science as a self-conscious career activity came into being in the wake of industrialization following the middle of the century, the growing urbanization, and the great pressure on American agriculture to increase its productivity.

Perhaps one of the most important set of steps in the development of science was the promotion of scientific agriculture on the part of government to cope with the mounting food needs, and the milestone Morrill Act of 1862 establishing the land grant colleges.

Although there were some schools devoted to mechanical and agricultural arts, the land grant college gave new resources, dignity, and status to scientific activity. The creation of the land grant college led to a vision of an academy quite different from the academy of the church-related college.

The universities that were created or rejuvenated by, or redirected with, moneys from the great industrial fortunes—Vanderbilt University, Harvard University, University of Chicago, Stanford University, Clark University and others—came on the heels of the land grant colleges, all gracious to science.

Many of the old church-associated colleges were also transformed when the Carnegie Foundation offered to provide pensions for college teachers, but only if their colleges gave up their church affiliations. Thus, Wesleyan, Drury, Drake, Brown, and others surrendered their church affiliations and bent toward the new scientific orientation in order for the teachers to receive the Carnegie Foundation funds.

Thus, science became entrenched in the academy. And with this, there emerged what, for want of a better term, may be called the two-step vision of science. The two-step vision of scientific development is that knowledge is *first* developed by experiment and theory, and is only subsequently applied to concrete problems. The two-step notion is so firmly entrenched that one has difficulty imagining it to have been otherwise. Yet the two-step vision of science had difficulty in emerging. It deviated dramatically from the long-standing craft tradition in which theory and practice are so closely intertwined that the distinction is not even made. Indeed, it can be argued that modern technology owes more to the craft tradition than to science as we commonly understand it. Perhaps the single most important development to make modern technology possible was not what we would consider scientific advance at all. I am talking about the improvements in the late eighteenth and early nineteenth centuries in machine tools. As machine tools grew in their precision, it made possible the fabrication of parts that would fit and operate together without further adjustment. This opened the way for modern manufacture.

The method of assembly of standardized parts was pioneered by Eli Whitney—hardly a scientist in the modern sense—in the manufacture of guns in the early nineteenth century. Oliver Evans had created an extremely impressive fully automated flour mill in 1785, with conveyors, hoppers, and varieties of ingenious devices. Photography was developed without an understanding of the chemical processes involved. Craftsmen were cracking petroleum quite effectively before the researches on the effect of heat on hydrocarbons by Berthelot became known in 1867, the latter offering only an interpretation of what was common practice in the oil industry. A vast body of experience and observation for finding oil preceded the later more sophisticated science of geology.

The special modern case is electricity. It was largely in connection with the development of the use of electricity that the two-step vision received its greatest support, with the findings from the laboratory having played an extremely important role in the development of the large electric power plants and the distribution of electric power. As the two-step vision grew, so did the prestige of the academy. Industrial leaders became increasingly enthusiastic about the academy, and increasingly, the control of the academy came into their hands. Subtle but profound changes took place in the academy following the Civil War. Most importantly, the authority of the professor in the field of human conduct became almost completely submerged to his role of monitor of, or even developer of, fact. Policy in the affairs of men was not his business any longer. That was to be left to the increasingly powerful people in the spheres of trade, manufacture, finance, and politics.

It is in this context that experimental psychology was introduced into the academy. It was clearly a form of psychology that was sufficiently remote from human conduct as not to be bothersome to the new economic and political powers. Science was rising in prestige, and the moral psychology was declining. Psychology announced itself vigorously as a laboratory science and relentlessly stayed clear of all types of questions that might in any way be related to the more classical concerns of psychology of the nineteenth century. It dropped its role as authority on human conduct, freed itself from lingering moral surveillance, and could enjoy some of the advantages that its status as a science provided.

Let me skip quickly to World War II for appreciating the nature of the two-step notion of science. During World War II, the evident value of the two-step vision of the nature of science took a giant step. Scientists of every kind participated in the war effort. They clearly demonstrated that talent and research could be transferred from the laboratory to conducting and winning a war, from step one to step two. The scientists made notable contributions, such as penicillin, radar, and the proximity fuse, whereby bombs could be triggered by the proximity to the target instead of by the older, less reliable timing devices. The most dramatic contribution was the atom bomb. Military and political leaders learned that scientists not only could solve problems that the leaders provided but could indeed come up with strategies and devices that they could not even imagine.

The atom bomb, in particular, provided a special lesson in connection with the two-step view: *Scientists could make contributions even if they did not know what they were working on.* The atom bomb was created by severe division of scientific labor, with each scientist knowing only enough to do his particular assignment. Division of labor had become commonplace in manufacturing. Now it was evident that division of labor could also be useful in scientific research. The scientist's way of working, devoting attention only to what appeared as intrinsic, was no handicap to the achievement of the ends of the military and the political leaders. Quite the contrary. It gave even greater prerogative in the fulfillment of military and political objectives. Ironically, at the same time, the scientists experienced themselves as having received an increase in autonomy.

Following the war, severe anxiety arose with respect to the scientific enterprise. The world had certainly been impressed with the power of science. This led to efforts to bring the scientist, his knowledge, his thoughts, and his loyalties under control. Those seemingly abstruse and remote details with which the scientist occupied himself had extraordinary consequences even for the very safety of the nation. Loyalty oaths were required. There was close surveillance of the habits and attitudes of the scientists. There was fear and suspicion of any deviance from total personal conformity on the part of scientists. The rising tendency on the part of the scientists to participate in policy decisions was severely opposed. In 1954 Robert Oppenheimer, who had directed the Los Alamos Laboratory during the war, was deprived of his security clearance and was barred from access to classified material. The death penalty for peacetime espionage was introduced.

On the other hand, pressures toward granting yet greater autonomy to scientists also mounted. With Sputnik and the explosion of an atomic bomb by Russia, it became clear that the recruitment and functioning of scientists was not to be trifled with and that the harassment of scientists would only restrict scientific recruitment and productivity. Thus the two-step notion was vigorously revived. Basic research had strategic advantages. The nation could develop and stock-pile scientific research and talent. The transferability from step one to step two had been more than adequately demonstrated, and there was a firm belief that scientific research and talent would be available when and if needed for applied purposes. Basic research was to science what flight hours were in keeping pilots prepared. The scientists, on their part, could devote themselves to their problems quite unharassed by the extremes of McCarthyism and even its less fanatical versions. Scientists would devote themselves to the production of fact-modules, fact-bricks, and they needed not concern themselves with the utilization of such fact-bricks. They were quite convinced that whatever they developed would work toward the common welfare, and they did not have to concern themselves with that in a direct manner.

American psychology again rode in on the support of so-called basic research after World War II, much as it had come in on the support of science in the late nineteenth and early twentieth centuries. Between World War I and World War II, psychology had established a strong experimental laboratory tradition. The recruits to psychology prior to World War II had come largely from rural areas, heavily conditioned by the successes of the mechanization of American agriculture. They were people who were heavily cathected on apparatus, and thus the laboratory was very congenial. The *Popular Mechanics* mentality of metal- and woodworking and work with electricity, motors, and gears was congruent with the experimental, behavioristic ideology. And these psychologists from their rural backgrounds were comfortable with animals. The possibility of vertical social mobility into the ever-widening vocation of scientist attracted increasing numbers of young men to the sciences, laboratory experimental psychology among them. With the decline in the possibility of hard-working and able young men becoming successful without access to capital, science was left as one of the important avenues still available for "rising to the top," as Andrew Carnegie put it. Hardly insignificant was the fact that the experimental psychological enterprise, combined with its behavioristic ideology, served the egalitarian spirit, not only with respect to personal rise, but also because of the seeming "fairness," for subjects and investigators alike, associated with attending only to current behavior. The observation of behavior was a game anyone could play. It was not dependent on any richness of cultural background, social class, or special education. In the experimental laboratory, the psychologists found that they could do a great deal with even the very limited capital equipment that they could scrounge, make out of common hardware, or buy with small sums of money that they could extract from their respective university administrations, and using volunteer subjects from among their students or animals that they could raise in the attic or basement of some old university building. With the kind of support they received in the decades after World War II, it became possible to acquire equipment of sophistication and complexity that had never before been possible.

The feeling of autonomy experienced by the scientist doing supported "basic research" was great. However, the basic fact-module orientation increasingly became the norm. Fact-module studies tended to win financial support. Smaller and narrower was better. Applications for grants for research were reviewed to eliminate "vague" proposals and those proposals which were not likely to produce fact-modules in a relatively short period of time. The mechanisms of support called for repeated review and repeated applications for further support.

The internal condition of the university worked equally to support the narrow-scope, fact-module orientation called basic research. Rapid publication of the findings of fact-modules and the bringing in of support funds to the university were rewarded. Administrators came to be extremely tolerant of neglect of the teaching enterprise and offered little or no objection to the narrowing of curricula to the teaching of fact-modules.

The selection of persons to occupy vacant posts came ever more strongly into the hands of existing faculty members themselves. Thus, one of the con, quences with respect to the staffing of academic posts was an extreme form of ideological vetting and the filling of academic posts with persons who would be sympathetic to the basic experimental ideology.

Within psychology, the characteristic and uncriticized parametric theory of the nature of human functioning articulated with the fact-module approach. The parametric theory asserts that all human functioning is the result of a set of identifiable variables. Research, then, is simply the work of identifying and studying the patterns of covariation among these parameters. Statistical methods, envisioned as somehow being capable of identifying the effect of variables over the noise, as it were, of other variables—that noise to be wiped out eventually by further research, presumably—became the methods of choice in psychological research. No examination of the parametric theory was ever seriously made. And the patent inadequacies of the statistical methods, even to serve the parametric theory, were regularly overlooked. What was more important was that the parametric theory appeared to be a ticket into the larger supported fraternity of scientists.

While this was going on inside the university, there was a lush growth of psychology taking place outside of the academy. It was largely Freudian. A good deal of it was expressed in fiction and other arts and in some political thought.

Consider the role of fiction in Western urban-industrial society. One of its main functions is to come to the ideological rescue of the individual against the depersonalizing forces of the social, political, and economic milieu. Urban-industrial fiction regularly emphasizes the unique, the personal, and the intimate nature of man, while the society stresses his parameters—his sex, age, vocation, marital status—and then his measurements on psychological variables, courtesy of the psychologist. In fiction, personality is more important than role. Indeed, a ubiquitous theme to be found in modern fiction is precisely the struggle—and often the victory—of the personal against the socially prescribed, parametrically expected role for the individual.

From the time of Freud's visit to the United States in 1909, American writers drew on his contributions in the fashioning of fiction. They liked such ideas as repression is the cause of neurosis and healing consists in overcoming oppression. They fully accepted the idea that the inner and psychic life of the individual was more vast and more complicated than had ever been previously imagined. Thus, largely through the efforts of writers of fiction, the image of psychology in the mind of the American public was more like Freudian psychology than like the psychology developed in the academy. The American academic psychologist rejected this Freudian "underground" psychology. He was not uncognizant of its presence. There even were some occasional academic efforts to tame some of the ideas and observations of psychoanalysis by subjecting them to experimental study. Although psychoanalysis was not widely accepted by the members of the medical profession, the few among them who availed themselves of it treated it as an arcane art, to be transmitted only orally to highly selected recipients holding M.D. degrees.

Virtually no funds were ever made available for psychological research that would be consonant with this psychology of the underground. Within the universities, battles were fought repeatedly between students—that is, undergraduate students who could yet be forgiven for indiscretion—whose view of psychology was informed by the underground, and their experimentally, behavioristically minded psychology teachers. Every introductory course in psychology was a battleground. Indeed, one of the major aims of the introductory course was to impress students with the possibility of a so-called scientific psychology and to derogate the ever-present enemy, the psychology of the underground. The selection of students for advanced work and for admission to graduate schools and the selection of faculty were all determined in large part on the basis of such "confession." "Wise" and career-oriented young people learned to overcome the "error of their youth," which had been influenced by the underground. Those who persisted in any interest in the underground were relentlessly weeded out.

Outside the academy, however, especially after World War II, there was a growing need for a professional class to cope with people who were not successful in adjusting to the claims of urban-industrial society. That was largely an unmet need. Psychiatrists were certainly not numerous, and prior to World War II, clinical psychology hardly existed at all as a profession. The difficulty, of course, has been that in the area of mental treatment those most in need of service are characteristically those least capable of paying for such services.

A turning point took place after World War II in connection with the treatment of war veterans. There arose a substantial attempt to develop and supply psychological services out of public funds. Government offered funds to psychology departments to train a cadre of clinical psychologists, some percentage of which, it was presumed, would work in veterans' hospitals and the like. Psychology departments accepted the funds for the support of clinical training, but usually with great ambivalence. The clinical concept had prevailed almost exclusively in the underground. There was virtually no tradition of education in clinical psychology, with the exception of psychometrics, some clinical child psychology, and educational psychology. The departments of psychology, suddenly experiencing an embarrassment of riches and ideological compromise, sought to keep the new enterprise of clinical psychology as second class and subject to the ideological control of the experimental psychologists. As the numbers of clinical psychologists grew within the American Psychological Association, the tension grew between the clinical psychologists, who wanted the association to serve its professional needs, and the experimental psychologists, who would keep psychology "pure."

The new clinical psychologist pioneers, fresh with their Ph.D.s, were met on the outside world, as it were, by the medical profession, whose attitude to them was one of petulance or, at best, sufferance. While the medical profession had hardly pursued the clinical psychological venture with vigour, it also resisted the encroachment of the clinical psychologists. There was conflict within institutions for power, prestige, and funds. And the medical profession hindered registration and certification legislation in state legislatures.

The new clinical psychologists were in an awkward position. Because of their association with the academy, they had received a credential by which, at the very least, they could be called "doctor." Their actual training in clinical psychology was often at best marginal—caused not the least by the simple fact that those who taught them were hardly strongly identified with, or experienced in, the clinical enterprise. Their teachers were characteristically experimental psychologists of some type, and under any circumstances, the typical socialization of the new clinical psychology Ph.D. entailed acceptance of the scientific superego which had developed in the academy over the decades. On confronting the hostility of the medical profession, they tended to drape themselves defensively in their credential, boasting that they had superior research backgrounds and somehow were in contact with some universe to which the mere medical practitioner could not hope to aspire.

The two-step idea of research that they had acquired in their university training occasionally led them to set up research units of one kind or another, for example, in mental hospitals—although most often there was only a remote relationship between these research projects and the kinds of problems which the clinical enterprise entailed.

The fact was that the clinical psychology lacked the kind of empirical, as contrasted with experimental, background which characterizes the development of every other service profession. The kind of empiricism represented in the work of such pioneers as Freud, Binet, Piaget, Rorschach, and others was the object of scorn by the academic teachers of the members of the new profession of clinical psychology. Clinical psychology could sneak some insight and technique from the underground, but it could not accept it openly. And there was little possibility of doing systematic empirical research of the case type. Such research was not honored. Clinical psychologists tended to do experimental research, distinguished only by some accompanying promissory notes suggesting ultimate clinical application. The fact is that to this day there is relatively little systematic empirical research going on among clinical psychologists. The practice of clinical psychology is characteristically extremely alienated, with very little of the necessary sharing of ideas and observations that the empirical mode needs in order to advance. And there are virtually no funds to bring people together into long sustained teams to work systematically, empirically, and energetically on the solution of clinical problems.

Since the journals were generally under the same taboos as the academy, there was relatively little opportunity for appropriate clinical and empirical materials to be reported in print. Indeed, because of the fact that *books* were considerably less under the taboos—the publishers were finding that there was some possibility of sale among the increasing number of clinicians, enough to make at least a reasonable profit—most of the published empirical material has been in the form of books rather than journal articles. The difficulty with this is simply that it is considerably harder, and takes a much more strenuous effort, to write a book than it does to write an article. Furthermore, journals allow a continuing flow of discourse on particular topics, which cannot be done in the same way by books.

I believe that some very significant change is currently possible. One important change is in the public attitudes to the scientific enterprise. Changes began toward the end of the 1960s and continue. By the end of 1969 and the beginning of 1970, the reaction against science had grown quite strong. Government support of the scientific enterprise weakened considerably, reflecting larger trends in the society. The idea that somehow scientific research could solve all problems that beset mankind had grown thin. The public fantasies of indefinitely sustained health, of flying cars, of personal collapsible pocket helicopters, of mechanized robots that would clean house and prepare meals, of inexpensive yet superb prefabricated houses and the like are virtually gone.

It was becoming evident that the payoff from science, together with the two-step approach, was less than expected. The returns were not commensurate with the huge amounts of money that had been spent. Chemistry has produced very little in the way of new products which would have any great advantages over the old. The multiplication of frivolous plastic products on the market has not enhanced the public image of the chemist. Indeed, the word "plastic" itself has come to mean "inauthentic" in the common language. Physics has produced little of great consequence except in aerospace. Exuberance over the moon landings was considerably dampened by the awareness of the wretched performance of science on planet Earth. The advances in quality control have not led to improved quality of products. Rather, they have been used to produce shabby products just at the margin of market acceptability and of timed obsolescence. Whereas huge sums of money had been spent in connection with military research, the war in Vietnam was not won with distinction, and the public became aware of such odious things as napalm, defoliants, and poison gases. The association of the scientific enterprise with the military establishment became conspicuous to those who would hope for better solutions to human problems than military ones in the next centuries. The scientist is viewed more and more in the image of Dr. Strangelove. The promise of science as the creator of varieties of new employment opportunities has hardly been realized. Organized labor sees science as wiping out jobs. Science has not produced a reliable and safe contraceptive method. The unwitting use of thalidomide that produced deformed babies severely reduced the prestige of medical research. There are daily reports of dangers in common products created by and not prevented by scientists. Research in dentistry has accomplished little in connection with the prevention of cavities—flouridated toothpaste notwithstanding. Computer developments led to the production of information systems that threaten the privacy of individual citizens in a way as to undermine the possibilities of democracy. The scientific evidence in connection with the effect of cigarette smoking presented to Congress—with scientists arguing among themselves—left Congress without the benefit of clear advice and left the image of the scientist as an "objective" observer quite tarnished. The neglect of science in connection with pollution has been notorious. The "rhetoric of imminent breakthrough," which scientists have become skilled in using, is met with increasing cynicism. There is boredom with reading about the imminent breakthroughs in cancer research, which appear in the newspapers with inexorable regularity. The promise of safe energy from the atom has not been realized in the more than 30 years and billions of dollars in research funds since Hiroshima and Nagasaki, while the threat of total destruction from atomic energy continues to be very real.

I am fully aware of the objection that enough time has not elapsed to be able to fully determine whether the strategy of recent science, the two-step approach, and so on, has been successful. Historians in the future may judge the progress in science of the last quarter of a century much differently than it is currently being judged. And certainly I do not mean to say that the field of experimental psychology should not be continued. Quite the contrary. One of the fundamental strategic lessons that emerges out of the contributions of Darwin is that the increase of variation is an extremely sensible way to meet an unknown future. At the same time, those historical efforts which restricted research in psychology in the universities need to be discouraged. It is the inhibiting influence that has been exerted that is objectionable.

Certainly the strategy of the two-step process has not been conspicuously successful in psychology. Preciously few of the findings from the laboratory, which often systematically delete the effect of social norm and of economic and political contexts, have been very consequential. Perhaps one of the outstanding failures that might be mentioned is the negligible and sometimes even damaging transfer from the psychology of learning to the field of education. And certainly, the various experimental studies in the field of personality have led to little in connection with the understanding of the functioning of human beings in their various paths. There has, however, been no shortage of the "rhetoric of imminent breakthrough" in the field of psychology.

The old motto "Nothing human is alien to me" would appear to be a good one to keep in mind for the future development of psychology. Instead of engaging in extreme efforts to satisfy a parametric model, and thereby trying to "study the effects of one variable at a time," the human world in its complexity needs to be examined and comprehended. Simpleminded presuppositions do not necessarily clarify nonsimple phenomena. The psychologist needs to overcome his aversion to the study of history and to fieldwork, and to look at things in other ways than those that yield fact-modules.

The psychologist needs especially to overcome the psychophobia that has characterized the history of academic psychology in America. The definition of psychology as the study of behavior needs to be replaced with the more classical definition of psychology as the study of thinking, feeling, and willing. Certainly, the psychologist should be interested in behavior. However, the critical linkages betweeen thoughts, feelings, and wishes, on the one hand, and behavior, on the other, need to be carefully examined, and the strategy of concentrating largely on behavior alone is unlikely to reveal the complex nature of those linkages.

It appears to me that the aim of "prediction and control," which has played such an important role in the culture of psychologists since its early formulation by John B. Watson, simply needs to be abandoned. In the light of the history of psychology, that aim has played its role more as a fantasy of power in lieu of real effectiveness than as real effectiveness. The role of that fantasy is analogous to a superman fantasy in a young boy who is actually quite ineffective in making circumstances conform to his will. Methodologically, that aim was converted into models of relationships with subjects of investigation in which the critical feature was *manipulation* of the subject by the experimenter. The experiment tended to become an experiment in the manipulation process. That strategy has not led to findings of distinction and has furthermore led to a severe injury of the capacity of the psychologist to be useful to society.

Behaviorism and Humanistic Psychology

How does psychology relate to human freedom and dignity? Humanistic psychology began its recent history in post–World War II America when the prevalent psychology of the academy was behaviorism. Behaviorism had a well-guarded monopoly in the academy that was defended in the name of science.

Behaviorism was, as John Watson boasted in an early presentation, "purely an American production" (1919, p. vii). Indeed, outside of a kinship with Pavlovian Russian psychology, behaviorism has always seemed to be indigenously American. One way to understand the great defensiveness of behaviorism in American academic institutions is to see it as an attempt to harden itself against other influences. But behaviorism was not American in a general sense—American means pluralistic. It was American in some special senses. It carried, within its academic institutions, the traces of American churches, which were the principal founders of the colleges and the universities in the nineteenth century.

The thought of John Wesley, the founder of Methodism, was important in the history of American culture. It was particularly important in the formation of many of the American colleges in the nineteenth century, particularly

in the American Midwest. The question of man's natural freedom and dignity
was extremely important to Wesley. He rejected the idea of man's natural
dignity and worth. The Fall from Grace in the Garden of Eden was his key to
understanding man's nature. Man was innately sinful. Man was totally unworthy. Man was fully dependent on Divine grace for any redemption. He
had no freedom in that regard. Moral development consisted only in achieving conviction of one's sin and one's dependence on the Divine.

The arrival of Darwinian thought in the second half of the nineteenth century served to confirm the prevalent doctrine of the natural depravity of man.
Darwin's thought was unacceptable to the fundamentalists because it challenged the Bible's authority. Yet, at a deeper level, Darwinism confirmed
Wesleyan thought, suggesting that man was not much better than a beast, presumed to be under the control of his instincts, lower passions, and appetites.
Darwinism, despite the manifest resistance, took firm root in American colleges, especially in the new American universities of the later nineteenth and
early twentieth centuries. The way had been prepared by the doctrine of
natural depravity. Behaviorism emerged as the leading psychology following
World War I, the product of Wesleyanism and Darwinism. It essentially provided a vision of man of the model of an incarcerated and essentially enslaved
rodent, whose name was a euphemism for depravity, completely under the
dominion of the laws of behavior he was divinely endowed with, living under
the constraints of his steward on Earth, the experimenter. His main project in
life was to selfishly grub for food. He lived in a universe dominated by a vend-
ing machine which was operated by somehow stumbling on the arbitrary law
of its operation contrived by his steward. This relationship to the steward was
essentially silent, all communication taking place through gross motor
responses, on the one hand, and "stimuli" and "reinforcements," on the other.

Human liberty has received its greatest challenge in history by technology.
Communication, transportation, and military science have endowed the
contemporary state with powers which would have been the envy of every
tyrant in the history of the world. Hitler and Stalin were rulers who took advantage of the capability for tyranny that modern technology made possible.
Certainly human liberty has been an issue in the history of the world for a
long time. But the widespread tyranny of the twentieth century has made the
issue of human liberty particularly acute.

There was a great assault on human liberty in post–World War II America.
There was McCarthyism, the attack on Oppenheimer, the uncontrolled
growth of the power of the FBI under J. Edgar Hoover, the excesses of the
CIA, Watergate, etc. There was also a great growth of petty tyrannies within
various institutions, elementary schools, high schools, colleges, universities,
government bureaus, and corporations.

Behaviorism in America and its cousin, Pavlovianism in Russia, are not
irrelevant to these developments. In spite of Pavlov's open and fearless
criticism of the Soviet government, he was nonetheless the darling of both

Lenin and Stalin. Lenin, for example, responded to Pavlov's request to leave Russia following the revolution with an order that Pavlov be treated as an honored Communist. His researches were supported virtually uninterruptedly through the revolution and the regimes of both Lenin and Stalin, until his death. Pavlov was the only non-American psychologist that Watson claimed any kinship to; and the intellectual connection to Pavlov's work has been openly acknowledged by Skinner. I should also point out that Skinner is distinguished among psychologists by having been awarded the National Medal of Science by the American government, granted to him by Lyndon B. Johnson in 1968.

What might be the connection between behaviorism–Pavlovianism, on the one hand, and the question of deprivation of liberty, on the other? The thought of Stalin may be suggestive toward answering this question. Stalin (1970), in his book *The Foundations of Leninism*, proudly asserted that the power of the Communist Party was transformed from being based earlier merely on "the power of ideas" to "the power of authority" (p. 108). This is a distinction that he credits Lenin with.

Stalin's clear interest was to substitute such "power of authority" for the "power of ideas." Now, one of the critical features of virtually all the research done under the aegis of either Pavlovianism or behaviorism is that the power of ideas in this sense is systematically set aside as a psychological factor. The transfer of ideas between experimenter and subject is rarely even alluded to. Rather, all interaction between the experimenter and the subject is conceptualized as contained in the presentation of physical stimuli and in the administration of rewards and punishments by the experimenter to the subject, and the physical behavior of the subject. Indeed, one of the most interesting features of the usual paradigm is that while the experimenter usually has an unlimited supply of rewards and punishments for administration to the subjects, the subjects, on the other hand, have no independent access to any supply. *The only reward that the subject can give the experimenter is deferential behavior*, and he has no way to punish the experimenter, except refusal. Through it all the subject remains the "subject" of the experimenter.

It is, on the other hand, in the common democratic tradition to celebrate "the power of ideas" in contrast to "the power of authority." Behaviorism and Pavlovianism conspired to undermine the validity of the power of ideas, and to assert the role of punishment. But by keeping the role of reward, it allowed the possibility of a kind of fascism with a friendly face, all the more culpable for its seeming humanitarianism.

The power of ideas is the power of persuasion. I think that there is value to point to a strange passage in Clark L. Hull's *Principles of Behavior* (1943), a classic in the history of behaviorism. In the introductory part of that book there is a small section that seems to have little bearing on the central substance of that book. It is a diatribe against the use of argument and persuasion.

Hull contrasts science with argumentation. Although there are similarities, he says, they differ radically from each other, and it is a mistake to confuse them. In italics he writes, *"The primary objective of argumentation is persuasion."* He then goes on to say that argumentation "is socially aggressive; one person seeking to influence or coerce another by means of a process of reasoning. . . . Underneath, however, the ultimate objective is usually to lead the recipient to some kind of action, not infrequently such as to be of advantage to the proponent or some group with which the proponent is allied [Hull, 1943, p. 8]."

It is ironic that Hull, seemingly in pursuit of the aim of protecting freedom, essentially reviles the use of dialogue and reason, the historical mainstays in the defense of human freedom.

But yet, as we hold this passage of Clark L. Hull against Stalin's expressed desire also to get rid of the possibility of the exertion of the "power of ideas," and note that Hull's theory of human behavior was based completely on the power of one person to dispense rewards and punishments to another on the basis of a formula contrived by the former, we cannot but wonder what the actual goal of the Hullian enterprise might have been. I think that if we examine this closely we can get some glimmer of the implicit politics of the generally avowedly nonpolitical behaviorism. Skinner, of course, and to his credit, has not disguised his views concerning the larger political implications of his views.

While, however, the power of behaviorism continued relatively strongly in the academic institutions, even through the post–World War II period, certain strong counterforces were also growing. These forces may, I believe, be appropriately appreciated as being both supportive of, as well as in some respects having been served by, the humanistic psychology movement.

There was a powerful demographic undercurrent following World War II. Between 1945 and 1946 the birth rate rose by about 25%. The birth rate stayed high, creating the so-called "postwar baby boom." When the 1960s opened, the leading edge of the postwar baby boom was entering the early teens. Many became involved in the Civil Rights movement. Some of the precocious ones created disturbances on the campuses of the most elite academies. That leading edge turned 19 in 1965. Nineteen is America's military age, and in 1965, hardly by coincidence, the government began sending massive numbers of troops to Vietnam. In 1968 masses of young adults congregated in the streets outside of the Democratic National Convention in Chicago.

This generation has been extremely important in changing the character of American culture. It sought conditions which were stimulating rather than discouraging of personal growth and development. It was impatient with patterns of education directed at specific goals which might become anachronistic quickly. It reacted negatively to those things which fostered alienation rather than communion. It embarked on a program of life experimentation which, by comparison, made the laboratory experimentation of the psychologist look contrived, trivial, frivolous, and foolish.

When the members of this generation were infants in the late 1940s, Professor Skinner invented the "Air-Crib," a Skinner box for babies. It was a large, soundproof, germproof, air-conditioned box for giving children mechanical care for the first 2 years of life. Almost as soon as this generation could sing their own songs they were singing sarcastic songs about being raised in "boxes made of ticky-tacky and they all looked just the same."[1] They took advantage of the one medium of expression which had not been quite so instrumentalized, rationalized, and bureaucratized, the medium of music. This was the one medium that seemed to remain sufficiently flexible to allow the expression of the perceptions, feelings, and desires of those young people.

Science, for this generation, appeared in the form of atom and napalm bombs, electronic eavesdropping, and thalidomide babies without arms. The scientist was Dr. Strangelove. They saw scientists displaying naked self-interest in serving the military and the corporations, grubbing for grants to carry out seemingly frivolous research, and engaging in unseemly bickering in the ugly public debates concerning the effects of tobacco on health. Rationality, for them, came in the form of benefit–cost ratios in which incalculable human costs played no role. Robert McNamara, who was sending them off to Vietnam, was represented to them as the supremely rational man. Numbers for them were Selective Service numbers. Probability theory was the chance of being drafted.

From about the middle 1950s to the present time, the humanistic psychology movement has responded variously to those kinds of problems which were characteristic for this generation, leaving more conventional psychologies, especially the psychology of the academy, very far behind. The psychology of the academy, throughout this period, was increasingly experienced by these young people as irrelevant and alien. I believe that had psychoanalysis ever been allowed to exist properly in the colleges and universities, there might have been some fuller articulation between the consciousness of this generation and psychology in their classes. However, psychoanalysis had been branded as heretical. It was subject to as severe a taboo as was ever put on any heresy in the history of the church. Correspondingly, the medical profession turned the teaching of psychoanalytic practice into an arcane art, as esoteric as any body of knowledge in the history of the world, restricted to the specially selected and initiated.

It is beyond the scope of this essay to deal in any detail with the characteristics of this academic psychology, such as its relentless exclusion of affect and volition and begrudging attention to cognition, or the celebration of the automatic man in both the investigatory procedures and in the conception of the nature of human behavior in general, or the systematic exclusion of any

---

[1] From *Little boxes* by Malvina Reynolds, Schroder Music Co. (ASCAP), 1963.

recognition of intention (which is universally regarded as important in distinguishing good from evil in man's actions), or the pretense that power was
unimportant in human relations, or that empiricism, which originally meant
an emphasis on experience, being turned around to mean its opposite.

I would like to conclude this presentation with a few observations concerning the role of statistics in connection with academic psychology. Quite aside
from the question of the intrinsic merits or demerits of statistics as a method
for psychology, the question of statistics played an extremely important role
in connection with the relative appreciation of the common academic
psychology. Statistics as a discipline signaled that psychology was "hard"
rather than "soft." It signaled that psychology was a "discipline," suggesting
as well the relative arduousness involved in having to acquire skill in connection with it. It signaled an association of psychology with other sciences for
which mathematics was part of their visible face to the world.

The fact is that from at least 1000 B.C. statistics has been understood as a
violation of human dignity. There is a very old tradition which sees in statistics one of the major instruments associated with tyranny. The classical locus
of this is to be found in the Bible. One of the very few mentions of Satan in
the Old Testament is to be found in the story of King David's initiation of a
military census told in I Chronicles, Chapter 21. It begins, "Now Satan, setting himself against Israel, incited David to count the people." The story continues indicating the protest and even partial failure to carry out David's order
on the part of his chief lieutenant, Joab. It follows with God expressing his
deep displeasure with David and proceeding to punish him severely. David, in
response, says to God, "I have done a very wicked thing: I pray thee remove
thy servant's guilt, for I have been very foolish [I Chron. 21:7-8]." And when
God proceeds to wreak further havoc on the people of Israel, David, falling
prostrate before God, says, "It was I who gave the order to count the people.
It was I who sinned, I, the shepherd, who did wrong. But these poor sheep,
what have they done? O Lord my God, let thy hand fall upon me and upon
my family, but check this plague on the people [I Chron. 21:17]."

But there was something more immediately deeply alienating about statistics. Deep cultural associations of statistics with the dehumanization and the
bureaucratization of man were somehow touched. And somehow the attitude that one took with respect to statistics seemed to indicate which "side"
one was on. As I have indicated, many of these young people had direct contact with statistics in terms of the number on their Selective Service cards, the
classification number which they were given by their draft boards, their rank
in class that had to be submitted to their draft boards by their colleges and
universities to determine whether their educational deferments would be continued, etc. For the very word, statistics, is etymologically related to the
word, state. In my dictionary it says of the word statistics that it was "originally 'political science dealing with state affairs' [American Heritage Dictionary, p. 1279]." Indeed the modern statistical movement had its origins quite

specifically in the huge increase in bureaucratization that took place in Victorian England, and the great efforts that were made to use numbers in coping with the various political and social problems there. And statistics became a major instrument in the late nineteenth and twentieth centuries in connection with public education in which the children of the working classes were pressed into the various factory-type educational institutions associated with the growing urbanization and industrialization (Cullen, 1975).

Conclusion

Psychology must align itself again with the historical aim of knowledge as serving emancipation. If psychology is to remain useful, it is essential that it make contributions to the understanding of the thinking and feeling and wishing of human beings and that it work to communicate that understanding to the community at large. For there is a great need in society for such an understanding. Many of the difficulties in the world may be traced to the fact that such an understanding by people of the nature of their own thoughts, feelings, and wishes, and the thoughts, feelings, and wishes of others, is inadequate to the complex problems of a world in which a very large number of people must share the planet at one time. Prediction and control, interpreted in such a manner as to imply manipulation, are simply unworthy aims for a contemporary science of psychology and are aims that will not and should not elicit the support of the community which science serves.

Let me conclude by saying that my argument is not one for a decreased autonomy but rather for an increased autonomy for the science of psychology. Historically, while psychology has often allowed itself to exclude larger considerations of its involvement with society at large, it has, in point of fact, been all the more under society's influence, in ways in which psychology itself has not been aware. At the present time, those same factors that have been influencing its direction are working in such a way as to threaten its very existence—precisely at a time when psychological understanding is critically needed by the community at large. It can no longer, for its own sake as an autonomous science and for the sake of the community which it serves, afford the luxury of innocence that the two-step view of science provided.

References

Cullen, M J. *The statistical movement in early Victorian Britain: The foundations of empirical social research.* New York: Barnes and Noble Books, 1975.

Hull, C. L. *Principles of behavior.* New York: D. Appleton–Century, 1943.

Stalin, J. V. *The foundations of Leninism.* Peking: Foreign Languages Press, 1970. (Originally published, 1924.)

Watson, J. B. *Psychology from the standpoint of a behaviorist.* Philadelphia: J. B. Lippincott, 1919.

Recommended Readings

Braginsky, B. M. & Braginsky, D. D., *Mainstream psychology: A critique*. New York: Holt, Rinehart & Winston, 1974.

Greenstein, F., *Personality and politics*. Chicago: Markham, 1969.

Kuhn, T. *The structure of scientific revolutions*. London: University of Chicago Press, 1962.

Rychlak, J. F. *The psychology of rigorous humanism*. New York: John Wiley, 1977.

HOWARD E. GRUBER **8**

Darwin on Psychology and Its Relation to Evolutionary Thought

*When we first begin to believe anything,
what we believe is not a single proposition,
it is a whole system of propositions. (Light
dawns gradually over the whole.)*
LUDWIG WITTGENSTEIN, 1969, p. 21

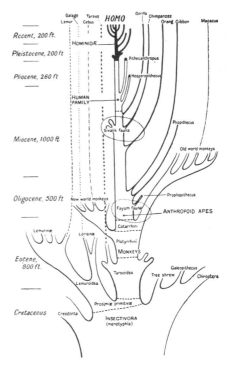

PSYCHOLOGY:
THEORETICAL-HISTORICAL PERSPECTIVES

ISBN 0-12-588265-3

Psychology and Evolutionary Thought

Muliply, vary, let the strongest live and the weakest die. —Charles Darwin, 1859.

This quotation from the *Origin of Species* was the astonishing title of a presidential address to the American Psychological Association (APA) in 1943 (Stone, 1943).

We may well ask, how much has the theory of evolution affected the history of psychology? If the theory could be adequately summarized in the stark selectionist doctrine just quoted, or in some other simple formula, we might cite a few such historical facts, write q.e.d., and pass on to the next question. But theories and their histories, like life, are never so simple.

Consider, for example, the stark contrast between the title of Calvin Stone's 1943 address and the 1909 APA presidential address of Charles H. Judd, entitled "Evolution and Consciousness," in which he wrote, "Psychology . . . deals in a broad way with the evolutionary processes by which consciousness arose and through which the trend of life has been changed from organic adaptation to intelligent conquest [Judd, 1910]."

As I have tried to show in *Darwin on Man: A Psychological Study of Scientific Creativity* (Gruber, 1974/1980), the theory of evolution through natural selection is an exceedingly complex system of ideas; its complexity and density are only matched by those of the creative thought process entailed in Charles Darwin's struggle to construct the theory.

The present essay deals not with the theory as a whole but only with the place of our species, *Homo sapiens*, in Darwin's argument. I try also to show the diverse social and intellectual forces with which he was contending.

The theory of evolution has indeed deeply affected almost every psychological theory since the beginnings of scientific psychology sometime in the nineteenth century. But without further examination this is not a very illuminating comment, since there is not one theory but a domain of theories of evolution. In most theories, natural selection operating on chance variations is the major factor. But chance can be construed in very different ways. At one extreme, there is the notion of mutations as relatively rare events due to forces extrinsic to and independent of the organism (such as radiation); at another extreme, there is the view of chance as the systematic exploration, albeit through blind trial and error, of all of the structural possibilities open to a given genic organization.

It would seem that a view of organic nature as undergoing perpetual change is the central idea of evolutionary theory. But this is not the idea that psychoanalysts and psychobiologists have drawn from it. On the contrary, in a style that owes more to Newton than to Darwin, they have stressed the existence of *constants* in nature, unvarying instinctual tendencies that lie at the bottom of all human behavior. This is certainly one way to approach the issue of continuity between *Homo sapiens* and other animals. But it is not the only way. There have been other thinkers who have tried to draw from evolutionary theory an understanding of the way in which our species' unusual cognitive capacities and emotional toughness and flexibility, leading to an enormous variety of cultures and societies, grew *out* of the more limited psychological capacities of our animal forbears.

Finally, there are different theoretical stances regarding the causal relations between behavior and evolution. On the one hand, it is possible to stress the idea that structural changes (through chance mutations) make possible new behavioral adaptations. On the other hand, Piaget is not alone in considering behavior to be the "motor" of evolution. This latter approach forms a congenial partnership with another idea: Upon the emergence of our species a genuinely new force appeared in nature, cultural evolution.

Now, in a few pages, I want to examine the very partial and disjointed assimilation of evolutionary theory in psychological thought. I will draw heavily upon APA presidential addresses and upon a few seminal writers (e.g., Freud, Piaget), because these sources give a sense of the main alternative theoretical pathways actually available to most psychologists and to their students. But the reader will notice that these pages are not a history of the subject they deal with. Ideas are not presented in chronological order but in a way intended to provide a sketch of some of the major theoretical landmarks in what remains a very contemporary scene.

APPROACHES STRESSING THE ROLE OF EVOLUTION IN SHAPING BEHAVIOR

Let us begin with Sigmund Freud and psychoanalytic theory. Freud (1930/1953) hailed Darwin, likened him to Copernicus for his part in dethroning our species from the grandiose view that we are the center of the universe and the highest object of God's creation:

> In the course of centuries the *naive* self-love of men has had to submit to two major blows at the hands of science. The first was when they learnt that our earth was not the centre of the universe but only a tiny fragment of a cosmic system of scarcely imaginable vastness. This is associated in our minds with the name of Copernicus, though something similar had already been asserted by Alexandrian science. The second blow fell when biological research destroyed man's supposedly privileged place in creation and proved his descent from the animal kingdom and his ineradicable animal nature. This revaluation has been accomplished in our own days by Darwin, Wallace, and their predecessors, though not without the most violent contemporary opposition [p. 296].

But Freud and other sociobiologists have borrowed one-sidedly from Darwin. They emphasize the animality of *Homo sapiens* at the expense of our humanity. Insisting on the essential identity of our mentality and behavior with the instinctual behavior of infrahuman species, they advance the idea that *Homo sapiens* is "nothing but" an animal. There is another way of thinking about the subject, more consonant with a fully evolutionary theory. Our long evolutionary prehistory can be viewed as providing the springboard for a radically new event in nature, the appearance of a species capable of elaborate language systems, of cumulative cultural history, and of reflective thought.

This view does not eliminate the task of understanding the relation between emotion and thought, but it does profoundly alter it. At every stage in the growth of an evolving system, the constantly changing relation between form and function opens the way for genuine novelty. In a double sense, the system of nature changes itself. On the one hand, it cannot go backward: Evolution consumes its own past, each moment destroys the conditions that made it possible. Thus, it is *impossible* for our species to revert to the instinctual forms of our precursors. On the other hand, every step of evolution makes a new future possible. Thus, it is not *necessary* for us to live within the confines of our past.

Although it is true that Darwin did much to show the "animal" nature of our species, he was equally at pains to explore the intellectual accomplishments of other organisms. Not only do we, as evolutionary latecomers, contain traces of the past, they contain promises of the future. It was this well-roundedness of Darwin's thinking about the continuity question that permitted him to close his book *The Descent of Man* with an evocation of man and his "god-like intellect."

Three important currents in psychological thought—behaviorism, psychoanalysis, and social Darwinism (now revised under the name of *sociobiology*)—all drew upon Darwin's work in a similar way. All three were movements that placed overwhelming emphasis on the animal origins of humanity, as against the "far more perfect creature" Darwin thought he saw in the making (Darwin, 1958).

Darwin's argument for the evolutionary continuity of human and animal mentality was steadily transformed into the antimentalism of behavioristic psychology. Skinner (1938) has acknowledged that this required three steps: Darwin ascribed mental powers to animals; Lloyd Morgan continued the development of comparative psychology by advocating the elimination of mind as a legitimate concept in the study of animal behavior; and J. B. Watson endeavored to "re-establish Darwin's desired continuity without hypothesizing mind anywhere [p. 4]." I believe that Darwin would have been happier with psychologists who, like the Gestaltists, preserved the idea of continuity by developing experimental methods for studying insightful problem-solving behavior in infrahuman species (see, e.g., Köhler, 1925).

By and large, the behaviorists exploited the Darwinian selectionist formula in a strict and narrow way. In his APA presidential address, Clark Hull (1936) began with an obeisance to Darwin. Then he presented his learning theory in the form of 18 definitions, 6 postulates, and 13 theorems. The fourth theorem states the principle of *variation:* "Organisms in simple trial-and-error situations may manifest spontaneous variability of reaction, the objective situation remaining constant [p. 325]." The seventh and eighth definitions state the principles of *selection:* "7. A *correct* or 'right' reaction is a behavior sequence which results in reinforcement. 8. An *incorrect* or 'wrong' reaction is a behavior sequence which results in experimental extinction [p. 320]." The choice of the term *extinction* clearly shows the evolutionary roots of behaviorist learning theory.

Nor is this kind of learning theory the only place in psychology where the narrow selectionist formula has been applied. For example, this is the theoretical schema underlying much of the experimental literature on creativity. Unable or unwilling to study the creative process as a whole, some psychologists have redefined their problem as the study of *originality*, or the production of unusual responses. The key experimental idea is to separate the processes of variation and selection from each other and to focus attention on the first phase, variation.

There have, however, been psychological theorists motivated by evolutionary thought who did not restrict themselves to the narrow selectionist formula.

In spite of the narrow selectionist focus of its title, Calvin Stone's address actually did grasp some of the open-endedness of behavioral evolution. More recently, M. Brewster Smith (1978), in another presidential address to APA, presented the kind of open, continuously evolving perspective of which I now write. Drawing on Jean Piaget, George Herbert Mead, and Karl Marx, he examines the way in which the growth of mind changes the material setting in which it evolves, and vice versa. He elaborates the theme that the growth of language and cognition permits the appearance and development of reflective selfhood, and vice versa. Finally, he conceives of all these as mutually synergetic processes at work in a continuous pattern of spiraling growth.

For Donald Campbell, the use of evolutionary theory as a tool for understanding all knowledge process—"evolutionary epistemology," as he terms it—has been an abiding passion and a productive enterprise. His APA presidential address in 1975 bore the complex title "On the Conflicts between Biological and Social Evolution and between Psychology and Moral Tradition" (Campbell, 1975). He wrote:

> The evolutionary theory I employ is a hard-line neo-Darwinian one for both biological and social evolution, the slogan being "blind-variation and systematic selective retention." . . . This model—which I summarize as "blind-variation-and-selective-retention"—is the only and all-purpose explanation for the achievement of fit between systems and for the achievement and maintenance of counterentropic form and order [p. 1105].

In spite of his epithet "hard-line," the careful reader will notice the use of the word *systems* in the plural. Campbell is not merely speaking of the adaptation of organisms to the system of nature. He has *two* systems in mind, the system of biological evolution and the system of cultural evolution. Their interplay creates complexities that cannot be dealt with through the simplistic use of a purely biological model of evolution. Campbell argues that any evolving system entails the operation of four kinds of mechanisms: variation, selection, retention, and duplication (or reproduction) of that which has been retained. But the exact nature of these mechanisms may be entirely different in a purely biological infrahuman system and in a human cultural system.

Although Campbell insists that variations are "blind," it is important to notice that this blindness is an epistemological constraint meaning only ignorance of the ultimate utility and impact of any innovation or variation. At the human cultural level, Campbell's epistemological blindness is not so different from the philosophers' "learned ignorance." It certainly does not mean that humans are unintelligent or mindless. We grope, but not mindlessly. This is a plea for "epistemic humility" (Campbell's phrase), not a denial of mind.

Campbell uses the same apparatus of evolutionary thought (variation, selection, retention, duplication) at both levels of his two-system model. The resultant situation is not a smoothly functioning coherent world, but one that is fraught with inherent contradictions: "1. Human urban social complexity has been made possible by social evolution rather than biological evolution. 2. This social evolution has had to counter individual selfish tendencies which biological evolution has continued to select as a result of the genetic competition among the cooperators [1975, p. 115]."

Thus, although Campbell's epistemological and social program is broad and subtle, the structure of his argument and the contents of his psychological theory are not so different from Freud's: Biologically evolved genetically determined instincts or tendencies are controlled by socially evolved cultural mechanisms; instincts that are supposed to have evolved over millions of years remain essentially unchanged.

APPROACHES STRESSING THE ROLE OF BEHAVIOR IN DIRECTING EVOLUTION

The anthropologist Washburn (1978) is among many who are critical of this sort of extrapolation from animals to humans. He writes

Students of animal behavior feel free to use the behaviors of nonhuman species when making points about human behavior. For example, in a recent book, the chapter on human behavior cites the behaviors of many nonprimates to make important points. The possibility of atavistic behaviors in human beings is illustrated by a picture of a musk-ox in a defensive position. To show how peculiar this habit of proof really is, consider what the reaction would be if I sent to a zoological journal a paper on the musk-ox with defensive positions illustrated by the British Squares at the Battle of Waterloo [p. 414].

There is a considerable group of anthropologists, evolutionists, and paleontologists who stress the explosive rapidity of recent evolution toward *Homo sapiens sapiens*, our species. A number of factors seem to have combined in multiplicative fashion to produce the qualitative leap to humanity. In general, this group of investigators tends to stress the role of behavioral changes in driving organic evolution, especially at the hominid level. For example, upright walking permits collecting food (by freeing the forelimbs, or hands); collecting food permits bringing it to a place where it can be shared with others; such sharing permits the development of a stable, homelike abode; this new (for primates) situation facilitates the transformation of a primarily emotional system of communication into true language. These evolutionary events do not happen in a linear sequence. Rather, a little progress along one front opens the way to change on some other front. Not only genes but protocultures are transmitted from one generation to another. Individuals and groups that invent and transmit valuable behavioral adaptations tend to survive; this allows time for neurological and other structural changes to evolve (through mutation and selection) that will make the recurrence and elaboration of these behaviors more probable. The traits that evolve and endure need not be highly specified behavior patterns. As Washburn (1978) writes about one much discussed trait, "There is, obviously, no need to postulate genes for altruism. It would be much more adaptive to have genes for intelligence, enabling one to be altruistic or selfish according to the needs of the moment [p. 416]."

The view that I have just sketched out for the evolution of behavior is quite similar to the geneticist Waddington's (1957) idea of *genetic assimilation*. At the ontogenetic level, organisms increase their chances of survival if they make appropriate phenotypic responses to environmental demands. The preferential survival of those individuals that have such responses within their range of reactions leads to the incorporation of their genic patterns in the gene pool of the population. It should be noted that Waddington still relied basically on natural selection and chance mutation to consolidate gains first achieved at the phenotypic, ontogenetic level.

Piaget goes even further. In his book *Le Comportement Moteur de l'Evolution*, (1976)—the title of which is inexplicably translated as *Behavior and Evolution* (1978) in the published English version, instead of *Behavior, the Motor of Evolution*—he argues that *all* evolution, not only human, is primarily induced by behavioral changes that lead to genetic changes. He insists that his position is not Lamarckian, and he advances a general hypothesis to explain how appropriate genetic variations could occur, tuned to environmental demands, without relying on occasional chance mutations (Piaget, 1978). Thus, he is arguing not only for the primacy of behavior in evolution but against the role of blind variation.

However, to see in just what measure Piaget rejects the idea of blind variation, we must examine the concept a little more closely. Piaget views the process of variation as a systematic exploration of a set of possibilities. This combinatorial attack or "organic logic" gives the initiative to the organism rather than submitting it to a process of waiting for the lucky environmental impact that produces an adaptive mutation.

Although the mechanism that Piaget proposes is novel, its consequences are fairly similar to the findings of recent research in genetics: There is far more variation than previously recognized. Many or even most genes exist in a number of allelic forms, expressing the biochemical structural variations of which each gene is capable (Piaget, 1978). Piaget uses this general biological position as a springboard for reiterating his argument that intellectual activity is a biological function and must follow the same law of organization and adaptation, assimilation and accommodation, as any living system. In his earlier treatise on the idea of *phenocopy*, he begins with the "Baldwin effect," well known to geneticists: Phenotypical adaptations arising in the individual life history are *replaced* by changes in the genotype having the same form and the same consequences. Piaget (1974) draws an important parallel between evolutionary genetic change and cognitive development. In cognition, too, we have phenotypic adaptations, such as imitation, which establish responses that can later be controlled by more fundamental changes in mental structures replacing the ones that give rise to the response, thus consolidating gains made. In this usage of the phenocopy argument, he is quite similar to Kurt Lewin (1935), who also used the terms *phenotype* and *genotype* to distinguish between outward behaviors and underlying structures that control them.

The main outlines of controversy have remained unchanged for nearly a century. In 1898, J. M. Baldwin's presidential address to the American Psychological Association was called "On Selective Thinking." He examined "the supply of thought–variations; . . . how certain variations are singled out for survival. . . ; and the criteria of selection [pp. 1–2]." In other words, he used the model of evolutionary theory for a theory of cognitive development. Far from casting *chance* variation in the role of prime mover, he criticizes this view sharply:

> We do not scatter our thoughts as widely as possible in order to increase the chances of getting a true one; on the contrary, we call the man who produces the most thought-variations a 'scatter-brain,' and expect nothing inventive from him . . . we succeed in thinking well by thinking hard; we get the valuable thought-variations by concentrating attention upon the body of related knowledge which we already have; we discover new relations among the data of experience by running over and over the links and couplings of the apperceptive systems with which our minds are already filled [p. 4].

Baldwin, of course, did not aim his criticism of blind variation at Donald Campbell, who was not born yet, but at Herbert Spencer, who not long before had applied evolutionary theory to learned behavior in a way that anticipated the behaviorism of 1910–1960. Baldwin went on to explain his theory of "organic selection." Some of its highlights are as follows:

1. Mental life, or knowledge, is highly organized; only those novelties can be assimilated into an enduring structure that can be responded to in a coherent way.
2. Of two main phases of the selective function, the first is "intra-organic selection". . . . this transfers the first selective function from the environment to the organism, requires the new experience to run the gauntlet of habitual reactions or habits which organize and unify the system of knowledges, before it can be eligible for further testing by action [p. 10]."
3. The second phase is "extra-organic selection or environmental selection, which is a testing of the special concrete character of the experience as fitted, through the motor variations to which it gives rise, to bring about a new determination in the system in which it goes [p. 10]." It is this phase in Baldwin's theory that is analogous to what is usually meant by *natural selection*.
4. Through this highly organized process of variation and selection the individual constantly rebuilds the "platform" on which further experience, action, and growth occur; this means that the variations that occur are not indiscriminate or blind but a function of the individual's whole life history of organized growth.
5. The growth of the internal organization of knowledge "gradually serves to free the organism from direct dependence upon the control of the environment [p. 21];" this means that the whole process of variation and selection becomes increasingly organized and directed as the person matures.
6. Baldwin, like Piaget, who admires him greatly, attempts to show how there could be an "organic logic" governing both biological and psychological growth.

To conclude this brief survey, it can be seen that there is today not one theory of evolution or of evolution and behavior but a wide array of possibilities. This means that the psychologist, as student of this subject, need not be intimidated by the seemingly greater rigor of the natural sciences. It remains true today as it was in Charles Darwin's day, that the study of organic evolution and of behavior can enrich each other.

Theories of the relation between mind and body have always been highly colored by their connection with broad social issues. This is especially true of the history of evolutionary thought, which has been seen as relevant to our understanding and ethical evaluation of war, capitalism, slavery, racism, and sexism. There is, in my opinion, no way of avoiding these connections. It may be helpful to be aware of them, to be sensitive to the social roots of all theories.

On the time scale of the history of psychology, a century or so, we see the same issues and theories cropping up more than once, in only slightly altered forms. On the time scale of intellectual fashion, a decade or so, we see a particular form of argument wax and wane in popularity: in one swing it is the heritability quotient, in another it is the sociobiology of aggression and altruism that is called upon to justify the claim that "you can't change human nature." On still longer time scales, there are always a few voices insisting that we *must* change ourselves. And the joint evidence of many disciplines suggests that over the long reaches of evolutionary time, *Homo sapiens sapiens* has changed human nature, that through our own behavior we have indeed made ourselves. The question remains, for the changes we must now make: Have we enough intelligence, courage, and time?

The Metaphorical Structure of Darwin's Argument

A scientific theory is a much denser structure than is generally recognized. Almost every component idea is itself an intricate structure, and the whole is a complex of interacting parts. In constructing the theory of evolution through natural selection, Darwin made use of a number of images or metaphors: tree of nature, war, wedges, artificial selection, tangled bank, and contrivance. Each of these has a specific function in illuminating a part of the theory. These images are not merely didactic or communicative devices, they seem to play a role in the actual generation of the theory: There is a complex and lively interaction between different levels of experience, such as the conceptual and the imaginal.

From a historical point of view, as one theory is assimilated by another, the earlier is necessarily distorted and only partially represented in the latter. As one consequence of this complexity, although some Darwinian ideas have been assimilated into psychological theories, one basic concept has been neglected. There is in the *Origin of Species* only one diagram. It represents Darwin's idea that in the panorama of nature "organized beings represent a tree *irregularly branched*," as he wrote in a notebook in 1837.[1] This was 15 months before he formulated the theory of evolution through natural selection. Darwin used this metaphor in many theoretically productive ways. Yet this conception of fundamental irregularity in nature remains foreign to psychology and other social sciences, which are still dominated by a largely

---

[1] Darwin's first notebook on Transmutation of Species (July 1837–February 1838), p. 21. The four notebooks on Transmutation of Species and the two notebooks on Man, Mind, and Materialism are kept in the Manuscript Room of the Cambridge University Library, where I have studied them. The transmutation notebooks have been published as "Darwin's Notebooks on Transmutation of Species," *Bulletin of the British Museum (Natural History), Historical Series* 1960–1961, Vol. 2 (Nos. 2–6); 1967, Vol. 3 (No. 5), edited by Sir Gavin de Beer with the collaboration of M. J. Rowlands and B. M. Skramovsky.

Newtonian world view. Some as yet unexploited implications of Darwin's metaphor have a bearing on the role of the individual in history and on the virtues of "weak theory."

In discussions of the philosophy of science, it has been commonplace to distinguish between the problems of justification and the problems of discovery. The latter can be further subdivided into procedural and substantive issues. This leaves us with a tripartite division: how to know if a proposition, once uttered or formulated is true; how to go about looking for propositions worth considering; and what sort of thing to look for. Within the context of discovery, something has been said about procedural matters. For example, writers in the vein of Hanson (1958) focus on the method of retroduction; writers in the vein of Polanyi (1958) stress intuitive and nonrational aspects of the process of discovery. But substantive matters—what to look for?—have received much less attention. In the older philosophical tradition, discussions of the nature of matter, objects, space, time, life, intellect, morals, humanity, and society were not considered matters for specialists in "other" disciplines but were part of a widespread exchange among intellectuals. This exchange, when it is active enough, helps maintain a general alertness to the mutual import of specialized inquiries and very general conceptions of nature.

The use by scientists of large metaphors and images plays a key role in such discussions, because it bears at once on the procedural and substantive matters referred to in the preceding paragraph. Even when expressed in very general form (vague, intuitive, poetic), such images have generative and regulatory power, both governing the search for more explicit formulations and giving rise to them. When the metaphor is invested with more precise form, it is transformed: We can call it a "model"; it guides analysis and invites the testing of hypotheses. These hypotheses are neither about the metaphor nor about nature, but about relations between them. The testing of hypotheses has been the glory of methodologists, but it remains a sterile glory so long as little or nothing is said of the primitive roots—both imaginal and ideological—from which testable ideas spring.

Experimental psychologists since the 1950s have become increasingly interested in imagery, but mainly at the level of reproductive images: Either some specific object is called up before the mind's eye, or some imagined relationship between specified objects serves as a mnemonic device, aiding in the recall of previously presented stimuli. The generative role of imagery in productive and creative thinking, unfortunately, still remains outside this universe of discourse. But generative images of wide scope become a central concern when we wish to understand the psychological processes involved in reflecting on the larger concepts of humanity, society, and nature that provide the framework for all scientific inquiry. In an older tradition, however, images of wide scope were not foreign to psychologists. Titchener (1909) begins an important work with an extended description of his image of science as an incoming tide on a sandy, rock-strewn shore.

THE DIFFERENTIAL UPTAKE OF IDEAS

A fundamental aspect of Charles Darwin's thought has been widely neglected by psychologists, because they are still guided by a highly deterministic view of nature, a simplistic view of science, and a Newtonian hope that their own universe of discourse can be shown to display the same underlying order, simplicity, and harmony that Newton claimed for his.

Although the connection between the tendency toward simplicity and the tendency toward determinism has not received the attention it deserves, a number of authors have drawn attention to the issue in a variety of ways (Sagan, 1977; Simon, 1962; Wimsatt, 1974). Sagan, for example, points out that some 300 million years ago the evolution of intelligence had progressed to the point where "there emerged an organism that for the first time in the history of the world had more information in its brains than in its genes [p. 47]." He estimates, also, that the human brain has some 10^{13} synapses and that this permits the brain to assume some $2^{10^{13}}$ different states, concluding:

> This is an unimaginably large number, far greater, for example, than the total number of elementary particles (electrons and protons) in the entire universe, which is much less than 2 raised to the power 10^3. It is because of this immense number of functionally different configurations of the human brain that no two humans, even identical twins raised together, can ever be really very much alike. These enormous numbers may also explain something of the unpredictability of human behavior and those moments when we surprise even ourselves by what we do [p. 42].

While rewriting this chapter for its present publication, I asked nine social scientists to take a brief test of free association, saying the first word that came to mind when I said the words "Thomas Kuhn." Of the nine, eight responded without hesitation, "paradigm." Upon discussion, all saw the irony that a book entitled *The Structure of Scientific Revolutions*—equally divided between Kuhn's concepts of normal science and of revolutionary science— should elicit such a one-sided response. For completeness, the ninth subject responded: "[Expletive]; *The Structure of Scientific Revolutions*; I suppose you want me to say 'paradigm.' "

This differential uptake of ideas has affected the history of psychology and kindred disciplines in a number of ways. White (1980) has described the halving of Wilhelm Wundt's work in the received history of psychology in a fashion that contributed to the false hope of constructing a Newtonian science of psychology. When the *Origin of Species* appeared, there was considerably greater readiness to draw from it lessons about the inevitability of progress than there was to accept Darwin's theory of the inherently chancy nature of the process (Allegård, 1958; Russett, 1976).

Maybe we psychologists trivialize our science by looking too hard and too soon for a few regularities in this diversity. Another strategy might be to find ways of catching hold of the diversity itself, of characterizing the unique functioning of each person. This is what Newell and Simon (1972) have in mind when they set about to construct "a theory of the individual" human problem solver.

Darwin's thought presents itself in two aspects, quite distinct from each other both in form and in aesthetic tone. On the one hand, there is the beautiful simplicity of the theory of evolution through natural selection. As early as 1838, Darwin could state it in 19 words expressing the three principles of heredity, variation, and superfecundity, from which, as he saw, natural selection and evolution followed inexorably.[2] On the other hand, there is his fascination with complexity and uncertainty, with nature seen as a multitude of small forces perpetually interacting and changing.

In Darwin's early notebooks and later in his published works, these two tendencies produced at least five metaphors, all of them necessary to express the whole of his thought. After providing some background material, I will discuss these in some detail. For the moment, I want only to introduce the idea that psychologists and other social scientists have been eager to borrow some of Darwin's ideas and imagery, especially the simplifying images of war and artificial selection, which seem to divide the world into winners and losers, or responses into successes and failures. But they have largely ignored the complexifying part of Darwin's thought.

Once it is recognized that organic nature always and in principle involves a dense web of intimately interacting processes, these tendencies toward simplicity appear in a new light. Of course, some simplicities can always be constructed, and it has been and will remain an important part of scientific work to construct them or, if you prefer, to wrench them out of nature. In moving beyond such simplicities, it is enjoyable first to contemplate the richness of the organic world. But it is also our task to search for ways to conceptualize nature in its richness, its variety, its complexity, and its interconnectedness.

It will be helpful to bear in mind the following chronology: Darwin was born in 1809 and died in 1882. The voyage of the Beagle, in which he circumnavigated the globe, began in 1831 and ended in 1836. In July of 1837, he began his first notebook on evolution, determined to construct a workable theory and probably believing that he already had the key to it, although this proved not to be the case. In July of 1838, he began his notebooks on man, mind, and materialism. This was an explosive moment for him, for during the same month he also undertook a demanding geological investigation; as Martin Rudwick (1974) has shown, this was not merely the narrowly specialized research that it seemed to be but bore directly on Darwin's most general views. On 28 September 1838, Darwin recorded his reading (or rereading?) of Malthus's *An Essay on the Principle of Population* (1826) and his own first excited insight into the theory of evolution through natural selection. I have elsewhere reconstructed the slow growth of Darwin's thinking leading up to

---

[2] Darwin's fourth notebook on Transmutation of Species (October 1838–July 10, 1839), p. 58.

that moment (Gruber, 1974/1980). By November of 1838, Darwin was able to reformulate the theory succinctly in the form of the three principles of heredity, variation, and superfecundity. Twenty years later, in 1858, Alfred Russell Wallace wrote to Darwin of his own discovery of the theory of evolution through natural selection, and joint publication of the two men's discovery was arranged. In 1859, finally, Darwin wrote and published the *Origin of Species*. But he remained silent about his views of man's place in nature until 1871, when he published *The Descent of Man*. *The Expression of Emotions in Man and Animals* followed, in 1872. Four of the five metaphors now to be discussed appeared in Darwin's notebooks by 1839 at the latest.

A PLURALITY OF METAPHORS

Virtually all discussion of metaphor until now has focused attention on the production or meaning of metaphors taken singly: What is a metaphor? How is one made? How do we know whether to call the item we are talking about a *metaphor, model, analogy, simile,* or *image?* But when we look at such productions in the context of a full-blown discourse, such as printed text, we see immediately that they do not come singly. Language and thought are permeated with them. It is of little avail to labor over differential definitions, for the idea that conforms neatly to some definition of *simile* in one paragraph turns up a little later as a particular kind of metaphor, or vice versa. It is not possible to arrive at a definitive count of the number of such productions in a given protocol, because they are nestled and interlaced with each other in ways that do not submit to item counts. For the moment, then, we need some strategy of approximation. First, although I will continue to use the term *metaphor,* the reader may wish to substitute some more generous phrase, such as *figure of thought.*[3] Second, in order to keep the number of figures discussed within reasonable bounds, we will aim for a certain "grain" in our analysis, the rather coarse grain that would appear if we sought for the ruling metaphor of each chapter or major section of a chapter of, say, the *Origin of Species*. Even this grain would give us far too much material to handle in one short essay, so there will be some simplification by some rather arbitrary omissions. The essential point will have been conveyed if the reader comes to see that the ensemble of metaphors working in one human mind, for example, Charles Darwin's, can be very complex indeed.

To these difficulties, I must add one further caveat. When we choose a term to stand for a given metaphor, the choice inevitably masks the fact that the actual idea is captured only by a family of metaphors. For example, we may speak of the metaphor of *war* in Darwin's thought, but this is only one member of a family that also includes *struggle* and *equilibrium*. Thus, there

---

[3] The poet Howard Nemerov uses the same phrase, which I had hit upon before knowing of his book. (Howard Nemerov, *Figures of Thought: Speculations on the Meaning of Poetry and Other Essays*. Boston: David R. Godine, 1978.)

exists not only the "between-metaphors" complexities of the previous paragraphs, but also a "within-metaphor" complication. Nor can we afford the luxury of believing that these are only our own peculiar difficulties, while for Darwin himself there was a "truly" central metaphor, simple and pristine, ruling over all his thoughts. As I will make clear with some other examples, Darwin was at least as aware as we are of the problems of metaphoric construction and choice that he had to solve in order to elaborate and clarify his ideas. And this should not surprise us.

I turn now to the enumeration of and discussion of some of the metaphors Darwin used in moving toward and writing the *Origin of Species*.[4]

Artificial Selection

Darwin was drawn to this subject because of his interest in variation and hybridization. He knew much about plant and animal breeding before 28 September 1838, but it was not until some time after that date that he took explicit note of the similarities between artificial and natural selection. In the *Origin*, he enlarged on this subject early in the book: The analogy between natural and artificial selection was as close as he could come to the application of the experimental method to the study of the process of evolution. By 1859, he could draw on his accumulated experience as a pigeon fancier and on many other strands of knowledge to dramatize the impressive cumulative changes that purposeful human beings could make in other species by selecting for the same trait over many generations. But he was also careful to point out that nature operates selectively not on one or a few favored characteristics but on the whole organism's adaptation to its natural environment and that it operates over immense reaches of time. Thus, his discussion of the similarities and differences between natural and artificial selection served to highlight the importance of cumulative change. Moreover, in the course of that discussion, he introduced a topic to which he devoted a separate chapter, the "correlation of growth," that is, the way in which the evolving organism remains a subtly coordinated system in which changes in one part engender or favor changes in other parts, in order to maintain this coordination.

War

The second human activity that Darwin took as a metaphor for natural selection was war. In this, of course, he was following Malthus, for the first volume of *An Essay on the Principle of Population* is very largely a catalog of human warfare and decimation. The key point for Darwin is the superfecundity principle, that population growth tends to outrun resources necessary for survival and that this necessitates both interspecific and intraspecific struggle. Thus, the metaphor of war served to emphasize the role of struggle in the pro-

---

[4] For another discussion of Darwin's metaphors, in quite a different context, see H. E. Gruber, Darwin's "tree of nature" and other images of wide scope, in *On Aesthetics in Science* edited by Judith Wechsler. Cambridge, Mass.: MIT Press, 1978.

cess of evolution. But Darwin's conception of struggle was not the kind that appears in other theories, not a titanic struggle between polar opposites—good and evil, oppressor and oppressed, Thanatos and Eros. For Darwin, struggle meant the total activity of each organism permitting it to survive long enough to reproduce its own kind. In this struggle the race is not only to the strong and the swift but sometimes to the well concealed, the prolific, the cooperative, the inventive, the adaptable. Since the theory aimed at explaining the evolutionary adaptation of species rather than of individuals, social characteristics of organisms could be flexibly taken into account. For example, sexual selection, the struggle between males of a species for possession of the females, is rarely a struggle to the death, since the defeated male is of potential use to the species only if he survives.

Wedges

This is the least known of Darwin's metaphors. It appears in the excited passage in his "transmutation notebook" written on 28 September 1838,[5] and it survives through various preliminary essays into the first edition of the *Origin of Species*, but it was deleted from the later editions, including the most widely read sixth, and last, edition. In Darwin's phrasing, the wedge image has two aspects. First, he speaks of "one hundred thousand wedges." By this he means to emphasize the point that the forces making for evolution are multitudinous, arising continuously out of the complex manifold of nature. Secondly, he speaks of these wedges as "splitting the face of nature." This phrase reflects Darwin's awareness of the small but vital difference between a God-ordained, perfectly harmonious order and a world in which small imperfections in adaptation constantly arise, serving as the motor of evolutionary change.

Tree

The three metaphors discussed so far all bear directly on the concept of natural selection. The remaining two are more general, reflecting even wider concepts of nature, providing the substratum necessary to think about evolution. Among all his metaphors, Darwin's image of the tree of nature as an irregularly branching tree certainly deserves pride of place. It appears early in the B-notebook (the first of the transmutation notebooks) and is then quickly redrawn to bring out Darwin's thought more precisely. (See Figures 8.1 and 8.2) Over the years, Darwin drew a number of tree diagrams, trying both to perfect it and to penetrate it—to learn what his own imagery could tell him. In a highly formalized version, the tree diagram is the only figure in the *Origin*, and Darwin refers to it over and over, throughout the book.

It is reasonably clear from the sequence of events that when Darwin drew his first tree diagram he was already a convinced evolutionist and that the

---

[5] Darwin's third notebook, pp. 134–135.

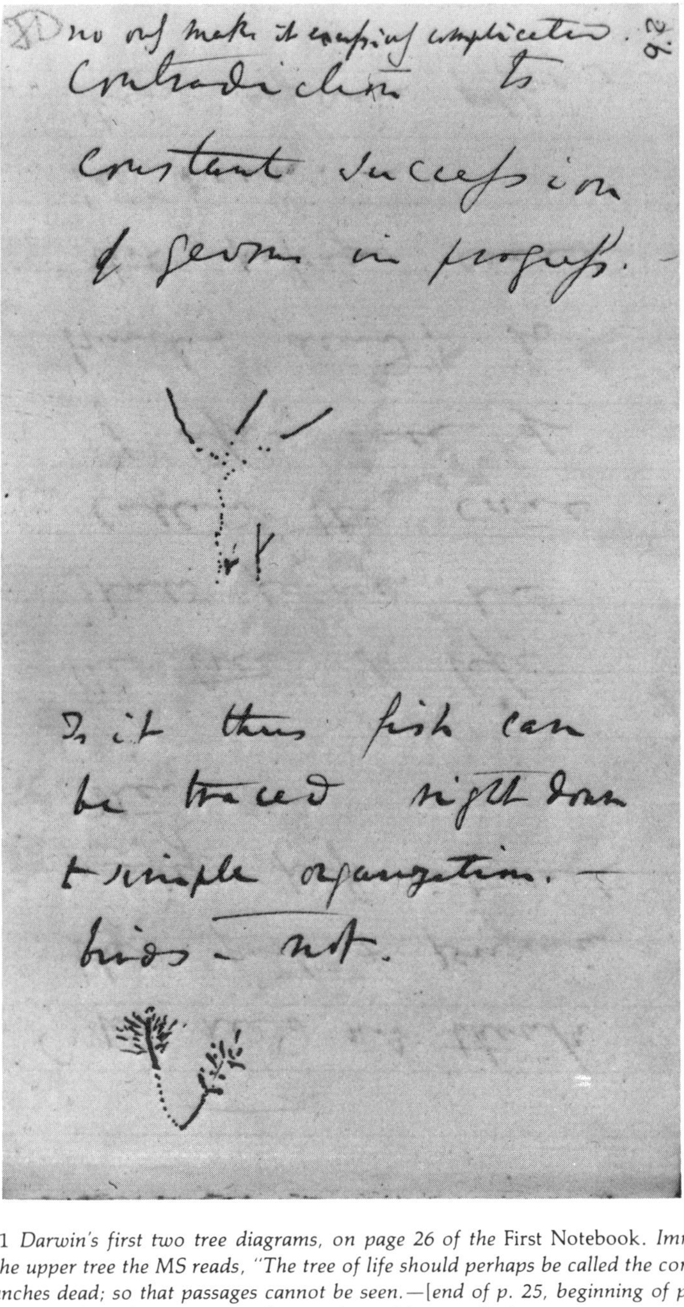

FIGURE 8.1 *Darwin's first two tree diagrams, on page 26 of the* First Notebook. *Immediately preceding the upper tree the MS reads, "The tree of life should perhaps be called the coral of life, base of branches dead; so that passages cannot be seen.—[end of p. 25, beginning of p. 26] this again offers ((no only makes it excessively complicated)) contradiction to constant succession of germs in progress." Words in double parentheses were inserted above the line by Darwin.*

Immediately preceding the lower tree the MS reads, "Is it thus fish can be traced right down to simple organization—birds—not." (Courtesy of the Syndics of Cambridge University Library.)

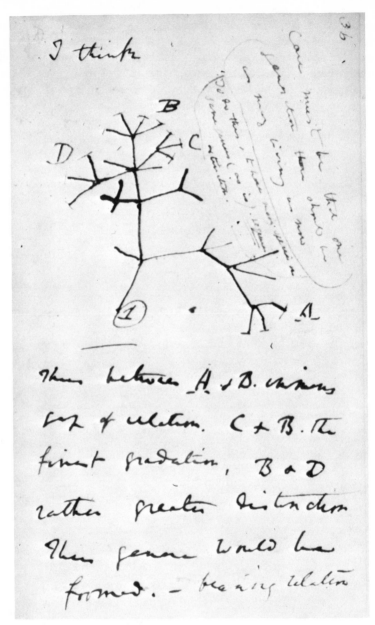

FIGURE 8.2. *Darwin's third tree diagram, on page 36 of the First Notebook. The MS reads, "I think" followed by the diagram. Then, "Thus between A & B immense gap of relation, C & B, the finest gradation, B & D rather greater distinction. Thus genera would be formed,—bearing relation [end of p. 36, beginning of p. 37] to ancient types." The marginal insertion alongside the tree diagram reads, "Case must be that one generation then should have as many living as now. To do this & to have many species in same genus (as is), requires extinction." (Courtesy of the Syndics of Cambridge University Library.)*

diagram expressed his view of a continuously evolving, freshly differentiating organic world. At the same time, he was drawing the tree diagram in order to grapple with a puzzling argument against evolution. If evolutionary change were everywhere continuous, there should be no gaps in the natural order: It should be possible for systematists to construct taxonomies in which there would be no "missing links." So Lamarck had believed, taking as fresh evidence for such continuity every new species brought back by the voyages of conquest and discovery. But others used the many apparent gaps in the system of nature as an argument against evolution; still others attempted to fashion "perfect" taxonomies in which the absence of any gaps would serve as evidence that the panorama of nature as a whole must be the handiwork of a divine artificer. In the tree diagram, Darwin saw another possibility: To be sure, there must be continuity in nature, but continuity does not necessarily require completeness. Beginning from some primitive form, evolution proceeds along diverging pathways; at every branching point, some species that exist are extinguished, and the species that these might have become never can evolve. There is thus a fundamental incompleteness in nature: Not everything that might have been will be.

Secondly, the tree diagram captures Darwin's profound conviction that nature is irregular. Among all those species that might evolve, the ones that do appear arise from happenstance. In some ways, Darwin grasped this point long before he grasped the principle of natural selection. Suppose, for example, members of a species migrate to a new habitat and there are isolated from other members of the species by the hazards of geography and of geological change (e.g., a land bridge used for migration can be submerged by the subsidence of the sea bottom, or a wind blows a seed or an insect or humans in a canoe to a place previously unvisited by that species). If they are isolated long enough, and if they adapt to their new milieu, they will form a new variant or race and eventually perhaps a new species. Darwin could carry the argument this far very early in his theoretical search, for it does not rest on the idea of natural selection. But the argument contains an important new point. The winds of chance, that produce the necessary isolation of a few individuals in a new habitat, have nothing to do with the intrinsic laws of development of members of that species. In that sense, some critical isolating events are accidents and therefore produce a fundamental irregularity in the tree of nature. This chanciness and irregularity, so much at odds with his predecessors' (and most of his contemporaries') search for a regular and harmonious order in nature, was explicit in Darwin's very first drawing of the tree diagram and in the accompanying commentary.[6]

Finally, of course, the tree diagram is the very image of some at first unspecified selection process. Some species are marked off as continuing, others as becoming extinct. A few months later Darwin saw, not too clearly,

[6] Darwin's first notebook on Transmutation of Species (July 1837–February 1838), p. 26.

that the tree diagram was also a model of exponential growth; if this idea is coupled with some constraints, such as a limit on the number of organisms or of species (i.e., the unit of analysis at work in the phase of the theory in question), a formal principle of selection necessarily follows. By *formal* I simply mean that, although no mechanism is specified, the occurrence of selection follows as a conclusion from the premises.

The Tangled Bank

The last metaphor I will discuss here is the "tangled bank," the image of the intricacy of nature at a moment in time evoked in the celebrated passage with which Darwin concludes the *Origin of Species*. It is difficult to specify the first appearance in Darwin's thought of this idea because it goes so far back. In the thousands of pages of notes he kept during the Beagle voyage, there is little or no trace of any concern for evolution, but there are many examples of his fascination with the ecological relations among species. Of course, the idea informs Gilbert White's *Natural History and Antiquities of Selborne* (1789), a book Darwin knew very early, and William Paley's *Natural Theology, or Evidences of the Existence and Attributes of the Deity Collected from the Appearances of Nature* (1802), which had excited Darwin during his student years at Cambridge. In a sense, then, the image of the tangled bank is the least specifically Darwinian of all the images I have discussed. But this does not mean that it is any the less fundamental in his thinking. We can get a better idea of its role in Darwin's thought if we compare the three authors just referred to. For White, there is no metaphoric use of this idea; it is the whole substance of his work. For Paley and for Darwin, some part of nature (e.g., the beehive, the tangled bank) is likened to the whole; in that sense we have a metaphor. But for Paley and the other natural theologians, the central point is harmony and perfection in nature and the beauty of the contrivances by which the Creator has achieved this order of things. This is certainly what struck the young Darwin. But for Darwin the evolutionist, the image is transmuted; it is the disharmony and imperfection that become the cutting edge of his theory.

Determinism in Psychology

It seems to me that Darwin had a very clear grasp of the relations between the two images, the tree and the tangled bank. One image describes events at a moment in time in one corner of the forest, with hundreds of species and thousands of individuals complexly interacting with each other, producing a kind of microevolution. Meanwhile, in another part of the forest, something similar is going on, but other organisms and a whole other set of contingencies are involved. From time to time, organisms from these two domains will come in contact with each other. Even though we may be able to speak of some lawful relations within each domain, these laws give us absolutely no way of knowing at what point in their respective evolutions organisms from the two sets will make contact, or what the outcome will be. In this way, the tree of nature becomes *fundamentally* irregular and unpredictable.

For example, we can "predict" that some early mammals, faced with a shortage of food near the ground and an abundance of foliage at higher elevations either will evolve some mechanism for reaching the available food or will perish. But even we, with our limited intellects, can conceive of many mechanisms by which the unexploited food supply might be attained, and nature is far more prodigal than we in its inventiveness. There is nothing in our theory that "predicts" the appearance of giraffes in the world. Likewise for the foliage; we can "predict" either that the tall trees will evolve in some way influenced by the fact that no herbivorous mammal has come along to exploit it or that they will evolve in some way affected by the arrival on the scene of the unpredictable giraffe.

In short, we are not talking about predictions at all, but about a point of view that helps us make some sense out of what has happened. The armamentarium of conventional science—creative simplification, hypothesis testing, lawmaking, prediction, and control—are tools to help us in this effort. I believe we can use these tools to better advantage if we keep in mind that in many key respects nature is irregular, nonrepeating, unpredictable, incomplete, indeterminate, complex, open ended, and inventive.

Unfortunately, our discipline, psychology, is still dominated by a highly deterministic point of view. There is an underlying belief in a potentially omniscient Being for whom the course of every droplet in the storm would be knowable and for whom the appearance of complexity would be understood in every detail as resulting from the operation of a finite set of simple laws. One might add, if we take the actual behavior of our colleagues as evidence, that they are hoping and searching for a small number of such laws. I do not want to cast the argument in the form of a Hobson's choice between an impossible hyperdeterminism and an obscurantist accidentalism. On some scales, we can all be determinists some of the time. But it does seem unfortunate that so much psychological work is directed by this vector toward simplistic determinism and so little toward concerted efforts to conceptualize complexity. In the space available, I can only mention briefly some of the major symptoms of this tendency.

1. In the heredity–environment controversy, the debate is still dominated by the view that development and behavior are the resultants of fixed entities with fixed properties. Thus, a certain number of "favorable genes" together with a certain "favorable environment" are supposed to lead to a certain predictable result. In contrast, geneticists insist that the significance of each gene depends *entirely* on its place in the whole genomic configuration and on a developmentally evolving sequence of

interactions with the environment. Nevertheless, many psychologists cling to the belief that there are favorable genes predisposing favorable outcomes. In this connection, I call your attention to geneticist Lewontin's (1976) criticism of psychologist Jensen's misuse of the concept of norm of reaction.

2. In discussions of the causes of behavior, the myth is still widespread among psychologists—and even more widely taught—that stimuli "cause" responses. With the emergence of cybernetic ideas, a fundamentally different approach has been freshly elaborated. As Powers (1976) put it: "Control theory changes our basic conception of human and animal nature, from that of a passive system driven according to the whims of the environment to that of an active system which more often than not drives the environment to conform with its own wishes, desires, intentions, goals, and basic requirements [p. 2]."

In a machine-worshipping world, once the feasibility of goal-guided machines has been admitted, it becomes possible to admit the reality of goal-guided people. But if this is granted, the system of their interactions (i.e., the social process) becomes largely indeterminate; it is the working out of an incalculable number of interactions. More important than their number, the social system is a highly differentiated, structured system in which some individuals are more important than others. Even more difficult for a highly deterministic approach, the configuration of the system changes from time to time, so that most "laws" of social behavior prevail only within severely limited boundary conditions. In *The Wealth of Nations*, Adam Smith (1776) proposed a theory in which he treated each individual as a social atom of equal value with all other atoms, the system operating according to very simple laws so that the net result is an equilibrium condition, similar to the way physical atoms operating according to the gas laws give an elastic container its shape and volume. To our sorrow, we read every day that all social atoms are not equal and that they are arranged in configurations that give some of them almost unbelievable influence over the shape of human affairs. Although it is not necessarily humanity's brightest dream, Smith's mythical free market might be better than today's reality. For better or worse, however, this reality does mean that some purposeful beings can have a greater effect than others on the course of human events.

3. In developmental psychology, all of the most influential theories—those of Freud, Erikson, Piaget—are cast in the form of single developmental pathways, that is, fixed sequences of stages. No matter how dynamic or interactionist a theory may be in other ways, insofar as it is a single pathway model, it is essentially deterministic.

4. In typological and taxonomic efforts by psychologists, what is most striking is the vector toward simplicity. Whole literatures are founded on simple dichotomies, on six-type taxonomies, or on lists of no more

than a few dozen traits. Meanwhile, our colleagues in biology think in terms of 3 million known species and an estimated 10 million extant species, not to speak of all those that have perished. Or they think in terms of many thousands of gene loci, with a growing number of known or suspected alleles at each locus (e.g., Neel, 1976).

There is a relation between simplistic taxonomies and deterministic theories that would be worth exploring. As long as the hope exists of reducing the variety of organisms under discussion to a comfortably compact number of types—roughly similar to the 100-odd elements of physics, or even fewer—a corresponding hope remains plausible. We may find a small set of laws governing the determination of each individual's type and then complete the strategy by using the type to explain behavior. But as the number of types approaches the number of individuals, the value of this strategy fades and it becomes incumbent on us to search for other approaches.

Now, you may argue that contemporary psychological thinking, rather than being deterministic, is highly probabilistic. Do we not teach our students that lawful regularities in nature are really statistical aggregates, and do we not insist on the careful use of statistical inference in drawing conclusions about these aggregates? Yes, of course. But the theoretical focus of attention is usually on the mean value or on shifts in mean values caused by some independent variable.

We recognize a kind of probability-in-the-small, but we look for regularity-in-the-large. This works well under certain simplified boundary conditions. In physics, the chancy dance of millions of molecules in a gas-filled balloon leads to certain average values for their collisions with the interior surface of the container, and this produces a highly regular and predictable result: a spherical balloon (if thickness is uniform) of a volume dependent on a few known variables. The essential requirements for this kind of regularity are: a closed system, a very large number of identical elements, and a very large number of equivalent events (e.g., collisions). In human affairs, none of these conditions is ever satisfied, and in living systems in general, only under very narrow ranges of conditions.

In recent research in population genetics, for example, the chanciness of the evolution of living systems seems to go well beyond the Darwinian image of nature that I have been sketching out. It is now widely believed that the number of variants extant in a population at any one time is far greater than called for by neo-Darwinian theory—greater perhaps by several orders of magnitude. Genetic drift produces much more variability in the gene pool than had been previously recognized (Kimura, 1976). (Variants of this kind owe their existence to protection from selection pressure; that is, they are not functionally significant, but as circumstances change, this immunity fades.) Hence, the hope is more remote than ever of achieving scientific progress by further refining our already advanced techniques for neglecting human individuality.

5. The disciplines of scientific and intellectual history and the history of technology ought to be closely related to psychology, especially cognitive psychology, since they also deal with the way human beings get ideas and elaborate them. In fact, psychologists have not paid much attention to these fields, except for a few seminal books, such as Kuhn's *The Structure of Scientific Revolutions* (1962), and some case studies emanating from the psychoanalytic tradition. More serious, the main ideas that psychologists have gleaned from these fields are part of the deterministic tradition I have been discussing: emphasis on the Zeitgeist and denial of the role of the individual in history. Justified criticism of the "great man theory of history" gives due recognition to the many less than great contributors and to the complex network of social processes involved in intellectual work; in so doing we need dismiss neither the less than great nor the great individual. Both are important in shaping history, each in his or her own way.

If important inventions were inevitable results of massive social forces, we should expect something simple and fundamental to have been invented and disseminated in every corner of the globe where a high civilization has appeared. Yet the whole American continent, from Alaska to Tierra del Fuego, with Aztec Mexico and Incan Peru included, was innocent of the wheel and the wheeled vehicle. The wheel, like all inventions, is really a synthesis, a bringing together of many component inventions. The unique combination necessary for the wheel was not an inevitable consequence of the mere existence of a civilization that could well have used it. High civilization, roads, cities, and so on were not enough to evoke the wheel. A certain rare event, a creative process, was also needed—in this instance, probably the confluence of a number of inventions.

We need to learn to look at such unique events. While, by definition, every unique event occurs only once, there are still a large number of interesting ones occurring all the time. If novelty springs from such events, we need some way of making them part of science, some way of asking: How did this happen? Why is it unique?

Lists of simultaneous and independent discoveries or inventions are often propounded as evidence for the deterministic view of intellectual and technological history. Without questioning the role of impersonal social forces or the occurrence of some such cases, my own work has led me to a certain skepticism. The Darwin–Wallace coincidence is one of the most often cited examples of independent discovery of a scientific idea. Yet they occurred exactly 20 years apart, they were not identical, and they were obviously not independent; when Wallace developed the idea of evolution through natural selection, it was to Charles Darwin and to Darwin alone that he sent his first sketch of it!

We are faced with some difficult conceptual choices. If we could think of living systems as operating through processes linked in one-way causal chains, we could retain a faith in science as the study of deterministic systems without giving up the idea of chance. Chance could operate through the unlooked-for-collisions of previously independent systems (e.g., alpha-particle × gene → mutation), leading to events not predictable from the study of the separate systems. Accidents of this type, although they upset our predictions, need not shake our faith in the principle of determinism.

But in systems containing a multitude of complex feedback loops (e.g., organism chooses environment; new environment changes organism; changed organism chooses new environment; etc.), our ability to predict is affected by the level of analysis at which we decide to work. In the short run, body temperature and belief systems both remain predictably stable, controlled by regulating mechanisms whose adaptive function is to maintain stability. In the longer run, some of us will produce unpredictable creative innovations that will direct the course of cultural and social evolution down uncharted pathways. In the far distant but quite predictable future, we will all be dead and our solar system will grow cold. Beyond that, something else will certainly happen somewhere.

Alternatives to Simplistic Determinism

If psychologists want to understand just how the individual relates to society, just how the unique creative product is at once unique, accidental, *and* a social product, there is one fundamental task they cannot escape; they must look to the individual. They must examine individual cases thoroughly in all their bewildering complexity and learn how to unravel them without destroying their meaning or their uniqueness.

In the field of artificial intelligence, as computers grow in power and humans in skill, complexity becomes more legitimate, and ways of conceptualizing it more urgently sought. A contemporary example is the idea of "scene" and "frame" being developed in artificial intelligence laboratories. We are far past the point where "bits" or even "chunks" of information are the units of analysis: Many complex images and scenes are stored, and problem solving requires a system for eliciting active exchanges among them. This is not unlike the arrangement of an exhibition at the Museum of Modern Art in New York City; in order to capture the feel of one quarter of Tokyo, Shinjuku, more than a dozen "experience maps" were used (each capturing a different aspect of the place), and no one would really suppose that this fascinating array exhausted the domain.

In a very different way, a paper by Estes (1976) represents a cautious move in the same general direction. Reflecting on the chaotic theoretical situation existing in the study of probability learning, he comments

> Evidently, the different models are capturing different aspects of a complex process, some aspects being more prominent in some situations. One would like to replace the collection of locally successful models with one general theory, but this objective may not be within our capabilities. A more feasible immediate goal may be to try to understand why different models are required to deal with different situations [p. 60].

In spite of this bow to a possible pluralism and complexity, the main effort of Estes's paper is unfortunately to find *the* boundary conditions within which *the* revised model will work.

The scientific implementation of the simplistic–deterministic vision of nature depends on an organization of scientific work into isolated specialties. Within such sub-subdisciplines, a larger view of nature seems a world well lost, narrow boundary conditions for research can be prescribed, and idealized laws pursued in comfort. It is not surprising that some of the criticism of this fragmentation has taken organizational form in such groups as the Group for Dialectical Psychology and the Social Science History Association. Realistically, however, these are still only splinter groups, and the main trends in social science are far from interdisciplinary or dialectical.

No one can pretend to real mastery in every branch of contemporary science and social science. But even ordinary polysensory mortals can keep an ear to the ground and a nose to the wind and stay in touch with general trends over areas much wider than their own specialties. So doing, it is not hard to accumulate expressions similar to my own dissatisfaction with simplistic determinism. In an address in 1974 on receiving the American Psychological Association's Distinguished Scientific Contribution Award, Lee Cronbach made a plea for observational studies and greater respect for descriptive results as against hypotheses testing, for exorcising the null hypothesis as too frequently leading to a waste of valuable descriptive data, for sensitivity to weak interactions, for avoiding research designs that conceal even strong interactions, for greater awareness of the boundary conditions within which nomothetic laws prevail, and for some recognition that we are often impotent to specify those boundary conditions. He closed with the following words:

> Social scientists are rightly proud of the discipline we draw from the natural-science side of our ancestry. Scientific discipline is what we uniquely add to the time-honored ways of studying man. Too narrow an identification with science, however, has fixed our eyes upon an inappropriate goal. The goal of our work . . . is not to amass generalizations atop which a theoretical tower can some-day be erected. . . . The special task of the social scientist in each generation is to pin down the contemporary facts. Beyond that, he shares with the humanist scholar and the artist in the effort to gain insight into contemporary relationships, and to realign the culture's view of man with present realities. To know man as he is is no mean aspiration [Cronbach, 1975, p. 126]."

Among other recent repressions of the same restlessness is the vigorous discussion in Marxist circles of the deterministic view of social process that relegates ideology to the "superstructure" and thereby fails to recognize that the human brain and its intellectual products are integral parts of the natural world.

If we press home such changes in our images of nature and of scientific knowledge, how might the actual practice of scientific inquiry be modified? I offer a few suggestions, none of them really new but perhaps gaining some new force from the foregoing reflections.

1. *"Weak theory."* Learn to live with the reality that the drive for strong and simple theories that make highly deterministic predictions may only lead us down the road to fiasco. Historians of the behavioral sciences could make a real contribution by documenting some of these failures. This might reduce the strength of the system of reinforcements that now regulates so much theoretical work.

2. *Sensitivity to boundary conditions.* Within limits, some deterministic laws are possible. (For example, under very specific stimulus conditions, height in the visual field corresponds to distance from the observer.) Inquiry cannot stop with discovering such laws. We need to go beyond them in two ways: (*a*) determine systematically the boundary conditions within which the laws operate; and (*b*) be not too bemused or self-satisfied by the laws themselves. We need to understand that our whole activity of detecting lawful relations and their boundary conditions is part of a still larger enterprise, forming and reforming our images of nature.

3. *Interdisciplinarity.* Piaget's reaction to uncertainties of the kind this chapter is concerned with has been a whole series of writings, not well enough known, on interdisciplinarity (e.g., Piaget, 1973). Each discipline makes assumptions that are not grounded or groundable within its own mode of operation. In principle, it must depend on other disciplines. One need not be a Renaissance person to pay attention to such relationships.

4. *Invention.* Another metaphor runs through all of Darwin's thought, the idea that the curious organs whose functions he loved to work out are "contrivances." As Darwin understood nature, it does not of course consciously contrive or invent; his use of the term is a metaphoric comparison with the human activity of invention.

   I believe it was Einstein who said that we know more than we can explain. By the same token, we can invent things without fully understanding how they work. Indeed, such invention is a far greater part of the scientific process than has been recognized. Without attempting to set up the most universal laws, we can still try to invent new ways of doing things; when we have created a novelty, we can try to understand it, and this understanding constitutes something like the conventional idea of scientific knowledge. This is how I appreciate the strategy of some workers in the field of artificial intelligence. In a first approximation, they forswear the goal of understanding the human mind; they are satisfied to invent a machine that carries out some functions similar to those of the mind. Then by examining what they have done, they may also shed light on the "natural" mind.

Considering invention as a part of science echoes Marx's (1845) aphorism: "Previous philosophers have only interpreted the world. The point is to change it [p. 199]." Invention (including, of course, social invention) is a form of world changing. Changing the world can be construed as part of our attempts to understand it.

5. *Individuality.* Rather than concentrating so much effort on looking for general laws of human functioning, look for laws of the individual. How does this person work? Cognitive psychology, in particular, needs new approaches to understanding each person as a unique system with its own mode of operation. With slight extensions, the same idea applies to the study of particular groups.

6. *Openness.* Give up all forms of the effort to characterize the person as a fixed entity. Become far more sensitive both to the changes that are actualized and to those that are just below the surface. Be more accepting of the role of chance in human growth and of interactions among loosely coupled systems.

7. *Humility.* Don't change nature too much. We do not know, and in principle cannot know, the effects of what we are doing. It's bigger than all of us . . . fortunately.

References

Allegård, A. Darwin and the general reader: The reception of Darwin's theory of evolution in the British periodical press, 1859-1872. *Acta Universitatis Gotheburgensis, Goteborgs Universitatis Arsskrift*, 1958, 64.

Ayala, F. J. The mechanisms of evolution. *Scientific American*, 1978, 239, 56-70.

Baldwin, J. M. On selective thinking. *Psychological Review*, 1898, 5, 1-24.

Campbell, D. T. Blind Variation and selective retention in creative thought as in other knowledge processes. *Psychological Review*, 1960, 67, 380-400.

Campbell, D. T. On the conflicts between biological and social evolution and between psychology and moral tradition. *American Psychologist*, 1975, 30, 1103-1126. (APA presidential address, 1975.)

Cronbach, L. J. Beyond the two disciplines of scientific psychology. *American Psychologist*, 1975, 30, 116-127.

Darwin, C. *The Origin of species.* London: John Murray, 1859.

Darwin, C. *The descent of man, and selection in relation to sex.* London: John Murray, 1871.

Darwin, C. *The expression of the emotions in man and animals.* London: John Murray, 1872.

Darwin, C. *The autobiography of Charles Darwin* (Nora Barlow, Ed.). London: Collins, 1958.

Estes, W. K. The cognitive side of probability learning. *Psychological Review*, 1976, 83, 37-64.

Freud, S. *A general introduction to psychoanalysis* (J. Riviere, Trans.). New York: Doubleday, 1953.

Gruber, H. *Darwin on man: A psychological study of scientific creativity together with Darwin's early and unpublished notebooks,* transcribed and annotated by Paul H. Barrett. (2nd ed.) Chicago: University of Chicago Press, 1980. (Originally published, New York: E. P. Dutton, 1974.)

Hanson, N. R. *Patterns of discovery.* Cambridge: Cambridge University Press, 1958.

Hull, C. L. Mind, mechanism, and adaptive behavior. *Psychological Review,* 1937, *44,* 1–32. (APA presidential address, 1936.) (Reprinted in E. R. Hilgard [Ed.], *American psychology in historical perspective,* Washington, D.C.: American Psychological Association, 1978.)

Judd, C. H. Evolution and consciousness. *Psychological Review,* 1910, *17,* 77–97. (APA presidential address, 1909.) (Quoted in E. R. Hilgard [Ed.], *American psychology in historical perspective,* Washington, D.C.: American Psychological Association, 1979.)

Kimura, M. Population genetics and molecular evolution. *Johns Hopkins Medical Journal,* 1976, *138,* 253–261.

Köhler, W. *The mentality of apes.* London: Routledge and Kegan Paul, 1925.

Kuhn, T. S. *The structure of scientific revolutions.* Chicago: University of Chicago Press, 1962.

Lewin, K. *A dynamic theory of personality* (D. K. Adams and K. E. Zener, Trans.). New York: McGraw-Hill, 1935.

Lewontin, R. C. The fallacy of biological determinism. *The Sciences,* March/April 1976, 6–10.

Malthus, T. R. *An essay on the principle of population.* 6th edition, 2 vols. London: John Murray, 1826. (This is the edition Darwin owned.)

Marx, K. *Theses on Feuerbach* No. 11. In F. Engels, *Ludwig Feuerbach and the end of classical German philosophy,* 1888. (Originally written, 1845.)

Neel, J. V. The circumstances of human evolution. *Johns Hopkins Medical Journal,* 1976, *138,* 233–244.

Newell, A., & Simon, H. A. *Human problem solving.* Englewood Cliffs, New Jersey: Prentice-Hall, 1972.

Paley, W. *Natural theology, or evidences of the existence and attributes of the Deity collected from the appearances of nature.* London, 1802.

Piaget, J. *Main trends in interdisciplinary research.* London: Allen and Unwin, 1973.

Piaget, J. *Adaptation vitale et psychologie de l'intelligence: Selection organique et phenocopie.* Paris: Hermann, 1974.

Piaget, J. *Le comportement moteur de l'evolution.* Paris: Gallimard, 1976.

Piaget, J. Phenocopy in biology and the psychological development of knowledge. In H. E. Gruber & J. J. Voneche (Eds.), *The essential Piaget.* New York: Basic Books, 1977.

Piaget, J. *Behavior and evolution.* (D. Nicholson-Smith, Trans.). New York: Pantheon, 1978.

Polanyi, M. *Personal knowledge: Towards a post-critical philosophy.* Chicago: University of Chicago Press, 1958.

Powers, W. T. Control theory, purpose, and determinism. Paper presented in a symposium on relevance and perspectives of cybernetics in psychology, American Psychological Association, Washington, D.C., 1976.

Powers, W. T. Quantitative analysis of purposive systems: Some spadework at the foundations of scientific psychology. *Psychological Review,* 1978, *85,* 417–435.

Rudwick, M. Darwin and Glen Roy: A "great failure" in scientific methods? *Studies in the History and Philosophy of Science,* 1974, *5,* (2).

Russett, C. E. *Darwin in America: The intellectual response, 1865–1912.* San Francisco: W. H. Freeman, 1976.

Sagan, C. *The dragons of Eden: Speculations on the evolution of human intelligence.* New York: Random House, 1977.

Simon, H. A. The architecture of complexity. *Proceedings of the American Philosophical Society,* 1962, (Reprinted in H. A. Simon, *The sciences of the artificial.* Cambridge: MIT Press, 1969.)

Skinner, B. F. *The behaviour of organisms: An experimental analysis.* London: Appleton-Century, 1938.

Smith, A. *Inquiry into the nature and causes of the wealth of nations.* 1776.

Smith, B. M. Perspectives on selfhood. *American Psychologist,* 1978, *33,* 1053-1063. (APA presidential address, 1978).

Stone, C. P. Multiply, vary, let the strongest live and the weakest die—Charles Darwin. *Psychological Bulletin,* 1943, *40,* 1-24. (APA, presidential address Psychological Association, 1943, not actually delivered, due to wartime conditions.)

Titchener, E. B. *Lectures on the experimental psychology of the thought-processes.* New York: Macmillan, 1909.

Waddington, C. H. *The strategy of the genes.* London: Allen and Unwin, 1957.

Washburn, S. L. Human behavior and the behavior of other animals. *American Psychologist,* 1978, *33,* 405-418. (APA invited address, 1977.)

White, G. *The natural history of Selborne.* London: Benjamin White, 1789.

White, S. H. *Psychology in all sorts of places.* In R. Kasschau (Ed.), *Psychology and practice* (tentative title). Houston: University of Houston Press, 1980.

Whyte, L. L. *Internal factors in evolution.* New York: Braziller, 1965.

Wimsatt, W. C. Complexity and organization. In K. F. Schaffner and R. S. Cohen (Eds.), *Boston studies in the philosophy of science* (Vol. 20). Dordrecht: Reidl Publishers, 1974.

Wittgenstein, L. *On certainty.* (G. E. M. Anscombe & G. H. von Wright, Eds.). New York: Harper & Row, 1969.

Recommended Readings

Burrow, J. W. *Evolution and society: A study in Victorian social theory.* New York: Cambridge University Press, 1970.

Campbell, D. T. On the conflicts between biological and social evolution and between psychology and moral tradition. *American Psychologist,* 1975, *30,* 1103-1126.

Coleman, W. *Biology in the nineteenth century: Problems of form, function, and transformation.* New York: Cambridge University Press, 1977.

Gruber, H. E. *Darwin on man: A psychological study of scientific creativity,* transcribed and annotated by Paul H. Barrett. Chicago: University of Chicago Press, 1980. (Originally published, New York: E. P. Dutton, 1974.)

Romanes, G. J. *Mental evolution in man: Origin of human faculty.* London: Kegan Paul, 1888.

Young, R. M. The role of psychology in the nineteenth-century evolutionary debate. In M. Henle, J. Jayres, & J. Sullivan (Eds.), *Historical conceptions of psychology.* New York: Springer Publishing Co., 1973.

Part III

Psychological Systems:
Past, Present, and Future

MARY HENLE **9**

The Influence
of Gestalt Psychology
in America

PSYCHOLOGY:
THEORETICAL-HISTORICAL PERSPECTIVES

ISBN 0-12-588265-3

In America, Gestalt psychology has always been a minority movement. A brief look at its history, both here and in Germany where it originated, will help us to understand why. It is well known that it began around 1910, when Wertheimer made his fateful stopover in Frankfurt to test his hypotheses about stroboscopic movement. Like the man who came to dinner, he remained for a number of years. Here he found Köhler and Koffka, and the three of them collaborated in what was to become Gestalt psychology.

The publication launching the new movement was Wertheimer's paper on the perception of movement (1912a). In 1911 Koffka left for Giessen, and work, particularly in perception, was soon coming out of his laboratory. Köhler, in 1913, was appointed director of the Anthropoid Station of the Prussian Academy of Sciences on the island of Tenerife; because of World War I, he was unable to return to Germany until 1920. By 1914 a few significant titles had been added to the literature of Gestalt psychology. But then Wertheimer and Koffka were engaged in war work. Only Köhler, in the isolation of Spanish Africa, was able to continue his psychological research.

In 1920 Köhler became acting director and, soon afterward, director of the Psychological Institute of the University of Berlin. Wertheimer was already there, as was Kurt Lewin, whose work bears a significant relationship to Gestalt psychology. From that time until the coming of the Nazis to power, Gestalt psychology flourished. Graduate students were coming to the institute from a number of countries; the *Psychologische Forschung*, the journal of the Gestalt psychologists, was founded, and work was progressing in many directions.

In 1922 Koffka introduced Gestalt psychology to America with his paper "Perception, An Introduction to the Gestalt-Theorie." Two years later, he came to the United States, settling in 1927 at Smith College, Northampton, Massachusetts.

Wertheimer moved his family out of Germany before Hitler came to power: He was quick to realize what was happening. Köhler remained for some 2 years of courageous struggle with the Nazi authorities, who harassed his students, dismissed his assistants, made appointments to the institute without consulting him.

By the end of World War II, the first generation of young Gestalt psychologists was essentially wiped out. For example, von Lauenstein was lost in the war, von Restorff died in Germany, Duncker in America, to name Köhler's last assistants in Germany. The others were scattered. A few migrated to America, England, the Scandinavian countries, Israel; Zeigarnik returned to the Soviet Union. Some went into practical work. For example, Paul Koseleff, one of the Nazis' first targets at the institute, became a psychoanalyst in Denmark; I recently learned that Krolik, whose perceptual experiments are among the most beautiful I know, became a school psychologist; Erich Goldmeier, who did excellent work on similarity and on memory change, practiced medicine in America. Others found positions in school, not university, teaching.

Could a second generation be started in the United States? Koffka, it will be recalled, was a professor at Smith College, an undergraduate institution; nevertheless, he gave one Ph.D., to Molly Harrower. Köhler went to Swarthmore, another undergraduate college in Swarthmore, Pennsylvania. And when Wertheimer arrived at the New School for Social Research, it was not yet giving degrees; only at the very end of his life were a few graduate students working with him for the Ph.D.

But it was not only the lack of graduate students that stood in the way of a new generation of Gestalt psychologists. Behaviorism was and—however modified—has remained the dominant psychology in America. Köhler (1953) relates an amusing anecdote:

> In 1925, soon after my first arrival in this country, I had a curious experience. When once talking with a graduate student of psychology who was, of course, a behaviorist, I remarked that McDougall's psychology of striving seemed to me to be associated with certain philosophical theses which I found it hard to accept; but that he might nevertheless be right in insisting that, as a matter of simple observation, people do this or that in order to reach certain goals. Did not the student himself sometimes go to a post office in order to buy stamps? And did he not just now prepare himself for certain examinations to be held next Thursday? The answer was prompt: "I never do such things," said the student. There is nothing like a solid scientific conviction [pp. 124–125].

Even when, years later, behaviorists became interested in cognitive problems, it was still a cognitive behaviorism, and the differences that distinguished Gestalt psychology from behaviorism remained. New developments were more closely related to behaviorism than to Gestalt psychology. As one example, the use of computer models of thinking still involves machine theory, no matter how sophisticated the machine. Machine theories of neural functioning have consistently been criticized by Gestalt psychologists.

Thus, the Gestalt immigrants found themselves in an intellectual atmosphere dominated by behaviorism and its relatives; they were mainly without graduate students; and several of them died too soon to have much influence on the psychology of their new country. It is scarcely surprising that a new generation of Gestalt psychologists did not grow up in America.

And it was hardly likely that Gestalt psychology would be understood, even when it was listened to politely or with respect. Misunderstandings may be seen as both cause and effect of the less than overwhelming influence that Gestalt psychology had in America. I would like to discuss a few of these.

Misunderstandings of Gestalt Psychology

The interesting thing about these misunderstandings is that, except for the first I will mention (which I have only recently begun to take as something other than a bad joke), they are not new. Gestalt psychologists have repeatedly spoken to these issues, but without effect. This problem of the persistence of misunderstandings is one that I hope will interest some future historian of ideas and one that the cognitive psychologist should not neglect.

The most grotesque current misunderstanding of Gestalt psychology is the notion that it has some relation to Gestalt therapy. I will not discuss this distortion of history and of ideas but will merely state that there is nothing in common between these two developments. The reader is referred to a previous analysis of this problem (Henle, 1978).

A second misunderstanding is this: Gestalt psychologists, because of their opposition to certain empiristic hypotheses, have repeatedly been called nativists: for example, by Piaget in the 1930s, by Boring in the 1940s, by Allport and Tolman in the 1950s, by the Mandlers in the 1960s. Here is a quotation from R. L. Gregory in 1970: "To the Gestalt writers, these Organising Principles were innate, inherited [p. 20]." Another perceptionist, writing in 1975, remarks: "By and large, the Gestalt psychologists were nativists [Rock, 1975, p. 20]." Considering the Gestalt psychologists' answer to the question of why units are perceived as units, he says:

> First, regarding the perception of the natural environment, evolutionary change has guaranteed that the brain will operate on the basis of laws that work, that is, that generally yield veridical perception. . . . Proximity and similarity evolved as laws of neural organization because of the nature of the environment in which animals evolved. In some other environment, different laws of organization would have evolved [Rock, 1975, p. 280].

This last quotation is particularly interesting because it spells out exactly the *opposite* of what Gestalt psychologists say about evolution and thus about nativism. In the 1920s, Köhler (1929) had already made his position clear. He left no room for doubt, in 1950, about what he thought evolution can do and what it cannot do (Köhler, 1950), and his last book, *The Task of Gestalt Psychology* (Köhler, 1969) contains perhaps the clearest statement of all. Gestalt psychologists are not nativists. I have no hope of being understood where the others were not, but I feel the obligation once more to state the position.

Nativism refers, of course, to explanations in terms of inherited mechanisms; we may consider in particular inherited features of the nervous system, though other parts of the anatomy are, of course, relevant. The nervous system exhibits certain histological structures because the organism is equipped with particular chromosomes—products of evolution. Thus, a nativistic explanation, say of perceptual facts, makes these facts the contribution of evolution.

In his examination of this theory, Köhler shows that evolutionary theory does *not* permit such an explanation. Although we most often think of evolution as a theory of change or of variance, it contains, as an essential part, a principle of invariance. If organisms develop from inorganic nature, they must have something in common with this nature; factors that apply to inanimate nature apply also to the organisms that develop from it. The alternative is vitalism or emergent evolution, which scientists have for the most part rejected.

What is it that organisms share with inorganic nature? General principles (like conservation of energy), forces, elementary processes such as electric currents. Thus electric currents occur in the brains of organisms as well as in streaks of lightning. Since they are found throughout nature, they must be independent of the genetic equipment of any species or any individual. Surely, nobody would maintain that electric or chemical processes corresponding to perception are inherited. As Köhler (1950) puts it, the principle of invariance states that "no essentially new kind of action appears in living systems [p. 292]." It is only constraints that are contributed by evolution—in our case, anatomical structures in the nervous system and elsewhere that exclude certain possibilities of action. But actions themselves owe nothing to evolution. "Any action in any organism involves the operation of factors which are entirely independent of evolution," writes Köhler (1950, p. 293). A nativistic interpretation can therefore not account for the facts of perception.

I started with a quotation that attributes to Gestalt psychologists the view that the laws of neural organization are a product of evolution. But evolution cannot possibly be responsible for such laws, since actions as such are independent of evolution. It is precisely the Gestalt psychologists who have pointed this out.

There is another, perhaps surprising, consequence of this application of the principle of invariance in evolution to psychological problems. It forces us to reject certain empiristic interpretations as well. We do not learn to see, to think, or to learn, nor are motives learned in the usual meanings of these expressions. For again, these are all forms of action. Thus, they involve the operation of factors that the organism shares with inanimate nature, with all species, and with all individuals—factors that must therefore be independent of the individual experiences of anybody.

This is, of course, *not* to deny a role to learning in all these cases. Each one exhibits important influences of experience. It is just that the *processes* themselves are no more learned than they are inherited.

To return to the main point, Gestalt psychologists are not nativists. They do not accept the nativism–empiricism dichotomy; there is a third class of factors, invariant dynamics, that applies to all of nature. In Köhler's (1969) words, "An enormous part of the business of living can never, as such, have been affected by the changes introduced during evolution [p. 87]." He continues:

> Why so much talk about inheritance, and so much about learning—but hardly ever a word about invariant dynamics? It is this invariant dynamics, however constrained by histological devices, which keeps organisms and their nervous systems going [p. 90].

I do not know why we find it so difficult to break out of the nativism–empiricism dichotomy. Are we unable to think in terms of trichotomies? If we are, we will continue to misinterpret Gestalt psychology and—more serious—our explanations will not do justice to our subject matter.

The criticism that Gestalt psychologists have neglected the role of past experience in psychological processes likewise has a long history, and once again, clarifications of their position do not seem to help. We still find statements like the following:

> A further feature of the theory was an almost complete denial of learning as important for perception [Gregory, 1973, p. 52].

> The Gestalt psychologists did not absolutely deny that past experience affects perception [Epstein, 1967, p. 101].

> As a matter of fact, the dialogue between the behaviorists and the Gestalt psychologists seems to have centered upon the relative importance of past experience and innate organizing properties of the brain [Kaufman, 1974, p. 21].

That Gestalt psychologists reject certain kinds of empiristic explanations has just been indicated. That they do not confine the issue to nativism versus empiricism has been sufficiently discussed. But that they deny an important role of past experience in perception, thinking, motivation, and so on is far from the case. The question they ask is: *How* does past experience operate in these connections; what role does it play? Space does not permit me to do more than refer you to the sources; consulting them would be a valuable exercise also for the critics I have been quoting.

Isomorphism has come in for its share of misunderstandings. This is the hypothesis that there is a structural similarity between percepts and corresponding brain events. Here is an example of a version of isomorphism by a critic of Gestalt psychology:

> When viewing a circle, there was supposed to be a circular brain trace; for a sphere a spherical brain trace, and presumably for a house a corresponding house-shaped trace.

> There is far more to perception than the recognition of shape. How does the 'isomorphism' idea cope with other perceptual features? Consider colour: are we supposed to believe that when we see a green traffic light, part of our brain turns green [Gregory, 1973, pp. 52–53]?

This same author asserts that "Gestalt writers did tend to say that there are pictures inside the brain [Gregory, 1966, p. 7]," and elsewhere he asks: If pictures, why not melodies? Another writer refers to the "picture-in-the-head Gestalt school," adding:

> This need not be a literal representation such that an actual recognizable picture of objects may be found in the brain if we know how to look for it. . . .
>
> Köhler . . . was the first to assert that there is a one-to-one topological correspondence between what goes on in experience and what goes on in the brain. This is like saying that there is a picture in the head which is in topological correspondence with the picture in the mind [Kaufman, 1974, pp. 7–8].

Gestalt psychologists do not know anything about pictures in the brain. Köhler, in particular, has taken pains to explicate the functional—not geometrical—meaning of isomorphism. One formulation of his is particularly relevant to the current interpretations I have quoted: "Certainly, the processes in our brain do not represent a geometrical picture of spatial visual experience [1930, p. 569]." Let us take an example from the same source. What is the functional meaning of "between?" "In cases of dynamic self-distribution . . . a local process of the functional context is 'functionally between' two other processes whenever mutual influence of these two is mediated by an alteration of the third." He offers an analogy:

> I tell Mr. A a story which is meant for Mr. F, whom for some reason I cannot address directly. Mr. A is in the same situation and hands the story down to Mr. B, Mr. B talks with C, C with D, D with E and, at last, E with F. Thus A, B, C, D, and E are "functionally between" me and F in this case of an influence. At the same time F may be nearer to me geometrically than D; for example, he may even be "geometrically between" me and D. Still, functionally, the opposite is true [pp. 568–569].

Other specific relations have likewise been analyzed.

Qualities, such as color, are not dealt with by isomorphism, which is a structural principle, since qualities do not possess structure. It is obvious that the brain does not turn green when we see that color: Colors do not exist in the physical world. Presumably, chemical reactions correspond to them, since these exhibit the required variety (cf. Köhler, 1938).

Isomorphism has proved to be a powerful heuristic, leading Köhler first to the investigation of figural aftereffects, then to the demonstration of steady cortical currents hypothesized to correspond to such effects and to the perception of segregated forms in general. Naturally, the theory of cortical currents has come under attack, notably by Lashley and by Sperry, with their co-workers. Why does everybody quote these criticisms, and why does nobody read Köhler's (1958, 1959, 1965) replies? One of the current texts I have been using does, in fact, after summarizing the work of Lashley and of Sperry, include the sentence: "There are, however, certain questions that can be raised concerning these experiments [Rock, 1975, p. 445]." What these questions are is never indicated. Another writer simply dismisses the theory of figural aftereffects as "no longer accepted," presumably because of Sperry's work (Kaufman, 1974, p. 511). It is interesting to note that the latest reference to Köhler's work in this volume is to a monograph of 1944, although the text was published 30 years later. Still another well-informed writer refers to the objections to the satiation theory already mentioned, omits Köhler's replies, and concludes (a bit more mildly than the others quoted): "While it cannot yet be discarded in its entirety, it is now evident that it cannot be retained intact, either as to substance or promise [Hochberg, 1971, p. 470]." Köhler (1965) himself has discussed unsolved problems in the field of figural aftereffects and has refined his concepts. But these considerations seem to have escaped the attention of the textbook writers on perception. It may be noted that the particular authors cited have been chosen, with one exception, not to be representative, but to be better informed than the average about the work of Gestalt psychology.

In the case of all the problems I have been discussing, why is one position so systematically ignored, or so consistently misinterpreted? We are concerned with developing a science not with winning a debate. Can we afford to ignore or to misinterpret the hypotheses of one group of scientists, particularly ones who have made such important contributions?

Some Contributions of Gestalt Psychology

It seems to be generally agreed that Gestalt psychology transformed the study of perception. In 1912, when Wertheimer's paper on stroboscopic motion appeared, the center of investigation was sensation; what we now call perception was accounted for, in one way or another, by the intervention of higher mental processes. A survey of some of the theories on the German scene can be found in Köhler's critical article of 1913 (Köhler, 1913). In America, Titchener was at his height; his context theory is formally similar to theories criticized by Köhler. While such theories are even now not extinct, the focus today is on the study of the objects and events of our phenomenal world. Both by their criticisms of the older views and by their demonstrations and experiments, Gestalt psychologists were most influential in effecting this change of direction. Beginning with stroboscopic movement—which Wertheimer refused to call by its then customary name, "apparent movement," because that term accorded it less reality than other movement from which it was phenomenally indistinguishable, Wertheimer and Koffka undertook their perceptual investigations. Köhler was meanwhile studying various perceptual functions in chimpanzees and in hens, now criticizing by empirical methods the theories that made of size constancy "apparent size," of color constancy "memory color." Once more, it was the phenomenal object, not sensations transformed by learning or other processes, with which his work was concerned. I think nobody will deny that it was mainly the Gestalt psychologists who turned the psychology of perception in this new direction. Gibson (1971), as one example, assessing Koffka's (1935) *Principles of Gestalt Psychology* 35 years after its publication, comments: "His book, more than any other book of its time, set the psychology of perception on the course it is now following [p. 9]."

Likewise in thinking, Gestalt psychology provided a fresh start. The old psychology of images was already beginning to give way to other approaches, but Wertheimer's (1912b) first use of the Gestalt principle in connection with the number concepts of "primitive peoples" represented a more radical departure. Köhler's work, published as *The Mentality of Apes* (1925), is an acknowledged turning point in the psychology of thinking. Departing from most paradigms then in use, Köhler gave his chimpanzees the opportunity to behave intelligently, and they did. But their curiously foolish errors were also illuminating. The concept of *insight* was introduced, and its role in thinking was progressively clarified after this early work. Insight has never been very popular among American psychologists, who even now tend to use protective quotation marks around the word, as if they suspected something mysterious about it. But insight, properly understood, may refer to the most commonplace cases as well as to more notable achievements. Duncker's (1945) work on problem solving is still widely known, and his term "functional fixedness" has become part of our psychological vocabulary. Wertheimer's (1945) major contribution to the psychology of the thought processes, *Productive Thinking*, has not yet had the influence it deserves; but it may still have an effect on theory if we ever have the courage to turn our attention from how computers solve problems and look to human thinking at its best.

I will return to theoretical and research contributions of the Gestalt psychologists, but I would like first to mention another kind of contribution. Since Gestalt theory did not fit the intellectual habits of American psychologists, attempts have repeatedly been made to reinterpret findings of this group in more familiar terms. Thus, issues for controversy were provided that, in turn, inspired new research. For example, the finding that animals and human beings often solve problems suddenly, often without previous fruitless efforts to reach the goal, did not fit the generally held theories of learning as an incremental process. There followed the long controversy over continuity in learning, and the result was much new research. Köhler's work on the nature of associations initiated a controversy, with Postman defending the traditional associationists' position and Asch continuing with experiments in the Gestalt tradition. We have thus acquired much new knowledge about the nature of associations. Attempts were made to reinterpret the Restorff effect (or isolation effect) in terms of association theory, and again new research was produced. Asch's work on the formation of impressions of personality, interpreted by him in organizational terms, led to a good deal of research that attempted to return it to the traditional fold. A very large body of research has grown out of attempts to reinterpret figural aftereffects.

Some of this work is difficult to evaluate at the present time. But however the issues are resolved—if they are resolved—controversy gives rise to new research. The supplying of issues for controversy is thus in itself an important contribution of Gestalt psychology. Controversy is good for psychology.

Some of the directions in which the Gestalt psychologists took their work were left strictly alone by American psychology. This is true of problems as diverse as values and cortical currents. Value seemed to many Americans best ignored in the interests of a value-free science, this despite Köhler's analysis of the concept within the framework of natural science. For very different reasons cortical currents were mainly ignored, except for the effort to show that they did not really correspond to perceptions anyhow: Technological advance had made it possible to stimulate the single cell, and attention was shifted away from more molar cortical events. In this case, physiologists will surely some day take up the problems if we do not; in the case of value, we seem to be leaving the task of analysis to philosophers. There are further examples of work that has been ignored. I wonder how many psychologists know that Gestalt psychologists have put forth a theory of recall and one of attention.

I think we must say, in short, that outside the field of perception and perhaps of thinking, the contributions of Gestalt psychology have been insufficiently utilized. I wonder if it is too optimistic to think that there is change in the air. That cognitive psychology has returned to prominence is well known. Even behaviorism can no longer turn its back on cognitive problems. But concern with cognition is one thing; *how* cognitive problems are dealt with is another. Cognitive behaviorism and computer simulation are still a long way from Gestalt psychology. Still, the stage may be set for a return to some of the conceptions of the Gestalt group.

Promising Contemporary Developments

A promising development is Jenkins's contextualism, as put forth in a paper entitled "Remember That Old Theory of Memory? Well, Forget It!" Jenkins (1974) describes the associationistic assumptions from which he started, remarking: "This view is so pervasive in American psychology that it is almost coextensive with being an experimentalist [p. 786]." But his own research forced him to what he calls a contextual position. "This means not only that the analysis of memory must deal with contextual variables, but also . . . that what memory is depends on context [p. 786]." There is no reference in this paper to Gestalt psychology, and the experimental paradigms illustrated differ considerably from those typically employed by the Gestalt investigators. But that Jenkins's own findings led him to abandon the atomism and the mechanistic assumptions of his earlier approach is an event of no little importance. Both atomism and mechanism have consistently been the targets of criticism by Gestalt psychologists.

Another small indication of change is what today is called interactionism in personality and social psychology. After a critique of the situationism of behavior theorists, Bowers (1973) defines his own position: "Interactionism argues that situations are as much a function of the person as the person's behavior is a function of the situation [p. 327]." Of course there is nothing new in this statement, and it took the Swedish psychologist Ekehammer (1974) to point out that it has a history. Certainly, the most relevant previous formulation is that of Kurt Lewin who, 40 or more years earlier, not only stated the relationship just quoted, but worked out concepts for person and environment that seem to be lacking in contemporary interactionism (Lewin, 1935). Still, here is a small step toward where we were 40 years ago.

Was Gestalt psychology ahead of its time—as some of these examples might suggest—or simply uncongenial to the American intellectual scene? Can we today make better use of the contributions of Gestalt theory than we have done in the past? Before trying to answer these questions, I would like to take another brief look back into history.

The Crisis of Science

Gestalt psychology arose, not only as a protest against the traditional psychologies of the time, but also as a response to a much more general intellectual situation. This was called the crisis of science; the German phrase, *die Krise der Wissenschaft*, is more exact, since it was not only the sciences, but academic knowledge in general that was involved. The academic disciplines could no longer take for granted the respect they had previously enjoyed. Why the crisis of confidence? Because scholars seemed to be unable to contribute to matters of human concern and indeed seemed to be uninterested in them. Science, by its very nature, seemed to exclude meanings and values and thus to exempt itself from pressing human problems.

In psychology, one solution to the crisis of science was to develop an understanding psychology that gave up scientific explanation and hoped, through understanding, to find an avenue to real life human concerns.

The solution of Gestalt psychology was different. Rather than abandon the scientific method, it undertook to reexamine it. It discovered that certain assumptions being made about this method were not a necessary part of it, that science did not require the atomistic and mechanistic approach prevailing in psychology. Problems excluded by these assumptions might be dealt with if psychology concerned itself with molar events, employed more natural methods of analysis, and adopted the scientific stance of field theory.

It seems to me that we are again in a crisis of science, at least in psychology.

To a large extent, we see the massive problems facing us today as human problems, and as psychologists we are able to do little about them. There is, it is true, one big difference from that earlier crisis of science: We want to help. The cry for relevance comes from within psychology itself. We have developed new fields of psychology in the face of our crisis: environmental psychology, community psychology, psychology of aging, population psychology. It is my impression that we have not learned how to formulate problems well out of practical necessity and that our new "relevant" psychologies are as much an expression of our own concern as areas of scientific achievement.

One solution to that earlier crisis is with us again. With the apparent failure of scientific psychology to solve human problems, we find advocates of an understanding approach to these problems. Occasionally such an author presents his program with a knowledge of that earlier history (e.g., Giorgi); more often, not. I hear from students today a question that was simply not expressed in the university a decade ago: Must psychology be a science? The understanding approach abandons or supplements the rational methods of natural science. It does not necessarily imply irrationalism, but today irrationalism is often one of its ingredients.

What is missing in our contemporary crisis of science is a radical reexamination of the scientific method. A reexamination of research paradigms—yes: field research versus experimental research, multivariate versus conventional analysis. We no longer want to deceive our subjects; indeed, we do not like to call them subjects, but rather research participants. We hear a great deal about paradigms these days. More important, there is discussion of outmoded philosophies of science on which we have relied: positivism, operationalism, and so on. But in a positive direction, what shall we do?

Here is my suggestion. It has been the theme of this chapter that, except for the field of perception and, to a lesser extent, that of thinking, Gestalt psychology has not been given a real hearing. It has been misunderstood, its findings reinterpreted as if nothing new had happened, parts of it have been ignored.

In this present crisis of science, let us see how far the scientific method will take us in psychology. But let us examine the method we use. It would be reasonable to start in the direction of Gestalt psychology's reexamination of science—which, if I am correctly interpreting the contemporary scene, has yet to be followed up. Perhaps terminology will have to be changed; doubtless, specific concepts require modification. Surely, they will be refined with further work. But this is still a direction that deserves to be explored by more than a few people. If such a revised psychological science is really tried and fails, I see two other courses open to us: a different kind of reexamination of science; or, failing that, we may be forced to agree with such thinkers as Sigmund Koch (1971) that a coherent discipline of psychology is not possible.

Summary

Gestalt psychology was very active and influential in Germany in the 1920s and early 1930s, but the first generation of young Gestalt psychologists was then wiped out by events in that country. Wertheimer, Köhler, and Koffka, the first three Gestalt psychologists, emigrated to America. There they were without graduate students, and the intellectual climate in psychology was dominated by behaviorism; thus, a new generation of Gestalt psychologists could not be established, and Gestalt psychology has remained a minority movement.

In the United States, Gestalt psychology has consistently been misunderstood. Some of these misunderstandings have been discussed in the preceding pages. Some contributions of Gestalt psychology have been reviewed, and a few promising developments in the same direction have been noted. It must be added that these new developments have been slow to recognize their relation to Gestalt psychology.

The crisis of science, out of which Gestalt psychology arose early in this century, seems still to be with us. It is here suggested that it might be resolved if Gestalt psychology were now given a real hearing.

References

Bowers, K. S. Situationism in psychology: An analysis and a critique. *Psychological Review,* 1973, *80,* 307–336.

Duncker, K. On problem-solving (L. S. Lees, Trans.). *Psychological Monographs,* 1945, *58,* (5, Whole No. 270).

Ekehammar, B. Interactionism in personality from a historical perspective. *Psychological Bulletin,* 1974, *81,* 1026–1048.

Epstein, W. *Varieties of perceptual experience.* New York: McGraw-Hill, 1967.

Gibson, J. J. The legacies of Koffka's *Principles. Journal of the History of the Behavioral Sciences,* 1971, *7,* 3–9.

Gregory, R. L. *Eye and brain.* New York: World University Library. McGraw-Hill, 1966.

Gregory, R. L. *The intelligent eye.* New York: McGraw-Hill, 1970.

Gregory, R. L. The confounded eye. In R. L. Gregory & E. H. Gombrich (Eds.), *Illusion in nature and art.* London: Duckworth, 1973.

Henle, M. Gestalt psychology and gestalt therapy. *Journal of the History of the Behavioral Sciences,* 1978, *14,* 23–32.

Hochberg, J. Perception. I. Color and shape. In J. W. Kling & L. A. Riggs et al. (Eds.), *Woodworth & Schlosberg's Experimental psychology* (3rd ed.). New York: Holt, Rinehart & Winston, 1971.

Jenkins, J. J. Remember that old theory of memory? Well, forget it! *American Psychologist,* 1974, *29,* 785–795.

Kaufman, L. *Sight and mind. An introduction to visual perception.* New York: Oxford University Press, 1974.

Koch, S. Reflections on the state of psychology. *Social Research,* 1971, *38,* 669–709.

Koffka, K. Perception, an introduction to the Gestalt-Theorie. *Psychological Bulletin*, 1922, *19*, 531-585.

Koffka, K. *Principles of Gestalt psychology*. New York: Harcourt, Brace, 1935.

Köhler, W. Über unbemerkte Empfindungen und Urteilstäuschungen. *Zeitschrift für Psychologie*, 1913, *66*, 51-80. (Translation in M. Henle [Ed.], *Selected papers of Wolfgang Köhler*. New York: Liveright, 1971.)

Köhler, W. *The mentality of apes* (E. Winter, Trans.). New York: Harcourt, Brace, 1925.

Köhler, W. *Gestalt psychology*. New York: Liveright, 1929.

Köhler, W. The new psychology and physics. *Yale Review*, 1930, *19*, 560-576. (Reprinted in M. Henle [Ed.], *Selected papers of Wolfgang Köhler*. New York: Liveright, 1971.)

Köhler, W. *The place of value in a world of facts*. New York: Liveright, 1938.

Köhler, W. Psychology and evolution. *Acta Psychologica*, 1950, *7*, 288-297.

Köhler, W. The scientists from Europe and their new environment. In F. L. Neumann, H. Peyre, E. Panofsky, W. Köhler, and P. Tillich, *The cultural migration: The European scholar in America*. Philadelphia: University of Pennsylvania Press, 1953.

Köhler, W. The present situation in brain physiology. *American Psychologist*, 1958, *13*, 150-154.

Köhler, W. Psychologie und Naturwissenschaft. *Proceedings of the 15th International Congress of Psychology, Brussels, 1957*. Amsterdam: North-Holland Publishing Co., 1959. (Translation in M. Henle [Ed.], *Selected papers of Wolfgang Köhler*. New York: Liveright, 1971.)

Köhler, W. Unsolved problems in the field of figural aftereffects. *Psychological Record*, 1965, *15*, 63-83.

Köhler, W. *The task of Gestalt psychology*. Princeton, N. J.: Princeton University Press, 1969.

Lewin, K. *A dynamic theory of personality*. (D. K. Adams & K. E. Zener, trans.). New York: McGraw-Hill, 1935.

Rock, I. *An introduction to perception*. New York: Macmillan, 1975.

Wertheimer, M. Experimentelle Studien über das Sehen von Bewegung. *Zeitschrift für Psychologie*, 1912, *61*, 161-265. (a) (Translation in T. Shipley [Ed.], *Classics in psychology*. New York: Philosophical Library, 1961.)

Wertheimer, M. Über das Denken der Naturvölker. I. Zahlen und Zahlgebilde. *Zeitschrift für Psychologie*, 1912, *60*, 321-378. (b) (Translation in D. N. Robinson [Ed.], *Significant contributions to the history of psychology. Series A. Orientations* [Vol. 11]. Washington, D.C.: University Publications of America, 1977.)

Wertheimer, M. *Productive thinking*. New York: Harper, 1945. (Enlarged ed., M. Wertheimer [Ed.], 1959.)

Recommended Readings

Heidbreder, E., *Seven psychologies*. New York: Appleton-Century-Crofts, 1933. (Chapter 9).

Heider, F. Gestalt theory: Early history and reminiscences. In M. Henle, J. Jaynes, & J. Sullivan, (Eds.), *Historical conceptions of psychology*. New York: Springer, 1973.

Henle, M., Jaynes, J., & Sullivan, J. J. (Eds.) *Historical conceptions of psychology*. New York: Springer, 1973.

Köhler, W. *The task of Gestalt psychology*. Princeton, N.J.: Princeton University Press, 1969.

Krantz, D. L. *Schools of psychology: A symposium*. New York: Appleton-Century-Crofts, 1969.

Wertheimer, M., *Productive thinking*. New York: Harper & Row, 1945.

B. F. Skinner   **10**

The Experimental
Analysis of Operant Behavior:
A History

PSYCHOLOGY:
THEORETICAL-HISTORICAL PERSPECTIVES

ISBN 0-12-588265-3

I was drawn to psychology and particularly to behaviorism by some papers which Bertrand Russell published in the *Dial* in the 1920s and which led me to his book *Philosophy* (1927) (called in England *An Outline of Philosophy*), the first section of which contains a much more sophisticated discussion of several epistemological issues raised by behaviorism than anything of John B. Watson's. Naturally I turned to Watson (1924) himself, but at the time only to his popular *Behaviorism*. I bought Pavlov's *Conditioned Reflexes* (1927) shortly after it appeared, and when I came to Harvard for graduate study in psychology, I took a course which covered not only conditioned reflexes but the postural and locomotor reflexes of Magnus and the spinal reflexes reported in Sherrington's *Integrative Action of the Nervous System* (1906). The course was taught by Hudson Hoagland in the Department of General Physiology, the head of which, W. J. Crozier, had worked with Jacques Loeb and was studying tropisms. I continued to prefer the reflex to the tropism, but I accepted Loeb's and Crozier's dedication to the organism as a whole and the latter's contempt for medical school "organ physiology." Nevertheless, in the Department of Physiology at Harvard Medical School, I later worked with Hallowell Davis and with Alexander Forbes, who had been in England with Adrian and was using Sherrington's torsion-wire myograph to study the reflex control of movement.

By the end of my first year at Harvard, I was analyzing the behavior of an "organism as a whole" under soundproofed conditions like those described by Pavlov. In one experiment, I quietly released a rat into a small dark tunnel from which it could emerge into a well-lighted space, and, with moving pen on a moving strip of paper, I recorded its exploratory progress as well as its retreat into the tunnel when I made a slight noise. Some of my rats had babies, and in their early squirmings, I thought I saw some of the postural reflexes stereoscopically illustrated in Magnus's *Körperstellung* (1924), and I began to study them. I mounted a light platform on tight wires and amplified its forward-and-backward movement with an arm writing on a smoked drum. I could put a small rat on the platform and record the tremor of its leg muscles when I pulled it gently by the tail, as well as the sudden forward leap with which it often reacted to this stimulation.

I decided to do something of the sort with an adult rat. I built a very light runway about 8 feet long, the lengthwise vibration of which I could also amplify and record on a smoked drum, and I induced a rat to run along it by giving it food at the end. When it was halfway along, I would make a slight noise and record the way in which it came to a sudden stop by the effect on the runway. I planned to watch changes as the rat adapted to the noise;

possibly I could condition another stimulus to elicit the same response. My records looked a little like those made by a torsion-wire myograph, but they reported the behavior of the organism as a whole.

This was all pretty much in the tradition of reflex physiology, but quite by accident something happened which dramatically changed the direction of my research. In my apparatus, the rat went down a back alley to the other end of the apparatus before making its recorded run, and I noticed that it did not immediately start to do so after being fed. I began to time the delays and found that they changed in an orderly way. Here was a *process*, something like the processes of conditioning and extinction in Pavlov's work, where the details of the act of running, like those of salivation, were not the most important thing.

I have described elsewhere (Skinner, 1956) the series of steps through which I simplified my apparatus until the rat simply pushed open the door of a small bin to get a piece of food. Under controlled conditions and with pellets of food which took some time to chew, I found that the rate of eating was a function of the quantity of food already eaten. The title of my first experimental paper, "On the Conditions of Elicitation of Certain Eating Reflexes" (Skinner, 1930) shows that I was still applying the concept of the reflex to the behavior of the organism as a whole.

Pushing open a door was conditioned behavior, but in order to study the process of conditioning, I needed a more clearly defined act. I chose pushing down a horizontal bar mounted as a lever. When the rat pressed the lever, a pellet of food was released into a tray. The arrangement was, of course, close to that with which Thorndike had demonstrated his Law of Effect, and in my first paper, I called my apparatus a "problem box," but the results were quite different. Thorndike's cat learned by dropping out unsuccessful bits of behavior until little or nothing remained but the successful response. Nothing of the sort happened in my experiment. Pavlov's emphasis on the control of conditions had led me to take certain steps to avoid disturbing my rat. I gave it plenty of time to recover from being put into the apparatus by enclosing it first in a special compartment from which I later quietly released it. I left it in the apparatus a long time so that it could become thoroughly accustomed to being there, and I repeatedly operated the food dispenser until the rat was no longer disturbed by the noise and ate as soon as food appeared. All this was done when the lever was resting in its lowest position and hence before pressing it could be conditioned. The effect was to remove all the unsuccessful behavior which had composed the learning process in Thorndike's experiment. Many of my rats began to respond at a high rate as soon as they had depressed the lever and obtained only one piece of food.

Conditioning was certainly not the mere survival of a successful response; it was an increase in rate of responding, or in what I called reflex strength. Thorndike had said that the cat's successful behavior was "stamped in," but his evidence was an increasing priority over other behavior which was being "stamped out." The difference in interpretation became clearer when I disconnected the food dispenser and found that the behavior underwent extinction. As R. S. Woodworth (1951) later pointed out, Thorndike never investigated the extinction of problem-box behavior.

Though rate of responding was not one of Sherrington's measures of reflex strength, it emerged as the most important one in my experiment. Its significance was clarified by the fact that I recorded the rat's behavior in a cumulative curve; one could read the rate directly as the slope of the curve and see at a glance how it changed over a considerable period of time. Rate proved to be a particularly useful measure when I turned from the acquisition of behavior to its maintenance, in the study of schedules of intermittent reinforcement. Theoretically, it was important because it was relevant to the central question: What is the probability that an organism will engage in a particular form of behavior at a particular time?

I was nevertheless slow in appreciating the importance of the concept of strength of response. For example, I did not immediately shift from "condition" to "reinforce," although the latter term emphasizes the strengthening of behavior. I did not use "reinforce" at all in my report of the arrangement of lever and food dispenser, and my first designation for intermittent reinforcement was "periodic reconditioning."

Strength or probability of response fitted comfortably into the formulation of a science of behavior proposed in my thesis. Russell was again responsible for a central point. Somewhere he had said that "reflex" in psychology had the same status as "force" in physics. I knew what that meant because I had read Ernst Mach's (1893) *Science of Mechanics,* the works of Henri Poincaré on scientific method, and Bridgman's (1928) *The Logic of Modern Psychics.* My thesis was an operational analysis of the reflex. I insisted that the word should be defined simply as an observed correlation of stimulus and response. Sherrington's synapse was a mere inference which could not be used to explain the facts from which it was inferred. Thus, a stimulus might grow less and less effective as a response was repeatedly elicited, but it did not explain anything to attribute this to "reflex fatigue," Eventually, the physiologist would discover a change in the nervous system, but so far as the behavioral facts were concerned, the only identifiable explanation was the repeated elicitation. In my thesis (Skinner, 1931), I asserted that in the intact organism "conditioning, 'emotion,' and 'drive' so far as they concern behavior were essentially to be regarded as changes in reflex strength," and I offered my experiments on "drive" and conditioning as examples.

One needed to refer not only to a stimulus and a response but to conditions which changed the relation between them. I called these conditions "third variables" and represented matters with a simple equation:

$$R = f(S, A)$$

where A represented any condition affecting reflex strength, such as the deprivation with which I identified "drive" in the experimental part of my thesis.

The summer after I got my degree, Edward C. Tolman was teaching at Harvard, and I saw a great deal of him. I expounded my operational position at length and the relevance of third variables in determining reflex strength. Tolman's book *Purposive Behavior in Animals and Men* (1932) was then in press, and in it, he speaks of "independent variables" but only as such things as genetic endowment or an initiating physiological state. Three years later he published a paper (Tolman, 1935) containing the equation:

$$B = f\,(S,\, H,\, T,\, P)$$

in which B stood for behavior, as my R stood for response, S for "the environmental stimulus setup" (my S), H for heredity, T for "specific past training" (my "conditioning"), and P for "a releasing internal condition of appetite or aversion" (my "drive"). Woodworth later pointed out that these equations were similar. There was, however, an important difference: What I had called a "third variable," Tolman called "intervening." For me the observable operations in conditioning, drive, and emotion lay *outside* the organism, but Tolman put them inside, as replacements for, if not simply redefinitions of, mental processes, and that is where they still are in cognitive psychology today. Ironically, the arrangement is much closer than mine to the traditional reflex arc.

Although rate of responding, in the absence of identifiable stimulation, had no parallel in Sherrington or Pavlov, I continued to talk about reflexes. I assumed that some features of the lever were functioning as stimuli which elicited the response of pressing the lever. But I was unhappy about this, and I began to look more closely at the role of the stimulus. I reinforced pressing the lever when a light was on but not when it was off and found that in the dark the behavior underwent extinction. Turning on the light then appeared to elicit the response, but the history behind that effect could not be ignored. The light was not *eliciting* the behavior; it was functioning as a variable affecting its rate, and it derived its power to do so from the differential reinforcement with which it had been correlated.

In the summer of 1934, I submitted two papers for publication in separate efforts to revise the concept of the reflex. In "The Generic Nature of the Concepts of Stimulus and Response" (Skinner, 1935a), I argued that neither a stimulus nor a response could be isolated by surgical or other means and that the best clue to a useful unit was the orderliness of the changes in its strength as a function of "third variables." In "Two Types of Conditioned Reflex and a Pseudo-Type" (Skinner, 1935b), I distinguished between Pavlovian and what I would later call operant conditioning. Quite apart from any internal process, a clear difference could be pointed out in the contingent relations among stimuli, responses, and reinforcement.

I was forced to look more closely at the role of the stimulus when Konorski and Miller (1937) replied to the latter paper by describing an experiment they had performed in the late 1920s which they felt anticipated my own. They had shocked the paw of a dog and given it food when it flexed its leg. Eventually the leg flexed even though the paw was not shocked. I replied that true reflexes seldom have the kinds of consequences which lead to operant conditioning. Shock may be one way of inducing a hungry dog to flex its leg so that the response can be reinforced with food, but it is an unusual one, and an eliciting stimulus can in fact seldom be identified. (As to priority, Thorndike was, of course, ahead of us all by more than a quarter of a century.)

In my reply (Skinner, 1937), I used the term "operant" for the first time and applied "respondent" to the Pavlovian case. It would have been the right time to abandon "reflex," but I was still strongly under the control of Sherrington, Magnus, and Pavlov, and I continued to hold to the term doggedly when I wrote *The Behavior of Organisms* (1938). It took me several years to break free of my own stimulus control in the field of operant behavior. From this point on, however, I was clearly no longer a stimulus–response psychologist.

The lack of an identifiable eliciting stimulus in operant behavior raises a practical problem: We must wait for behavior to appear before we can reinforce it. We thus start with much less control than in respondent conditioning. Moreover, there is a great deal of complex behavior for which we shall certainly wait in vain, since it will never occur spontaneously. In human behavior, there are many ways of "priming" an operant response (that is, evoking it for the first time in order to reinforce it), and one of them is also available in lower organisms: Complex behavior can be "shaped" through a series of successive approximations. To reinforce pressing a lever with great force, for example, we cannot simply wait for a very forceful response, but we can differentially reinforce the more forceful of the responses which do occur, with the result that the mean force increases.

I used a simlar programming of contingencies of reinforcement to shape complex topography in a demonstration (reported in *The Behavior of Organisms*) in which a rat pulled a chain to release a marble, picked up the marble, carried it across the cage, and dropped it into a tube. The terminal behavior was shaped by a succession of slight changes in the apparatus. Later my colleagues and I discovered that we could avoid the time-consuming process of altering the apparatus by constructing programmed contingencies while reinforcing directly by hand.

I soon tried the procedure on a human subject—our 9-month-old daughter. I was holding her on my lap one evening when I turned on a table lamp beside the chair. She looked up and smiled, and I decided to see whether I could use the light as a reinforcer. I waited for a slight movement of her left hand and turned on the light for a moment. Almost immediately, she moved her hand again, and again I reinforced. I began to wait for bigger movements, and within a short time, she was lifting her arm in a wide arc—"to turn on the light."

I was writing *Walden Two* (Skinner, 1948) at the time, and the book is often cited as an essay in behavioral engineering, but I believe it contains no example of the explicit use of a contrived reinforcer. The community functions through positive reinforcement, but the contingencies are in the natural and social environments. They have been carefully designed, but there is no continuing intervention by a reinforcing agent. The only contrived contingencies are Pavlovian: Children are "desensitized" to frustration and other destructive emotions by being exposed to situations of carefully graded intensity.

I began to analyze the contingencies of reinforcement to be found in existing cultures in an undergraduate course at Harvard in the spring of 1949. *Science and Human Behavior* (1953) was written as a text for that course, and in it, I considered practices in such fields as government, religion, economics, education, psycho-therapy, self-control, and social behavior—and all from an operant point of view.

Practical demonstrations soon followed. A graduate student at Indiana, Paul Fuller, had reinforced arm raising in a 20-year-old human organism which had never before "shown any sign of intelligence," and in 1953, I set up a small laboratory to study operant behavior in a few backward patients in a mental hospital. Ogden R. Lindsley took over that project and found that psychotics could be brought under the control of contingencies of reinforcement if the contingencies were clear cut and carefully programmed. Ayllon, Azrin, and many others subsequently used operant conditioning in both management and therapy to improve the lives of psychotic and retarded people.

At the University of Pittsburgh in the spring of 1954, I gave a paper called "The Science of Learning and the Art of Teaching" (Skinner, 1954) and demonstrated a machine designed to teach arithmetic, using an instructional program. A year or two later, I designed the teaching machines which were used in my undergraduate course at Harvard, and my colleague James G. Holland and I wrote the programmed materials eventually published as *The Analysis of Behavior* (1961). The subsequent history of programmed instruction and, on a broader scale, of what has come to be called applied behavior analysis or behavior modification is too well known to need further review here.

Meanwhile, the experimental analysis of operant behavior was expanding rapidly as many new laboratories were set up. Charles B. Ferster and I enjoyed a very profitable 5-year collaboration. Many of our experiments were designed to discover whether the performance characteristic of a schedule could be explained by the conditions prevailing at the moment of reinforcement, including the recent history of responding, but administrative exigencies drew our collaboration to a close before we had reached a sound formulation, and we settled for the publication of a kind of atlas showing characteristic performances under a wide range of schedules (*Schedules of Reinforcement*, Ferster & Skinner, 1957). The subsequent development of the field can be traced in the *Journal of the Experimental Analysis of Behavior,* which was founded in 1958.

Several special themes have threaded their way through this history, and some of them call for comment.

Verbal Behavior

I began to explore the subject in the mid-1930s. The greater part of a manuscript was written with the help of a Guggenheim Fellowship in 1944–1945, from which the William James Lectures at Harvard in 1947 were taken. A sabbatical term in the spring of 1955 enabled me to finish most of a book, which appeared in 1957 as *Verbal Behavior.* It will, I believe, prove to be my most important work. It has not been understood by linguists or psycholinguists, in part because it requires a technical understanding of an operant analysis, but in part because linguists and psycholinguists are primarily concerned with the listener—with what words mean to those who hear them and with what kinds of sentences are judged grammatical or ungrammatical. The very concept of communication—whether of ideas, meanings, or information—emphasizes transmission to a *listener.* So far as I am concerned, however, very little of the behavior of the listener is worth distinguishing as verbal.

In *Verbal Behavior,* verbal operants are classified by reference to the contingencies of reinforcement maintained by a verbal community. The classification is an alternative to the "moods" of the grammarian and the "intentions" of the cognitive psychologist. When these verbal operants came together under multiple causation, the effect may be productive if it contributes, say, to style and wit, but destructive if it leads to distortion and fragmentation. Speakers manipulate their own verbal behavior in order to control or qualify the responses of listeners, and grammar and syntax are "autoclitic" techniques of this sort, as are many other practices in sustained composition. A technology of verbal self-management emerges which is useful both in "discovering what one has to say" and in restricting the range of controlling variables—emphasizing, for example, the kinds of variable (characteristic of logic and science) most likely to lead to effective practical action or the kinds found to be more productive of poetry or fiction.

The Nervous System

My thesis was a sort of declaration of independence from the nervous system, and I restated the position in *The Behavior of Organisms.* It is not, I think, antiphysiological. Various physiological states and processes intervene between the operations performed upon an organism and the resulting behavior. They can be studied with appropriate techniques, and there is no question of their importance. A science of behavior has its own facts, however, and they are too often obscured when they are converted into hasty inferences about the nervous system. I would still say, as I said in *The Behavior of Organisms*, that no physiological fact has told us anything about behavior that we did not already know, though we have been told a great deal about the relations between the two fields. The helpful relation is the other way around: A behavioral analysis defines the task of the physiologist. Operant theory and practice now have an important place in the physiological laboratory.

Psychopharmacology

At Minnesota, W. T. Heron and I studied the effects of a few familiar drugs on operant behavior, and in the early 1950s, Dr. Peter Dews of the Department of Pharmacology at the Harvard Medical School, became associated with my laboratory and co-workers. At about the same time, many of the ethical drug companies set up operant laboratories, some of which contributed to the present armamentarium of behavior-modifying drugs. Operant techniques are now widely used in the field, as well as in the study of drug addiction and related medical problems.

Ethology

Ethologists often assert that their work is neglected by behaviorists, but Watson's first experiments were ethological, and so were mine. The process of operant conditioning itself is part of the genetic equipment of the organism, and I have argued that reinforcers are effective, not because they reduce current drives (a widely held view), but because susceptibilities to reinforcement have had survival value. Species-specific behavior may disrupt operant behavior, but the reverse is also true.

In *Science and Human Behavior*, I pointed out that contingencies of survival in natural selection resembled contingencies of reinforcement in operant conditioning. Both involve selection by consequences, a process which, in a work in progress, I argue to be particularly relevant to the question of whether human behavior can indeed take the future into account. Phylogenic contingencies which could have shaped and maintained, say, imitative behavior resemble the contingencies of reinforcement which shape similar behavior in the individual, but one repertoire does not evolve from the other. An experiment on imprinting has shown how an operant analysis may clarify field observations and correct conclusions drawn from them: The young duckling does not inherit the behavior of *following* its mother or an imprinted

object; it acquires the behavior because of an innate susceptibility of reinforcement from being close.

A Theory of Knowledge

I came to behaviorism, as I have said, because of its bearing on
epistemology, and I have not been disappointed. I am, of course, a radical
rather than a methodological behaviorist. I do not believe that there is a world
of mentation or subjective experience that is being, or must be, ignored. One
feels various states and processes within one's body, but these are collateral
products of one's genetic and personal histories. No creative or initiating function is to be assigned to them. Introspection does not permit us to make any
substantial contribution to physiology, because "we do not have nerves going
to the right places." Cognitive psychologists make the mistake of internalizing
environmental contingencies—as in speaking of the storage of sensory contacts with the environment in the form of memories which are retrieved and
responded to again at some later date. There is a sense in which one *knows* the
world, but one does not *possess* knowledge; one behaves because of one's exposure to a complex and subtle genetic and environmental history. As I
argued in a final chapter in *Verbal Behavior*, thinking is simply behaving and
may be analyzed as such. In *About Behaviorism* (Skinner, 1974), I attempted
to make a comprehensive statement of the behaviorist's position as I
understood it 46 years after I first entered the field.

Designing a Culture

Walden Two was an early essay in the design of a culture. It was fiction,
but I described a supporting science and technology in *Science and Human
Behavior*. I was made aware of a basic issue when *Walden Two* was immediately attacked as a threat to freedom. Its protagonist was said to have
manipulated the lives of people and to have made an unwarranted use of his
own value system. I discussed the issue in a paper called "Freedom and the
Control of Men" in 1955 and in a debate with Carl Rogers in 1956. The control of behavior became especially critical with the rise of an applied
behavioral analysis in the 1960s, and I returned to the issue in *Beyond
Freedom and Dignity* in 1971. Unfortunately, that title led many people to
believe that I was opposed to freedom and dignity. I did, indeed, argue that
people are not in any scientific sense free or responsible for their
achievements, but I was concerned with identifying and promoting the conditions under which they *feel* free and worthy. I had no quarrel with the
historical struggle to free people from aversive control or from punitive
restrictions on the pursuit of happiness, and I proposed that that struggle be

continued by shifting to practices which employed positive reinforcement, but I argued that certain aspects of the traditional concepts stood in the way. For example, to make sure that individuals receive credit for their actions, certain punitive practices have actually been perpetuated. I believe that a scientific formulation of human behavior can help us maximize feelings of freedom and dignity.

There is a further goal: What lies beyond freedom and dignity is the survival of the species, and the issues I first discussed in *Walden Two* have become much more pressing as the threat of a catastrophic future becomes clearer. Unfortunately, we move only slowly toward effective action. A question commonly asked is this: When shall we have the behavioral science we need to solve our problems? I believe that the real question is this: When shall we be able to use the behavioral science we already have? More and better science would be helpful, but far more effective decisions would be made in every field of human affairs if those who made them were aware of what we already know.

References

Bridgman, P. W. *The logic of modern physics*. New York: Macmillan, 1928.

Ferster, C. B., & Skinner, B. F. *Schedules of reinforcement*. New York: Appleton-Century-Crofts, 1957.

Holland, J. G., & Skinner, B. F. *The analysis of behavior*. New York: McGraw-Hill, 1961.

Konorski, J., & Miller, S. On two types of conditioned reflex. *Journal of General Psychology*, 1937, *16*, 264–272.

Mach, E. *The science of mechanics*. Chicago: Open Court, 1893.

Magnus, R. *Körperstellung*. Berlin: Springer, 1924.

Pavlov, I. P. *Conditioned reflexes*. London: Oxford University Press, 1927.

Rogers, C. R., & Skinner, B. F. Some issues concerning the control of human behavior: A symposium. *Science*, 1956, *124*, 1057–1066.

Russell, B. *Philosophy*. New York: W. W. Norton, 1927.

Sherrington, C. S. *Integrative action of the nervous system*. New Haven: Yale University Press, 1906.

Skinner, B. F. On the conditions of elicitation of certain eating reflexes. *Proceedings of the National Academy of Sciences*, 1930, *16*, 433–438.

Skinner, B. F. The concept of the reflex in the description of behavior. Thesis. Harvard University Library, Cambridge, Massachusetts 1931. (Part One reprinted in B. F. Skinner, *Cumulative record* [3rd ed.]. New York: Appleton-Century-Crofts, 1972, along with 47 other papers.)

Skinner, B. F. The generic nature of the concepts of stimulus and response. *Journal of General Psychology*, 1935, *12*, 40–65. (a)

Skinner, B. F. Two types of conditioned reflex and a pseudo-type. *Journal of General Psychology*, 1935, *12*, 66–77. (b)

Skinner, B. F. Two types of conditioned reflex: A reply to Konorski and Miller. *Journal of General Psychology*, 1937, *16*, 272–279.

Skinner, B. F. *The behavior of organisms*. New York: Appleton-Century, 1938.

Skinner, B. F. *Walden Two*. New York: Macmillan, 1948.

Skinner, B. F. *Science and human behavior*. New York: Macmillan, 1953.

Skinner, B. F. The science of learning and the art of teaching. *Harvard Educational Review*, 1954, *24*, 86-97.

Skinner, B. F. Freedom and the control of men. *American Scholar*, Winter 1955-1956, *25*, 47-65.

Skinner, B. F. A case history in scientific method. *American Psychologist*, 1956, *11*, 221-233.

Skinner, B. F. *Verbal behavior*. New York: Appleton-Century-Crofts, 1957.

Skinner, B. F. *Beyond freedom and dignity*. New York: Alfred A. Knopf, 1971.

Skinner, B. F. *About behaviorism*. New York: Alfred A. Knopf, 1974.

Tolman, E. C. *Purposive behavior in animals and men*. New York: Century, 1932.

Tolman, E. C. Philosophy versus immediate experience. *Philosophy of Science*, 1935, *2*, 356-380.

Watson, J. B. *Behaviorism*. New York: W. W. Norton, 1924.

Woodworth, R. S. *Contemporary schools of psychology*. New York: Ronald Press, 1951.

Recommended Readings

Skinner, B. F. *Science and human behavior*. New York: Macmillan, 1953.

Skinner, B. F. *Verbal behavior*. New York: Appleton-Century-Crofts, 1957.

Skinner, B. F. *Beyond freedom and dignity*. New York: Appleton-Century-Crofts, 1971.

Skinner, B. F. *Cumulative record*. Third Edition. New York: Appleton-Century-Crofts, 1972.

Skinner, B. F. *About behaviorism*. New York: Alfred A. Knopf, 1974.

Skinner, B. F. *Particulars of my life*. New York: Alfred A. Knopf, 1976.

Skinner, B. F. *The shaping of a behaviorist*. New York: Alfred A. Knopf, 1979.

WILLARD F. DAY, JR. **11**

The Historical Antecedents
of Contemporary Behaviorism

*The verbal processes of logical and scien-
tific thought deserve and require a more
precise analysis than they have yet received. One of the ultimate accomplishments of a science of verbal
behavior may be an empirical logic, or a
descriptive and analytical scientific
epistemology, the terms and practices of
which will be adapted to human behavior
as a subject matter.*
B. F. SKINNER, 1957, p. 431

CONDITIONED REFLEXES

AN INVESTIGATION OF

THE PHYSIOLOGICAL ACTIVITY

OF THE

CEREBRAL CORTEX

BY

I. P. PAVLOV, FOR. MEM. R.S.

Director of Physiological Laboratories in the Russian Academy of Sciences
and the Institute of Experimental Medicine,
formerly Professor of Physiology at the Military Medical Academy, Petrograd

TRANSLATED AND EDITED

BY

G. V. ANREP, M.D., D.Sc.
Lecturer in Physiology in the University of Cambridge

OXFORD UNIVERSITY PRESS: HUMPHREY MILFORD
1927

PSYCHOLOGY:
THEORETICAL-HISTORICAL PERSPECTIVES

ISBN 0-12-588265-3

My purpose in what follows is to identify, and to discuss briefly, certain perspectives in the history of philosophy and psychology that bear on an understanding of contemporary behaviorism. In this, my interest will not be primarily to trace lines of historical influence. Instead, I will concentrate upon certain epistemological issues that need to be understood if one is to appreciate the dimensions involved in current discussions among contemporary behaviorists. I will also restrict my consideration of contemporary behaviorism largely to a concern with the thought of B. F. Skinner and to issues that need to be correctly assessed in order to place his thought in appropriate intellectual perspective. At the turn of the 1980s, psychologists who regard themselves as behaviorists are likely to look to B. F. Skinner as the standard-bearer of their cause, and although he is now retired from his formal teaching duties, Skinner continues to exercise his preeminent authority among behaviorists from his offices at Harvard University. At the present time, behaviorism is an active and aggressive orientation within professional psychology. In 1978 the Midwestern Association of Behavior Analysis formally changed its name to the Association for Behavior Analysis (ABA) and began publication of *The Behavior Analyst*, the official organ of that association. The annual conventions of the ABA are becoming increasingly important as focal points for the intellectual and social organization among behaviorists, where not only is there an exchange of information in regard to the frontiers of behaviorist thinking and research, but there are also discussions directed toward implementing appropriate social change along behaviorist lines.

Behaviorism has had a highly influential role to play in the history of psychology, particularly in the United States. Consequently, *behaviorism* can mean different things to different people. In the strong sense, in which behaviorism can be identified, say, with the interests of the ABA, contemporary behaviorism manifests itself with three somewhat contrasting faces, each associated with a different professional journal. There is first the "pure science" aspect of contemporary behaviorism, spoken of as *the experimental analysis of behavior*. Research representative of this approach is most commonly published in the *Journal of the Experimental Analysis of Behavior, or JEAB* (pronounced JAY-ab). There is second the area of *applied behavior analysis*, where the effort is made to change human behavior in concrete situations, generally by the judicious application of contingencies of reinforcement. Such clinical application of reinforcement principles is often spoken of as "behavior modification." Research related to this work, as a rule making

FIGURE 11.1 *John B. Watson.*

use of single-subject and baseline methodologies, is characteristic of the material published in the *Journal of Applied Behavior Analysis,* or *JABA* (pronounced JAH-bah). A third area of interest in behaviorism, in the strong sense of the term, is concerned largely with conceptual issues pertaining to behaviorism—that is, with the philosophical underpinnings and ramifications of behaviorist epistemology, with naturalistic approaches to ethical questions and value judgments, and with proposals for methodological innovation in behaviorist research. Work of this kind is published in the journal *Behaviorism.*

In a considerably weaker sense, people may mean by *behaviorism* psychological formulations that retain certain features of the behavior-theoretical emphasis of the 1940s and 1950s, and yet that are more or less self-consciously irrelevant to the systematic interests of Skinnerian behaviorism. Much of the current research on efforts to clarify the distinction between classical and instrumental conditioning, or on the instrumental conditioning of autonomic responses, can be regarded as behavioristic in this sense (e.g., Coleman & Gormezano, 1979; Roberts, 1978). Similarly behavioristic are certain important theories of perception and of the organization of behavior (e.g., Gibson, 1969; Hebb, 1972). On an applied level, numerous behavior-oriented approaches toward psychotherapy exist, and although they are non-Skinnerian in formulation, they may properly be regarded as behavioristic (e.g., Eysenck, 1964; Wolpe, 1969). Also behaviorist in this weaker sense are certain systematic formulations that to one or another degree are derivative from Skinner's thought, such as "cognitive behavior modification" (Meichenbaum, 1974), "social behaviorism" (Staats, 1975), "self-perception theory" (Bem, 1972), and "social learning theory" (Bandura, 1977). On the level of a concern with conceptual issues, certain views within professional philosophy are often spoken of as "philosophical behaviorism." These views have in common an opposition to Cartesian dualism and a belief that all psychological and mental terms are somehow capable of analysis in terms of behavior (see Kaufman, 1967). Current professional work that is behaviorist in this weaker sense will not be discussed in what follows. All such manifestations of the heritage of behaviorism can be said to contrast, in one way or another, with *radical behaviorism*, an expression often used to refer to the integrated conception of behaviorism associated directly with the thought and work of B. F. Skinner.

In a still weaker sense, one may mean by *behaviorism* simply the commitment to objectivity and the use of objective research methods that is widely regarded as central to standard experimental procedures in psychology today (Murphy & Kovach, 1972, p. 251; Wertheimer, 1979, p. 129). When behaviorism is thought of in this way, as simply a name for the commitment to the use of objective procedures in testing psychological hypotheses by controlled experimentation, it is generally spoken of as *methodological behaviorism*. (In a narrower usage, *methodological behaviorism* may refer specifically to the epistemological thesis that knowledge of conscious states, or of mental processes generally, is obtainable only as an inference from publicly observable behavior.) (See Day, 1976a, 1977b; Hebb, 1972.)

Many texts trace developments within behaviorist thinking since the time of Watson, and there is no need to go over that material again here. An in-depth history of behaviorism that is adequate to the needs of issues involved in current discussion does not exist. Texts in the history of psychology rarely move very far away from a perspective toward the field that seems to have become widely accepted during the 1950s. In terms of that perspective, the real history of psychology is taken to close with the victory of methodological behaviorism as the outcome of the period of the competing classical schools of psychology. Material after that time is treated by reviewing the empirical and theoretical developments in the various subdisciplines within professional psychology. For example, in the text by Murphy and Kovach (1972), the work of the major behavior theorists from Thorndike to Skinner is presented in a chapter on the "Psychology of Learning." Undoubtedly the best psychological treatment of the history of behaviorism up to 1950 is that of E. G. Boring (1950). Centrally important developments in the history of philosophy for that same period are discussed in detail by Tatarkiewicz (1973), although from a distinctly continental perspective. Misiak and Sexton (1966) carry their discussion of behaviorism as an integrated perspective up until the middle

1960s, and their treatment reflects a sensitivity to the relevance of philosophical considerations that is uncommon among psychologists.

For the serious student of the history of behaviorism, particularly if there is an interest in the conceptual issues currently under discussion, the best thing to do is to look at the increasing number of scholarly papers that review the history of behaviorism in the light of a specific intellectual question that needs to be addressed. Although contained in a paper unsympathetic to behaviorism, Koch's (1976) distinctions among successive stages in behaviorist thought (from behaviorism, to neobehaviorism, to "deflated neobehaviorism," to neo-neobehaviorism, or "post-deflated behaviorism" or "inflated behaviorism" [pp. 486–487]) are drawn with a deep sensitivity to the range of epistemological concerns now under discussion within the behaviorist community. Work of a more constructive nature is done by Kitchener (1977) in his historical review of what behaviorists have taken themselves to mean by *behavior*. Equally valuable is Boden's (1972) review of the sense in which major figures in the history of behaviorism can be regarded as reductionist in their views. The papers by Powell and Still (1979) and by Tweney (1979) are useful in view of the increasing interest among behaviorists in the functional analysis of verbal behavior. A paper by Herrnstein (1972) is of interest because it focuses on the intellectual climate at Harvard at the time when Skinner was formulating his ideas and points out certain interesting relations between Skinner's thought and that of William McDougall.

At this point, I might clarify my own perspective on the history of behaviorism. Personally, I view behaviorism as a social development that took place within professional psychology during the second decade of this century and that, having become somewhat institutionalized in academic circles, has continued to advocate a certain range of intellectual and professional values since that time. Thus, I do not take behaviorism to be a fixed position that can be given definitive statement. Rather, I regard it as a professional perspective that is continually in evolution and that takes its character at any particular period in history in terms of the contrast it must make with other professional perspectives influential at that time. An important feature of the classical behaviorism of John Watson was the stance it took against the authority of the German tradition in psychology, particularly as this was manifest in the introspectionism of E. B. Titchener. At the present time, behaviorism takes its form in contrast to a number of semiinstitutionalized, vested professional interests in psychology, the most conspicuous of which are cognitive psychology, humanistic psychology, phenomenological psychology, dialectical psychology, and agency psychology. In connection with epistemological and methodological issues, behaviorism contrasts even with standard experimental psychology. The best place to look for an overview of the competing intellectual perspectives that make up the current scene in psychology is *The Nebraska Symposium on Motivation, 1975* (Arnold, 1976).

If I were asked to list the salient features of the behaviorism of the present, I would say: (a) a focal interest in the study of behavior, *as a subject matter in its own right;* (b) antimentalism; (c) a commitment to biological evolutionism; and (d) a commitment to materialistic determinism. (A somewhat different list is found in Murphy & Kovach, 1972, p. 251.) A commitment to biological evolutionism and materialistic determinism is not all that unusual in today's scientific world. However, strong advocacy of the first two of the aforementioned characteristics is very close to the heart of what is interesting about contemporary behaviorism.

Since methodological behaviorism—that is, the view that no matter what it is that interests one about people the only thing one can work with in doing experimental research is objectively observable behavior—is very widely taken for granted in psychology today, the notion of being interested in behavior as a subject matter in its own right may take some getting used to. Today's behaviorist is interested in behavior, not for what can be inferred from it about other underlying psychological processes, but for the orderliness and lawfulness it can be seen to possess by observing it directly. Contemporary behaviorists are interested in cumulative records of the rate of key pecking in pigeons, not so much because key pecking can be viewed as an example of instrumental learning, but because the rate of key pecking in a controlled experimental chamber shows a number of consistent patterns and regularities that vary systematically with environmental manipulation in a fashion that is interesting in its own right. Research in the experimental analysis of behavior is very much of this character, and it is not a trivial thing for Skinner to say that behaviorism is the philosophy of the experimental analysis of behavior (1974, p. 8).

However, it is behaviorism's unrelenting stance against mentalism that continues to be the source of most of the intellectual controversy concerning the position. Basically, for Skinner, mentalism is taking feelings and inner states to be the causes of behavior (see Day, 1976a, pp. 88–92). Thus, it would be mentalistic for someone to explain why he was reading a particular book by saying that he was *interested* in reading that sort of material or that he *wanted* to find out what the book had to say. A contemporary behaviorist would argue that such explanations actually do not explain anything at all (Skinner, 1974, p. 224) and that a satisfactory explanation would involve reference to how contingencies of reinforcement have operated in the past to make reading of the book highly probable for that person.

The root of the controversy concerning behaviorism's opposition to mentalism centers on the issue of *intentionality*, or, roughly, the extent to which it is true that the concepts used in describing and explaining action must *always* involve some reference to motives and purposes, if only implicitly (see Boden, 1972, pp. 307–321, 334–338). What philosophers mean by *intentionality* is a difficult thing to grasp, and considerable space will be devoted to discussion of its implications in the pages that follow. However, the concept of mind can be taken to be essentially coextensive with the range of application of intentional concepts, so that a vigorous antimentalism seems to fly in the face of our capacities to make sense of any behavior at all in an ordinary way. Yet it has been forcefully argued that the central behaviorist concept of *reinforcement* satisfies the criteria for intentionality necessary to mediate an intelligible explanation of behavior (Ringen, 1976). The upshot of the current situation is put nicely in the following remarks:

> Radical behaviorism appears to be the only serious existing alternative to common-sense mentalism, and serious conceptual analysis of its technical terms will contribute to our understanding what the alternatives are. If current assessments of the revolutionary character of operant behaviorism are correct, such a clarification will be no small task. It will require something of at least the magnitude of Galileo's critical discussion of Aristotelian physics and cosmology [Ringen, 1976, p. 250].

Historical Antecedents of Contemporary Behaviorism within Philosophy

ANCIENT PHILOSOPHY

The antecedents of behaviorism within the history of philosophy are best taken to be simply those factors that contributed to the emergence of experimental psychology in general in the last quarter of the nineteenth century. One can then look back on this philosophy, if one wants, and see in the work of certain thinkers points of view that share conspicuous common features with the behaviorism of a particular period. However, concerning the antecedents of experimental psychology in general, Wertheimer's (1979) presentation is representative of the consensus of scholarly opinion: Three major philosophical trends have been involved—(a) the *critical empiricism* movement; (b) the *associationist* tradition; and (c) *scientific materialism*. Boring's (1950) treatment gives a good account of this history from a psychological perspective. The revised one-volume edition of Brett's *History of Psychology* by R. S. Peters (1962) is particularly to be recommended as relevant discussion from a philosophical perspective. Peters regards *atomism*, or analysis into elements, as one of the most central practices brought to behaviorism from its empiricist heritage, an orientation that behaviorism shared with its archenemy introspectionism. "Like the Introspectionists, whom they attacked, [the early behaviorists] believed that the task of the scientist was to analyse the experimental data into atomistic units and then to find some general principles which determined the binding together and regular sequences of these units [Peters, 1962, p. 697]."

Behaviorism, as with all professional psychology, is a product of Western civilization. Western civilization can properly be said to have begun with the culture of ancient Greece, which had become sophisticated by around 600 B.C. Modern scientific perspectives have developed out of the refined intellectual considerations of the philosophy stemming from Greek thought, and the basic dimensions of this philosophy as we can trace it historically were forged by Plato and Artistotle, a substantial portion of whose work has been preserved. In the differences between Plato and Aristotle, we can see the beginning of the deep-seated conflict between idealism and naturalism that can be traced throughout the history of Western philosophy. Plato was the idealist, and Aristotle the naturalist, in the pair. As Webster's puts it simply, idealism is "any theory which affirms the central importance of mind, or the spiritual and ideal, in reality"; naturalism is "a theory that expands conceptions drawn from the natural sciences into a world view and that denies that anything in reality has a supernatural or more than natural significance." Behaviorism, of course, comes down squarely on the side of intellectual naturalism, and in its thoroughgoing antimentalism, it is the most outspoken opponent in psychology today of the pervasive influence of idealistic perspectives in current conceptions of human nature. A good place to see this is in the field of ethics, where Skinner staunchly insists upon a naturalistic conception of statements representative of moral and value judgments (see Day, 1977a; Garrett, 1979; Graham, 1977).

Platonic patterns of thought were important in theologizing the beliefs of the early Christians, and since the civilizing and subsequent development of Europe took place within a largely Christian perspective, an essentially Platonic conception of mind has come to be very deeply embedded in the conceptual equipment with which ordinary people in the West make sense of the world. It is tempting, therefore, to wonder what the intellectual climate in Greece was like before the course of world affairs made the thought of Plato and Aristotle so deeply influential. Actually, there is a reason for contemporary behaviorists to be especially interested in pre-Socratic philosophy. This reason is not for any influence of the pre-Socratics on the development of behaviorist thought. It is rather that in considering the range of pre-Socratic, yet still Greek, formulations one can come to have a glimpse of what sort of differing intellectual stances were possible, even in the West, before the dimensions along which philosophical discussion would henceforth take place became formalized in the work of Plato and Aristotle.

Pre-Socratic philosophy began with the Milesian school (Thales, Anaximander, and Anaximenes), and it was their invention "to seek a universal explanation of the world along rational lines" and to construct an account in terms of "universal and discoverable law" (Guthrie, 1967, p. 442). From the Milesians, we inherit the concept of *nature* as the object of scientific study and of *natural law* as the achievement of scientific investigation. Yet might we not conceive of the aim of controlled experimental research in some other light than as a search for the ultimate laws of nature? The Pythagoreans looked at nature and saw it as something intrinsically harmonious, with a structure best made intelligible by reference to mathematical relations. In contrast, Heraclitus took the image of fire as the most accurate model of the world, where the focus of attention was drawn to anything but harmony: conflict, strife, opposition, constant movement, flux, and change. However, for the great Parmenides, both motion and change were entirely impossible in the real world. A reaction to Parmenides was the atomism of Leucippus and Democritus, who broke reality apart into innumerable particles of matter that, in their turn, could not be broken apart and that were in constant motion in empty space. What is involved here is the matter of believing one can explain something by breaking it into parts or elements and then talking about interrelationships among the parts. The issue is relevant to behaviorism because of the widespread objection to conceptual *reduction*; it is reductionist, for example, to try to conceive of action exclusively in terms of the movements of muscles and glands or to try to describe behavior, which is inherently intentional in nature, in terms of purely physical measurements (see Boden, 1972). For some contemporary behaviorists, all these issues force attention to such questions as: What do we mean by *analysis*? What is actually going on when analysis is productive? Is analysis necessarily the breaking of something into parts that are then said in sum to constitute the original whole? What do we expect of an analysis when we speak of, say, a "functional analysis of behavior" or "the experimental analysis of behavior?"

Of particular interest to the radical behaviorist should be the perspective of Protagoras, who took an entirely different approach from any of the natural scientists. Protagoras made his living by teaching people verbal skills that would be useful to them in practical life. Russell (1945) says of Protagoras that "he is chiefly noted for his doctrine that 'Man is the measure of all things. . . .' This is interpreted as meaning that *each* man is the measure of all things, and that, when men differ, there is no objective truth in virtue of which one is right and the other wrong [p. 77]." It is the opposition to a simple notion of objective truth that is relevant to contemporary behaviorism. Protagoras' approach to truth is similar to that of pragmatism and thus indirectly to the epistemology implicit within Skinner's book *Verbal Behavior* (1957), not to mention his 1945 paper on operationism. For Kerford (1967), at the heart of Protagoras' doctrine lies the notion "that all perceptions are true and the ordinary view is mistaken, according to which, in cases of conflict [between reported perceptions] one person is right and the other person is wrong [p. 505]." Such a rock bottom epistemological reliance on perceptions unique to the situation of the observer is similar to the analogous reliance of radical behaviorists on the unique capacities for discriminative responding brought to bear upon the observation of behavior by each observing scientist (see Bennett, 1978).

In assessing the significance of such a similarity between Protagoras and radical behaviorism, the student should keep in mind that "perception" cannot simply be equated with "discriminative responding." I will have much occasion in what follows, particularly when discussing nineteenth-century thought, to talk about epistemologies focally centered upon "perceptions," "sensations," or other terms taken to refer to states of consciousness. Relations to radical behaviorist thought mediated through the concept of discriminative responding should be drawn carefully and with a sensitivity to the sophistication involved in the radical behaviorist analysis. The simplest analogy would be between what, on the one hand, might be spoken of as "a report of what one perceives" and what, on the other hand, a radical behaviorist would speak of as "a tact of the environment." Catania's presentation of the relevant radical behaviorist analysis in his book *Learning* (1979, Chap. 10) is both up to date and reliable.

However, to return to our concern with the Greeks, if the concept of mind is a contribution of the ancient Greeks, it is possible to consider how mental concepts came to be used to explain behavior even before the development of pre-Socratic philosophy. For Skinner, the conception of mind is a human *invention*, not a discovery (see 1974, p. 104). According to him,

> Plato is said to have discovered the mind, but it would be more accurate to say that he invented one version of it. Long before his time, the Greeks had constructed an elaborate explanatory system, a strange mixture of physiology and metaphysics. A pure mentalism was not long in making its appearance, and it has dominated Western thinking for more than two thousand years [1974, p. 31].

In view of the focal opposition of Skinnerian thought to mentalistic explanation, one might well wonder what form a scientific account of behavior might have taken had the concept of mind never emerged. In any case, the gradual development of the concept of mind out of the earliest Greek thought is the subject of a book by Bruno Snell, *The Discovery of the Mind* (1953; see also Dodds, 1951).

MODERN PHILOSOPHY

Modern philosophy is said to have begun with Descartes, who was just 32 years younger than Galileo, so that the development of modern philosophy is associated with the rise of science following the Renaissance. Although the historical antecedents of experimental psychology within philosophy have been nicely traced in the standard texts, there are a few matters that should be highlighted because of their relevance to a special concern with behaviorism. Descartes is important because he reaffirmed dualism, that is, the notion that mind and body are different in nature, and thus he ensured that the mind–body problem would continue to be a source of concern in efforts to apply the new scientific perspective to interests in human nature. It is significant that while Descartes restricted mentality to humans, he held that our bodies, and all the behavior of animals, functioned as automata, as machines strictly determined by the principles of mechanics. Thus Descartes is regarded as the father of psychologies based upon the reflex arc, and indeed Skinner frequently introduces his discussion of respondent behavior by reference to Descartes (e.g., 1953, p. 46).

One of Descartes's contemporaries who objected to his views was the English materialist Thomas Hobbes, more of interest today for his political than his psychological views. Hobbes advocated a thoroughgoing determinism of behavior, and he constructed a psychology that attempted to be rigorously mechanistic. For this reason, he is sometimes linked with behaviorism (e.g., Robinson, 1976, p. 288). However, in the long run I believe the assessment by Peters (1967) will prove more useful: "Hobbes's psychology was not behavioristic, as it has sometimes been said to be, except insofar as behaviorism has often been associated with a materialistic metaphysical theory or with mechanical modes of explanation. Hobbes stressed the indispensability of introspection in the analysis and explanation of human behavior [p. 37]." It is uninformed to believe that Skinner regards animals and humans as "machines" (see Skinner, 1974, pp. 222 ff). Mechanistic explanation is usually contrasted with purposive explanation, yet for Skinner (1974) "operant behavior is the very field of purpose and intention [p. 55]."

Descartes argued that we are born with the capacity to have the ideas of mind, matter, and God; that is, these ideas are innately given to us and do not have to be acquired by experience. Later in the seventeenth century, the English philosopher John Locke vigorously denied that our minds come equipped with innate ideas of any kind, asserting instead that all our ideas come from experience. Thus was born the tradition of British empiricism (from Locke, through Berkeley and Hume, to Hartley in the eighteenth century), and according to Boring (1950) "it is this tradition [of empiricism and associationism] more than any other which has influenced modern psychology [p. 168-169]." Empiricism and associationism have been conspicuous in the theories of a number of behaviorists who have focused, in their theories, upon conditioning and other associative forms of learning. For example, the psychological perspective of D. O. Hebb (see, e.g., Hebb, 1972), a variety of methodological behaviorism in its insistence that all knowledge of mind is an inference based on the observation of behavior, is still a very useful integration of what we know about human functioning. Yet the connection of Hebb's theory with British empiricism is very direct, for instance in its conception of thinking as the functioning of associations among cell-assemblies having an ultimately sensory origin. On the other hand, Noam Chomsky, perhaps the most outspoken and influential of Skinner's critics, bases his attack broadly on what he takes to be the pernicious influence of empiricism in general on contemporary social science, and he advocates an explicit return to Cartesian dualism, replete with innate cognitive capacities (see, e.g., Chomsky, 1968).

However, I have brought up the matter of empiricism and associationism in part in order to call attention to the eloquent opposition of Thomas Reid to British empiricist theorizing in the same century. Reid was the founder of the Scottish school of "common sense" philosophy, and he objected to the ludicrous artificiality of the speculative theories of mind constructed by the empiricists. His opposition to theory construction was not unlike that of Skinner: "He had a fairly elaborate theory of perception, though 'theory' was not his word for what he regarded as a plain description of the facts of perception with the gaps where knowledge is necessarily unobtainable left unbridged by conjecture [Grave, 1967, p. 120]." Reid objected to a principle in the empiricist theory of ideas that he thought had "the very general, if not universal, sanction of philosophers. This principle asserts that we can know nothing of anything outside the mind except by means of some representative substitute for it within the privacy of the mind [Grave, 1967, p. 119]." This is very similar to Skinner's objection to what he calls the "copy theory" of perception (Skinner, 1974, pp. 80 ff). For Reid, as with Skinner, we perceive the world directly and not as an inference built up from an association of more basic sensations. For radical behaviorists, the meaningfulness of our perceptions is bound up in our learned capacities for discriminative responding. This is important in the experimental analysis of behavior, since the analysis of cumulative response curves depends critically upon the capacities of the researcher to discriminate meaningful changes in the rate of response. Even the specification of operant classes depends fundamentally upon the discriminative capacities of the observer (see Catania, 1979, p. 137). Other interesting relations between contemporary behaviorism and the thought of Thomas Reid are discussed by Robinson (1976, pp. 229–237).

Historical Antecedents of Contemporary Behaviorism within Science

NINETEENTH-CENTURY PSYCHOLOGY IN GERMANY

Much has been written on the founding of experimental psychology, as a discipline separate from experimental physiology, in the establishment of the Psychologisches Institut at the University of Leipzig by Wilhelm Wundt in 1879. The range of depth of treatment in the standard texts is nicely varied to match the various levels of interest of the student. For our purposes here of a concern with behaviorism, it is necessary only to highlight certain features of the opposition, during the late nineteenth century, that existed among intellectuals interested in psychology to the vision concerning the nature of the new discipline that was held and promoted by Wundt.

Murphy and Kovach (1972) characterize the new experimental psychology of Wundt as "a union of the long-established introspective methods with methods borrowed from nineteenth century physiology [p. 161]." I have already mentioned the similarity between the German introspectionist tradition and classical behaviorism in their interest in the atomistic analysis of psychological subject matter into its constituent elements, with subsequent integration accounted for by the formation of associations. This *structuralist* character of the Wundtian introspective experimental work was very different in orientation from the *functionalist* outlook of William James, who found

Wundt's pedantic system-building and authoritarian influence over his students very distasteful. The place to look for an appreciation of the nature of the opposition in Germany to the authority exercised by Wundt over the direction being taken in the developing new field is in the extensive correspondence between James and a German psychologist of the period, Carl Stumpf. This fascinating correspondence is reproduced in the biography of William James by Ralph Barton Perry, a distinguished professor of philosophy at Harvard while Skinner was a graduate student there. In one of these letters, James mentions a remark in a Berlin newspaper that makes reference to the "psychological pope of the old world, Wundt, and the psychological pope of the new world, James" (Perry, 1935, p. 145). Stumpf, for his part, responds in one of his letters to James as follows:

> Wundt leads students and some others to believe that the ever-repeated measurement of reaction-time marks the beginning of an entirely new "experimental psychology" from which one can look back upon the old psychology only with scorn and derision. . . . As though anything important at all could follow from time measurements as such; as though these themselves did not have to be interpreted by inner observation; as though, finally, numbers, rather than clear concepts, were the chief thing [Perry, 1935, p. 67]!

Undoubtedly, the famous Wundt–Stumpf controversy is no longer as famous as it once was; yet it illustrated nicely the nature of the opposition among certain German psychologists to the direction being taken in the "new psychology" under Wundt's leadership. This controversy, which was extremely acrimonious, is described briefly by Boring (1950, p. 365). Yet the heart of the dispute was Wundt's insistence that primary value was to be attached to the results of experimental work, which analyzed experience into its sensory elements, and Stumpf's insistence that more to be valued were reports of experience as directly given in perception, even if these contradicted the results of reductive experimental findings. At any rate, Stumpf's view is representative of the *phenomenological*, as opposed to the reductionistic or atomistic, approach to psychological research that was a vocal force in German psychology in the nineteenth century. Two of Stumpf's students were Köhler and Koffka, both instrumental in the development of Gestalt psychology, who by vigorously insisting that "the whole is greater than the sum of its parts," were outspoken critics of the reductionism of classical behaviorism. The antipathy between phenomenological interests and the Wundtian analytical approach led to the establishment of the Würzburg School, standing in opposition to the Leipzig tradition, which in turn led in the latter part of the century to the contrasting psychologies of act (functional) and content (structural).

I am interested in calling attention here to the opposition of German functional and phenomenological interests to Wundtian structuralism because of the central concern of contemporary behaviorism with the *functional* analysis of behavior. Similarly, at the present time, there is a certain professional interest in relations between contemporary behaviorism and phenomenology (see, e.g., Fourcher, 1979; Giorgi, 1975). Contemporary phenomenological psychology regards itself as historically derived from the thought of E. G. Husserl, who was also a student of Stumpf. Husserl had formerly been a student of Franz Brentano, another opponent of Wundtian psychology, whose relevance to issues in contemporary behaviorism is of the first importance and to whose work we must now turn.

The idea from Brentano that must be understood is that of *intentionality*, a conception that is as difficult for the beginner to grasp as it is important. Let me introduce Brentano by a collection of sentences from two standard historical texts:

> The year 1874 is important in psychology because it is the date of Brentano's book [*Psychology from an Empirical Standpoint*] and of the completed first edition of Wundt's handbook. These two books both represent attempts to formulate the "new" psychology and to formulate it as a science. The contrasts, however, interest us more than the similarities. . . . We have already seen that [Brentano's] "empirical" psychology is not "experimental" psychology. Brentano had respect for the results of experiment, but he believed that all this stressing of experimentation led to an overemphasis upon method and blindness for the main issue. In this view he resembled William James [from Boring, E. G., *A History of Experimental Psychology* (2nd ed.), copyright © 1950 by Appleton-Century-Crofts, New York, pp. 357–359].

> We have given some attention to the revolt against the fundamental tenets of that modern structuralism which had begun with Locke and had been perfected by associationism, by Wundt, and by Titchener. . . . One of the great leaders [of the revolt] was Brentano (1874), who built up a psychology in which the "act" rather than the content of experience was central. . . . Brentano [drew a distinction between] experience as a structure and . . . experience as a way of acting. For example, in the case of sensation, there is a difference between the quality "red" and the *sensing* of "red." The true subject matter of psychology, said Brentano, is not, for example, "red," but the process of "experiencing red," the act which the mind carries out when it, so to speak, "reddens." The experience as we look at a red object is a way of behaving, and this way of behaving is to be distinguished from the quality of redness as such, which is a purely passive thing. For Brentano, the content of mind points to something outside itself ("intentionality") within the framework of the act, and mind can never be reduced to content [from Murphy, G., & Kovach, J. K. *Historical Introduction to Modern Psychology* (3rd ed.), copyright © 1972 by Harcourt Brace Jovanovich, New York, pp. 222–223].

With respect to the difficult concept of intentionality, the important things to concentrate upon in the preceding quotation are the claims that the content of mind points to something outside itself *within the framework of the act* and that mind can never be reduced to content. The relevance of intentionality to behaviorism lies precisely in this: What can be said to be true about *mind* in this claim can be said to be equally true about *behavior*. Thus, these claims can be relevantly translated for behaviorists as follows: "The content of action points to something outside itself within the framework of the act, and behavior can never be reduced to movements capable of adequate description in purely physical terms."

For Brentano, all psychological concepts are inherently different in nature from the concepts used in the natural sciences. For him, all psychological concepts, unlike the concepts of physics, are inherently "intentional," in the sense that they are intelligible only because they point toward an *object* intrinsically relevant to the psychological act. Thus, one cannot simply "think"; one must think *something*. One cannot simply "believe"; one must believe *something*. One cannot simply "see"; one must see *something*. One cannot simply "say"; one must say *something*. A pigeon cannot simply "peck"; it must peck at *something*, like a key. With respect to behavior, the inherent intentionality of action concepts would carry the consequence that we cannot classify separate instances of behavior as the same or different unless *we* make some sort of sense of what the organism is doing: For example, it is opening the door; it is pressing the lever; it is pecking the key; it is jumping into another compartment, etc.

William Baum (1979), a researcher currently active in the experimental analysis of behavior, has commented as follows on the relation between Brentano and Skinner: "It seems to me that Skinner clearly is an act psychologist a la Brentano, even though he disagrees as to the roles of experiment and introspection and as to the importance of the *object*." However, I would argue that even for Skinner the intentional object is always present in the conceptualization of units of behavior as such. This is because what amounts to an intentional object is automatically brought into play in the specification of reinforcing consequences necessary for the identification of any operant class. The intentional object for an operant class consists of its reinforcing consequences. "The essential feature of an operant is the correspondence between a class of responses defined by its consequences and the spectrum of responses generated by these consequences [Catania, 1979, p. 121]."

These matters are of relevance to contemporary behaviorism because behaviorists are frequently criticized for their inclination to think that classes of behavior ("operants," if you will) can be defined strictly in terms of physical measurements. The discussion by Mary Midgley (1978) is representative:

That language works in this way has long been a subject of grievance to behaviorists. Thus, Skinner complains that "the vernacular is clumsy and obese" because it does more than record what is actually before us. "Many of its terms," as he says in *The Behavior of Organisms*, "imply conceptual schemes. . . . The term 'try' must be rejected because it implies the relation of a given sample of behavior to past and future events; but the term 'walk' may be retained because it does not. . . ." But this is sweeping back the sea with a feather duster. "Walk" is no better for this purpose than "try": how could one be said to walk without any implication of earlier and later walking? We see a figure in a certain posture and say "he is walking." This is to class him as someone who *can* walk . . . and it is to place him as going from A to B. . . . Far more drastic efforts would be needed to avoid these implications. One would have to proceed by using, as far as possible, words that apply naturally to physical objects rather than people. Thus, instead of "he walked across the road," one would have to say something like "section of protoplasm, measuring 1.76 meters vertically, emerged at 2:06 P.M. from hole in building at point *x* on plan and moved northward, its extremities landing alternately on concrete substratum, finally entering hole in further building, at point *y* on plan, at 2:09 P.M." The effect of this kind of thing is disappointing, since the listener's only chance of making any sense of it is to grope around for a usable conceptual scheme, which will make it possible finally for him to shout, "Oh I *see*—you mean that a man walked across the road [from Midgley, M. *Beast and Man: The Roots of Human Nature,* copyright © 1978 by Cornell University Press, Ithaca, N.Y., pp. 109–110].

At the present, there is controversy among behaviorists as to the legitimacy of thinking that even in strictly experimental situations behavioral terms can be adequately defined in purely physical language. I have argued that the specification of stimulus and response classes *always* depends on the involvement of the discriminative capacities of the scientist investigating the behavior (Day, 1976b, p. 4; 1977a, p. 225). According to Catania (1979), "the close correspondence between the class of responses with consequences and the class of responses generated by the consequences is the criterion for speaking of an operant class [p. 136]." Yet I would argue that it takes human discriminative responding on the order of tacting to determine what constitutes "close correspondence." Sidman (1979) goes even further in discussing the problems involved in identifying controlling stimuli. "We can, of course, observe and measure a single instance of any stimulus, but we can never know except by inference whether we are actually observing a particular controlling relation between two stimuli or between a stimulus and a response. Unlike individual stimuli and responses, controlling relations are not directly observable [p. 123]."

On the other hand, Schnaitter (1978) regards definition in physical terms as satisfactory for experimental work on lower animals, while acknowledging that "social stimuli (e.g., smiling) require human observation for their identification [p. 4]." Harzem and Miles, however, strongly support efforts to describe behavior in language that is as close to the purely physical as possible, by advocating "a language without extra-episodic words" that would be useful for research purposes only. They give as an example of description without extra-episodic words use of the term *walk*—regarded as in some sense a description in physical terms since walking "could be photographed by a cine camera" (Harzem & Miles, 1978, p. 61). Yet this example fails to meet the aforementioned objections of Midgley, which explicitly call attention to the intentionality of *walk*. I will return shortly to further discussion of the Harzem and Miles proposal. However, the book *Purposive Explanation in Psychology* by Margaret Boden (1972) provides an excellent, and in-depth, discussion of the philosophical difficulties one faces in attempting to describe behavior in purely physical (or physiological) terms. All of this discussion is of considerable importance, since it bears on the problem of how research findings in the experimental analysis of behavior can actually pertain to behaviorist interpretations of complex human functioning in everyday social or environmental situations.

THE INFLUENCE OF THE THEORY OF NATURAL SELECTION AND INTERESTS IN ANIMAL BEHAVIOR

The enormous effect of Darwin's theory of the evolutionary origin of species on all biological science is, of course, well known to everyone. However, the effect of this theory on the development of psychology was also very great. For our present purposes, I need only call attention to certain influences of the theory of natural selection upon the contemporary behaviorist outlook, and to certain specific developments that took place in the course of research on animal behavior, given its impetus to begin with by the widespread intellectual response to Darwin's views. I will take up shortly the relevance to contemporary behaviorism of the views of William James and of the American school of functional psychology, both of which were very strongly influenced by the Darwinian perspective. The background of behaviorism in evolutionary thinking, in the interest in doing research on animal behavior, and in functional psychology is very thoroughly discussed by Boring (1950) in his *History*, and the serious student is well advised to be thoroughly familiar with this material.

It is undoubtedly true that most psychologists today, in light of the broadly humanistic temper of these times, assume that an evolutionary perspective on the origins of the human innate endowment can more or less be taken for granted. In current behavioral biology, theories of the mechanisms involved in natural selection have become very technical, and they form the groundwork upon which complex accounts of the genetic contribution to human social and ethical interaction have been constructed (see Midgley, 1978; Wilson, 1975). However, the perspective of natural selection has also become important, although in a considerably less technical way, in contemporary behaviorism. During the 1970s, Skinner's writing has come to manifest an increasingly explicit reliance upon the concept of natural selection as a general orientation within which his systematic views can be conveniently integrated. In *About Behaviorism* (1974), Skinner conceptualizes behaviorism broadly as a special science concerned only with the effects of the environment upon the adaptive capabilities of the organism and its species:

> The relation between organism and environment is, in short, a separate scientific field. It can conveniently be divided into two parts:
>
> 1. The interaction with the environment during the evolution of the species produced the so-called genetic endowment, the behavioral aspects of which are studied by ethologists.

2. The environment to which a person is exposed during his lifetime changes that endowment, with the result that the person behaves in new ways on new occasions. What happens during the lifetime of an individual is much more accessible than what has happened during the evolution of the species. . . .

Historically, theories of the inner determination of behavior have dominated the field, and their abandonment means a sweeping change. A new and unfamiliar conception emerges of man as a species and as an individual member of a species. Many questions concerning ethical, religious, governmental, economic, and other interrelations among people are raised. Cultural practices are features of the environments in which people live and must be analyzed accordingly, and decisions which need to be made in designing new practices involve so-called value judgments. The resolution of these problems may have a bearing on the future of the species [from Skinner, B. F. *About Behaviorism* (College ed.), copyright © 1974 by Alfred A. Knopf, New York, pp. xii–xiii].

Skinner's conceptualization in *About Behaviorism* involves two kinds of natural contingencies: There are not only the familiar *contingencies of reinforcement*, there are also *contingencies of survival*. In his discussion of contingencies of survival, Skinner calls attention to how it is that old-fashioned notions of cause and effect relations are no longer adequate to the needs of a science of behavior:

Darwin simply discovered the role of selection, a kind of causality very different from the push–pull mechanisms of science up to that time. The origin of a fantastic variety of living things could be explained by the contribution which novel features, possibly of random provenance, made to survival. There was little or nothing in physical or biological science that foreshadowed selection as a causal principle.

Contingencies of survival are often described with terms which suggest a different kind of causal action. "Selection pressure" is an example. Selection is a special kind of causality which is not properly represented as a force or pressure [pp. 36–37].

Skinner makes use of the concept of natural selection in even more difficult patterns of reasoning in considering the problem of how values are to be assessed in designing a culture. An inability to be comfortable with thinking from an evolutionary perspective has led people to misinterpret Skinner as advocating simple *survival* as the ultimate social value (e.g., Matson, 1964, p. 75). Yet for Skinner, two kinds of evolutionary processes are at work in human affairs—cultural, as well as biological, evolution.

The important thing to recognize is that survival as a value in Skinner's analysis is not derived from the reinforcement-based values of individual persons, even though individual persons may be genuinely and seriously interested in social planning and cultural design. The two evolutionary processes differ in their unit of analysis: at the biological level the unit is behavioral; at the cultural level the unit is "social practices" [Day, 1977a, p. 17].

I turn now to certain historical matters pertaining to the development of research on animal behavior. Darwin's *Origin of Species* was published in

1859. However, it was his books *The Descent of Man* (1871) and *Expression of the Emotions in Man and Animals* (1872) that were important in stimulating psychological research on the behavior of animals, since in them he argued for the continuity of mental life between men and animals. In 1882, Darwin's friend George Romanes published *Animal Intelligence,* in which the expression "comparative psychology" was used for the first time. In this book, "Romanes reinforced the argument for continuity [of mental life between man and animals], bringing forth carefully selected anecdotal material which exhibited instances of animal intelligence and purposive action [Boring, 1950, pp. 622–623]." The interest in "indications of purposive action" is significant, since the criteria for purposiveness in behavior are generally taken to be closely connected with the criteria for consciousness in animals (see, e.g., Hebb, 1972, pp. 250 ff). The burgeoning interest in animal research that was stimulated by Romanes's book was often explicitly associated with an effort to determine whether or not consciousness could be legitimately attributed to animals at one or another level along the phylogenetic scale. Boring's discussion of this interest (1950, pp. 623 ff) is particularly interesting.

Romanes's work was severely criticized on methodological grounds by Lloyd Morgan (1894), in a book that was to be exceptionally influential in shaping professional values associated with animal research. Morgan objected not only to the "anecdotal" nature of the evidence reported by Romanes, but also to his flair for "anthropomorphizing," that is, for interpreting animal behavior by reading into it mental states that are commonly called upon to explain human functioning. There are few psychologists today who are not familiar with "Lloyd Morgan's Canon," which states that "in reasoning from behavior to consciousness, the investigator must always choose the simplest kind of mind that is adequate as an explanation of the observed facts [Boring, 1950, p. 623]." However, Morgan's own work, while hardly "anecdotal," was not what one would want to call experimental.

All [Morgan's] books contain many accounts of the author's own experiments upon animals, experiments which lie midway between the observation of the naturalist in the field and observation by way of artificial but controlled situations in the laboratory. They consist in the careful observation of animal behavior when the usual environment has been modified so as to create special situations. Thus, to say that experimental animal psychology began with Thorndike's use of puzzle-boxes in 1898 is to limit the meaning of the word *experimental* to the formal laboratory with apparatus [Boring, 1950, p. 475].

Of course, in its commitment to the experimental analysis of behavior, contemporary behaviorism is outspoken in its advocacy of research in "the formal laboratory with apparatus." Yet I have already mentioned how difficulties centering around the inherent intentionality of behavioral concepts, even at the purely descriptive level, arise in seeing precisely in what ways findings in the experimental analysis of behavior become connected with the behavioral interpretation of complex human behavior in everyday, real-life situations. Consequently, there are, at the present, pressures within radical behaviorism to develop new and innovative research strategies capable of assessing variables controlling behavior in nonlaboratory situations. There is a growing interest in relating a behavioral analysis to techniques of semina-turalistic observation and ethological and phenomenological research. Often the focus of interest in this work is on refining techniques for the analysis of verbal behavior. The recent work of Lahren (1978) and McCorkle (1978) is representative of this interest.

Thorndike's laboratory research on animal behavior was published in his monograph *Animal Intelligence* (1898), a work which bears the same title as Romanes's book. However, the important thing to see about Thorndike's research is the question he was addressing in the work. Whereas earlier work had more or less taken the continuity of mental life between man and animals for granted, Thorndike raised the question of whether it was necessary to bring in the concept of mental life at all, in accounting for the learning and problem solving of cats and dogs. In concluding that his experimental subjects learned "by trial and error, and accidental success," and in formulating his famous Law of Effect, Thorndike reasoned that it was not necessary to call upon consciousness, and conscious thought processes, to explain performance of this kind. Thus, the stage was set for Watson to take the stance, 15 years later, that psychology could do its job very nicely without taking con-sciousness, or other mental states and processes, into account at all.

Thorndike's Law of Effect and Skinner's notion of operant reinforcement are often taken to amount to much the same thing (e.g., Hebb, 1972, p. 25; Hilgard, 1956). Similarly, the concept of reinforcement is often taken to mean essentially the same thing as "reward." These practices are unfortunate. The historical linkage between the work upon which Thorndike's Law of Effect was based and Skinner's development of the concept of operant reinforcement appears to be quite indirect. Skinner reviews the major intellectual controls over the development of his professional behavior in his own contribution to the present volume, and these direct antecedents are discussed by him in more detail in *A Case History in Scientific Method* (1956), in the editorial introduc-tions to his papers reprinted in the first edition of *Cumulative Record* (1959), and in his contribution to *A History of Psychology in Autobiography* (1967). In *The Behavior of Organisms* (1938), Skinner appears to have regarded Thorndike's work as a contribution to "the traditional field of learning [p. 111]" and his own work as an attempt to establish a systematic approach to the analysis of behavior, where the analysis of operant behavior happened to help explain what Thorndike had found (p. 111). What Thorndike meant in the Law of Effect was that the cat's success in getting out of the puzzle box "stamped in" the *learning* of a particular stimulus–response connection; he went on to argue that what was important about the success was its pleasant or satisfying nature. The notion of a pleasant, satisfying success is close to what we mean by *reward*. Yet in 1953, Skinner discusses the Law of Effect in terms of the more appropriate concept of *consequence*, and *consequence* remains today the ordinary language concept most appropriately used in setting the stage for the technical concept of *reinforcer*. Incidentally, in a text on learning from a perspective of the experimental analysis of behavior, Catania (1979) argues that the effect of reinforcing consequences upon behavior is not to cause "learning": "Reinforcement, then, does not produce learning; it produces behavior. . . . The consequences of responding are critical to our understanding of learning *not because learning follows from them but because they are what is learned* [p. 86]."

If the direct historical influences on Skinner's work have little to do with Thorndike, they have much to do with another line of research that began around the time of Lloyd Morgan. According to Boring (1950), Morgan took a "psychological" approach to animal research in view of his concern with their mental capacities, and he was followed in this by H. S. Jennings, who took a functional outlook toward the nature of consciousness and suspected the possibility of consciousness even in protozoa. (In Baum's opinion, "It is easy to misunderstand Jennings by reading Boring, because Boring presents his views simplistically. Jennings took a view almost operational by today's standards. He considered consciousness in an organism worthy of consideration if it was *useful* in understanding its behavior [1979].")

On the other hand, a strictly "mechanistic," as opposed to "psychological," approach to accounting for the behavior of animals began to influence American psychology at the turn of the century through the work of Jacques Loeb. Loeb's work on lower organisms was extended to the behavior of mammals by W. J. Crozier, and it was Crozier's perspective that, in part, gave to Skinner's work an orientation that is strikingly different from most other manifestations of behaviorism in psychology.

> Crozier, Jacques Loeb's disciple at Harvard, arrived in 1925 to become chairman of the short-lived Department of Physiology. For about a decade, Crozier and his students showered the scientific community with paper after paper (mostly in the *Journal of General Physiology*, which Loeb had co-founded) on the simple "tropisms" of meal-worms, tent caterpillars, water scorpions, slugs, and other invertebrates. More complex response systems, in rats and mice, were depicted as the interaction of multiple sources of stimulation, but still conforming to the Loebian conception of mechanistic determination. Crozier seemed to be fleshing out Loeb's stark conceptual framework with quantitative, empirical fact. He contributed more than data, however, for his version of Loebian biology was more distinctive. In Crozier's hands, it became especially *mathematical* in the sense of functional relations between the physical measures of stimulus and response. . . , concerned more with *behavior as behavior* rather than as a manifestation of something else (such as a nervous system). . . , and *experimental* rather than statistical. . . . The line of behaviorist descent as regards actual research passes more conspicuously from Loeb *via Crozier* to Skinner, than *via Watson* [from Herrnstein, R. J., Nature as nurture: Behaviorism and the instinct doctrine. *Behaviorism*, 1972, *1*, 45–46].

The characteristics of Crozier's approach as highlighted by Herrnstein in the preceding quotation with italicized expressions (*mathematical, behavior as behavior,* and *experimental*) are the salient features of Skinner's *The Behavior of Organisms* (1938), as an effort to systematize, or to integrate within a single coherent system, the experimental analysis of behavior. In a nicely written overview of the experimental analysis of behavior and its origins, Kazdin (1978) has pointed up the close connection between the orientation of Loeb and Crozier and the development of Skinnerian research strategies.

Crozier's influence on Skinner seems particularly noteworthy. Crozier, who had been a student of Loeb, extended the research of his mentor by studying the responses of diverse animals to various stimuli such as light. General and specific features of Crozier's approach to research bear similarity to Skinner's position. Initially, and perhaps most importantly, Crozier advocated study of the organism as a whole. This focus derived directly from Loeb, who had published a book entitled *The Organism as a Whole* (1916). Skinner also studied the behavior of the organism as a whole and its relationship with the environment. He was interested in behavior in its own right rather than the processes of the nervous system to which it might be related.

Another similarity between Crozier and Skinner was their general attitude toward theory. Crozier tended to eschew theory in favor of a strong base of empirically established relationships between independent and dependent variables after which interpretation of behavior was possible (Crozier and Hoagland, 1934). Skinner, too, has emphasized the priority of establishing empirical relationships rather than generating theory.

Features of Crozier's research methodology also were apparent in Skinner's subsequent work. Crozier advocated single-organism research. Experimental control could be demonstrated by obtaining measures of the individual organism as a number of values or parametric variations of the experimental condition were invoked. He believed that the variability of an organism's response at any time was a function of external conditions and changes in that organism. He viewed variation as lawful rather than random. The task of research was to determine the factors of which such variation was a function. Crozier advocated looking at experimental effects over time in light of intrasubject variability of behavior rather than merely comparing means across conditions or characterizing the variability statistically. Skinner's research has amplified the importance of studying the individual organism, its variations in behavior, and the conditions of which the variation is a function [from Kazdin, A. E., *History of Behavior Modification,* copyright © 1978 by University Park Press, Baltimore, pp. 92–93].

Skinner (1938) succinctly contrasts his own approach with that of Crozier in *The Behavior of Organisms:*

A system of behavior based upon the concept of the tropism seems to satisfy the requirements of a system in [my own] sense on the point of generality. In the extensive experiments of Crozier and Pincus . . . variables have been isolated which are capable of being treated quantitatively and which behave in lawful ways. . . . But any system which takes orientation or oriented progression as the only property of behavior to be accounted for and which regards a stimulus only as a field of force is seriously circumscribed. In the case of the higher organisms at least it is presumably possible to set up an independent descriptive system based upon the concept of the reflex that will yield an equally satisfactory result. Where behavior is largely orientation and where stimuli are fields of force, we may prefer the concept of the tropism on grounds of simplicity while at the same time rejecting it in the case of more complicated organisms [from Skinner, B. F., *The Behavior of Organisims*, copyright © 1938 by Appleton-Century-Crofts, New York, p. 435].

WILLIAM JAMES AND ERNST MACH

I have already mentioned that in his own lifetime William James could be regarded as the pope of American psychology, in contrast to the papacy of Wundt in European psychology. However, as admired as James was, and as influential as he is taken to have been in the formulation of American psychology, at the present time an appreciation of James is most commonly tempered by a reminder that he was not first and foremost an experimentalist and that his antipathy to the elementalist structuralism of Wundt was also associated with a distrust on his part of too narrow a confidence in simple experimentation itself. For James, psychology could not yet be regarded as a science. In 1950, well after behaviorism had played its card and appeared to have won the game, Boring could still say, "There can be no doubt that James is America's foremost psychologist, in spite of the fact that he was but a half-hearted experimentalist influencing a predominantly experimental trend [pp. 509–510]." In 1972 it could be written, "For a long time it seemed silly to remark that James was America's greatest psychologist; for in the judgment of scholars and of laymen alike, any second to him was a poor second. But it must be remembered that even at the height of his powers he rejected the trends that were most popular in American psychology [Murphy & Kovach, 1972, p. 206]." In 1976 Robinson would write, "In the first two decades of the present century, the most influential figures in American psychology were William James and E. B. Titchener [p. 352]." Then Robinson goes on to deliver a searing attack on the narrow commitment of current psychology to experimentalism per se.

Now, it is unmistakable to anyone surveying the contemporary psychological scene that there is hardly a vestige of the program envisaged by Titchener and James. . . . The contemporary psychologist, if only insensibly, has made a *metaphysical* commitment to a method and has, per force, eliminated from the domain of significant issues those that cannot be embraced by that method.

The method itself is not simply some variant of the experimental method. Titchener and James both subscribed to that. The method referred to here is broader than a set of actions or procedures. It includes a way of thinking about problems and a way of talking about them. The method needs a label and the one most commonly applied to it is *empirical*. . . . *Empirical*, if the contemporary usage is to be captured, must also suggest measurement, practicality, impersonality, ethical neutrality, (ironic) "antimetaphysical*ness*." Contemporary journals, whether devoted to neuropsychology, clinical practice, animal learning, or family counseling, strive to reflect these "empirical" features [from Robinson, D. N., *An Intellectual History of Psychology*, copyright © 1976 by Macmillan, New York, p. 353].

The character of James's thought, both in its psychological and philosophical aspects, was very much influenced by evolutionary theory. For James,

> The mind is a tactical power which reveals itself in the struggle with its environment. The only kind of world in which minds can conceivably develop and be found is one in which success is neither automatic nor impossible. . . . The notion of mind as an instrument within the general economy of purpose and resistance to purpose, a notion which has justly been called "biological" and "Darwinian," is simply an ungeneralized expression of pragmatism [Earle, 1967, p. 243].

There is generally taken to be a direct line of descent from James to the formulation of functionalism, as one of the classical schools of American psychology. "The conception of function was explicit in James' psychology. . . . Mind has a use and it can be observed in use. Thus we find in James what came later to be the central tenet of American functionalism [Boring, 1950, p. 515]."

However, James was also concretely influential on the thinking of certain individuals who are important in the history of behaviorism. "Both John Dewey and William McDougall admitted that the early development of their own thinking could be attributed largely to having read James's *Principles* [Misiak & Sexton, 1966, p. 135]." E. B. Holt, the great behaviorist at the time of Watson, was so interested in James's approach that for a time he was thought to be planning a revision of the *Principles* (Boring, 1950, p. 646). In his behaviorism, Holt was articulate as a philosopher, and around 1910 he was a dominant figure in propounding a "new realist" philosophy that was related to the metaphysical views of William James (see Robischon, 1967). Holt's perspective is generally thought to be the immediate precursor of the systematizing work of E. C. Tolman, one of the major contenders among the grand behavior theorists of the 1940s. "It is clear that Tolman was carrying on from Holt. He was also influenced by Gestalt psychology, for he was writing about *molar* behavior, the total action of the whole organism, and not about the 'molecular behavior' of reflexology [Boring, 1950, p. 720]." Yet Gestalt psychology, in turn, is thought to have been anticipated by James (Boring, 1950, p. 513). McDougall, Holt, and Tolman are all significant persons in the history of behaviorism; yet their work constitutes a *purposive behaviorism*, in contrast to the more elementalistic, reflexological, and reductive behaviorism that was the legacy of Watson. However, it is the purposive, and not the atomistic, branch of behaviorism that is relevant to contemporary behaviorism. In an important paper, Herrnstein (1972) has called attention to conceptual interdependencies between the work of Skinner and that of McDougall: "A comparison of McDougall's theory of instinct and Skinner's reinforcement theory—representing nature and nurture—shows remarkable, and largely unrecognized, similarities between the contending sides in the nature–nurture dispute as applied to the analysis of behavior [p. 24]." In an equally insightful work, W. S. Verplanck (1954), who prepared the in-depth critique of Skinner's system for the Dartmouth Conference (to be discussed later), has had the following to say:

> That Skinner's concepts have often been misunderstood and misinterpreted probably stems from his choice of a set of terms. Implicative and associational values turn up frequently in the selection of a theorist's terminology. To the "Tolmanite," conditioned responses are *mere*, or *mechanical*. To the "Hullian," *expectancy* and *cognition* carry the suggestion of the capricious intervention of entities extraneous to behavior. . . . In his choice of terminology, Skinner has assured that his works and those of his fellows will be read easily by the followers of Hull and Guthrie and only with emotion, if not with difficulty, by those who have selected the organismic-field-Gestalt-force family of words to work with. Skinner's conditioned responses seem to many readers just as *mere* as those of Pavlov or Hull, with the extraordinary result that he has been classed with Hull rather than with Tolman, with Guthrie rather than with Lewin, in his general position [from Verplanck, W. F., in Estes *et al., Modern Learning Theory*, copyright © 1954 by Appleton-Century-Crofts, New York, p. 307].

The metaphysical views of James that were of particular interest to the behaviorist E. B. Holt were similar in important ways to the conception of the nature of science that was developed by the physicist Ernst Mach, who was James's contemporary. An understanding of Mach is enormously important for an understanding of Skinner. According to Baum (1979):

> There are several either mysterious or controversial aspects to Skinner's thinking that become understandable on reading Mach: his method of extension in the absence of data (e.g., the entire book, *Verbal Behavior*), his indifference to the circularity of the law of effect, his approach to selection of units for measurement, his intolerance of mentalism, his linking of explanation to description of behavior and to the study of behavior as a subject matter in its own right, and his so-called "antitheoretical" position, which actually disallows only a certain type of theory and leaves plenty of room for theory that grows from observation. Skinner follows Mach's lead: to describe is to explain, and the real value of scientific knowledge lies in the power it gives to describe. [Skinner] has told me himself . . . how profoundly he was influenced by reading Mach's *Science of Mechanics*.

Mach was a positivist, yet his positivism differed significantly from the logical positivism of the Vienna Circle that was so influential in the formation of methodological behaviorism in the 1930s (see Boring, 1950, pp. 655ff).

> The characteristic theses of positivism are that science is the only valid knowledge and facts the only possible objects of knowledge; that philosophy does not possess a method different from science; and that the task of philosophy is to find the general principles common to all the sciences and to use these principles as guides to human conduct and as the basis of social organization. Positivism, consequently, denies the existence or intelligibility of forces or substances that go beyond facts and the laws ascertained by science. It opposes any kind of metaphysics and, in general, any procedure of investigation that is not reducible to scientific method [Abbagnano, 1967, p. 414].

At first glance, it would seem that James and Mach must surely be at opposite poles from one another. Yet the point of contact comes in their mutual interest in the analysis and description of experience. In both James and Mach, there is an emphasis on the importance of description, yet James goes far beyond Mach in what he takes to be involved in describing facts as they are directly given in the experience of an observer.

> If the *Principles* is to be regarded as primarily a descriptive work, one must be clear about what is involved in description as James understands it. He was convinced that pure description in the manner of phenomenology is impossible. Description cannot be other than conceptual; concepts, in turn, are tools of classification that have inexpugnable conventional and theoretical elements. Concepts do not passively mirror; they select according to human interests and purposes. Assumptions, James maintained, have a way of establishing themselves "in our very descriptions of the phenomenal facts. . . ." James's frequent use of the expression "part of experience" was not meant to suggest that experience has an atomistic constitution. Indeed, James constantly argued against the "pulverization" of experience in British empiricism. . . . There are therefore many levels of fact, and words like "part," "whole," "unity," "concrete," "abstract," "particular," and "individual" do not qualify any reality simply or always. These words are definable only within purposive contexts [from Earle, W. J., in P. Edwards (Ed.) *The Encyclopedia of Philosophy*, copyright © 1967 by Macmillan, New York, pp. 242–248].

However, Mach's views on the analysis of experience were *phenomenalistic*, in the sense that he felt that the observable facts of science, and hence ultimately all its laws, were capable of reduction to sense-perceptions, by an analysis of the observer's experiences. "Mach identified experience with sensations, making sensations into the observational data of both physics and psychology [Boring, 1950, p. 442]." Since the difficulties people sometimes have in understanding Skinner's work often stem from its methodological connection with Mach's views, it is important to understand how different Mach's phenomenalism was from the "common sense" approach to science that is generally taken in psychology. If the methodology of Skinner's radical behaviorism has been strongly influenced by Mach's phenomenalism, then the outlook of methodological behaviorism is essentially that described by Blackmore (1972) as *causal realism*.

> Let me clarify three different epistemological positions that must be understood in order to obtain perspective in understanding the development of Mach's philosophical ideas. Most people normally behave as *naive realists*, describing nature in presentationalist terms (apparent physical objects are physical objects) and explaining in representationalist terms (innate forces are causes). Most people's best or most consistent understanding, or what I will call "common sense" . . . , is *causal realism* which is representationalist in both description and explanation (conscious experience provides evidence and allows us to infer the characteristics of physical objects and causes that lie entirely outside conscious experience). *Phenomenalism* is presentationalist in both description and explanation. Like causal realism it identifies *apparent* physical objects with sensations, and like naive realism it is presenta-

tionalist in describing nature, but unlike both naive and causal realism it rejects causes as forces or agents in favor of explanation in terms of "laws," "mathematical functions," or "regular sequences of events" [from, Blackmore, J. T., *Ernst Mach*, copyright © 1972 by University of California Press, Berkeley, pp. 10–11].

Blackmore's book *Ernst Mach* (1972) is the thing to look at to develop an understanding of Machian philosophy of science and Mach's relation to the philosophical climate of the turn of the twentieth century out of which behaviorism emerged. Relevant to our interests here are the remarks it contains about the relationship between Mach and James. James visited Mach in Prague in the fall of 1882.

Mach and James corresponded and remained friends for the next twenty-eight years until the latter's death. Mach even dedicated a book to him. Nor were Mach's ideas without influence on William James's subsequent philosophy. . . . It seems very possible that Mach's phenomenalism and theory of "biological needs" encouraged James to develop his theory of experience and, with Peirce, helped lead him to his notorious special philosophy, Pragmatism. . . . Mach's theory of "biological needs" was compatible with James's Pragmatism, and, as we have already mentioned, probably helped develop it, but again, as with phenomenalism, James exploded his views so far beyond Mach, that eventually the resemblance seemed feeble to the point of virtual disappearance. In spite of the fact that Mach justified scientific investigation and his philosophy of science in terms of how well they satisfied human "biological needs," in practice, he tended to ignore this ultimate goal almost entirely and concentrated on the "internal" goal of science, to describe the appearance in the simplest way possible, as if that were an end in itself. James, on the other hand, took "biological needs" seriously and insisted that there were other ways to satisfy them than by following a narrow scientific methodology [from Blackmore, J. T., *Ernst Mach*, copyright © 1972 by University of California Press, Berkeley, pp. 77, 127–128].

It is well to keep in mind that *The Science of Mechanics*, Mach's history of that branch of physics, must be regarded as the work by Mach that most influenced Skinner. However, it is *The Analysis of Sensations* (in the English translation of 1914) that is quoted by Skinner in *The Behavior of Organisms* (1938, p. 432), and it is in this book that Mach discusses most fully his phenomenalism, or "sensationalism." Mach developed his notions concerning the dependence of sensations on "biological needs" out of an interest in making a bridge between his early "strong suspicion. . . that the world consisted only of sensations [Blackmore, 1972, p. 26]" and Darwin's evolutionary ideas, and out of a fear that in reducing science to relations among sense-perceptions he was coming perilously close to solipsism. Similarly, there is a tendency toward what might mistakenly be regarded as "subjectivism" in Skinner's work, a tendency that is not all that successfully concealed by the "superscientistic" stance with which the experimental analysis of behavior at times presents itself. The approach to experimentation that is presumably most Skinnerian is that displayed in his two books that report experimental findings, *The Behavior of Organisms* (1938) and *Schedules of Reinforcement* (Ferster & Skinner, 1957). However, a striking feature of the research reported in these books is the critical reliance that is made in the analysis of the data upon simple visual inspection of discriminable patterns in cumulative response records. At the heart of the method of analysis of the data is the very Machian reliance upon relations among various "sense-perceptions" of the experimenter in looking at the data.

> In choosing rate of responding as a basic datum and in recording this conveniently in a cumulative curve, we make important temporal aspects of behavior *visible*. Once this has happened, our scientific practice is reduced to simple looking. A new world is opened to inspection. We use such curves as we use a microscope, X-ray camera, or telescope. This is well exemplified by recent extensions of the method. . . . It is no longer necessary to describe avoidance and escape by appeal to "principles," for we may *watch* the behavior develop when we have arranged the proper contingencies of reinforcement, as we later watch it change as these contingencies are changed. . . . In these experiments you see the effect of a treatment as directly as you see the constriction of a capillary under the microscope [Skinner, 1956, pp. 229-230].

Such a fundamental reliance upon the discriminative capacities of the researcher has tended to become attenuated with the passage of time in the development of the experimental analysis of behavior as a special field of research. Both Skinner (1976) and Ferster (1978) have bemoaned the decreasing professional interest in the direct observation of cumulative records, and Poling (1979) presents a graph of the number of figures showing cumulative records in the *Journal of the Experimental Analysis of Behavior* as a function of year of publication. His conclusion: "The data in Figure 1 seem to underscore a question raised by Ferster (1978) and others: are operant conditioners getting bored with behavior? Time alone will tell, but it is apparent that a collective fondness for a direct and graphic depictor of ongoing behavior—the cumulative record—has faded [p. 126]." Even though there are radical behaviorists who feel that the experimental analysis of behavior is becoming increasingly indistinguishable from methodological behaviorist investigations of the psychology of learning (see Day, 1977b), many articles currently published in JEAB still show a Machian reliance on perceptual and other judgments of the experimenter that function to determine the course of the research as it is actually carried out. At times, for instance, an experimenter will observe behavior patterns on the part of his experimental animals that will lead him to adjust the course of the research in midstream. Research is frequently reported that bears no relationship to hypotheses conceived and specified in advance, so that they might well strike a methodological behaviorist as experiments that have been inadequately designed. Baum (1979) has responded to this situation as follows:

> One need not rely on cumulative records to satisfy Mach's requirements. Scientists work with data in many different forms. Cumulative records are only one form. The crucial issue is not the form, but how the scientist treats the data. I myself use

cumulative records little, but I work with my measures in a way that I think Mach would find agreeable. I make many graphs, always looking for the visual display that makes sense.

On the other hand, there are now researchers, operating under the banner of radical behaviorism, who advocate research procedures focally centered upon displaying the way in which the discriminative capacities of the researcher are brought to bear upon the simple observation of behavior, even at the expense of the controlled manipulation of experimental variables (see, e.g., McCorkle, 1978). The aim of such research is to facilitate directly changes in the researcher's own verbal and nonverbal behavior, by bringing the researcher's behavior self-consciously under the control of interesting behavioral phenomena as they are directly observed. Reports of such research are likely to contain a record of changes in the researcher's tacting behavior as they actually develop. Research of this kind is likely to be regarded by methodological behaviorists as distastefully "subjective" in character. However, the "objective–subjective distinction" itself does not fit comfortably within the verbal practices of radical behaviorist epistemology. The concentration on "objectivity" as a professional value became important for methodological behaviorism, and hence for psychology in general, as a consequence of the climate of discussion at the time of Watson's attacks upon introspectionism, as we shall see.

For Mach, the focal point of interest in science is direct *description*. "He held that it is the aim of science to give concise, economical descriptions of phenomena. He was also prepared to say that these descriptions constitute scientific explanation [Alexander, 1967, p. 118]." Bradley (1971) calls attention to two representative quotations from Mach's *Popular Scientific Lectures:*

> What is called a *theory* or a *theoretical idea,* falls under the category of what is here termed indirect description. . . . Does description accomplish all that the inquirer can ask? In my opinion, it does.
>
> Again, to save the labor of instruction and of acquisition, concise, *abridged description* is sought. *This is really all that natural laws are* [pp. 207, 208].

It was also characteristic of Mach to take a historical approach to the origin of scientific concepts, and he felt it was helpful in eliminating the "metaphysical" component of scientific theories to trace the origins of scientific concepts back to their sources in man's primitive experiences in adapting to his environment (Blackmore, 1972, p. 33). For Mach, "The origins of science lie in our experiences in the manual arts and in our need to communicate these experiences. . . . Men also desire to simplify and abridge their descriptions [in the construction of verbal rules for action], in order to reduce the labor of communication [Alexander, 1967, p. 115]."

All this is very close to Skinner. For Skinner, expressions in ordinary language involving reference to goals and purposes are "abbreviations" of adaptive natural contingencies (1953, p. 90). In Skinner's writings, there are many Machian-like speculations concerning the historical origins of scientific relations in natural contingencies (e.g., 1931, pp. 427 ff; 1953, p. 14; 1974, pp. ix ff). Skinner's scientific approach is often differentiated from that of other behaviorists as being "purely descriptive" and "antitheoretical" (see, e.g., Hilgard, 1956, p. 117). Skinner's focally descriptive aim is particularly apparent in *The Behavior of Organisms* (1938), where he says his "directly descriptive science of behavior [p. 5]. . . confines itself to description rather than explanation [p. 44]." Even today it is common to characterize Skinner's position as simply "descriptive behaviorism" (e.g., Chaplin & Krawiec, 1979, p. 296; Lundin, 1979, p. 205). Day (1969b) has called attention to the latent professional power that is to be found in the radical behaviorist's focal interest in the direct observation and description of behavior in a broadly phenomenological sense, and McCorkle (1978) has pointed up affinities between radical behaviorism and ethological and naturalistic observation and description.

However, Malone (1975) has sharply criticized Skinner for his penchant, in his interpretative writings, for offering possible explanations of human behavioral phenomena in advance of their having been carefully described. "Skinner is not particularly interested in phenomenal description, or even in careful objective description of the behavior of others. His goal seems to lie in convincing his readers that whatever the phenomenon and whether it has been well described or not, his analysis can deal with it [pp. 146–147]." Malone calls attention to the basic compatibility of Skinner's orientation with that of William James; yet he points out the central role that is played in James's thought by his careful and detailed descriptions.

> The weakness [in Skinner's interpretative work] lies in his efforts to apply a very tentative and specific formulation to the explanation of cursorily described phenomena. This invites comparison with James' excellent descriptions. . . . Comparing James and Skinner further, I suggest that Skinner's "analyses" often amount to mere translations to conditioning language [p. 150].

Yet the extent to which behavior adequately described by the inherently intentional vocabulary of ordinary language is capable of being satisfactorily translated into "conditioning language" is very much the issue under current discussion.

There is no question that research in applied behavioral analysis often begins with the painstaking observation and description of real life human behavior (see, e.g., Patterson, 1974). However, such descriptions are quickly converted to classes of behavior that lend themselves conveniently to "objective" measurement. Such classes are then "defined" in terms suggestive of possible measurement in terms of "the language of physics." Research by Bernstein and Ebbesen (1978) is representative:

> Response categories were defined in terms of body position and contact with appropriate materials. For example, "sewing" was recorded if the subject was touching any cloth, thread, patterns, or equipment designated for sewing, and the subject's

head was directed towards the materials. Similarly, "reading" was recorded if the subject was looking at and holding a copy of the reading matter [p. 245].

The origins of this practice undoubtedly lie in the stance taken by Skinner in *The Behavior of Organisms* (1938) concerning the limited utility of ordinary language for the descriptive needs of a science of behavior.

> The important objection to the vernacular in the description of behavior is that many of its terms imply conceptual schemes. . . . This does not mean that we must entirely abandon ordinary speech in a science of behavior. The sole criterion for the rejection of a popular term is the implication of a system or of a formulation extending beyond immediate observations. We may freely retain all terms which are descriptive of behavior without systematic implications. Thus the term "try" must be rejected because it implies the relation of a given sample of behavior to past or future events; but the term "walk" may be retained because it does not [pp. 7–8].

As we have seen, the unsatisfactory nature of the reasoning in this passage from *The Behavior of Organisms* has been pointed out by Midgley (1978) in material quoted earlier (see pp. 217–218). Strictly analogous difficulties with Mach's effort to describe experience in purely phenomenal language have been pointed out by Alexander (1963, p. 112) and discussed by Bradley (1971, p. 214). I have made reference earlier to the heroic, if unsuccessful (see Rachlin, 1979; but see also Begelman, 1979), effort by Harzem and Miles (1978) to defend the practice in the experimental analysis of behavior of using only the simplest possible language in the description of behavior. Harzem and Miles appear to sense the difficulty of defending coherently the intelligibility of a language that is descriptive of behavior yet completely free of intentional implications, since they present the language they have in mind as an "ideal":

> A language which is fully specific and contains no extra-episodic words should perhaps be regarded as some kind of ideal limit, since there may not in practice be any form of words which relates solely to the here-and-now and gives every possible detail. Even "X walked" does not tell us precisely what bodily movements were involved, while "X coughed" does not tell us if the noise which he made was "ahem" or something different, while the very act of naming a person or object presupposes belief in a degree of permanence and regularity which could in principle turn out to be mistaken. This point, however, does not affect our central thesis. It is still the case that certain words entail extra-episodic commitment more than others. It is therefore quite legitimate, for research purposes, to aim at a language which makes such commitment minimal, without being drawn into argument as to whether there could ever be no commitment at all [from Harzem, P., and Miles, T. R., *Conceptual Issues in Operant Psychology, copyright* © 1978 *by John Wiley, New York, pp.* 62–63].

Harzem and Miles justify their advocacy of the use of such simple descriptive language "for research purposes" essentially on the grounds that such language is generally employed in operant research and that such research has already been found to be professionally productive. Yet a concern to eliminate extraepisodic descriptions is not an accurate way to characterize the commitment to objective procedures of measurement that is generally made in research in the applied analysis of behavior. Indeed, Malone (1978) has gone so far as to argue that the chief accomplishments of behavioral technology are better understood if the Skinnerian conceptual scheme—and specifically the concept of "reinforcement"—is abandoned entirely in favor of the behaviorism of E. R. Guthrie. And when it comes to the experimental analysis of behavior, one of the most persistent objections raised by his critics to Skinner's analyses of human behavior is that concepts meaningfully defined in controlled experimental research on lower animals cannot legitimately be extended in any straightforward way to the interpretation of complex human affairs (see, e.g., Chaplin & Krawiec, 1979, p. 296; Chomsky, 1959, p. 30). Sigmund Koch has been quite outspoken in insisting upon this point. Speaking of *About Behaviorism* (Skinner, 1974), Koch (1976a) says:

> This is a book that offers a portentious [sic] redefinition of man and society on the basis of no discernible arguments . . . intrinsic to the text. Authoritatively but distantly in the background, however, is "the experimental analysis of behavior"—a repository of hard knowledge constantly alluded to by the author as the scientific bedrock of his assertions. . . . But this will simply not do . . . ! It is one thing to identify an "operant" (like lever depression) in an experimental setting . . . ; quite another when the operant is a putative unit of complex human behavior. . . . The remarkable detail in which "schedules of reinforcement" and other relationships have been worked out for rate fluctuations of the bar-pressing and key-pecking behaviors studied in the foundational experiments should not mask the astronomical analogical distances between the "laws" and such contexts of application [p. 456].

In any case, it is surely safe to say that at the present time enormous tension exists among radical behaviorists over how best to specify the nature of the relationship between the empirical research findings obtained in the experimental analysis of behavior and the interpretative behavior commonly engaged in among radical behaviorists in the assessment of human behavior in everyday situations. Baum's (1979) comment on this tension is interesting: "Understanding this tension requires understanding Skinner's following of Mach's model. His extensions are Mach's descriptions."

A possible way out of all these difficulties may lie in another centrally important connection between radical behaviorism and the thought of William James. The connection is an epistemological one, and it has to do with James's development of pragmatism as a view toward the nature of knowledge. It can be seriously misleading to attempt to characterize a philosophical position too succinctly; yet that of Murphy and Kovach will be helpful at this point. James's "*Pragmatism* (1907) and *The Meaning of Truth* (1909) . . . mark the beginning of that contemporary pragmatist school which places its emphasis upon the relativity of knowledge, the impossibility of obtaining absolute truth, and the essentially adaptive nature of all thought [Murphy & Kovach, 1972, p. 205]." It has been said of pragmatism that it "is the only unique contribution American philosophy has made to the tradition known as Western philosophy [E. C. Moore, 1961, p. vii]." In any case, it "was the most influential philosophy in America during the first quarter of the twentieth century [Thayer, 1968, p. 3]." There was thus every opportunity for pragmatism to have a marked influence on the character of Skinner's epistemological thinking, although such an influence, if it exists, would have to be regarded as a very indirect one, since Skinner has made no mention so far of intellectual indebtedness to James. Pragmatism can no longer be regarded as the dynamic movement within philosophy that it was during Skinner's formative period: "Pragmatism as a movement . . . cannot be said to be alive today [Thayer, 1967, p. 435]." In the 1930s psychology assumed an epistemological orientation that was dominated by logical positivism, and as a result, most experimental psychologists today are comfortable with efforts to clarify the meaning of psychological concepts by their "objectification" in "operational definitions." Yet logical positivism and pragmatism have very different stances when it comes to the issues of meaning and truth.

For the [logical] positivist, value terms are meaningless. They have no cognitive import. The only meaning they have is emotive meaning. Thus, for the positivist, science, or intelligent inquiry, can have no connection with problems relating to the determination of ultimate values. For the pragmatists, on the contrary, the problem of the relation between value problems and science is one of the major problems in philosophy, if not the major problem [E. C. Moore, 1961, p. 265–266].

For Skinner, of course, the analysis of values in terms of reinforcement plays a central role in the forceful advocacy he makes of a planned society (see Skinner, 1971, Chap. 6). However, the background of current experimental psychological approaches to the clarification of meaning in logical positivism, at the expense of pragmatism, has led to the situation where Skinner's epistemological views, particularly with respect to the nature of scientific knowledge, have been hardly appreciated at all. The following quotations can be regarded as representative of the pragmatist aspect of Skinner's thought:

Scientific knowledge is verbal behavior, though not necessarily linguistic. It is a corpus of rules for effective action, and there is a special sense in which it could be "true" if it yields the most effective action possible. But rules are never the contingencies they describe; they remain descriptions and suffer the limitations inherent in verbal behavior. [A] proposition is "true" to the extent that with its help the listener responds effectively to the situation it describes [1974, p. 235].

The extent to which the listener judges [a verbal response] as true, valid, or correct is governed by the extent to which comparable responses have proved useful in the past [1957, p. 427].

In many ways, then, this seems to me to be a better way of talking about verbal behavior, and that is why I have tried to get the reader to talk about it in this way too. But have I told him the truth? Who can say? A science of verbal behavior probably makes no provision for truth or certainty (though we cannot even be certain of the truth of that) [1957, p. 456].

I should at least mention that at the present time certain technical views of the philosophers Goodman and Quine are spoken of as pragmatism (see Aune, 1970, p. vii) and that these views are at times also associated with the thought of Skinner (see, e.g., Kretzmann, 1967, p. 402; Margolis, 1975, p. 24).

It was said earlier that James's pragmatism involved not only an emphasis upon the impossibility of obtaining absolute truth but also upon the essentially adaptive nature of all thought. James's insistence on the adaptive nature of all our capacities for knowledge reflects, of course, his deep interest in Darwin. For James, as well as for the functionalist school of psychology that followed him, all knowledge was basically *functional* in nature, in the sense that all our capacities for knowing things are shaped in us by the practical needs we face in adapting to our environment. Skinner's epistemological views concentrate even more fundamentally than James's upon the basically functional, or adaptive, nature of whatever it is that we can be said to know.

An explicit concern with epistemological issues, that is, with the nature of our capacities to know things, is not all that frequently a matter of detailed attention on the part of professional psychologists. An obvious exception to this rule would be the evolutionary epistemology of Jean Piaget (see, e.g., Robinson, 1976, p. 337), and Sigmund Koch continues to call with increasing intensity for a professional epistemology based upon a psychological understanding of the knowing process to replace the "official" epistemology derived from logical positivism that has become so taken for granted in experimental psychology (see Koch, 1976a, pp. 510 ff). Interestingly, Koch's emphasis upon the discriminative capacities of the observer in underlying our professional knowledge has very much the same thrust as the discriminative foundations of radical behaviorist epistemology (see Bennett, 1978; Day, 1976b). However, the explicit interest of Skinner in a functional epistemology is very strong. As he puts it in his contribution to this book: "I came to behaviorism, as I have said, because of its bearing on epistemology, and I have not been disappointed [see p. 200]."

Skinner's interest in epistemological issues has been a characteristic concern throughout the course of his career (e.g., 1945; 1953, pp. 138ff; 1964; 1969, pp. 157 ff; 1974, Chap. 9). However, the most important and internally coherent statement is contained in *Verbal Behavior* (1957), when the book is regarded as a whole. Skinner continues to regard *Verbal Behavior* as possibly his most important work (see his statement to that effect on p. 198 of this book), and I would argue that this is because the book exemplifies his functional epistemology put into practical application.

Of particular interest is the chapter in *Verbal Behavior* specifically dealing with "Logical and Scientific Verbal Behavior" (pp. 418 ff). This chapter gives an overview of how a rigorously functional approach may be taken to giving an account of the realities of scientific practice. What one finds in this chapter are the first steps in giving a functional analysis of the practices actually involved in carrying out research that conforms to accepted scientific methodology. What the profession needs to know, when it comes to making sense of the "thin" descriptive language employed in operational definition, is what sort of consequences and sources of stimulus control actually function to shape and maintain this practice. For example, it is easy to suggest that the practice of defining "sewing" as "touching any cloth, thread, patterns, or equipment designated for sewing [with] the subject's head . . . directed towards the materials" may well be supported by the ease with which measurements of observer reliability may be made. Yet what is the *functional* meaning of such concepts as "reliability" and "validity" when regarded within the framework of a pragmatist epistemology? What is needed in the defense of any proposed strategies of research in connection with the experimental analysis of behavior is an effort to clarify specifically what the practical consequences of the use of such a methodology happen to be. I have argued these matters in somewhat more detail elsewhere (Day, 1979), and a step in the direction of this kind of functional analysis of experimental method has been made by Michael (1974) in an effort to discuss the utility of statistical tests in research bearing on the applied analysis of behavior. In any case, the most important thing a student of contemporary behaviorism can do at the present time is to be sure he or she understands the relationship between the epistemology contained in Skinner's *Verbal Behavior* and the functional epistemologies of James and Mach.

AMERICAN FUNCTIONALISM

James's influence was carried very forcefully into professional psychological affairs after the turn of the century by the pragmatists John Dewey and George Herbert Mead and the psychologists James Rowland Angell and Harvey Carr. These persons formed the leadership of the functionalist school of psychology, which was associated with the University of Chicago, where they worked. Functionalism is commonly regarded as one of the five "classical schools" of psychology, the others being structuralism, behaviorism, Gestalt psychology, and psychoanalysis. Yet there seems to be little reason these days for the student to be in awe of this particular classification. Nowadays a concern with the "classical schools" of psychology is likely to be more basically a vehicle either for organizing material in the history of psychology for the first third of this century (see, e.g., Murphy & Kovach, 1972) or for initiating discussion of a range of theoretical or other "systematic" stances deemed relevant to an overview of the profession at any particular time (see, e.g., Marx & Hillix, 1973, p. 68).

In 1929 Boring mentions Carr only in a footnote as "the comparative psychologist at Chicago" in a list of notable psychologists who had taken their degree under Angell (p. 564). Angell had presented functionalism not as a special school but as an interpretation of psychology in general, especially in its justification of "animal psychology" (Boring, 1929, p. 544). Thus, in 1929 Boring assesses functionalism in the following way:

> Although this school was limited at first geographically and later, as its members migrated to other places, in its personnel, it was nevertheless in a broad way an expression . . . of the epistemological attitude in American psychology in general. . . . When behaviorism came along, with assimilative powers equal to those of functionalism, functional psychology gradually faded out of the picture. Angell himself . . . made no reference to functional psychology as a particular kind of psychology when he wrote his *Chapters from Modern Psychology* in 1912 [pp. 538, 544].

In 1931 R. S. Woodworth published the first text specifically devoted to the psychological "schools." Functionalism is not one of the five schools that are each discussed in a separate chapter, and it is mentioned only briefly in the chapter on behaviorism, largely by way of calling attention to Watson's opposition to it (Woodworth, 1931, pp. 45–47). Although by 1950 Woodworth had come himself to be viewed as a functionalist from what was now regarded as the Columbia school of functional psychology, the final chapter of his 1931 book is devoted to what he calls "The Middle of the Road," a position with which he clearly aligns himself (p. 215). In 1933 a second text devoted to the schools appeared, written by Edna Heidbreder. In this book, seven schools are distinguished, with a chapter devoted to each. There is a chapter on "Functionalism and the University of Chicago." However, there is also a chapter on "Dynamic Psychology and Columbia University," a perspective preeminently associated with the views of Woodworth. To go back only a few years, in 1926 the first of what was hoped would be a continuing series of invited lectures on "contemporary theoretical psychology" appeared under the editorship of Carl Murchison. "We have here a genuine cross-section of contemporary theoretical psychology. Here are the norms with which future psychologies can be compared. Here are the principles which are up-to-date through the year 1925 [Murchison, 1926, p. x]." In this series, six schools are differentiated, none of which is functionalism. Woodworth (1926) has a paper under the heading "Dynamic Psychology," in which he mentions a contrast between "the 'structural' and 'functional' psychology of twenty years ago [p. 111]." In 1930 the second, and final, series of such papers edited by Murchison appeared. There is a paper by Carr on "Functional Psychology" (as well as one by Woodworth in a separate section called "Dynamic Psychology"). However, Murchison (1930) advises the reader that

> Associationism, Act Psychology, and Functionalism have been included in their historical setting, but the reader should not presume that these three schools are discussed by partisans in the same way as are the other schools. Professors Brett and Carr have acted largely as historians only in bringing these three schools to the convenient attention of students of this book, though Professor Carr himself is certainly in the direct line of descent from Functionalism [p. ix].

I have gone into all this detail about what the professional perception of functionalism was like at the turn of the 1930s because I want to concentrate upon functionalism as the chief legacy to professional psychology of William James and of such immediately succeeding pragmatists as Dewey and Mead. My point is that by 1930 that legacy of pragmatism to professional psychology could be widely regarded as a matter of history. It is true that in 1949 a three-part series of articles on "Psychology and Scientific Research," published in the journal *Science*, attempted to spell out the relevance to the conduct of psychological research of pragmatist epistemology (Cantril, Ames, Hastorf, & Ittelson, 1949). These epistemological papers were authored by psychologists whose interest in the Ames demonstrations in perception is relatively well known today. However, the epistemological perspective toward scientific research advocated by Cantril *et al.* has been, to my knowledge, utterly without impact upon the conception of psychological research that is widely shared among experimental psychologists today. A salient feature of the current conception of research in psychology is that it should be satisfactorily "objective" in character. Yet how would one proceed to clarify *precisely* what we mean by "objectivity" in this context? I have already suggested that an empirical, functional analysis of research behavior exemplifying accepted experimental method would be the direction in which radical behaviorism would attempt to move in answering this question.

Functionalism had its day in the sun largely as the first strong protest in this country to the German structuralist and introspective tradition, then under the leadership of E. B. Titchener. However, in 1913 an even stronger blow was struck at the structuralist tradition by the behaviorist manifesto of J. B. Watson (Watson, 1913). For an appreciation of how both functionalism and classical behaviorism played a part in the overthrow of the authoritative introspectionist tradition, the student should consult the papers by Krantz, by Heidbreder and by Herrnstein in Krantz (1969). A knowledge of the papers in this book, edited by David Krantz, is absolutely essential for anyone seriously interested in the "classical schools" of psychology: The papers are written not only by the acknowledged authority in the history of the particular school; they are also written recently enough to entail familiarity with the use of historical material by the authors of texts in theories and systems of psychology. In his discussion at the end of the book, Gardner Murphy (1969) speaks of functionalism in this way:

> We seem to be, then, at a point at which some sort of a serious concern has to be expressed for *system-building which is free of ossification*. In some cases the ossification, as in American functionalism, has reached the point actually of a sort of dried up starfish on the coast which is of interest to the collector, but which is very different from the living starfish which the biologist is interested in [pp. 128–129].

Krantz, in his fascinating paper on the bitter debate in 1895–1896 between the functionalist J. M. Baldwin and E. B. Titchener over how best to make sense of the results of certain experiments on reaction time, shows clearly how by that time the professional climate had become such that even rational communication between the German tradition and the interests of American psychology was barely possible. However, the interests of American psychology at the turn of the twentieth century were such that they could be nicely captured and inspired by Watson's outspoken call in 1913 for something new—for behaviorism (Figure 11.1). The background of professional interests and values that Watson could call upon in mediating the ultimate shift in fundamental professional commitment from the German tradition to behaviorism can be seen in the chapter on "Behavioristics" in the 1950 edition of Boring's *History* (Boring, 1950,Chap. 24).

Herrnstein's paper for Krantz's book shows very clearly how the thrust of Watson's appeal lay in his demand for objectivity at the heart of psychological research. In his preface to the book, Krantz (1969) characterizes the upshot of Herrnstein's paper in the following way:

> The systematic position of behaviorism was in part as one of the assimilators of the functionalist viewpoint. Added to this incorporation was an attack upon the study of "mind" which shifted the field from an analysis of consciousness to the investigation of behavior. By considering the background and developing thought of J. B. Watson . . . , Dr. Herrnstein, a contemporary behaviorist and historian of this period, indicates that this shift was not a revolutionary one but rather that the behaviorist's position was at the crest of an existing trend toward objectivism in psychology [p. vii].

In current usage the concept of *objectivity* contrasts most easily with that of *subjectivity*. Herrnstein devotes considerable attention to the historical antecedents of the objective–subjective distinction in psychology. However, he points out that "Spencer's distinction between objective and subjective psychology was a matter of method, rather than anything more profound [Herrnstein, 1969, p. 55]." It is in behaviorism conceived as the commitment to objective method that classical behaviorism has its most pervasive influence in psychology at the present time. In the historical factors that have led psychologists to take objectivity to contrast primarily with subjectivity, one can see the source of the propensity among psychologists today to assume, incorrectly, that any attack upon the epistemological presuppositions of methodological behaviorism must thereby involve an advocacy of subjective research methods. However, as I have mentioned previously, the objective–subjective distinction does not accommodate itself comfortably within radical behaviorist epistemology without further analysis. Is verbal behavior subjective, or is it objective, when it tacts the presence of stimuli and responses observable in the environment, or when it tacts relations between responses and reinforcing consequences, or between responses and controlling antecedent stimuli? The objective–subjective distinction becomes intelligible for radical behaviorism only when the adaptive consequences have been specified that support and maintain research behaviors identified as objective or subjective by the professional community.

The functional epistemology of William James was carried forward in psychology, as far as it went, by the classical school of American functionalism. By 1930 this school could be regarded as no longer professionally viable. At that time, the epistemological imagination of the field was captured by the objectivist orientation of classical behaviorism. To the extent, then, that there is a significantly pragmatist element in radical behaviorist epistemology, Skinner's work can be expected to be difficult for the general professional community to understand, since that community is now on the whole methodological behaviorist in epistemological orientation.

Some Comments on the History of Professional Behaviorism

During the 1930s, the professional commitment to objective research methods became wedded to logical positivism, as a philosophy of science, and to "operationalism," which differs from logical positivism largely in that "operationalism seems to associate meaningfulness with linkability to experimental activities, whereas the principle of verifiability [in logical positivism] is satisfied if an expression is anchored to mere passive observation [Schlesinger, 1967, p. 545]." The historical details of the incorporation of logical positivist epistemology within the newly victorious behaviorism have been outlined by Boring (1950, pp. 653 ff), and the professionally counterproductive consequences of this merger continue to be commented upon by Sigmund Koch (see, e.g., 1964; 1976a, pp. 511 ff). However, as important as a logical-positivist-derived epistemology may continue to be in rationalizing the research strategies currently associated with methodological behaviorism, "logical positivism . . . is [now] dead, or as dead as a philosophical movement ever becomes [Passmore, 1967, p. 56]." It has been replaced, within empiricist philosophy of science, by what is often spoken of as "analytical" or "ordinary language" philosophies, derived from the later thought of the philosopher Ludwig Wittgenstein. I have myself discussed elsewhere the relation between radical behaviorism and Wittgenstein's later thought (Day, 1969a; 1976a).

Throughout the 1940s, then fading out as the 1950s came to a conclusion, the imagination of experimental psychology was captured by the promise of the great behavior theories of the day. During the summer of 1950, an important event took place. Under the sponsorship of the Social Science Research Council, the Carnegie Corporation of New York provided funds for a "seminar" to be held on the campus of Dartmouth College, the purpose of which was to provide a detailed, in-depth critical assessment of the dominant learning theories in light of the then reigning logical-positivist-derived "logic of theory construction," in which there was much confidence. "The 'seminar' consisted of seven men, all young and of approximately the same age, academic rank, and prestige. Their attitudes toward science in general and toward psychology in particular were sufficiently uniform to furnish a common basis for group discussion [Poffenberger, 1954, p. vi]." These seven men are now, after 30 years, all very distinguished psychologists (as can be seen from the names of the authors of the book in which the results of the conference were published: Estes, Koch, MacCorquodale, Meehl, Mueller, Schoenfeld, & Verplanck, 1954). These persons are notable in the history of psychology, since they represent the living of the life of behaviorism while it was the most prestigious intellectual orientation in the profession. Five theories were subjected to critical analysis, those of Hull, Tolman, Skinner, Lewin, and Guthrie. The book produced by the Dartmouth conference, *Modern Learning Theory* (Estes *et al.*, 1954), is of exceptional interest as a historical document, not only because of the unusual intellectual integrity of the work involved, but because the book is an example of the unity of professional orientation that was possible within behaviorism at its finest hour. Verplanck's paper on Skinner's "theory" is the finest critical assessment of *The Behavior of Organisms* that has been made to date.

Of particular historical importance is the analysis by Sigmund Koch of the theoretical work of Clark Hull. Much more than any other theory, that of Clark Hull (e.g., Hull, 1943) had fired the enthusiasm of the aspiring behaviorists of the day. This was not only because the theory was explicitly hypothetico-deductive in orientation and led easily to the formulation of experiments that could be brought to bear upon its possible verification, but because Hull's attempt at the explicit statement of postulates in mathematical form, from which corollaries could be derived by logical deduction, afforded a vision of a comprehensive theory of behavior that could match in mathematical elegance those of the physical sciences. Koch, in turn, had quickly acquired a professional reputation as a young behaviorist of exceptional promise by the publication in 1941 of a theoretical paper on "The Logical Character of the Motivation Concept," which had been part of his master's thesis, written under the supervision of the eminent logical positivist Herbert Feigl. In 1944 the *Psychological Bulletin* published a "Special Review" by Koch of Hull's *Principles of Behavior* (1943). The review could hardly be regarded as other than enthusiastic: The "few final [critical] evaluative comments . . . are offered as constructively motivated suggestions rather than objections [Koch, 1944, p. 283]." Other comments by Koch in 1944:

> *Principles of Psychology* is one of the most important books published in psychology during the twentieth century. No psychologist, whatever his affiliation, can afford the luxury of not reading this immensely challenging work [p. 269].

> *Principles of Behavior* arrives at a time when the withering *corpus* of the social sciences requires radical therapy. The war has seen a widespead resurgence of anti-scientific, metaphysical and theological speculation in the social sciences. There are

some who mistakenly believe that the application of scientific methods to behavior and society has been tried and—witness the present social crisis—has failed miserably. Nothing could be further from the truth. If the social "sciences" have not realized their promise, this is primarily due to the *absence* of rigorous scientific method. The remedy is to make the social sciences more scientific, not less so. As a concrete step in this direction, the importance of *Principles of Behavior* cannot be overemphasized [p. 286].

Koch's analysis of Hull's theoretical work for the Dartmouth conference, including again the *Principles of Behavior*, was a Herculean achievement. It was 176 printed pages in length, taking up essentially half the book in which it was published (Koch, 1954). In this work, Koch set himself the task of assessing the nature of Hull's theory, of examining the orienting commitments and methods that underlay the theory's construction, and then determining the extent to which the resulting theoretical structure turned out to conform to Hull's theoretical objectives. He commented on the importance of this task as follows:

Hull's theory is the product of a period of heroic optimism in recent theoretical psychology. The keynote of this era is the belief in the imminent feasibility of comprehensive theory, having an unrestricted range of application to the major phenomena of organismic behavior. This era—dating roughly from 1930—seems distinctly on the wane. Yet, it would not be quite correct to say that it is over. If, within recent years, we have learned that the major "theories" which dominated psychology during the thirties and forties were, in reality, over-extended *programs* towards theory, we have not yet arrived at a clear perception of the enormity of the distance separating such programs from theory, nor have we settled on the characteristics of those programs and objectives which might mediate realistic progress. . . . *For these reasons, it is of the first importance to test Hull's formulations against the criteria of rigorous natural science theoretical procedure—eminently fair criteria, in Hull's case, because he explicitly adopted them* [from Koch, S., in Estes *et al., Modern Learning Theory*, copyright © 1954 by Appleton-Century-Crofts, New York, p. 3].

The upshot of Koch's exceedingly detailed analysis—Koch called his documentation "interminable" (p. 166)—was that Hull's theory failed in its achievement to meet its objectives. The following material is extracted from Koch's concluding remarks:

In the preceding part of the report, we have done what may be construed as a nasty thing. We have proceeded on a literal interpretation of some such proposition as: "Hull has put forward a hypothetico-deductive theory of behavior." It can be fairly maintained, when a twentieth-century psychologist claims he has a "general" theory of behavior . . . , that the world "general" is necessarily meant with reservation and that "theory" is a metaphor. . . . Unfortunately, the only way to measure the "dimensions" of the metaphor is to proceed from a *literal* interpretation of what the metaphor asserts. . . .

We have raised, in some form, most of the types of questions that can be asked in characterizing the status of a scientific theory. We have inquired into the adequacy of all classes of definition of all classes of the theoretical variables. We have inquired into the postulated interconnections among all classes of variables. We have looked into the methods of postulate construction, of quantification, of derivation. We have examined the induction basis, and the general state of the evidence, for certain of the assumptions. Under close scrutiny, not a single member of a single class of such theoretical components satisfied the requirements for rigorous scientific theory of the sort envisaged within the theorist's explicit objectives. . . .

This analysis has not been intended to destroy Hull's reputation, or minimize his very great contributions. It has seemed a necessary job because of the paramount importance of making explicit the limits within which it is feasible to aim for theory in the current phase of psychology. . . .

In this report, we have therefore tried to locate specific sources for Hull's inevitable failures, as he faced the manifold problems of building theory. We have tried to show that he failed not *merely* because he aimed at a comprehensive theory, or because relevant empirical knowledge is too painfully slim to justify even far more limited attempts. We have tried to show that he failed because he did not adequately meet concrete problems of *empirical definition*, of *measurement*, of *quantification*, of *intervening variable function construction*, and various subspecifications of all of these. He could not meet these problems because no one else had met them, or currently can meet them. And this is the case because such problems have as yet received only the vaguest definition, while anything approaching useful resolution is still far out of sight [from Koch, S., in Estes *et al.*, *Modern Learning Theory*, copyright © 1954 by Appleton-Century-Crofts, New York, pp. 159–161].

In the last paragraph of his report, Koch identified what "all of us most want: 'genuine' quantification of behavioral relationships [p. 167]." Thus, it was natural some nine years later, in 1963, for Koch to have been chosen, along with B. F. Skinner, to represent behaviorism in the debate with phenomenology at the Rice Symposium on Behaviorism and Phenomenology, a landmark symposium in the history of psychology, which had been organized by the Division of Philosophical Psychology to "mark its inception as a new division of the American Psychological Association" (Wann, 1964, p. viii).

By this time, however, Koch had come to see, and to become convinced by, the implications for behaviorism in general of his own critical assessment of Hull's work in his contribution for the Dartmouth conference. When Koch delivered his paper for the Rice symposium, it turned out to be an impassioned attack upon behaviorism, rather than a defense, in what remains today a historical assessment of behaviorism of considerable relevance to the philosophical issues involved. In commenting on Koch's paper, "Skinner spoke of his feeling of loneliness at the symposium. He had looked over the people on the symposium to see where he could find a little support and had 'felt perhaps Sig Koch might be my man—but you see now how little I have to expect from him' [Wann, 1964, p. 42]." In the discussion following one of the papers in the symposium, Koch had the following to say, in remarks that seemed to some extent to reflect his reaction to the symposium as a whole: "I would be happy to say that what we have been hearing could be characterized as the death rattle of behaviorism, but this would be a rather more dignified statement than I would like to sponsor, because death is, at least, a dignified process [Wann, 1964, p. 162]." In the discussion following Koch's paper, a member of the audience remarked that what Professor Koch presented did not seem "truly representative of what Skinner has to say" (Wann, 1964, p. 42) and implied that Koch's analysis of behaviorism did not engage correctly the philosophical issues involved in Skinner's work. I have myself discussed elsewhere the bearing of Koch's analysis on Skinner's radical behaviorism and the relation it bears to phenomenological concerns in general (Day, 1969b). Even so, I should perhaps remark that I often advise my students that the easiest way to assess the historical progress of methodological behaviorism, as opposed to radical behaviorism, is to follow closely the professional fortunes of Sigmund Koch.

Skinner's *The Behavior of Organisms* was published in 1938. There were three significant critical reviews, and they place the book nicely within the professional research context of the period (Finan, 1940; Hilgard, 1939; Krechevsky, 1939). The book was clearly accepted at once into the community of such already established learning theorists as Hull, Tolman, Guthrie, and Lewin. All three reviews commend the value of the new research findings that are reported, particularly in connection with extinction and intermittent reinforcement. Krechevsky is the most extreme about this. Agreeing with some comments by the publisher, he says: "These data mark . . . a new 'high' in experimental achievement. [The] book 'represents the most successful description of the behavior of the individual organism thus far achieved' [p. 404]." However, the dominant underlying tone of the three reviews is that in its systematic and methodological perspectives the book is "outside the trends currently popular in psychology" (Hilgard, 1939, p. 121), "nonconformist" (Finan, 1940, p. 443), and "queer" and "self-contradictory" (Krechevsky, 1939, pp. 405, 407).

The ground upon which the reviews attempt to base their reservations with respect to *The Behavior of Organisms* are particularly interesting to see today, since they indicate an awareness even then of aspects of Skinner's thought that continue to be troublesome areas of tension between radical behaviorism and the general professional community at the present time. The authors of all three reviews are outraged at Skinner's apparent refusal to see any relation between his own work and the extensive research being carried out by others at the time in the experimental investigation of learning. "It is to be profoundly regretted that Skinner did not attempt to tie up his work and his thinking with the rest of psychology's data and concepts. He should have given us a more 'social' and a more generalized product [Krechevsky, 1939, p. 407]." Yet the epistemological cleavage between Skinner's thought and that of the rest of psychology continues to make it very difficult to bring the research findings of the rest of psychology to bear upon the radical behaviorist perspective. This is not to say that the scope of Skinner's psychological interests is too restricted to permit the accommodation of research findings obtained in general experimental psychology, as is witnessed by the breadth of coverage in such works as *Science and Human Behavior* (1953) and *About Behaviorism* (1974). The difficulty in accommodation occurs because Skinner's thought differs from that of the rest of the profession at an epistemological, or conceptual, level. It is only very recently that findings from experimental research can be seen to be affecting the conceptual structure associated with contemporary behaviorism (see Catania, 1979). However, these findings continue to come largely from research that would be regarded as one or another aspect of the experimental analysis of behavior, and as increasing attention is given to findings in other areas, this can be seen generally to involve a reinterpretation of those findings in terms of contemporary behaviorist conceptual equipment. For example, Krechevsky (1939) called Skinner to task for neglecting "all the relevant work of Tolman and his students on the phenomenon of latent learning, where responses seem to be acquired *without* specific and differential reinforcements [p. 405]." Yet in 1979, Catania returns to an explicit consideration of the research findings on latent learning. The conceptual nature of the basis of the controversy is pointed out. "Even in principle the argument could not be resolved and latent learning gradually faded away as a critical experimental issue [p. 87]." Catania then goes on to show how the latent learning findings can be plausibly interpreted in terms of conceptual distinctions he had made earlier in his text between a functional and a structural analysis (see pp. 86–88, 357–358).

Other objections raised in the reviews of *The Behavior of Organisms* also indicate that epistemological sources contributed to the difficulties the reviewers found in the book. There is, of course, the usual complaint that there has been no use of statistical procedures. Yet this issue is raised as part of a more general puzzlement, at an epistemological level, concerning what sort of criteria are needed in order to establish lawfulness of data in a "pure case" (Finan, 1940, pp. 443–444). Hilgard (1939) objects that the kinds of "laws" found in *The Behavior of Organisms* are not the kind of laws of general interest in doing scientific research:

> They do not appear to the reviewer to be laws at all, but collections of variables probably correlated in such ways that laws might be looked for. To describe them as laws of behavior is like speaking of a 'law of moisture' or a 'law of sunshine' as laws of growth at the stage when little more is known than that moisture and sunshine favor growth. . . . If this interpretation is correct, the laws were merely definitions of variables to be investigated, and experimental verification means not that the laws are proved or disproved, but merely that the variables chosen were convenient to direct inquiry [pp. 122–123].

In these comments on behavioral "laws," the failure of communication between Hilgard and Skinner hinges on the epistemological issue of in what sense the results of experimental research can be taken to "verify" purportedly behavioral "laws" or "hypotheses." The focus of Finan's (1940) objections is on analogous epistemological differences concerning the meaning of such concepts as truth ("validity") and "reliability."

> In the present study where the operationalistic outlook throws so much weight on procedure, and where in addition raw data and theoretical interpretations are so close to the methods by which they were obtained, it becomes increasingly important that the methods of experimentation be examined for reliability and validity. The importance of such analysis is further indicated by somewhat divergent results obtained with the same technique, with the same species, and with utilization of the same experimental variables, in other laboratories [p. 443].

Yet I have already pointed out in the preceeding discussion how it is that the epistemological characteristics of Skinner's thought call for a *functional analysis* of such vested professional interests in the "validity" and "reliability" of research findings, if the utility of such concepts in radical behaviorist research is to be clarified.

I should also at least mention, in view of the attention I have given here to the necessary intentionality of concepts employed in the description of behavior, that Krechevsky, in his review, devotes over one-third of his discussion simply to establishing the point that, in spite of the impression Skinner appears to want to give to the contrary, his analysis in terms of the "reflex" is not a reductive, "molecular" one, but a "molar" one. He wishes

> merely to emphasize the point that Skinner's reflex is *not* a 'molecular' unit, as understood and criticized by Gestalt psychologists. . . . Again we find Skinner following in the best traditions of Tolman, Lewin, Koffka, *et al.*; for if he stops with his process of analysis at a point beyond which no *psychological* sense can result, he is not differing from the Gestaltist's concept of what is proper analysis [Krechevsky, 1939, pp. 406–407].

Hilgard's review of *The Behavior of Organisms* was followed in the next year by the publication of the first edition of his influential text with Marquis, *Conditioning and Learning* (Hilgard & Marquis, 1940). In this text, *The Behavior of Organisms* is cited 26 times, which shows the relatively easy professional assimilability of the experimental work reported in it. In 1948 Hilgard published the first edition of his equally influential text, *Theories of Learning.* This book contains a balanced and lucid overview of what goes on in *The Behavior of Organisms*, insofar as it can be "understood in relation to the theories of Guthrie and Hull . . . , as an avowed behaviorism making use of conditioning principles [p. 116]." Discussion of controversial epistemological issues is avoided. The book can be recommended for use today as a guide for students who are making their way through *The Behavior of Organisms* for the first time, a comment that cannot be made with respect to subsequent editions of the same text. In noting the "present insulation [of Skinner's position] from other systematic viewpoints," Hilgard has this to say:

"Skinner has not yet presented his system in a form to make it fully accessible to others, because he has avoided the transformations which would show its relevance to what others are doing and thinking [p. 143]." In considering the extension of Skinner's research to human affairs, Hilgard cites Skinner's contribution to the Symposium on Operationism, organized by E. G. Boring and published as a single issue of the *Psychological Review* in 1945 (see Boring, 1950, p. 663). However, this citation is made, not out of any appreciation of the heavy epistemological importance of Skinner's paper on operationism, but only to note that Skinner has "promised a volume on verbal behavior" (Hilgard, 1948, p. 144).

Skinner's paper for the Symposium on Operationism, "The Operational Analysis of Psychological Terms," can be regarded as a paper of the first importance in the history of radical behaviorism. In it, Skinner draws for the first time the distinction between radical and methodological behaviorism (1945, p. 294), and the major work done in the paper is to offer a solution to the problem of how the verbal community in which we learn to use language can teach us how to talk about our own private experiences, an argument that Skinner characteristically employs throughout his career in distinguishing radical from methodological behaviorism (see Day, 1977b). The paper is consistent with a functionalist or pragmatist epistemology throughout, and consequently, it has been difficult for conventional psychologists to make sense out of it easily. Dr. Boring's (1945) response to the paper is characteristically honest:

> *Skinner* is full of his unpublished book and that makes difficulty. He can not get away from the complexities in which his thought is now at home, nor present them fully in the space at his disposal. Again and again I want the referents for his terms. Can many of us be sure what is meant by the sentence: "A verbal community which has no access to a private stimulus may generate verbal behavior in response to it"? In general, I think I follow Skinner, who has limited himself to a discussion of how operationally privacy may be invaded, and agree with him. But he scares me. He has probably implied something that I missed [p. 278].

The material of particular epistemological interest in this paper is found both in its opening section (Skinner, 1945, pp. 270–272) and also in Skinner's remarks by way of "rejoinders and second thoughts" (pp. 291–294). Skinner defines operationism in a passage that is frequently quoted, the upshot of which is that operationism is essentially a matter of talking only about what one observes and about what is involved in coming to make those observations (p. 270). To say the same thing by means of radical behaviorist conceptual equipment, operationism is basically talking largely under the control of observable events. If one is interested particularly in giving operational *definitions*, Skinner says that this involves a procedure that can, and presumably should, be used in clarifying the meaning of any term. "There is no reason to restrict operational analysis to high-order constructs; the principle applies to all definitions. This means that we must explicate an operational definition for every term unless we are willing to adopt the vague usage of the vernacular [p. 270]." The clarification of the meaning of a term requires no less than, and precisely, a functional analysis of the control of the use of the term as a part of someone's verbal behavior.

> Meanings, contents, and references are to be found among the determiners, not among the properties, of response. The question "What is length?" would appear to be satisfactorily answered by listing the circumstances under which the response "length" is emitted (or, better, by giving some general description of such circumstances). If two quite separate sets of circumstances are revealed, then there are two responses having the form "length" . . . , since a verbal response-class is not defined by phonetic form alone but by its functional relations [pp. 271–272].

That Skinner is speaking here from an epistemological perspective that is quite different from that of his colleagues can be seen in the way in which he calls attention to the incoherence of the commonly accepted philosophy of science of the day:

> No very important positive advances have been made . . . because operationism has [so far had] no good definition of a definition, operational or otherwise. It has not developed a satisfactory formulation of the effective verbal behavior of the scientist.
>
> The operationalist . . . has not improved upon the mixture of logical and popular terms usually encountered in casual or even supposedly technical discussions of scientific method or the theory of knowledge. . . . *Definition* is a key term but is not rigorously defined. . . . Instead, a few roundabout expressions recur with rather tiresome regularity whenever this relation is mentioned. We are told that a concept is to be defined *"in terms of"* certain operations, that propositions are to be *"based upon"* operations, that a term denotes something only when there are *"concrete criteria for its applicability,"* that operationism consists in *"referring any concept for its definition* to . . . concrete operations . . . ,"* and so on. . . . Modern logic, as a formalization of "real" languages . . . can scarcely be appealed to by the psychologist who recognizes his own responsibility in giving account of verbal behavior [from Skinner, B. F., The operational analysis of psychological terms, *Psychological Review*, 1945, *52*, 270–271].

Thus, the epistemological cleavage between Skinner's functional conception of knowledge and that of the conventional professional psychologist has meant that the radical behaviorist and the methodological behaviorist have two entirely different conceptions of operational definition (see, e.g., J. Moore, 1975). For the methodological behaviorist, operational definition involves essentially taking a psychological term to mean the operations by which it is measured or manipulated as a variable in an experiment. For the radical behaviorist, operational definition involves a functional analysis of the control of the use of the term as an aspect of verbal behavior.

In 1956 Hilgard published the second edition of his *Theories of Learning*. The author states that the chapter on Skinner has been "thoroughly rewritten"

(p. v), and this involves largely an expansion of the perspective taken on Skinner's views made possible by the publication of *Science and Human Behavior* by Skinner (1953) and *Principles of Psychology* by Keller and Schoenfeld (1950). Hilgard speaks of *Science and Human Behavior* as a "textbook of general psychology" (p. 82), and this is in line with the disposition adopted toward the book by the profession in general. The book was reviewed favorably in 1954 along with six other texts in a special review on "Textbooks and General Psychology" for the *Psychological Bulletin* (Finger, 1954). However, it was wise indeed for Hilgard to look closely at *Science and Human Behavior* for clues pertaining to the structure of Skinner's thought as "learning theory." With remarkable perspicacity, he spots, and highlights in his text (Hilgard, 1956, p. 103), obscurely presented material on "behaviorial atoms." Yet this presentation is all we have to rely on now in order to comprehend certain fine details in the major work *Verbal Behavior* (see, e.g., Skinner's discussion of "minimal tacts," 1957, p. 333). Interest in Skinner's thought as "systematic behavior theory," as it was conceived of in the 1940s, appears not to have survived the passage of time; interest in Skinner now centers on the implications of his thought for a functional and experimental analysis of behavior. However, in a number of ways, *Science and Human Behavior* can be regarded as the most detailed and comprehensive statement of Skinner's views as a systematic psychologist. For example, the arguments regarded as so inflammatory when presented in *Beyond Freedom and Dignity* (1971) are much more carefully and reasonably argued in *Science and Human Behavior* (e.g., 1953, Chap. 18).

Discussion of epistemological issues in the second edition of Hilgard's *Theories of Learning* is confined largely to commentary on Skinner's "antitheory argument," as based on his well-known paper "Are Theories of Learning Necessary?" (1950). Hilgard again calls attention to Skinner's interest in verbal behavior, even though the book *Verbal Behavior* had not yet appeared. He cites with interest Skinner's report of early experimentation with the "verbal summator," makes reference to the William James Lectures that Skinner gave in 1948 on the analysis of verbal behavior, and notes that "the best available treatment at the time of writing is the section on verbal behavior in Keller and Schoenfeld (1950)" (Hilgard, 1956, p. 107). The reference to Skinner's 1945 paper on operationism, which was present in the first edition, is dropped in the second edition and all subsequent editions.

A third edition of Hilgard's *Theories of Learning* appeared in 1966, this time coauthored with Gordon Bower (Hilgard and Bower, 1966). The important thing to note about this edition is that it is essentially unchanged from the edition of 10 years previously. The significance of this lies in the fact that as late as 1966 it was possible for the profession to regard Skinner's thought, and the experimental work associated with it, as something aimed in the same direction as that of traditional "learning theory." There is no appreciation at all of the possibility that critical epistemological issues might be involved in Skinner's "fresh start" approach to psychology:

> Skinner's "fresh start" approach to psychology has made it difficult for him to use the data collected by others, and, on principle, he rejects their concepts. His role in reference to the theories of others—insofar as he has paid any attention to their claims—has been chiefly that of a trenchant critic. He has felt no responsibility for the task of inter-investigator coordination. In his book *Science and human behavior* (1953), written as a textbook, he used no literature citations, and he mentions by name, among writers with some place in learning theory, only Thorndike, Pavlov, and Freud [Hilgard and Bower, 1966, pp. 141–142; also identical in Hilgard, 1956, p. 116].

In the third edition several pages are added to the treatment of schedules of reinforcement in direct response to the publication in 1957 of *Schedules of Reinforcement* by Ferster and Skinner, "a large book concerned exclusively with variations on the themes of ratio reinforcement, interval reinforcement, and mixed schedules [Hilgard and Bower, 1966, p. 117]." At this point in the text, after noting that "the followers of Skinner have become a fairly large in-group in psychology [p. 117]," the authors call attention to the formation of a special journal (JEAB, in 1958) and a special division of the American Psychological Association (Division 25, in 1963) devoted to the experimental analysis of behavior.

Ever since the first edition of his text in 1948, Hilgard had anticipated the publication of Skinner's work on verbal behavior. It appeared in 1957, the year following Hilgard's second edition. Yet the assessment in 1966 remained the same as that of 1956, with the addition simply of a definition of autoclitic behavior and the following remarks:

> In essence, our verbal behavior is "shaped" by the reinforcement contingencies of the verbal communities in which we live.

> The book on *Verbal behavior*, while certainly a serious effort, has not proved to be very influential. This may have come about because it was not well received by the professional linguists, whose rapidly developing linguistic science has made great strides by means of analyses different from Skinner's (e.g., Chomsky, 1959). Or it may be that the interest in programed learning, coming to a head about the time when this book appeared (1957), siphoned off the interest and debate that the book might otherwise have provoked. If that should prove to be the case, we may some-day see a revived interest in the book [Hilgard and Bower, 1966, p. 133].

It is at least possible to read the preceding assessment as an understated expression of "disappointment." However, to take the thrust of Skinner's interest in verbal behavior to lie basically in the claim that our verbal behavior is shaped by contingencies of reinforcement is to approach the book from the perspective of someone looking for a contribution to learning theory. It is thus to miss the challenge posed to the profession by the book of undertaking the functional analysis of verbal behavior. Chomsky's famous review of *Verbal Behavior*, to which Hilgard and Bower make reference in the preceding quotation, had a devastating effect, not only upon the professional reception of the book itself, but also upon the general intellectual credibility of any kind of Skinnerian behaviorism. Chomsky's review was widely read among philosophers, who at the time were becoming increasingly interested in the philosophy of mind and the philosophy of action, and the damaging effects of Chomsky's review contributed to a general disengagement of serious professional philosophical attention to the epistemological dimensions of Skinner's thought at a time when it was needed most. Ten years later, a behaviorist reply was made to Chomsky's review by Kenneth MacCorquodale (1969, 1970). MacCorquodale's point is that Chomsky's analysis is in many ways irrelevant to Skinner's work because of basic disengagement at an epistemological level. "Chomsky's criticisms of Skinner are, then, necessarily methodological. The disagreement is fundamentally an epistemological one, a 'paradigm clash' [MacCorquodale, 1970, p. 840]." "Unfortunately for his purposes Chomsky did not grasp the differences between Skinner and Watsonian–Hullian behaviorism, and his criticisms, although stylistically effective, were mostly irrelevant to *Verbal Behavior* [MacCorquodale, 1969, p. 851]." However, it is more characteristic of the behaviorism of the present to take an integrative approach to these problems. In 1972 Catania published a paper on "Chomsky's Formal Analysis of Natural Languages: A Behavioral Translation." In this paper, Catania attempts to show how the findings of psycholinguistic research can be conceptualized in a fashion essentially compatible with a functional approach derived from the experimental analysis of behavior. This perspective is developed in considerable detail in his book *Learning* (Catania, 1979).

And then—to continue our interest in the course of events as monitored by the Hilgard texts—something happened. In 1975 a fourth edition of the text appeared (Hilgard & Bower, 1975). This time we have something really quite different from all the others. Although there are certain structural similarities to the earlier editions, and a certain amount of basic information is retained, the material on Skinner has been very much reworked, much as if it had been entirely thought through again. This time topics pertaining to underlying epistemological issues are raised, and they are raised in a context suggestive of productive professional discussion. The introduction points to the relevance of the entire range of Skinner's thought:

> Skinner is also one of the most sophisticated and persuasive protagonists of the *behaviorist methodology* that psychology has ever seen. He rejects mentalistic or "cognitive" explanations of behavior, or explanations attributing behavior causation to "inner psychic" forces of any kind. . . . Mentalistic explanations are incomplete, and their acceptance simply postpones doing a proper functional analysis of the behavior. A "functional analysis" of a given behavior means that we attempt to identify and isolate the environmental variables of which the behavior is a lawful function. . . . Skinner has also defended a particularly compelling behavioristic

position regarding the analysis of common-sense psychological terms such as *self*, *self-control*, *awareness*, *thinking*, *problem-solving*, *composing*, *will power*, and many of the psychodynamic concepts. . . . He has taken his ideas a step further in the analysis of the notions of *free will*, *inner determination*, and *social values*, and has discussed how one might arrange cultural practices by design so as to engineer a society that is "better" according to certain humanitarian values [from Hilgard, E. R., and Bower, G. H., *Theories of Learning* (4th ed.), copyright © 1975 by Prentice-Hall, Englewood Cliffs, N.J., pp. 206–207].

In this edition, Hilgard and Bower point to the relevance of a large amount of ongoing research, covering a range of species and involving a wide variety of contexts, both basic and applied. However, particularly interesting to note is the fact that the material contains a special section on "self-attribution and self-awareness." Here the discussion in Skinner's 1945 operationism paper of how "a verbal community which has no access to a private stimulus may generate verbal behavior in response to it"—once, as we have seen, so incomprehensible to Dr. Boring—is explained simply and lucidly, and in Hilgard and Bower's own words.

This time, the professional impact of Chomsky's review is straightforwardly assessed: "However, Skinner's book *Verbal Behavior* has not been very influential. This may have come about because it was not well received by professional linguists, and was given a renowned and relentlessly negative review by Chomsky (1959) [p. 234]." As the chapter approaches its end, and "difficulties for Skinner's position" are taken up for consideration, fully two and a half pages are devoted to Chomsky's views on the matter: "Perhaps the most effective critiques of Skinner's systematic position and his extrapolation of it to human affairs have been provided by the linguist Noam Chomsky [pp. 245–246]." Yet the authors appear to sense the relevance of underlying epistemological issues. The chapter ends with a forceful presentation of the tension that exists between the Skinnerian and the traditional experimental approaches on methodological grounds. An attempt is made to resolve the issue in terms of professional interest:

It may be noted that the split between the two methodologies depends on the focus of interest. . . . The main division thus remains theoretical preference—or, rather, a preference for theorizing on one side versus an active antipathy to theorizing within the operant conditioning group. This comes down to the matter of deciding what are the proper goals of a scientific psychology. And here we come again upon the empiricism–rationalism schism of antiquity. There is a fundamental opposition between scientists who believe that progress is to be made only by rigorous examination of the actual behavior of organisms and those who believe that behavioral observations are interesting only insofar as they reveal to us hidden underlying laws of the mind that are only partially revealed in behavior. Is psychology to be the science of the mind, or the science of behavior? Is physics the science of physical things, or the science of meter readings? Do behaviorists confuse the subject matter of the field with the evidence available for drawing inferences about this subject matter? . . . This contemporary clash between alternative views illustrates how very fundamental are these essentially historic and philosophic assumptions [from Hilgard, E. R., and Bower, G. H., *Theories of Learning* (4th ed.), copyright © 1975 by Prentice-Hall, Englewood Cliffs, N.J., p. 250].

I might simply point out that when Hilgard and Bower end their discussion of Skinner's views by asking, "Is psychology to be the science of the mind, or the science of behavior?" and "Do behaviorists confuse the subject matter of the field with the evidence available for drawing inferences about this subject matter?" they epitomize very nicely the heart of the distinction drawn earlier in this chapter between methodological and radical behaviorism.

Conclusion

It has been my purpose in this chapter to examine the "fundamental . . . and essentially historic and philosophic" issues, as Hilgard and Bower put it, that underlie an understanding of contemporary behaviorism. A wide range of intellectual concerns have been considered, and the picture that has emerged may well not conform to the stereotype that many people have of what behaviorism involves. In my account of the antecedents of contemporary behaviorism, I have taken the following to be important:

1. The challenge of contemporary behaviorism to the Greek concept of mind, so ubiquitously called upon in Western culture in the making sense of human affairs;
2. The problem of reductionism, or analysis into elements, so widely associated with behaviorism in the past, and its relative irrelevance to Skinnerian radical behaviorism;
3. The importance of the philosophical concept of intentionality, and its implications concerning the impossibility of describing behavior in exclusively physical language;
4. The significance of the fact that the concept of reinforcing consequences successfully mediates intentionality, thereby accounting for the intelligibility of radical behaviorist translations;
5. The importance in Skinnerian patterns of explanation of the Darwinian conception of adaptation to the environment;
6. The enormous influence of Crozier and Mach in giving a structure to Skinner's understanding of science that is very different from that tacitly assumed by most other psychologists;
7. The relevance of philosophical pragmatism to an understanding of Skinner's adaptational conception of human knowledge;
8. The difference between the primary systematic concerns of functionalism and behaviorism as classical schools of psychology, and the emergence with behaviorism of a focal interest in "objectivity" as a central orienting value for research in the profession;

9. The very great difference between the radical behaviorist conception of operational definition as the functional analysis of language in use and the understanding of what is involved in operational definition that is held by most other psychologists;
10. The revolutionary centering of radical behaviorist epistemology on the functional analysis of verbal behavior, in particular on the pivotal role of verbal discriminative responding—tacting—in conducting psychological research.

These 10 emphases would seem to differ so significantly from what is generally held to be important in behaviorism that the question may well arise as to whether it is appropriate to regard Skinner's orientation as a true form of behaviorism at all, as opposed, say, to viewing it as some further development within psychology of classical functionalism, or of act psychology. Is it legitimate to regard Skinner's perspective as a true form of behaviorism?

Actually, it is absurd on the face of it for me to raise such a question: It is the heart of Skinner's professional stance to present himself as the champion of behaviorism, and in this claim he is challenged among psychologists by no contender. The question becomes relevant only because of the particular emphases I myself have felt it wise to make in order to contrast Skinner's thought with widespread and popular misconceptions. However, it is not entirely aside from our purpose to consider briefly what it takes for a psychological perspective to be regarded properly as behaviorism.

Here we can turn to Sigmund Koch for assistance. In setting the stage for his in-depth analysis of Hull's theory for the Dartmouth conference, Koch found it appropriate to enumerate the central and salient features of behaviorism. Such a statement of the defining features of behaviorism produced in the early 1950s is particularly valuable for our purpose, since at that time professional interest in the orientation was at its peak. Koch's (1954) characterization is as follows:

It is fashionable to label Hull a "neo-behaviorist." In order to understand his most general orientative ideas, it becomes necessary to determine wherein Hull is a "behaviorist," and wherein "neo."

The "classical" behaviorism of Watson, Weiss, Holt, etc., which achieved the peak of its influence in the mid-twenties, was itself little more than a set of orientative attitudes. Behaviorism was a vocal and energetic movement towards theory, but not a single behavioristic writer put forth a concrete theory. . . . Individual behaviorists were often far apart on concrete empirical issues. The core of the movement was a common set of orientative attitudes, the most prominent of which were the following:

1) *The insistence on inter-subjective (objective) techniques for securing and expressing empirical data.* This was held to be incompatible with the continued use of "introspective," "subjective," or "anthropomorphic" methods.
2) *The advocacy of stimulus and response variables as the only legitimate indepen-*

dent and dependent variables in which to express the results of psychological research, and formulate theory. In line with this, the task of psychology was represented (by Watson and others) in some such way as "given the stimulus, to predict the response, and given the response to infer the stimulus."

3) *The commitment to conditioned response principles, or some related form of S–R associationism, as the basic laws of learning.* In writers like Watson, this commitment went little further than the assertion that learning could be accounted for by [conditioned reflex] principles, and the absence of an attempt to elaborate conditioning theory in a systematic or detailed way was conspicuous. . . .

4) *A strong emphasis on "peripheral" determinants of behavior.* This emphasis is, of course, related to the S–R orientation, the plausibility of which behaviorists tried to buttress by showing how all effective behavior determinants and processes could be gotten into S–R terms. . . . It is not unfair to note a certain coherence between the behavioristic insistence on "objective" methods and the stress on peripheral theorizing.

5) *An emphasis on extreme environmentalism* [from Koch, S., in Estes *et al.*, *Modern Learning Theory*, copyright © 1954 by Appleton-Century-Crofts, New York, pp. 5–6].

Koch concluded that "Hull operates within the general frame of reference defined by the first four behavioristic orientative attitudes . . .—but he holds and applies all these attitudes with a *difference* [p. 6]." Now, it seems to me that very much the same sort of thing should be said with respect to Skinner. Skinner operates within the broad frame of reference defined by these five orienting attitudes, but with very substantial differences. These differences arise largely from his functional epistemology, his Mach-like conception of science, and the large differences in the current professional climate from that of the 1920s with respect to which behaviorism must now contrast itself. The most salient features of Skinner's behaviorism are its robust antimentalism and its restriction of psychological interest to the analysis of behavior as a subject matter in its own right. To adopt these two stances forcefully would alone make any psychologist a behaviorist.

What do I take to be the direction in which radical behaviorism is likely to move in the immediate future? Personally, I think that the current trend in radical behaviorism is to try to bring patterns of thinking derived from Skinner to bear somewhat more concretely than in the past upon the broad research and applied interests of psychologists not primarily behaviorist in orientation. A good place to see this is in Catania's book *Learning* (1979). Although the author's purpose in the book is simply to provide a text that "surveys the major areas in the psychology of learning from a consistent behavioral point of view [p. ix]," the book can nevertheless be regarded as a major advance in the manifestation of radical behaviorist patterns of thinking, much as the introductory textbook *Principles of Psychology* by Keller and Schoenfeld could be regarded as a major theoretical advance in 1950. One of the most fascinating things about the book is the un-self-conscious way in which Catania leads the reader to follow easily, and to understand, a perspective on experimental findings that is intelligible only within a radical behaviorist conceptual framework. An example would be Catania's conceptualization of simple discriminative responding on the part of pigeons as tacting behavior. "Is there any reason why the pigeon's performance should not be called the tacting of red, blue, and green? . . . Although the pigeon's pecks in the presence of red and blue and green may be relatively trivial instances of verbal behavior, they are legitimate illustrations of the tact relation [p. 237]." An important feature of the book is that it cannot be regarded simply as a rehash of Skinner. Instead, the conceptual equipment of radical behaviorism is brought to bear in an interestingly original way upon the making sense of representative findings in the experimental psychology of animal and human learning, and to this extent it must be regarded as an important advance.

Similarly, I expect radical behaviorists to become increasingly interested in making explicit what they take Skinner to be saying in obscure or controversial aspects of his writings. Associated with this is a growing interest, particularly on the part of younger members of the profession, in examining the nature of the conceptual moves employed in radical behaviorist analysis. Actually, I have made reference to a number of papers of this kind in this chapter. If such an interest continues to develop, a lot more behaviorists will be reading a lot more books, and of a considerably larger scope, than is suggested by the image of a narrow commitment to experimentalism with which behaviorism is often associated.

In any case, the place to follow firsthand the future evolution of radical behaviorism is at the annual conventions of the Association for Behavior Analysis. These conventions are self-consciously engineered to facilitate the efficient exchange of new ideas and new research findings. The atmosphere at the conventions is cordial and congenial, and opportunities for effective intercommunication are maximal. As almost any psychologist, behaviorist or otherwise, would agree, these conditions are precisely the environmental circumstances under which professional behavior, in its more significant aspects, is most likely to evolve.

References

Abbagnano, N. Postivism. In P. Edwards (Ed.), *The encyclopedia of philosophy* (Vol. 6). New York: Macmillan, 1967.

Alexander, P. *Sensationalism and scientific explanation.* London: Routledge & Kegan Paul, 1963.

Alexander, P. Mach, Ernst. In P. Edwards (Ed.), *The encyclopedia of philosophy* (Vol. 5). New York: Macmillan, 1967.

Arnold, W. J. (Ed.) *Nebraska Symposium on Motivation, 1975.* Lincoln: University of Nebraska Press, 1976.

Aune, B. *Rationalism, empiricism, and pragmatism: An introduction.* New York: Random House, 1970.

Bandura, A. *Social learning theory.* Englewood Cliffs, N.J.: Prentice-Hall, 1977.

Baum, W. M. Personal communication, 25 July 1979.

Begelman, D. Review of Harzem & Miles's *Conceptual issues in operant psychology*. *Behaviorism*, 1979, 7, 113–122.

Bem, D. J. Self-perception theory. In L. Berkowitz (Ed.), *Advances in experimental social psychology* (Vol. 6). New York: Academic Press, 1972.

Bennett, M. L. *A conceptual analysis of radical behaviorist epistemology*. Master's thesis, Western Michigan University, 1978.

Bernstein, D. J., & Ebbesen, E. B. Reinforcement and substitution in humans: A multiple-response analysis. *Journal of the Experimental Analysis of Behavior*, 1978, 30, 243–253.

Blackmore, J. T. *Ernst Mach*. Berkeley, Cal.: University of California Press, 1972.

Boden, M. A. *Purposive explanation in psychology*. Cambridge, Mass.: Harvard University Press, 1972.

Boring, E. G. *A history of experimental psychology*. New York: Apple-Century-Crofts, 1929.

Boring, E. G. The use of operational definitions in science. *Psychological Review*, 1945, 52, 243–245; 278–281.

Boring, E. G. *A history of experimental psychology* (2nd ed.). New York: Appleton-Century-Crofts, 1950.

Bradley, J. *Mach's philosophy of science*. London: Athlone Press, 1971.

Cantril, H., Ames, A., Jr., Hastorf, A. H., & Ittelson, W. H. Psychology and scientific research. *Science*, 1949, 110, 461–464, 491–497, 517–522.

Catania, A. C. Chomsky's formal analysis of natural languages: A behavioral translation. *Behaviorism*, 1972, 1, 1–15.

Catania, A. C. *Learning*. Englewood Cliffs, N.J.: Prentice-Hall, 1979.

Chaplin, J. P., & Krawiec, T. S. *Systems and theories of psychology* (4th ed.). New York: Holt, Rinehart & Winston, 1979.

Chomsky, N. Review of Skinner's *Verbal behavior*. *Language*, 1959, 35, 26–58.

Chomsky, N. *Language and mind*. New York: Harcourt, Brace & World, 1968.

Coleman, S. R., & Gormezano, I. Classical conditioning and the "Law of Effect": Historical and empirical assessment. *Behaviorism*, 1979, 7, 1–33.

Crozier, W. J., & Hoagland, H. The study of living organisms. In C. Murchison (Ed.), *Handbook of general experimental psychology*. Worcester, Mass.: Clark University Press, 1934.

Darwin, C. *The descent of man*. New York: Appleton, 1871.

Darwin, C. *Expression of the emotions in man and animals*. London: J. Murray, 1872.

Day, W. F. On certain similarities between the *Philosophical investigations* of Ludwig Wittgenstein and the operationism of B. F. Skinner. *Journal of the Experimental Analysis of Behavior*, 1969, 12, 489–506. (a)

Day, W. F. Radical behaviorism in reconciliation with phenomenology. *Journal of the Experimental Analysis of Behavior*, 1969, 12, 315–328. (b)

Day, W. F. Contemporary behaviorism and the concept of intention. In W. J. Arnold (Ed.), *Nebraska Symposium on Motivation, 1975*. Lincoln: University of Nebraska Press, 1976. (a)

Day, W. F. *The concept of reinforcement-history and explanation in behaviorism*. Paper presented at the annual meeting of the American Psychological Association, Washington, D.C., September 1976. (b)

Day, W. F. Ethical philosophy and the thought of B. F. Skinner. In J. E. Krapfl & E. A. Vargas (Eds.), *Behaviorism and ethics*. Kalamazoo, Mich.: Behaviordelia, 1977. (a)

Day, W. F. *On the difference between radical and methodological behaviorism*. Paper presented at the annual meeting of the Midwestern Association of Behavior Analysis, Chicago, May 1977. (b)

Day, W. F. *The behavioral analysis of experimental method*. Paper presented at the annual meeting of the Association for Behavior Analysis, Dearborn, Mich., June 1979.

Dodds, E. R. *The Greeks and the irrational*. Berkeley, Cal.: University of California Press, 1951.

Earle, W. J. James, William. In P. Edwards (Ed.), *The encyclopedia of philosophy* (Vol. 4). New York: Macmillan, 1967.

Edwards, P. (Ed.) *The encyclopedia of philosophy* (8 vols.). New York: Macmillan, 1967.

Estes, W. K., Koch, S., MacCorquodale, K., Meehl, P. E., Mueller, C. G., Schoenfeld, W. N., & Verplanck, W. S. *Modern learning theory*. New York: Appleton-Century-Crofts, 1954.

Eysenck, H. J. *Experiments in behavior therapy*. Oxford: Pergamon Press, 1964.

Ferster, C. B. Is operant conditioning getting bored with behavior? A review of Honig and Staddon's *Handbook of operant behavior. Journal of the Experimental Analysis of Behavior*, 1978, *29*, 347–349.

Ferster, C. B., & Skinner, B. F. *Schedules of reinforcement*. New York: Appleton-Century-Crofts, 1957.

Finan, J. L. Review of Skinner's *The behavior of organisms. Journal of General Psychology*, 1940, *22*, 441–447.

Finger, F. W. Review of Skinner's *Science and human behavior. Psychological Bulletin*, 1954, *51*, 86–88.

Fourcher, L. A. Human ethology and phenomenology. *Behaviorism*, 1979, *7*, 23–36.

Garrett, R. Value conflict in a Skinnerian analysis. *Behaviorism*, 1979, *7*, 9–16.

Gibson, E. J. *Principles of perceptual learning and development*. New York: Appleton-Century-Crofts, 1969.

Giorgi, A. Convergences and divergences between phenomenological psychology and behaviorism: A beginning dialogue. *Behaviorism*, 1975, *3*, 200–212.

Graham, G. On what is good: A study of B. F. Skinner's operant behaviorist view. *Behaviorism*, 1977, *5*(2), 97–112.

Grave, S. A. Reid, Thomas. In P. Edwards (Ed.), *The encyclopedia of philosophy* (Vol. 7). New York: Macmillan, 1967.

Guthrie, W. K. C. Pre-Socratic philosophy. In P. Edwards (Ed.), *The encyclopedia of philosophy* (Vol. 6). New York: Macmillan, 1967.

Harzem, P., & Miles, T. R. *Conceptual issues in operant psychology*. New York: Wiley, 1978.

Hebb, D. O. *Textbook of psychology* (3rd ed.). Philadelphia: W. B. Saunders, 1972.

Heidbreder, E. *Seven psychologies* (Student's ed.). New York: Appleton-Century-Crofts, 1933.

Herrnstein, R. J. Behaviorism. In D. L. Krantz (Ed.), *Schools of psychology: A symposium*. New York: Appleton-Century-Crofts, 1969.

Herrnstein, R. J. Nature as nurture: Behaviorism and the instinct doctrine. *Behaviorism*, 1972, *1*, 23–52.

Hilgard, E. R. Review of Skinner's *The behavior of organisms. Psychological Bulletin*, 1939, *36*, 121–125.

Hilgard, E. R. *Theories of learning*. New York: Appleton-Century-Crofts, 1948.

Hilgard, E. R. *Theories of learning* (2nd ed.). New York: Appleton-Century-Crofts, 1956.

Hilgard, E. R., & Bower, G. H. *Theories of learning* (3rd ed.). New York: Appleton-Century-Crofts, 1966.

Hilgard, E. R., & Bower, G. H. *Theories of learning* (4th ed.). Englewood Cliffs, N.J.: Prentice-Hall, 1975.

Hilgard, E. R., & Marquis, D. G. *Conditioning and learning*. New York: Appleton-Century-Crofts, 1940.

Hull, C. L. *Principles of behavior*. New York: Appleton-Century-Crofts, 1943.

Kaufman, A. S. Behaviorism. In P. Edwards (Ed.), *The encyclopedia of philosophy* (Vol. 1). New York: Macmillan, 1967.

Kazdin, A. E. *History of behavior modification*. Baltimore: University Park Press, 1978.

Keller, F. S., & Schoenfeld, W. N. *Principles of psychology*. New York: Appleton-Century-Crofts, 1950.

Kerferd, G. B. Protagoras of Abdera. In P. Edwards (Ed.), *The encyclopedia of philosophy* (Vol. 6). New York: Macmillan, 1967.

Kitchener, R. F. Behavior and behaviorism. *Behaviorism*, 1977, *5*(2), 11–71.

Koch, S. Hull's *Principles of behavior. Psychological Bulletin*, 1944, *41*, 269–286.

Koch, S. Clark L. Hull. In W. K. Estes, S. Koch, K. MacCorquodale, P. E. Meehl, C. G. Mueller, W. N. Schoenfeld, & W. S. Verplanck, *Modern learning theory.* New York: Appleton-Century-Crofts, 1954.

Koch, S. Psychology and emerging conceptions of knowledge as unitary. In T. W. Wann (Ed.), *Behaviorism and phenomenology.* Chicago: University of Chicago Press, 1964.

Koch, S. Language communities, search cells, and the psychological studies. In W. J. Arnold (Ed.), *Nebraska Symposium on Motivation, 1975.* Lincoln: Univeristy of Nebraska Press, 1976. (a)

Koch, S. Review of Skinner's *About behaviorism. Contemporary Psychology,* 1976, *21,* 453–457. (b)

Krantz, D. L. (Ed.). *Schools of psychology: A symposium.* New York: Appleton-Century-Crofts, 1969.

Krechevsky, I. Review of Skinner's *The behavior of organisms. Journal of Abnormal and Social Psychology,* 1939, *34,* 404–407.

Kretzmann, N. Semantics, history of. In P. Edwards (Ed.), *The encyclopedia of philosophy* (Vol. 7). New York: Macmillan, 1967.

Lahren, B. *An exploratory functional analysis of stimulus control in descriptive verbal behavior.* Doctoral dissertation, University of Nevada, Reno, 1978.

Loeb, J. *The organism as a whole, from a physicochemical viewpoint.* New York: Putnam, 1916.

Lundin, R. W. *Theories and systems of psychology* (2nd ed.). Lexington, Mass.: D. C. Heath, 1979.

MacCorquodale, K. B. F. Skinner's *Verbal behavior:* A retrospective appreciation. *Journal of the Experimental Analysis of Behavior,* 1969, *12,* 831–841.

MacCorquodale, K. On Chomsky's review of Skinner's *Verbal behavior. Journal of the Experimental Analysis of Behavior,* 1970, *13,* 83–99.

Mach, E. *The analysis of sensations.* English translation. Chicago: Open Court Publishing Co., 1914. (Reference as cited in Skinner, 1938, p. 448.)

Mach, E. The science of mechanics, a critical and historical account of its development. LaSalle, Ill.: Open Court Publishing Co., 1942. Reference as cited in Skinner, 1967, p. 413.

Malone, J. C., Jr. William James and B. F. Skinner: Behaviorism, reinforcement, and interest. *Behaviorism,* 1975, *3,* 140–151.

Malone, J. C., Jr. Beyond the *operant* analysis of behavior. *Behavior Therapy,* 1978, *9,* 584–591.

Margolis, J. Mental states. *Behaviorism,* 1975, *3,* 23–31.

Marx, M. H., & Hillix, W. A. *Systems and theories in psychology* (2nd ed.). New York: McGraw-Hill, 1973.

Matson, F. W. *The broken image.* New York: George Braziller, 1964.

McCorkle, M. *A radical behaviorist study of "women's experience of conflict."* Doctoral dissertation, University of Nevada, Reno, 1978.

Meichenbaum, D. *Cognitive behavior modification.* Morristown, N.J.: General Learning Press, 1974.

Michael, J. Statistical inference for individual organism research: Mixed blessing or curse? *Journal of Applied Behavior Analysis,* 1974, *7,* 647–653.

Midgley, M. *Beast and man: The roots of human nature.* Ithaca, N.Y.: Cornell University Press, 1978.

Misiak, H., & Sexton, V. S. *History of psychology: An overview.* New York: Grune & Stratton, 1966.

Moore, E. C. *American pragmatism: Peirce, James, and Dewey.* New York: Columbia University Press, 1961.

Moore, J. On the principle of operationism in a science of behavior. *Behaviorism,* 1975, *3,* 120–138.

Morgan, C. L. *Introduction to comparative psychology.* London: W. Scott, 1894.

Murchison, C. Preface. In C. Murchison (Ed.), *Psychologies of 1925.* Worcester, Mass.: Clark University Press, 1926.

Murchison, C. Preface. In C. Murchison (Ed.), *Psychologies of 1930*. Worcester, Mass.: Clark University Press, 1930.

Murphy, G. Discussion. In D. L. Krantz (Ed.), *Schools of psychology: A symposium*. New York: Appleton-Century-Crofts, 1969.

Murphy, G., & Kovach, J. K. *Historical introduction to modern psychology* (3rd ed.). New York: Harcourt Brace Jovanovich, 1972.

Passmore, J. Logical positivism. In P. Edwards (Ed.), *The encyclopedia of philosophy* (Vol. 5). New York: Macmillan, 1967.

Patterson, G. R. A basis for identifying stimuli which control behaviors in natural settings. *Child Development*, 1974, *45*, 900-911.

Perry, R. B. *The thought and character of William James* (Vol. 2). Boston: Little, Brown, 1935.

Peters, R. S. (Ed.) *Brett's History of psychology*. New York: Macmillan, 1962.

Peters, R. S. Hobbes, Thomas. In P. Edwards (Ed.), *The encyclopedia of philosophy* (Vol. 4). New York: Macmillan, 1967.

Poffenberger, A. T. Foreword. In W. K. Estes, S. Koch, K. MacCorquodale, P. E. Meehl, C. G. Mueller, W. N. Schoenfeld, & W. S. Verplanck, *Modern learning theory*. New York: Appleton-Century-Crofts, 1954.

Poling, A. The ubiquity of the cumulative record: A quote from Skinner and a frequency count. *Journal of the Experimental Analysis of Behavior*, 1979, *31*, 126.

Powell, R. P., & Still, A. W. Behaviorism and the psychology of language: An historical reassessment. *Behaviorism*, 1979, *7*, 71-89.

Rachlin, H. Skinner and the philosophers. Review of Harzem and Miles's *Conceptual issues in operant psychology*. *Contemporary Psychology*, 1979, *24*, 184-185.

Ringen, J. Explanation, teleology and operant behaviorism. *Philosophy of Science*, 1976, *43*, 223-253.

Roberts, L. E. Operant conditioning of autonomic responses: One perspective on the curare experiments. In G. E. Schwartz & D. Shapiro (Eds.), *Consciousness and self-regulation*. New York: Plenum, 1978.

Robinson, D. N. *An intellectual history of psychology*. New York: Macmillan, 1976.

Robischon, T. Holt, Edwin Bissell. In P. Edwards (Ed.), *The encyclopedia of philosophy* (Vol. 4). New York: Macmillan, 1967.

Romanes, G. J. *Animal intelligence*. London: Kegan Paul, Trench & Co., 1882.

Russell, B. *A history of western philosophy*. New York: Simon & Schuster, 1945.

Schlesinger, G. Operationalism. In P. Edwards (Ed.), *The encyclopedia of philosophy* (Vol. 5). New York: Macmillan, 1967.

Schnaitter, R. Private causes. *Behaviorism*, 1978, *6*, 1-12.

Sidman, M. Remarks. *Behaviorism*, 1979, *7*, 123-126.

Skinner, B. F. The concept of the reflex in the description of behavior. *Journal of General Psychology*, 1931, *5*, 427-458.

Skinner, B. F. *The behavior of organisms*. New York: Appleton-Century-Crofts, 1938.

Skinner, B. F. The operational analysis of psychological terms. *Psychological Review*, 1945, *52*, 270-277; 291-294.

Skinner, B. F. Are theories of learning necessary? *Psychological Review*, 1950, *57*, 193-216.

Skinner, B. F. *Science and human behavior*. New York: Macmillan, 1953.

Skinner, B. F. A case history in scientific method. *American Psychologist*, 1956, *11*, 221-233.

Skinner, B. F. *Verbal behavior*. New York: Appleton-Century-Crofts, 1957.

Skinner, B. F. *Cumulative record*. New York: Appleton-Century-Crofts, 1959.

Skinner, B. F. Behaviorism at fifty. In T. W. Wann (Ed.), *Behaviorism and phenomenology*. Chicago: University of Chicago Press, 1964.

Skinner, B. F. B. F. Skinner. In E. G. Boring & G. Lindzey (Eds.), *A history of psychology in autobiography* (Vol. 5). New York: Appleton-Century-Crofts, 1967.

Skinner, B. F. *Contingencies of reinforcement*. New York: Appleton-Century-Crofts, 1969.

Skinner, B. F. *Beyond freedom and dignity*. New York: Alfred A. Knopf, 1971.

Skinner, B. F. *About behaviorism* (College ed.). New York: Alfred A. Knopf, 1974.

Skinner, B. F. Farewell, my LOVELY! *Journal of the Experimental Analysis of Behavior,* 1976, 25, 218.

Snell, B. *The discovery of the mind* (T. G. Rosenmeyer, Trans.). Oxford: Basil Blackwell, 1953. (Originally published, 1948.)

Staats, A. W. *Social Behaviorism.* Homewood, Ill.: Dorsey Press, 1975.

Tatarkiewicz, W. *Twentieth century philosophy* (1900–1950) (C. A. Kisiel, Trans.). Belmont, Cal.: Wadsworth, 1973.

Thayer, H. S. Pragmatism. In P. Edwards (Ed.), *The encyclopedia of philosophy* (Vol. 6). New York: Macmillan, 1967.

Thayer, H. S. *Meaning and action: A critical history of pragmatism.* Indianapolis: Bobbs-Merrill, 1968.

Thorndike, E. L. Animal intelligence: An experimental study of the associative processes in animals. *Psychological Review Monograph Supplements,* 1898, 2(4).

Tweney, R. D. Reflections on the history of behavioral theories of language. *Behaviorism,* 1979, 7, 91–103.

Verplanck, W. S. Burrhus F. Skinner. In W. K. Estes, S. Koch, K. MacCorquodale, P. E. Meehl, C. G. Mueller, W. N. Schoenfeld, & W. S. Verplanck, *Modern learning theory.* New York: Appleton-Century-Crofts, 1954.

Wann, T. W. (Ed.) *Behaviorism and phenomenology.* Chicago: University of Chicago Press, 1964.

Watson, J. B. Psychology as the behaviorist views it. *Psychological Review,* 1913, 20, 158–177.

Wertheimer, M. *A brief history of psychology* (Rev. ed.). New York: Holt, Rinehart, & Winston, 1979.

Wilson, E. O. *Sociobiology.* Cambridge, Mass.: Harvard University Press, 1975.

Wolpe, J. *The practice of behavior therapy.* Oxford: Pergamon, 1969.

Woodworth, R. S. Dynamic psychology. In C. Murchison (Ed.), *Psychologies of 1925.* Worcester, Mass.: Clark University Press, 1926.

Woodworth, R. S. *Contemporary schools of psychology.* New York: Ronald Press, 1931.

Recommended Readings

Cohen, D. J. *B. Watson: The founder of behaviorism.* London: Routledge & Kegan Paul, 1979.

Day, W. Contemporary behaviorism and the concept of intention. In J. K. Cole *et al.* (Eds.), *Nebraska Symposium on Motivation, 1975.* Lincoln: University of Nebraska Press, 1976.

Heidbreder, E., *Seven psychologies.* New York: Appleton-Century-Crofts, 1933.

Krantz, D. L. (Ed.), *Schools of psychology: A symposium.* New York: Appleton-Century-Crofts, 1969.

Rychlak, J. F. *The psychology of rigorous humanism.* New York: Wiley, 1977.

Smith, K. R. *Behavior and conscious experience: A conceptual analysis.* Athens, Ohio: Ohio University Press, 1969.

MAURICE GREEN
R. W. RIEBER

12

The Assimilation
of Psychoanalysis
in America

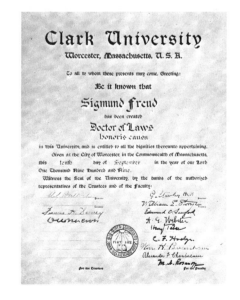

PSYCHOLOGY:
THEORETICAL-HISTORICAL PERSPECTIVES

ISBN 0-12-588265-3

Origins and Groundwork

The groundwork for psychology in America before the Civil War, described in Chapter 6 by Rieber, establishes the development of the American dream and psychology's role in it. This groundwork consisted of the democratic way of embodying a belief in the equal opportunity and right of everyone to participate in the shaping of their own lives and destinies. This is basically compatible with the democratic government of agrarian capitalism first and with industrial capitalism later. All scientific discoveries were valued because they were seen as applied to the good of each and every individual as well as to the nation at large.

The second important part of the groundwork consisted of the belief that every individual had the capacity to change for the better in accordance with his needs and desires—the "do-it-yourself" philosophy embodied in the children's story of the Little Red Hen. This change of personality was seen not as some arbitrary and capricious activity but as a morally serious behavior directed toward the benefit of all mankind. Education of course, was a necessary and important instrument of all this for the cultivation of both the body and the mind. The family as an institution played a key role in providing discipline, moral training, and the knowledge and skill required by the growing society.

The third important part of the groundwork was religious faith and lifestyle, extremely varied but usually true to the ethnic origins of the families.

The deity was to be appreciated not only by the study of the Scriptures but also by the accurate study of nature—the work of the Creator. This lay the connection for the belief in the value of the inner life of the individual and in the importance of self-knowledge. All this groundwork was brought to America in its very beginnings by the Puritan Pilgrims and has remained alive to the present day. These very factors allowed for the easy assimilation of psychoanalysis in America as well as the assimilation of many earlier "fads," such as Darwinism, phrenology, and mesmerism. With the casting of this mold, psychoanalysis had to be shaped in its American assimilation to conform to this preexisting framework in some considerable measure. We shall see how the beginnings of psychoanalytic thinking developed in Europe, what similar work was developing in America, and how the specific work of Freud and his associates in Vienna and Zurich was received and assimilated into the early and persisting American dream.

Hegels's personification of society—his view of the state as a single organism, like a person—is reflected by Freud and Jung in their notions of the collective unconscious, of group psychology, and of the archaic ego, the inherited deposit of racial history. His dialectic thesis, antithesis, and synthesis also influenced Freud, especially in his preoccupation with polarities of opposites, such as male and female, love and hate, life and death, and passive and aggressive.

During the early nineteenth century, the unconscious part of the mind received increasing attention, and by the mid-1880s, the term unconscious, which originally had meant simply to be unaware of something, had come to denote a separate part of the mind existing outside of awareness. However, this meaning still lacked respectable, scientific status. This was less true of psychology itself. But Immanuel Kant's criticism of psychology still held great weight. Kant had denied that psychology could ever become an exact natural science, for an exact science depends on accurate measurements that are impossible to achieve in dealing with internal phenomena of mental activity. There is no weight, size, or volume to thought, Kant asserted; its only dimension is duration, which is inadequate by itself as a unit of measurement.

The nineteenth-century German philosopher Johann Friedrich Herbart attempted to answer Kant's objection by adding the dimension of force or intensity. Ideas have force, as well as duration, and conflict with each other. On the basis of these two dimensions, he argued, mental activity can be measured. In this way, Herbart sought to establish a truly scientific psychology that could be formulated in quantitative mathematical terms. This ideal was never completely realized, but quantitative concepts played an increasingly important part henceforth in general psychology as well as in psychoanalytic thought. The same search goes on today, where statistics and other mathematical tools are important in psychological research.

Herbart elaborated Kant's unknowable reality by assuming it to be made up of separate entities constantly disturbing and reacting against each other. The soul of man, in Herbart's view, is such an entity: The ideas of conscious and unconscious life are the reactions of our unknowable, real soul to the disturbing impingement of other entities, such as other unknowable souls. Ideas, here, mean all mental activity, including sensations, impulses, feelings, images, and words. These ideas react against or support each other, and their behavior determines the content of consciousness. Imagine consciousness to be a beam of light shining through a window; the turbulent motes of dust seen rising up, bumping against each other, and falling down and disappearing below this beam of light are the ideas struggling with each other for the threshold of attention. When an idea is overcome by an opposing idea, Herbart says, it is pushed back or repressed below the light of conscious attention. He thus introduced the term repression in the sense that Freud later used it, to refer to this forceful pushing back of something into the unconscious. He also stated that when something is repressed, it regresses or returns to a more primitive form; for example, a word becomes an image, an image becomes a feeling.

Herbart also described a notion of an apperception mass—namely, a compact, organized, unconscious group of ideas present in the mind that determines whether new ideas will be retained or not. Jung later elaborated a similar notion, to which he applied the term psychic complex and which is reflected today in the terms inferiority complex, oedipal complex, etc. An inferiority complex, so to speak, draws ideas that contain the feeling of inferiority, or the compensation for it, and it excludes ideas that would conflict with these feelings.

Freud used Herbart's popular textbook in his own studies at the university and was undoubtedly influenced considerably by him. Herbart also had an influence on American education, and a National Herbart Society honoring him was formed here.

A Herbart section of the National Education Association was formed, and his authoritarian pedogogical German model of educational method had profound influence throughout America until challenged by John Dewey, who laid the foundations for the interactional approach in education and the interpersonal approach in psychiatry and psychoanalysis. It was popular and traditional by that time to eulogize nature and the natural (as "unconscious") in man. A famous study by the German philosopher Hartmann, *The Philosophy of the Unconscious* appeared in 1869 and was widely translated in many different countries and reappeared in many editions. It described the action of unconscious forces manifested in feelings, instincts, personality changes, historical events and processes, religion, art, language, and literature in much the same way later described by popular psychoanalytic writers.

Sigmund Freud's voice was well received in the book he did with Breuer, *Studies in Hysteria* (Breuer & Freud, 1895), and was dismissed as he became preoccupied with the so-called polymorphous perverse infantile sexuality and its role in later life. However, contrary to his posture, he was not a lonely solitary truth sayer unfairly discriminated against in a hypocritical puritanical conventional world. In Germany and in eastern Europe in the last two decades of the nineteenth century, there was a preoccupation with the dark side of sexuality in the work of many writers. The extremely popular and widely read book on sexual perversions by Krafft-Ebing is only the best known of these; it is still being reprinted.

In the Ukraine, whence hundreds of people moved to Vienna, there was a group of realist writers led by Stanislaw Przybyszewski, who treated sexual themes in a bold way and preached that every individual is an absolute law unto himself, a direct inheritance from Rousseau, of course. (Freud's notion of a primal father reflects this same idea.) Sexual preoccupations pervaded the sophisticated literary and bohemian society of the Austro-Hungarian Empire, in which Freud grew up. Figure 12.1 shows Freud at various times of his life. In Vienna during his early professional career, there were three principal literary personalities—Hermann Bahr, Hugo von Hofmannsthal, and Arthur Schnitzler. Bahr was a pronounced atheist and realist. Hofmannsthal was intensely fascinated by disease and mental illness, which gave his work a morbid quality. Schnitzler was a brilliant analyst of character, preoccupied with mental and emotional aberration. His writings were pervaded with skepticism, nihilism, and lust for pleasurable sensations. These writers faithfully reflected the Weltanschauung of cultivated Viennese society. They had many imitators. Freud's work fits into this context clearly.

Medical practitioners joined realist writers such as Zola in France and Dickens in England in this concern over the degradation and deterioration of the quality of human living consequent to the harsh and rigid industrial urban development. They were also constantly on guard against losing the ground they had won for scientific authority over the authority of superstition and religion, and they celebrated their anatomical and physiological discoveries frequently in popular literature. By and large, the medical profession still enthusiastically believed that these discoveries pointed the way to eventual command over sickness. This accounts for the emphasis placed on physical factors in disease and for the rather considerable weight given in medical opinion to the view of disease as the result of a weakness or defect in man's physical constitution. Mental illness was thought to be caused by such physical factors as inherited constitutional defects, infections, and tumors, although some recognition was also given to social, psychological, and other factors as contributing causes.

The wide popularization of these medical theories explains in part the gloomy preoccupation with sickness in the closing decades of the nineteenth century. Physical illness in many respects came to represent man's human situation and to substitute in popular thought for moral weakness. Popular presses rapidly sold out works on depravity and perversion. Krafft-Ebing's *Psychopathia Sexualis* (1886/1909) was a bestseller for decades. Freud's case histories are very superior examples of this same approach. Investigators of this period coined many new words: All the terms now used to designate the phobias (hemato-, agora-, claustro-) and the manias (hypo-, hyper-, klepto, eroto-) first came into use at this time, as did also the terms paranoia, sadism, and masochism, which were coined by Krafft-Ebing. In other words, much of the language of modern psychiatry and psychoanalysis began here in this period and in this medical context.

Included among the stigmata or signs of degeneration were the loss of moral sense, excessive originality, morbid vanity, mystical tendencies, religious enthusiasm, and revolutionary ideas. Evidently only a hardworking, hardheaded type of middle-class person could qualify as healthy here. The causes of degeneration were variously described—climate, industry, social and political upheavals, large cities, and alcohol all come in for a share of the blame. The treatment recommended was hypnosis, autosuggestion, changes in diet travel, hot baths, narcotics, rest, work, and lemonade. For the worst cases, sterilization was recommended. Some investigators also recommended amputation of the clitoris for nervous women. There was some real basis for castration anxiety with one's physician in those days.

FIGURE 12.1 *Sigmund Freud. a. Age 8, 1864. b. Age 16, 1872. c. Age 35, 1891. d. Age 60, 1916. e. Age 64, 1920. f. In his early seventies.*

The studies of degeneration were particularly concerned with the genius. Morel in the 1850s wrote that the genius is a neurotic, a sublime fool. Hence, such a weakness in itself was conventionally given a certain prestige as a mark of artistic sensitivity or creative potential. This led to a kind of conventional

e   f

FIGURE 12.1 (continued.)

splitting of the human personality into a physically degenerate, emotional, oversensitive soul, separated from a physically healthy, insensitive, aggressive one. Sickness itself thus became both a sign of genius and a mark of destiny—evidence of the delicate superiority of the poet over the physically vigorous and strong but morally inferior businessmen and industrialists.

Ironically, then, the discoveries of anatomical and physiological research that had seemed in the early nineteenth century to promise the conquest of human illness came into support of a general escapist and self-indulgent tendency in the closing decades of the century. Many conservative medical writers contributed to this development by their tendency to call everyone and everything of which they did not approve "sick"—a useful label for evading political and social choices.

Psychological theory was strongly influenced by the views on the nature and cause of sickness advanced by Benedict Morel. In his *Traité des Dégénérescences, Physiques, Intellectuelles et Morales de L'Espèce Humaine* (1853), Morel attributed what he called degenerations in the human species to the following causes: (a) physical deformity and arrested development (later reflected by Alfred Adler in his organ inferiority theory); (b) perversions of normal function (reflected in Freud's theory of infantile sexuality); (c) disturbance of intellectual and emotional faculties (reflected in Jung's theory of introversion); (d) adverse conditions in the physical and social environment (taken up by all later theories). On the basis of this theory of the nature and cause of sickness, Morel attempted to explain the fall of civilizations. Society

and morals decayed and deteriorated, he asserted, because of the constitu-
tionally sick individuals, such as Nero in ancient Rome, who were the leaders.
In 1860 Morel expanded his concept of degeneration to include not only
alcoholism, drug addiction, mental deficiency, languor, inertia, apathy,
melancholy, malaise, and suicidal tendencies but also pyromania, klep-
tomania, erotomania, nymphomania, and necrophilia. These degenerations,
according to Morel, could be caused by unfortunate love affairs or thwarted
ambition or could be simply the inevitable consequences of advancing
civilization. (The inhibiting force of advancing civilization was a causal agent
that Freud later made central to his own theories about sexual inhibitions.)

Morel's work set the stage for the psychological investigations of the latter
part of the nineteenth century. Moll, Moebius, and Krafft-Ebing all followed
the precedent set by him, the scientific convention of making detailed descriptions of individual patients and then drawing inferences from these descriptions. Krafft-Ebing's and others' compilations of such descriptions of sexual
behavior of men and women in history were published to show evidence of
degeneracy in their personalities and physiques. These writers were also concerned with unmasking the superior intellectual powers. (Psychoanalytic
studies, such as Freud's study of Leonardo da Vinci (1947) continued this approach.) Lombroso, for example, stated unequivocally that genius is merely a
sublime form of insanity, and he implied that intellectual activity in general
might be a kind of refinement of criminal propensities. There was general
agreement on the relation of art to insanity.

Freud's work was misidentified perhaps in the popular literature of pre-
World War I as synonymous with the rhetoric of sexual liberation associated
with many of the movements for reform and revolution in America and
Europe. He was publicly endorsed by Leon Trotsky and was popular among
many of the Marxist–Leninist circles then, although later strongly rejected by
the Communists and Marxists as a representative of bourgeois decadence.
Recently, Marxist–Leninist writers in France, such as some members of the
structuralist movement, and the radical writers represented by Marcuse and
Lasch in America have again taken up Freud as a "revolutionary liberator."

Freud himself was basically opposed to Marxism and socialism, having had
Wilhelm Reich ostracized from the psychoanalytic establishment for this
reason. He maintained by and large a conservative position identified with
medicine, in spite of his defense of lay analysis, and practiced the popular
techniques of his time, such as shocking people's limbs with faradic currents
and using hypnosis. He was familiar with the work of J. Hughlings Jackson,
Spencer, and Darwin, and had translated some of the work of J. S. Mill into
German. These writers undoubtedly influenced his evolutionary and ontogenetic approach.

After he studied the work of Charcot and Bernheim in France, Freud
assimilated what he learned to his early education with Herbart's thought,
thereby developing notions of primary and secondary process, unconscious

fantasy, and the determining force of childhood memories. The notion of condition prime, or primary condition, was frequently used in hypnosis to refer to the natural state of the subject, uninfluenced by the force of hypnotic instructions; the term secondary condition referred to the conditioned state in which the original natural state is modified by hypnotic influences. Substitute reality for hypnotic and one has Freud's primary process and secondary process, more or less. Frederick W. H. Meyers and E. Gurney of England in the 1880s described the unconscious strivings of another self apart from the conscious self, which they called the subliminal self. They believed every human being had this kind of divided personality. Writers of fiction portrayed this theme—for example, Dostoevsky in *The Double* and Stevenson in *Dr. Jekyll and Mr. Hyde*. In America in the 1880s and 1890s, Boris Sidis, Morton Prince, Joseph Jastrow, and others were investigating these aspects of personality under the leadership of William James.

The important turning point from hypnotic therapy to psychoanalysis occurred in Breuer's experience in treating Anna O. In fact, in his lectures given at Clark University in Worcester, Massachusetts, in 1909, Freud credited Breuer with being the true founder of psychoanalysis. There was a period in the course of what Freud referred to as the "talking-out treatment" when Anna O. spoke again and again of her thirst. Then one day she went into a trance state in which she remembered a childhood experience of her nurse letting a dog drink out of Anna's drinking glass. With the recall of this incident, she became very angry at the nurse and expressed this anger toward Breuer directly. After this, her symptom of thirst disappeared. The point was, Freud emphasized, that simply to talk about the incident involving the nurse and the dog was insufficient for cure. What was required was that Anna O. express the strong feeling of anger that she had felt toward the nurse. She expressed this anger toward Breuer. Breuer named this expression of emotion "abreaction"—the patient now reacted toward the psychiatrist with the earlier emotion felt toward the traumatic figure. He distinguished this from catharsis, which was simply the relief experienced at talking out the fantasies that were imagined or remembered.

Freud paid special attention to this phenomenon of emotional discharge, even though Breuer was more interested in the different types of states of consciousness in which these reactions were originally formed and later expressed. Freud had been dedicated under Brücke to the understanding of all living phenomena, physiological and psychological, in terms of basic physical forces struggling with each other for the light of consciousness. He made this emotional discharge a quantitative item like Herbart's force or intensity. He called it the charge, the sum of excitation, the quantity of excitation, the quantity of affect—these are all terms that he used in his attempt to abstract the fundamental or physical event from the communication between the patient and the doctor.

This emotional discharge was a certain something analogous to the "electric current" that he was later to call the libido. He identified it with the intensity of feeling abstracted from the meaning that might be observed in a patient or communicated by a patient. As Breuer traced the thirst of Anna O. to her repressed anger toward her nurse, so Freud traced Lucy R.'s symptom to her repressed love for her employer. In both cases, the repressed emotions were thought to represent quantities of a kind of electrochemical fluid that was held back somewhere in the organism, prevented from flowing out or discharging. Freud (1946) developed this notion of excitation in repression further in his important paper in 1894, "The Defence Neuropsychoses" (pp. 59–75).

Freud early sought to generalize these ideas into an all-embracing medical philosophy. All real causes, he believed, are symbolized in science by the word "force." Progress in knowledge has reduced all forms of force to attraction and repulsion. This applies to man, as Freud saw it, as well as to all other organisms and to the physical–chemical universe. The unity of science and physical force, taught by Brücke, was something that Freud believed in with passion from his earliest writings to his last published work, *An Outline of Psychoanalysis* (1940/1949a). Until his dying day, Freud sought to make psychoanalysis a science in the same sense that physics was a science.

Studies in Hysteria (Breuer & Freud, 1895) was widely and enthusiastically endorsed. The concept of the unconscious put forth in these studies referred mainly to the past experiences, memories, and feelings that the individual cannot or will not communicate because of shame or fear of ridicule or condemnation. Soon, however, Freud began to develop a less personal and less individual concept of the unconscious—a concept that had more to do with electrochemical forces and with the romantic Absolute or Will. This grew out of his increasing interest in the sexual history of his patients and his recognition of the part it played in the origin and development of their neurotic illnesses. In tracing memories further and further back to the patient's earliest traumatic experience, he found childhood sexual experiences that very much impressed him. This led to the discovery of infantile sexual traumas, reported in his paper "Further Remarks on the Defence Neuropsychoses" (1896). On the basis of this early incomplete work, Freud assumed that he had discovered here the principal cause of these mental illnesses. Cure would follow, he believed, upon the complete analysis of every individual symptom by tracing back associations until one came to the primary cause, the early sexual trauma.

The long collaboration with Breuer that resulted in the *Studies in Hysteria* was ended on the issue of Freud's conviction that sexuality is the only key to an understanding of all neuroses. Freud now went on to formulate his theory of psychoanalysis, with its emphasis on inhibited sexual excitation as the exclusive etiological agent in psychopathology. This was poorly received in the scientific and medical communities not because of Victorian prudery as Freud alleged but because of its inadequate scientific base.

The work with Breuer, from which some of the early roots of psychoanalysis grew, was itself deeply rooted in the mechanistic science, hypnotic studies, and romantic tendencies of the nineteenth century. These same influences carried over into psychoanalytic theory and practice. In particular, as J. Rioch and others have pointed out, psychoanalysis reflects Freud's early orientation in hypnotic therapy. He continued to conceive of his role as essentially that of the hypnotist. In hypnotic therapy, the patient's memories and fantasies were supposedly something completely apart from the hypnotist. Similarly, in psychoanalysis, Freud assumed that he himself—who he was and what he did—had no reflection in the content of the patient's memories and communications. Later he also thought that, just as hypnotic subjects acted out their memories with the hypnotist, his patients presented their memories in their behavior with him rather than in their speech. For example, the patient acted out in his feelings toward him, Freud discovered, some past experiences with his own father without recognizing it as a memory or communicating it as such. Freud called this process "transference"—that is, the wish or feeling of some earlier experience was transferred from past figures onto the figure of Freud himself, the therapist. Through the process of transference, the psychoanalyst was able, like the hypnotist, to recapture childhood memories by evoking the behavior and feelings of the child in the adult. This then became another method of making the unconscious conscious.

In abandoning the hypnotic technique, Freud never abandoned the hypnotic aim—that of relieving the symptoms of mental illness by recovering lost memories of the painful experiences out of which the symptoms had arisen; psychoanalysis, as Freud conceived of it, was simply a more effective technique for achieving this aim. This may account for the role he implicitly assigns to the psychoanalyst—that of a composite figure, half detached doctor–scientist and half romantic mesmerist, rescuing a painful sexual life from a stifling civilization in the name of science.

Classical psychoanalysis began to attain popular acceptance in America, and in small circles in Europe, in the first decade of the twentieth century. This decade was an extraordinarily fruitful period in many other fields of human endeavor also. Revolutionary currents that had begun in the previous century with the disintegration of older conventional forms, traditions, and values now emerged rich in energy and creative potential. By 1900, for example, the Moscow Art Theatre had been founded by Stanislavsky, who declared war on all previous conventions of the theatre. By 1900, also, John Dewey had established his experimental school at the University of Chicago, which repudiated Herbart and the prevailing conventions of education. By 1904 Isadora Duncan had set up her school near Berlin, dedicated to freeing the art of the dance from confining classical conventions. In 1905 Einstein published his *Theory of Relativity*, which profoundly undermined long-established scientific conventions. Between 1900 and 1910, Picasso and others struck out in a number of new directions in painting, and Debussy, Stravinsky, and Schoenberg introduced revolutionizing new forms of music. Gertrude Stein, during this same period, was waging her own personal revolution against the established conventions in poetry, and Frank Lloyd Wright was initiating a revolution in architecture with his new concepts of functional form. Is it any wonder that Freud, in the context of this social, political, scientific, and aesthetic revolution, sought to overthrow the established conventional point of view in psychiatry? Whether or not Freud was aware of these movements is irrelevant; for any individual, as widely read and intellectually accomplished as Freud, would have felt the impact of these developments.

The great American psychologist and philosopher, William James, was as painfully aware as Freud of the essentially tragic quality of human existence. "We are all potentially sick men," he wrote in 1895.

> The sanest and best of us are of one clay with lunatics and prison-inmates. And whenever we feel this, such a sense of the vanity of our voluntary career comes over us, that all our morality appears but as a plaster hiding a sore it can never cure, and our well-doing as the hollowest substitute for that well-being that our lives ought to be grounded in, but alas! are not [Perry, 1954, p. 265].

Freud saw the tragedy of human existence in the irreconcilable conflict between man's instinctual sexual nature and civilization; in line with his strict determinism, his only answer to this was enlightened resignation. James saw this tragedy in the shortness of the life that man is given in which to learn so much and in the necessity for so much to be painfully learned again and again in every generation. In spite of these limitations, however, he believed that both the individual human being and the human race can grow by looking at each new situation afresh, seeking novelty and adventure. This attitude gave a forward thrust to his pragmatic psychology, which at times appeared as a kind of naive optimism; but nothing could be further from the true stoic spirit with which James bravely faced the fact of pain and suffering in human experience. "I can't bring myself, as so many men seem able to do, to blink the evil out of sight, and gloss it over," he wrote in 1870. "It's as real as the good, and if it is denied, good must be denied too. It must be accepted and hated and resisted while there is breath in our bodies [Perry, 1954, p. 388]."

The pragmatic psychology of Peirce, James, and Dewey, with its emphasis on the social and interpersonal quality of man's very being, profoundly influenced American psychological thought in the late nineteenth and early twentieth centuries. This influence is conspicuous, for example, in the theory of personality advanced by Thorstein Veblen. Although Veblen is known primarily as an economist, his theory of personality, first formulated in the 1890s, has contributed significantly to an understanding of personality dynamics. Like James—and like Adolf Meyer, whose work will be considered later—Veblen saw the fallacy of explaining human behavior in terms of the pleasure–pain principle; he emphasized the social context in which all individual personality must be grounded. Habits of thought molded by this social context and its institutions, rather than any inherited instinctual patterns per se, he asserted, are the dynamic factors in human behavior.

Like the pragmatists, too—and also like the romantics, including Freud—Veblen was bitterly critical of particular processes and institutions in the social order that are destructive of human values and impose obstacles to personality development. The gist of his criticism is that the existence in modern society of a moneyed prestige class that does not produce and that asserts its importance by conspicuous expenditure on wasteful leisure activity has led to the development of a social order based on exploitative mechanisms and hypocritical frauds. In this social order, the context in which personality is grounded, everyone's success in life is measured by the extent to which he is able to imitate this leisure class. Consequently, the importance of social class membership determines all social values and becomes a dynamic factor in human behavior. This "accepted scheme" of things, Veblen believed, lies at the root of many of the problems of individual personality development in modern society.

Independently of Freud, Veblen arrived at his own idea of repression in terms of the individual's adaptation to his social class. "Such human material as does not lend itself to the methods of life imposed by the accepted scheme," he wrote in 1899,

> suffers more or less elimination as well as repression. The principles of pecuniary emulation (imitating the rich) and of industrial exemption (exemption of the leisure class) have in this way been erected into canons of life, and have become coercive factors of some importance in the situation to which men have to adapt themselves [p. 212].

Veblen did not influence psychiatry directly in his own day, but he anticipated in some ways the later psychiatric developments of Sullivan, Fromm, and Horney. His penetrating analysis of the corrosive effect of business ideology on human life made a great impact on the creative searching minds of his time, and his influence is reflected in the thinking of many of the New Dealers who helped shape the social revolution of the 1930s in the United States.

Actually, the attack on status climbing, hypocritical conformity, wasteful leisure, and sterile dogma in American culture, so eloquently voiced by Veblen, has been made with curious frequency in American literature and philosophy from the earliest days of the Republic down to present times—from Thomas Jefferson down through Emerson, Thoreau, Whitman, Mark Twain, Theodore Dreiser, H. L. Mencken, and William Faulkner, to cite only a few examples. This characteristic attitude accounts for the eager audience that European critics of the American scene have always found here. It may also explain why American psychiatrists and psychologists were the first official group to recognize the importance of Freud's contributions. For

Freud, in spite of his many shortcomings, was also trying to penetrate the disguises of conventional society. His detailed case histories, however narrowly he interpreted them in terms of his libido theory, were impressive in their clinical candor and social realism.

But independently of Freud, psychiatric treatment based on the recovery of dissociated memories and feelings was being carried on in America as well as in Europe during these years. Boris Sidis, a former student of William James and one of the founders of the New York State Psychiatric Institute, published many articles and a couple of books on the problems of dissociation at the turn of the century. Like Pierre Janet and Freud, he abandoned the technique of hypnosis for that of a sympathetic rapport, encouraging a free flow of associations from his patients. "The patient is simply asked to tell the nature of ideas and images that entered his mind," he wrote in 1897 (Sidis, 1902, p. 107). William Alanson White, who studied with Sidis for several years, described his own adaptation of the technique he had learned from him as follows:

> I had Mr. X sit in a room only dimly lighted and very quiet, in a semi-reclining position, and then assuring him that memories would return (influence of suggestion), asked him to fix his attention on the events just related, more particularly at that point where memory ceased, and see if he could not recall additional facts [Sidis, 1902, p. 108].

With this technique, White arrived at an understanding of neurotic symptoms and behavior that had previously seemed imcomprehensible. He said of another patient with whom he used this technique:

> It is noteworthy in this connection, that all of her acts and sayings which had previously seemed to have no foundation and reasons, but on the contrary had every appearance of being quite incoherent, could be traced back in each instance to an adequate cause, and thus what appeared as chaos on the surface was reduced to order [cited in Sidis, 1902, p. 153].

George M. Parker, Boris Sidis's assistant, wrote of Sidis's approach in 1902:

> It definitely points out the great importance of bringing all the dissociated memories out of the depths of the subconscious and reassociating them in the synthesis of the upper personality, restoring all the lost psychic material to the contracted active personal consciousness, and thus bringing about a state of former mental activity which will maintain the formed synthesis [cited in Sidis, 1902, p. 319].

The emphasis here on the synthetic over the analytic aspects of psychotherapy anticipated Jung's emphasis on synthesis by many years. Freud later introduced this in his ego psychology.

In *The Psychology of Suggestion* (1898), Sidis formalized his thinking about the role of the subconscious in mental illness and health. Here he described subconscious mental activity as an unquestionable fact in human experience. There is, he asserted, a subconscious mind capable of memory and even intelligence. He further asserted that this subconscious mind is the medium through which all messages of perception or sensation come to the conscious self. And he asserted the importance of a human relationship in effecting a change in that self (Sidis, 1898). Sidis characterized the subconscious mind as follows: It lacks all critical sense; it follows the letter rather than the spirit; it accepts any suggestion; it lacks all sense of the true and the rational; it is devoid of all morality; it has no will; and it is essentially a brutal self, such as one sees manifested in crowds and mobs.

Sidis, White, and Parker thought the pathological dissociation on which mental illness is based to be caused by a combination of psychic trauma and characteristic tendencies of the personality. There are, first of all, the previous tendencies of the patient toward such things as daydreaming, sleepwalking, and exaggerated emotional display; the present illness is then precipitated by some psychic trauma that occurs either in waking life or in the subconscious. Once the dissociation occurs in this way, it tends to extend, to grow and develop, unless it is arrested by good fortune or interrupted and healed by treatment.

Another former student of William James, Morton Prince, published many studies on dissociation in the 1890s and later. His classic work, *The Dissociation of Personality* (1905/1957) described at length a case of multiple personality that he successfully treated over a period of many years. He demonstrated in this work how, under conditions of emotional strain and fatigue, dissociated systems can emerge into greater prominence and activity in the personality. (Prince is also known as the founder of the *Journal of Abnormal and Social Psychology* and of the Harvard Psychological Clinic. In 1910 he joined with Boris Sidis, who shared these interests, in founding the Psychopathological Association.)

However, the most profoundly learned psychiatrist of this period in America was undoubtedly Adolf Meyer. During the same time that Freud in Vienna was developing his libido theory and gathering around him a small group of disciples, Meyer was developing his theory of psychobiological reactions. Under the influence of Peirce, James, and Dewey, he rejected not only the idea, so popular among the Germans, that mental processes can be separated into affect and ideas but also the whole tendency of his time to model theories of human behavior, as Freud and others attempted to do, on laboratory studies of the nerve cell. He likewise rejected the search for the Absolute—the *ding an sich*, or thing-in-itself, that haunted European psychologists and made them distrust the phenomenal appearance of the patient's experience. Under this unfortunate legacy of Immanuel Kant, they wanted to reduce all the phenomena to the "ultimate reality," and thing-in-itself, of their particular dogma. Meyer, in contrast, exhorted psychiatrists to formulate their observations experimentally in terms of their own experiences with individual patients, rather than dogmatically, so that their conclusions could be brought to a test.

In 1896, the year after Freud and Breuer published their *Studies in Hysteria,* Meyer published a paper that marked the beginning of his psychobiological orientation in psychiatry. Like Peirce and James, he viewed the psychological reactions of man as continuous with and inseparable from physiological, chemical, and anatomical reactions. He said here

> All life is reaction, either to stimuli of the outside world or of the various parts of the organism. We recognize death by the absolute absence of these reactions. In our mental life these reactions are pictured as if in a mirror. (Our thoughts are like reflections of our experience in the mirror of our mind.) But not every reaction appears in this mirror, in other words, becomes conscious. Most of the reactions during sleep, all during epileptic fits, during syncope (fainting spells), remain unconscious; in other words, we do not remember having been aware of them and do not give any evidence of consciousness at the time. In our daily life, in walking and working, we heed many things without thinking of them. Further, many reactions take place in our mind which are not expressed. They take the form of "simple" thought. They seem, indeed, purely mental, and create the appearance on which the idea of mind independent from the body is built [from, Meyer, A., *The Commonsense Psychiatry of Dr. Adolf Meyer* (A. Lief, Ed.), copyright © 1948 by McGraw-Hill, p. 89].

If we trace back some of these "simple" ideas that seem to just flit across our minds, we see that they are part and parcel of our own movement of living, of what we feel and do and respond to in our everyday life.

Meyer deplored equally both the exclusive emphasis placed by philosophers on the psychological processes and the exclusive emphasis placed by the physicians and psychiatrists of his acquaintance on physiological and structural conditions. He exhorted the medical schools particularly to offer a much more thorough training in psychology and to integrate this psychological training with the physiological and anatomical methods in the medical schools. This is the essence of his psychobiological position.

Some of the differences that are present today in psychiatric and psychoanalytic thought have a historical continuity with the differences apparent in the views of Meyer and Freud, two giant figures of the early twentieth century. Classical psychoanalysis stems more or less continuously from Freud. The interpersonal approach, as represented particularly in the work of Sullivan and his associates, stems largely from Meyer. His work laid the foundation on which this distinctively American development of psychoanalytic theory and practice is based.

Adler and Jung were the two most important associates of Freud, and they were widely appreciated in America, especially Adler with his easy colloquial style and democratic interest in the mental health of school children. He was admired in Vienna much more than Freud was, and he established child guidance clinics in the Vienna school system. He introduced Rank and others to the Freudian circle before becoming disenchanted with it.

Adler, a highly respected general practitioner in Vienna, first became acquainted with Freud about 1900 through *The Interpretation of Dreams* (Freud, 1900/1955a), which he later publicly defended in a reply to a scornful review. Freud, touched by this, sent him a postcard thanking him and inviting him to join the discussion circle of psychoanalysis. In spite of his sympathetic admiration of Freud's work, Adler doubted that they were in agreement; but Freud nevertheless persuaded him to join the group (Bottome, 1957). At the time of the break between the two men some years later, Adler was president of the Freudian Society and editor of its journal, *Zentralblatt für Psychoanalyse.*

As early as 1907, Adler, whom Freud had come to consider one of his most promising followers, began to challenge Freud's position in his work entitled *Study of Organ Inferiority and Its Psychical Compensation* (Adler, 1917). Adler observed here that there is an inherent tendency to compensate for inferior organic structures that leads to exaggerated developments of particular functions and related activities. For example, a person who has a weak right arm in childhood tends to develop an extremely strong right arm in later life in compensation for the earlier weakness, and with this added strength come other abilities, such as dexterity. This axis of relative weakness and subsequent compensation, he asserted, runs through all physical and personality development as a powerful motivational factor. On the basis of this observation, he concluded that the successful and effective functioning of the body, or part of the body, along this axis of compensation gives in itself an intrinsic pleasure that has no relation to sexual excitation but might be mistaken for it. He implies here that, in ascribing a sexual significance to the pleasurable functioning of nongenital parts of the body, Freud had mistaken this satisfaction in effective bodily activity for a sexual instinct. Adler then postulated his concept of a separate compensatory striving in all human beings, which he called the aggressive instinct.

In 1908 he formulated this concept in more general and psychological terms by defining what he called the aggression drive as an overall coordinating function of human living. There is, he asserted, a general psychological orientation, drive, or tendency directing an individual to master the difficulties of living in his environment; this drive for mastery is a more important motivational force in human behavior than the sexual instincts. Here he comes close to Adolf Meyer's focus on adjustment or adaptation, on dealing effectively with the situations of one's life. Adler based his concept of anxiety on this theory of aggressive striving; he defined anxiety as "a phase of the aggression turned upon the self" because of encountering frustration, rather than a consequence of sexual frustration and repressed sexual excitation. "The various signs of anxiety come about," he wrote in 1908, "because the aggression drive, which is at the basis of anxiety, can take hold of various systems [Ansbacher & Ansbacher, 1958, p. 36]." In other words, the aggression drive can use motor systems and be manifested as tremor, shaking, or cramps; it can use the vasomotor system and be manifested as palpitations, paleness, or blushing; and so on (Ansbacher & Ansbacher, 1958).

Adler at this time also took the position that the need for affection is an innate human need and that the wish for fondling, love, and praise must be interpreted in terms of the fulfillment of this need in itself, rather than in terms of sexual release, as Freud interpreted it. He considered this need for affection to be a lever in education, the earliest social feeling. In contrast to Freud, who insisted that the libido is originally autoerotic or narcissistic, Adler insisted that autoeroticism is a compensation for failure in the real relationship. The importance of interpersonal relationships in human development is thus taken for granted by Adler here. The feelings of people, he asserted, are of more significance in the treatment of psychopathology than the interpretation of their instincts.

Adler at this time also took the position that the need for affection is an innate human need and that the wish for fondling, love, and praise must be interpreted in terms of the fulfillment of this need in itself, rather than in terms of sexual release, as Freud interpreted it. He considered this need for affection to be a lever in education, the earliest social feeling. In contrast to Freud, who insisted that the libido is originally autoerotic or narcissistic, Adler insisted that autoeroticism is a compensation for failure in the real relationship. The importance of interpersonal relationships in human development is thus taken for granted by Adler here. The feelings of people, he asserted, are of more significance in the treatment of psychopathology than the interpretation of their instincts.

In 1910 Adler developed his concept of the basic role played by inferiority feelings in all human development and his notion of the "masculine protest" as a widespread response to these feelings (Ansbacher & Ansbacher, 1958). This represents a shift in emphasis from biological conditions and drives to subjective feelings in his view of personality dynamics. Feelings of inferiority, Adler asserted, are inherent in the relative weakness of the child, both physically and intellectually, in an adult world; and they may be intensified by heredity, accidental, or environmental factors. These feelings carry over into later life and are primary determinants of adult personality traits and attitudes. They may be expressed in the adult personality by attitudes of timidity, indecision, shyness, cowardliness, and submissive obedience. Or they may be concealed by compensatory and defensive attitudes, such as impudence, impertinence, rebellion, stubbornness, defiance, ideas of grandeur, and destructiveness. Adler called the response to unconscious feelings of inferiority the "masculine protest." He advanced the view that the wish to deny these feelings through compensatory modes of behavior is the major motivating factor in all human behavior and the root of all neurosis.

By 1911 Adler had outspokenly criticized Freud's theory of sexuality on four basic issues. First, he took the position that the sexual function in itself is restricted more or less to the genitals. The more general feelings of pain and pleasure are actually protective functions of the human organism rather than sexual functions (Ansbacher & Ansbacher, 1958). They must be regarded, Adler believed, as defensive reactions of adaptation rather than in terms of instinctual discharge. Here, again, he is close to Meyer's view. Second, he related the libido to the masculine protest. "Sexual impulses (are) never causes," he said, "but worked over material and means of personal striving [Ansbacher & Ansbacher, 1958, p. 60]." Here he anticipated later thinking in viewing sexual behavior as a manifestation of the whole person, with his strivings, ambitions, and character traits, rather than as a separate part of the person. Third, he called Freud's theory of organic repression an example of circular reasoning that was entirely inadequate for a theory of neurosis. Fourth, he criticized Freud's separation of ego drives from libido drives; the concept of ego drives, he said, was a redundant and empty concept, for ego drives can be just as "libidinal" as sex drives. (Freud later incorporated Adler's criticism in his invention of ego-libido; in his essay, "On Narcissism," the distinction between ego-libido and object-libido replaces his earlier distinction between ego drives and libido drives. However, he never abandoned his category of separate ego drives.)

In addition to taking issue with Freud's theoretical position, Adler charged at this time that the emphasis in therapy on infantile sexual pleasures tends to reify and freeze the psyche, preventing its forward movement into the future. The concentration on traumas and guilts about enjoying the activities of the anus, mouth, urethra, and so on, he said, keeps patients preoccupied with the past rather than leading them to face their problems of growth and learning.

Adler saw as the driving force of human life the desire to be significant in a particular society, culture, and family. The striving for this significance can inhibit or repress some drives and can intensify others. One can strive for significance in one's living with others through submissiveness, rebellion, or independence. The main obstacle to achieving it, Adler believed, is imposed by the person's own safeguarding tendency, which he sometimes referred to as a depreciation tendency. Persons whose early striving for significance has been blocked or frustrated will pretend to depreciate themselves in order to hold back from new experiences and growth. Belittling oneself serves as a good excuse for not trying.

In line with this view, Adler dismissed the Oedipus complex as "only a small part of the overpowering neurotic dynamic, a stage of the masculine protest, a stage which in itself is insignificant though instructive in content [Ansbacher & Ansbacher, 1958, p. 69]." In other words, the child's wish to kill the father and sleep with the mother is, according to Adler, only a minor phase of his total attempt to compensate for his relative immaturity and weakness in a world of adults—only one aspect of the person's striving for greater human significance in his living with himself and others.

Thus, on the fundamental issue of the predominance of the sexual instincts in the etiology of neuroses, Adler took a position during these years that was clearly and irrevocably opposed to Freud's. The actual break between the two men was precipitated by a paper presented by Adler before the Freudian Society in 1911, "The Masculine Protest as the Nuclear Problem of Neurosis." In a heated debate over this paper, Freud criticized Adler's views harshly, but nevertheless showed his respect for Adler's integrity. "I feel the Adlerian teachings are incorrect and dangerous for the development of psychoanalysis," he said. "They are scientific errors due to false methods; still they are honorable errors. Though one rejects the content of Adler's views, one can recognize their consistency and meaning [Ansbacher & Ansbacher, 1958, p. 72–73]." In the following committee meeting, Adler resigned his position as president of the society because, he said, "of the incompatibility of my scientific position with my post in the Society." The society later elected Freud president and voted to thank Adler for his activities, to regret his departure and to differ with him on his opinion of his incompatibility. Adler continued, however, to be a member of the society and coeditor of the *Zentralblatt für Psychoanalyse* until Freud wrote to the publisher saying that his name must be dropped from the journal unless Adler's was taken from the title page. Adler then immediately resigned his editorship and withdrew altogether from Freud's group.

To provide a forum for a wider freedom of scientific inquiry, Adler then formed the Society for Free Psychoanalytic Research, the name of which was later changed to the Society of Individual Psychology; and in 1914 he founded his own journal, the *Zeitschrift für Individual Psychologie.*

It is interesting to note that in 1913, when Freud published his paper "Predisposition to Obsessional Neurosis" (reprinted in Freud, 1946, Vol. 2), he tended to accept Adler's principle of a separate aggressive striving; he refers to it in this paper, without reference to Adler, as the general instinct of mastery. However, he never abandoned his early convictions about the structure of the psyche. In this same paper he said, "Psychoanalysis stands or falls by the recognition of the sexual component-impulses, of the erotogenic zones, and by the consequent expansion of the idea of the 'sexual function' as opposed to the narrower one of a 'genital function' [Freud, 1946, Vol. 2, p. 128]." After all, it was the most truly original notion that Freud developed, however unscientific it was.

Adler came increasingly to regard the desire for self-esteem as the basic motivational principle in all human behavior. He had recognized very early in his work the important influence exerted by feelings of inferiority and responses to them in determining personality traits and attitudes. These feelings of inferiority, according to his later thinking, are not based on any organic defects or inherited instinctual disposition. They arise out of the situation of relative weakness in which every child finds himself; they are consequences of the child's feeling of powerlessness in his early world of the all-powerful adult.

We shall not consider the later developments of Adler's thought nor the work of his school in Europe and America, which continues to the present day. Here in America, it is represented most prominently by the work of Rudolph Dreikurs in Chicago and Kurt Adler, Alexandra Adler, and Helena Papanek in New York. These later developments do not bear on the central thesis of this work. However, Adler, unlike Freud, made many visits here and was a very popular lecturer throughout the United States in the late 1920s.

Carl Jung, on the other hand, never undertook lecture tours in America and was never popular with physicians here. His greatest appeal was to artists and literary intellectuals. Jung, who was associated with Bleuler at the Burghölzli clinic in Zurich, was one of Freud's most devoted and promising disciples in the opening years of the twentieth century and, at Freud's express wish, was the first president of the International Psychoanalytic Association. Over the years, however, he found himself increasingly at variance with Freud on fundamental aspects of psychoanalytic theory.

In 1912 Jung gave a series of lectures (1928) at Fordham University in New York that revealed how pervasive and far-reaching the differences between the two men had by this time become. Here he criticized the theory of early sexual trauma, which Freud had not completely abandoned, as far too narrow an explanation of neurosis. Neurotic phenomena, he insisted, are much too complicated to be accounted for in terms of a single trauma long past or even in terms of a small series of such traumas; to arrive at an understanding of them, one must consider hereditary predispositions and environmental factors in all their complexity.

He also criticized Freud's theory of the erogenous zones and infantile sexuality. Freud, he said, conceived of the erogenous zones as so many "genitals" out of which the streams of sexuality flow together; the mouth is like a genital, the anus is like a genital—all these "genitals" accumulate excitations and flow into the penis or its castrated equivalent at puberty. In this connection, Jung strongly objected to Freud's definition of libido, which restricted its meaning to the sexual desires; Freud used the term libido for referring to sexual want, he said, as the term hunger is used for referring to want for nourishment. But long before Freud, Jung pointed out, this term had been in usage as a general term for all passionate desire. Jung wanted to revive the earlier meaning of libido and generalize it even further to refer to all energic processes of the human psyche, just as the term energy is used by physicists to refer to the kinetic, potential, and other energic processes in mechanics.

He rejected the theory of infantile sexuality on the grounds that the nutritional and growth processes, rather than the sexual processes, are the important processes in infancy. Sexuality, he asserted, does not play a significant part in these early years of life. Since he rejected the notion of infantile sexuality, he also rejected Freud's view of the period before puberty as the period in which sexuality is repressed (Freud, 1946, Vol. 3, p. 473–581). In contrast, he believed that it is during this period, which Freud called the latency period, that sexuality begins. A further criticism Jung made of the libido theory was that it failed to explain the symptoms and pathology of dementia praecox (or schizophrenia). He considered this an additional reason for either redefining the term libido to give it a wider meaning or replacing it with the broader term, psychic energy.

Jung differed sharply also with Freud's view that the determining factor in the etiology of neuroses is the conflict between ego instincts and sexual instincts. He stressed, instead, the conflict consequent upon the failure of a person's emotional development to keep pace with his physical, chronological development as the determining factor. The emotionally immature person—the person whose emotional development has been arrested at some earlier stage—is unable to meet the demands made on persons of his physical and chronological maturity in later life. The resulting disharmony lays the foundation for the dissociation of the personality seen in neurosis. In neurosis, the psychic energy, according to Jung, is taken up by childish, unrealistic fantasies that are ill suited for adaptation to everyday life. Jung called this state "introversion." Introverted patients, he said, live in a world that in truth belongs mostly to their past—a world in which the personalities of their parents play the most important determining part. In other words, these patients continue to live in their adult years as though they were little children still living with their parents.

In his emphasis on the unconscious influence of the members of the family on each other, Jung anticipated the interpersonal conception of mental illness as something that develops between people, rather than as a walled-off intrapsychic occurrence in an isolated individual. He called this factor of the parents and family life the parent complex. The parent, he believed, is a far more important factor than the Oedipus complex in the development of psychopathology. On the other hand, he reinterpreted the Oedipus complex in terms of the possessive, jealous attitude of children of either sex toward the mother as a protecting, providing, comforting being. In other words, the Oedipal wish is not a wish for sexual intercourse with the mother but a wish for the exclusive possession of this protective and comforting being.

Jung also took issue with Freud's views on infantile amnesia. Freud attributed the failure of patients to remember early childhood experiences to the repression of their infantile sexuality. Jung considered the general amnesia of infancy to be simply due to immaturity and not analogous to the amnesia of neurosis. The failure to recall the events of early childhood, he said, is due not only to repression but also to the inability in early years to formulate events in a way that makes them available for memory and recall later. We are best able to remember that which we are able to formulate for ourselves at the time. If we cannot organize an experience in our own mind, we cannot remember that experience. It can be recalled then only as isolated fragments of sensations and images (see Schachtel, 1959).

In contrast to Freud's emphasis on the patient's early history, Jung emphasized the actual present in the etiology of neuroses. He rejected Freud's view of neurosis as determined exclusively by infantile situations. Present situations, he insisted, can also play a large part in the development of neurotic illness. His criticism of Freud's theory of regression is closely linked with this view. Freud regarded regression entirely in terms of the earlier pregenital instincts; he described it as the release of the dammed-up libido—frustrated sexual excitation—along the pathways of early fixation or constitutional predisposition. Jung regarded it as a pathological way of dealing with a present problem or obstacle by replacing a real action with a childish illusion; it is a form of self-deceit that the person employs to preserve his self-esteem by hiding from a knowledge of his limitations. In this view of regression as a maladaptive way of dealing with a problem, Jung comes close to Adolf Meyer's notion of substitution, Ferenczi's notion of a false character, and Adler's notion of fictional final goals. All these notions refer to distortions of reality and evasions of appropriate action.

In the Fordham lectures, Jung defined the aim of psychoanalysis as that of achieving individual freedom and independence for the patient. "Modern humanity demands moral autonomy," he said. "Psychoanalysis has to allow this claim and refuses to guide and advise." The highest ambition of the analyst, he emphasized, is to put his patients on their own feet (1928).

During the same year, 1912, that Jung lectured in America on his deviations from Freud, he published his first work in Europe describing these deviations, his *New Paths in Psychology*. He called his approach "analytic psychology" to distinguish it from the depth psychology of Bleuler, the individual psychology of Adler, and, of course, the psychoanalysis of Freud. In this work, he emphasized the unconscious insight of individuals into the social and ethical reality of their time. People are much more in touch, he said, with the social and ethical problems of their group, community, and society than they are conscious of. And, to a considerable extent, neurosis is an expression of the individual's genuine attempt to solve these problems as they are manifest in his own life situation. (For example, our own society today is struggling with the problem of using its energies and resources for the good of the people; but, as Galbraith has pointed out, there is an overproduction of material goods and a paucity of resources for the nation's educational needs. Each person must also struggle with his own choices between education, expensive cars, and so on.) The symptoms of the neurotic illness express the false answers as well as the creative struggle of the individual for a true solution.

Like his former teacher, Pierre Janet, Jung regarded neurosis as essentially a self-division or a dissociation of the self. The moral part of a person as well as the immoral part may be repressed in the unconscious, he asserted, and lead to the development of autonomous complexes. Not only hate and lust are buried in the unconscious, not only infantile instincts; creativity, truth, and love may also be repressed. Jung, more than anyone else, pointed up the creative, positive effort that the neurotic person is making to deal with the real problems of living his life. He was also among the first to stress moral values in his theory and practice. Where Freud, because of his particular biophysical bent, attempted to reduce moral issues to infantile narcissistic strivings, Jung emphasized love and respect as goals to achieve in the treatment of mental illness. These goals exist, not only in relation to one's own nature, but also in relation to others; in order to have love and respect for others, one must have love and respect for oneself.

We have discussed the major contributions of Jung, Adler, and Meyer. Jung was the first to recognize that positive and constructive aspects of the personality, as well as hate and lust, may be repressed. In this way, he gave a new meaning to repression and pointed out a valuable new approach to it in therapy. He was also one of the first to talk about the mutual enrichment of the analyst and the patient in their relationship with each other. In addition, he brought an erudite scholarship to the illumination of myths, folklore, and religious symbols, discovering ancient wisdom in the dreams of everyday man.

Adler was the first to discard completely the sexual theory of neurosis. His emphasis on the purposeful role of the ego and the involvement of the total personality of the patient over the determinism of the biological instincts might justifiably have been described as the wave of the future in psychoanalysis. He also laid the basis for later psychoanalytic thought in stressing the problem-solving, anticipatory function of the dream. His view of the dream as an attempt to work out the problems facing the individual in everyday life anticipated the work of Thomas French and others in this field by about 40 years.

The contribution of Adolf Meyer to psychoanalytic thought is the most difficult one to summarize. In his later years, his antagonism to the narrow, exclusive theory of classical Freudian psychoanalysis gave him the reputation among many analysts of a man who was prejudiced against without being informed of psychoanalytic thought. Actually, Adolf Meyer played a leading role in encouraging the dynamic point of view characteristic of psychoanalytic thought to prevail in American psychiatry. When classical psychoanalysis was in its beginning, Meyer demanded an open-mind and an appreciative hearing for it. Later, when it became crystallized in various schools of dogma, he turned away from it impatiently to develop further his own dynamic orientation under the label of psychobiology. Psychobiology is a term still used today for the integration of genetic, biochemical, neurophysiological, intrapsychic, interpersonal, and social aspects of human disorders.

The Americanization Process (1910–1940)

The importance Freud attached to *The Interpretation of Dreams* can illuminate for us the development of psychoanalysis in the twentieth century following the publication of that book and the Americanization of psychoanalysis that took place following World War II. This matter, unwittingly or otherwise, can be taken as a political manifesto for the development of the psychoanalytical movement. Freud wrote, quoting from the Aeneid, "Flectere si nequero superos, Acheronta movebo," translated by David Bakan as "If the gods above are no use to me, then I'll move all hell." Bakan (1975) recognized that as manifestation of the idea that within every person's subconscious is a pact with Satan, suggesting that the devil is the permissive part of a person that allows him to violate the precepts of his superego. Freud's reference to "gods" clearly summarizes his attitude toward the university medical establishment, where he had failed to gain recognition and announces his intent to obtain the support elsewhere, wherever it may be found, in order to create his scientific revolution. This interpretation is not incompatible with Bakan's understanding of Freud's meaning.

In America, the status of psychoanalysis as a scientifically respectable enterprise depended completely on its acceptance by clinical medicine (Hale, 1971). The well-known physician, Isador Coriat, joined with the ministers of the Emmanuel Church in Boston at the turn of the century (completely independent of Freud's influence) to found a Christian ministry for treating nervous disorders. This ministry, called the Emmanuel Movement (after the church), was short lived after Freud's strictures against it (1909–1912) (Hale, 1971). It set the stage, however, for scientific psychotherapy following Freud's visit to America.

The roots of the Emmanuel Movement, which William James referred to as the "mind-cure movement" (James, 1920), had its origins in early American work on animal magnetism and mesmerism. This is in contrast to two earlier approaches from the works of Thomas Upham and of Isaac Ray still current in that same period. (see Rieber, Chapter 6). The work of Rev. Dr. W. R. Evans (1869, 1872, 1876, 1885), which dealt with such subjects as primitive mind cure and transcendental medicine, constitutes the most direct link to the Emmanuel Movement (Worcester , 1908). [It took almost a hundred years to move from transcendental medicine to transcendental meditation.]

From the beginning of the century, the psychotherapeutic movement in America had been led by medically supported psychologists—William James, J. M. Baldwin, Joseph Jastrow, Boris Sidis, and Morton Prince. That the Americanization of Freud was already in process during his only visit to America was evidenced by William James greeting him as an allied functionalist in the contest between functionalists and structuralists. Freud severely disappointed William James, as James expressed in his letter to Flournoy, the famous Swiss psychologist (28 September 1909) (James, 1920).

Freud himself rejected the attempts to use psychoanalysis in America to fight the structural school of Titchener, insisting that Freudian psychoanalysis itself be the most dominant school in its own right. This probably explains the slowness of the professional assimilation of psychoanalytic thought in America and the predominance in this period (1910–1920) of such eclectic books as *Psychotherapeutics* (Prince *et al.*, 1909) and *Subconscious Phenomena* (Munsterberg *et al.*, 1910).

By far the most important event of 1909 for American psychiatry was Freud's series of well-attended lectures at Clark University in Worcester, Massachusetts, to celebrate the school's twentieth anniversary (Figure 12.2). The effect was quick—after 2 years, the Emmanuel Movement was not mentioned again; within 5 years, hypnotism, mesmerism, and suggestion were out of fashion; and by 1918 almost 50 articles about psychoanalysis had appreared in such popular magazines as *McClure's, Ladies Home Journal* and even in *The Nation* and *The New Republic.* Some 170 articles were published about psychoanalysis in the medical journals of America between 1912 and 1918. Coriat (1917) warned against the misuse of psychoanalysis in one of the first popularizations and primers of psychoanalysis (also see Hale, 1971). Led by Adolf Meyer, W. A. White, and Joseph Jastrow (1932) the university medical centers throughout most of the country published increasingly persuasive critiques of Freud's libido theory in spite of its vogue in the popular literature.

THE INFLUENCE OF SULLIVAN

Harry Stack Sullivan, influenced by Meyer and White, also attacked the misleading ideas of Freud's libido theory. Sullivan came out of the American tradition grounded in the work of G. H. Mead, J. M. Baldwin, and John Dewey. White (1919) had already substituted the cognitively oriented concept of interest for the narrow sexual libido concept of Freud. In 1926 Sullivan

FIGURE 12.2 *Group of psychologists at Clark University Conference, 1909.*

wrote a paper criticizing Freud's libido theory, called "Erogenous Maturation" (Sullivan, 1926). He said:

> The Oedipus complex must be recognized as a distortion, not a biological development normal to the male child. It is a fraudulent symbol situation, the result of multiple vicious features of our domestic culture, the greater number of which can in turn be referred to the working of sexual sin in the personality of the mother and often too in that of the father. It is not from the preadolescent sexual competition in any meaningful use of the words with the father for the mother as a sex object, but from a blind effort at achieving a coherent word representation, especially of the mother and father, amid the welter of fraudulent attitudes, contradictory motives and domestic infelicities [p. 14]."

He added that in the juvenile period the child moves away from a self-centered existence toward intimacy with others. The sexual curiosity becomes aroused at this time, and society often fails him.

Sullivan said: "He has a wealth of contradictory and incoherent symbols plus his life experience, insofar as the latter exists in spite of distortions, and this latter factor gives him rapport with boys, just as the former interferes with the process of heterosexual adaptation soon to be demanded of him [p. 14]."

In other words, Sullivan felt rather bitterly and violently about the fraud and hypocrisy of adult society, and the impact of this fraud and hypocrisy on the growing child. It was this society that was responsible for the Oedipus complex, which was the best the child could do to try to make sense out of what he was presented with. The experience that he managed to accumulate in the face of all this hypocritical and distorting influence could prepare him for some kind of comfortable experience with his own peer group, but this was not usually adequate for a genuinely intimate relationship with the opposite sex. The Oedipus complex itself is a product of our kind of distorting culture. When one enters into relations with the opposite sex, there is very little basis, then, because of all this distortion, for a fully human experience of intimacy. The so-called resolution of the Oedipus complex—or what Freud saw as a solution to the Oedipus complex—is really a sadomasochistic orientation. Freud, like most of us, was a victim of his society.

In 1927 Sullivan published a paper describing his research work during 1925–1926 at Shephard and Enoch Pratt Hospital in Towson, Maryland. In this paper, entitled "Affective Experience in Early Schizophrenia," he deplored any description of mental life in terms of separate entities or structures of thinking, feeling, and willing. He preferred to regard mental life in terms of different aspects of an underlying unity; he did this by abstracting these aspects from life experience and naming them cognition, affectivity, and conation. He defined life experience simply as anything lived, undergone, or the like. He insisted on combining minute, painstaking observation of the patient and the milieu with a careful report, by the patient, of his own experience. In his observations, Sullivan used both slow-motion movie cameras and phonograph recordings to study the changes in speech, tone of voice, enunciation, gesture, muscular tensions, posture, and especially subtle changes in facial muscles and expression.

He discovered that there were striking similarities in the facial expression around the lips and corners of the mouth between so-called apathetic schizophrenic patients and individuals who pretended to express affects they did not actually experience. He inferred from this that the schizophrenic patients were concealing intense affect rather than failing to experience any.

His inquiry confirmed this inference. In fact, these patients by and large had suffered intensely for many years with a variety of extremely uncomfortable, unpleasant desires and experiences. During their psychoses, they continued to run the gamut of human emotions; all these emotions were entirely appropriate to the patient's conscious experience. As Meyer had pointed out many years earlier, a detailed life history of these patients usually revealed that the psychosis itself was only an incident in a lifetime of difficulties, at home, at school, and at work, marked by massive compensatory and substitutive thought processes. During these difficulties, they felt the most severe fears and pain.

Sullivan related these results of his investigations to warps in the personalities of the psychiatrists themselves. This is the first time, we believe, that such warps found any place in psychoanalytic literature—the first time that it was taken for granted that psychiatrists had warps in their personalities that must be accepted and worked with.

Sullivan stood out for his persistent effort to establish the human relatedness that is at the very core of character and personality. It is only in this relation between separate persons that an ego can emerge and grow. We use the term "ego" in his chapter to refer to the experience of the self and its value. The ego comes into being through object relationships (see the most recent developments along this line in the Chicago school of psychoanalysis [Kohut, 1977]); it emerges as relationships mature, and its strength develops with the development and continuity of interpersonal relationships. The ego is formed by human interaction, although it is genetically rooted in the biological equipment for perception and sensorimotor coordination. For Sullivan, the symbolic elaboration of the infantile experience of body exploration and coordination is the beginning personification of what is later called "Me" and "Mine." The recall and anticipation of sensations of sucking a thumb and feeling a thumb being sucked and the recall and anticipation of the movements and kinesthetic sensations of eyes, hands, mouth, feet, and so on are the beginning of a sense of independence and of autonomy. This is associated early in infancy with the beginning personifications of "Good Me," "Bad Me," and "Not Me," and the personifications of the "Good Mother" and "Bad Mother" are associated with this notion of "Mine," "My Body," and

"Not-My-Body" in the earliest experience of what is to be "Myself," the rudimentary ego. By personification, Sullivan means the symbolic elaboration of organized experience anticipatory of particular kinds of interpersonal events. For example, a personification of the "Good Mother" for a 6-month-old infant may be a vague organization of the recall of pleasant sounds, touch, the nipple in his lips, and so on, which are anticipatory of the satisfactions of hunger, thirst, and tenderness provided by mothering persons. The personification of the "Bad Mother" at the same age might be formed from the recall of loud voices and frightening sensations or facial expressions, which are anticipatory of a state of disorganized fearfulness or anxiety evoked by mothering persons. The "Good Me" at this age is simply the personification of "My Body" associated with the recall of behavior that frequently called forth the "Good Mother." "Bad Me" is the personification of "My Body" associated with behavior that makes the mother increasingly anxious and forbidding. "Not Me" is a poorly elaborated primitive type of uncanny, dreadful experience analogous to the nightmare. Much later on in development, all these personifications fuse more or less into personification of the self, such as "Me," "Mine," and "I," and the personification of mother, father, sister, and so on. The achievement of these personifications occurs during the development of language and other communicative behavior and marks, for Sullivan, the end of infancy and the beginning of childhood. The personified self continues to develop and grow as the personification "Me" and "We" are added to by an increasingly rich and more complex body of experience with the important persons in the child's life. The thrust of biological maturation, the eager play and curiosity, and the exciting responsiveness of the child to the world about him bring further and more rapid transitions in the personifications of the child. Important additions occur early here simply on the basis of gender, whether the child is a boy or a girl. The way the child's play is approved or not, the kind of clothes he or she is dressed in, the kind of behavior that is viewed as feminine or masculine, and how it is endorsed or scorned by the authority figures—all this adds up to a considerable and enduring influence on the personified self. Other important additions occur in later childhood, with the personification of the playmates; in preadolescence, with the personification of the "best friend" and in adolescence, with the personification of preferred sexual partners. Insofar as these stages have been successful, one's growth progresses with a deepening sense of respect for one's self and others, with a wider and more expansive relationship to one's fellowman and the world about.

The total experience of the self in its perceived value is the organized aggregate of all these various developmental personifications—both within and outside the field of conscious awareness. This aggregate of personifications is never fixed but evolves and is modified by experience in the course of one's lifetime. The conscious part of this experience is referred to by "I," "Me," and "My," in talking or thinking about one's self, and is very important, particularly from later childhood and on, in establishing an adequate orientation in living. Even though no personification is a completely accurate description of an individual, the degree to which it is inadequate, false, and dissociated handicaps the individual for the process of living.

In relation to this handicap, Sullivan viewed anxiety as the main factor. Sullivan emphasized the traumatic nature of severe anxiety (the experience or anticipation of severe lowering of self-respect), likening it to a blow on the head, and made it a central organizing principle of what could be consciously formulated by a person. He called the organizing of experience directed at escaping anxiety the antianxiety system or self-system.

THE INFLUENCE OF THE MORE ORTHODOX PSYCHOANALYTIC WORK

Although Sullivan's work had little, if any, impact on psychology in America until the 1950s, the more orthodox psychoanalytic work had considerable influence on abnormal psychology, experimental psychology, social science, and pop culture. General experimental psychology during 1910–1940 stressed laboratory studies of the sensory processes, reaction time, and memory, whereas Freud dealt entirely with human suffering, neurosis, and mental pathology in the private office, clinic, and hospital. Very little was written about psychoanalysis in American psychology journals until after Freud's visit to Clark University. After that period, American psychology was treated to a heavy dose of psychoanalysis in the literature of American journals and textbooks of psychology.

Mechanisms of adjustment became the focus of the subject matter assimilated within American academic psychology (Hilgard, 1949). Another important area of Freud's work to be assimilated was the distinction between the manifest and latent that was reflected in the literature. These Freudian ideas were usually presented with no reference to Freud himself. Hilgard (1957) discusses John B. Watson's program of behaviorism in a similar vein, pointing out that Watson was much impressed by Freud's work even though he found Freud's language unacceptable. Psychosexual development and the Oedipus complex were taken up by both Watson and Freud with similar values but very different language. In 1928 Watson wrote his extremely popular book on child rearing. Hilgard (1957) pointed out that this work was based on a misinterpretation of Freud. Watson believed the danger inherent in the child-rearing process was excessive emotional attachment to parents through excessive pleasurable fondling but made no reference to a theoretical notion of an Oedipal triangle. Freud, on the other hand, viewed excessive pleasurable fondling of an infant by its mother as a direct enhancement of the Oedipal overattachment to the mother in rivalry with the father for sexual possession of her. These ideas of Freud and Watson lead to the excessive detachment ("hands-off policy") of the 1920s and 1930s by typical American parents.

Eventually, a more compatible relationship developed in America between academic psychology and psychoanalysis. McDougall (1926) said, "I believe Professor Freud has done more for the advancement of psychology than any student since Aristotle." In the next breath, he added that he regarded most current psychoanalytic dictums as "ill founded and fantastic." Joseph Jastrow (1932) in his brilliant critique of Freud, took a similar position to the latter statement. The academic psychologist Neal Miller, a behaviorist who went to Vienna to be psychoanalyzed in the 1930s, did much with a colleague, John Dollard, to cement the bond between academic psychology and psycho-analysis. The Yale group, under the leadership of Clark Hull, a leading behaviorist of that time, led seminars where both psychologists and an-thropologists learned psychoanalysis from John Dollard and Erik Erikson. A similar program was initiated by Henry A. Murray at Harvard.

ANTHROPOLOGY AND PSYCHOANALYSIS

Anthropologists became involved with psychoanalysis in the 1920s in England with W. H. Rivers, Geza Roheim, and Bronislaw Malinowski, basically in reaction to Freud's *Totem and Taboo*. There was a burgeoning of interest in psychoanalysis among such important anthropologists in America as Edward Sapir, Ruth Benedict, Margaret Mead, and Gregory Bateson. However, the scientific study of psychoanalysis and culture came directly from an American psychiatrist who had been analyzed by Freud, Abraham Kardiner. Kardiner was approached in the late 1930s by Cora DuBois, Margaret Mead, Ruth Benedict, and others to initiate a Columbia University seminar in this area. This led to the classical books in this field by Kardiner and his associates, *Individual and Society* and *Psychological Frontiers of Society*. This flirtation between anthropologist and psychiatrist proved tem-porary, and eventually this interdisciplinary cooperative group was ter-minated. The anthropologists decided that the interaction of personality and culture was a proper part of anthropology itself and did not require any leadership from psychiatrists. A. I. Hallowell's (1962) important contributions to personality and culture showed evidence of that break late in the 1940s and 1950s. However, at Harvard alone, Henry Murray, a psychiatrist, and Clyde Kluckhohn, an anthropologist, continued to collaborate productively. This was due mainly to the interdisciplinary structure in which Murray and Kluckhohn worked—Harvard's Department of Social Relations, which was terminated in the early 1970s. There has been a sad lack of progress in the past few decades apart from Murray and Kluckhohn in this area of psychoanalysis and culture except for the works of Robert LeVine (1973) and Whiting and Child (1953), both now at Harvard. This is an area ripe for historical research.

POPULAR BOOKS

As Bakan (1977) correctly pointed out, the significance of psychoanalysis in academic psychology and professional psychiatry must be distinguished from the influence of Freud in the popular media of the culture: "Mark Sullivan in

Our Times estimates that there were over 200 books on Freudianism in the decade that followed Freud's visit (1909) to the United States. This averages out to one book every two and a half weeks [p. 30]."

It must be noted that members of the famous Bloomsbury group of English intellectual writers took up Freud's ideas before World War I, and some were analyzed by him. James Strachey, after he went to Freud in Vienna, returned to found the Hogarth Press in 1917 with his old friend Leonard Woolf and his wife, Virginia Woolf. The importance of this publishing connection cannot be underestimated as a vehicle for spreading the psychoanalytic credo in America. For it was through Strachey's translations of Freud, which were superior to the American translations by A. A. Brill, that Freud's work became best known. Although the English translations were the most important to the professional readers, the Modern Library edition of Brill's translation made Freud's work available to the general educated public throughout America. Later, the International Universities Press served the same function for Strachey allowing for the dissemination of the new Freudian ego psychology throughout America.

D. H. Lawrence in novels and essays written in Wales and later in America, Thomas Mann in Germany in the 1920s and 1930s, as well as the Bloomsbury circle about Virginia Woolf at that time, furthered the popularity of Freudian ideas in American college literature courses, literary circles, and periodical literature. (Hopps, 1934, wrote a doctoral dissertation on the British poets who were influenced by Freud which was widely referred to in American Universities.) *The Forsythe Saga* by Galsworthy, published in the 1920s and widely read in the United States, reflects much of this popular literary preoccupation with Freudian throught. These people, together with many others, such as the famous writers Arnold and Stefan Sweig and the Bohemian circles around figures like Henry Miller, laid the foundation for the wave of popular interest in and expression of Freudian ideas in America following World War II.

Robert Lindner's bestselling novels *Rebel without a Cause* and *Prescription for Rebellion* reflected this postwar influence of psychoanalysis on the popular mind as an instrument for self-assertion in an expanding prosperous economy. Lionel Trilling, the well-known critic and professor of literature at Columbia University, wrote *Freud and the Crisis of Our Culture* (Trilling, 1955).

ART AND MOTION PICTURES

Freud wrote psychoanalytic essays on writers, poets, painters, and sculptors, mostly recognized masters but sometimes relatively contemporary artists, such as the Danish writer, Wilhelm Jensen, in *Gradiva*. The concern with attacking surface hypocrisies, cant, and outworn conventions to lay bare the unconscious conflicts beneath was manifested in the existentialist movement, arising from roots entirely separate from psychoanalysis in the nineteenth-century work of Husserl, Kierkegaard, and Nietzsche. Many psychoanalysts, such as Edith Weigert in Washington, D.C., and others here and abroad, assimilated existentialist thought into their psychoanalytic formulations.

Painters who attempted to lay bare their own unconscious in raw abstract forms clearly reflected the psychoanalytic ideal of making the unconscious conscious. The artists went one step further than the old psychoanalytic motto "Where Id was, there shall Ego be" into "Where Ego was, there shall Id be." Salvador Dali, the surrealist, used obvious psychoanalytic symbols in his paintings and was hired to design some of the sets for the famous popular film about a psychoanalytic treatment, *Spellbound.*

In order to fully appreciate the influence of Freud on film, one must go back to the *Cabinet of Dr. Caligari*, which came to America in 1921. This film is about a patient dreaming of a psychiatrist–hypnotist who murders people through command to a hypnotized agent. According to I. Schneider (1977), the first film about psychoanalysis itself—Pabst's film *Secrets of a Soul*, starring Greta Garbo—was made in Germany in 1926 with the collaboration of Karl Abraham and (unofficially) of Freud.

Ernest Jones stated that MGM offered Freud $100,000 in 1935 to collaborate in making a film about love. Since Freud refused to do it, resenting even further the attempts to Americanize psychoanalysis, MGM dropped the project. Outside of America, however, Freud gave his permission to Abraham, as just noted, perhaps feeling psychoanalysis would be less "diluted" in Germany. Freud had been concerned ever since his visit to America in 1910 that the purity of psychoanalysis would be contaminated by its use in America; and therefore he tried to protect it in its pure orthodox form.

The New Freudian Ego Psychology in America
(1940 to present)

It is important to know the profound change Freud made in his theory of psychoanalysis in the 1920s and 1930s in order to understand the use of this in the spectacular growth of psychoanalysis in America that took place in the 1950s and early 1960s.

Freud's notion of the death instinct had already been anticipated in his original asumption that excessive excitation was the pathogenic factor in neurosis. From the very beginning, he considered the pressure for release from painful excitation as the prime motive in psychopathology of all kinds. This closed system, of the materialist reductionist type, which is implicit in his early libido theory, is much more manifest in his ruminative speculative work on the death instinct. Here Freud, sensing the inadequacy of the pleasure principle and the sexual instinct theory for explaining either the holocaust of World War II or the spontaneity of a child's play, sought beyond the pleasure principle. He met the inevitable wall of his earlier materialist assumptions—matter, dead matter and energy, lifeless energy struggling with their own product, life itself, in an incessant struggle of blind forces for supremacy, as Herbart had described almost a hundred years earlier in Freud's schoolbook.

Identification, according to Freud, is a derivative of the early oral cannibalistic phase of libido development in which the child wants to devour the object of its love. In identification, this is expressed in terms of being like the loved one; instead of actually eating the flesh of his mother or father, the child modifies his behavior and models his own ego after that of the father. This can also recur regressively at a later age when an individual loses his love object, when the boy, let us say, loses his father. He then substitutes the early tie of identification for the later one. Freud refers to this as introjection, that is, absorbing the personality of the father into the personality of the child, analogous to eating the father's body.

He had previously described introjection in his paper, "Mourning and Melancholia," in which he explained the cruel, self-depreciation, relentless self-criticism, and bitter self-reproaches of melancholics as the activity of an ego divided against itself. The ego ideal attacks that part of the ego that introjected the lost object of its narcissistic love. In other words, the introjected, omnipotent father, the idealized father figure in the ego ideal, is cruelly, ruthlessly attacking the modified imitation of the real father figure, with all its weaknesses and faults, in the other part of the ego. Therefore, the superego is punishing its modified self in the place of punishing the lost love, by whom the ego was hurt or abandoned.

Furthermore, Freud says this very same introjection occurs in the everyday state of infatuation, of being in love. Like a hypnotized subject, the person in love is completely devoted, uncritical, subservient, and sexually unsatisfied.

The superego itself is made up of these identifications with the mother and the father, fear of the father, and inherited fear of the primal father and the primal siblings.

By means of the processes of fusion, defusion, transformation, incomplete fusion, and neutralization of instincts, Freud now explained many phenomena in terms of love impulses and hate impulses. Where the love and hate fuse together, we have an aggressive love. *Defusion* refers to the state wherein the aggressive love is defused, leaving only aggression and repression of love, or only love and repression of aggression. *Transformation* is where love is transformed into hate and vice versa. *Incomplete fusion* refers to the state wherein there is a certain amount of aggressive love, but there is also some naked hostility or some passive love. *Neutralization* refers to the state wherein the ideas of the instincts exist, but their energy cathexis is neutralized, displaced, or somehow manipulated into something else. For example, two rivals hate each other. They realize that they cannot kill without being killed in turn; that is very frustrating. Hence, according to Freud, the aggressive instincts are neutralized and the instinctually more satisfying relationship of homosexual love takes place.

We belabor these technical terms and their introduction into Freud's writings and the mainstream of psychoanalytic literature at that time because this new language that subordinated the sexual energies from the erotic zones of the body to more abstract and cosmic forces and more complicated and obstrusive interpretative language laid the foundation for the ego psychology that was introduced by David Rapaport in the 1940s. This foundation led to the systematic and rigid domination of psychoanalysis, particularly in America, by Anna Freud, Heinz Hartmann, Rudolph Lowenstein, and Ernest Kris. At the same time, Melanie Klein embraced Freud's work in primal aggression and the primal death instinct, assimilating these ideas to the object relations work of Abraham. The Kleinian group had a firm base in London and eventually survived the antagonism of the ego psychology group to become the dominant force in international psychoanalysis in the 1970s. W. R. D. Fairbairn's contribution, which held sway at the Taristock Clinic in London, had very much in common with Harry Stack Sullivan, who also began to be widely appreciated in the 1970s.

Hartmann's popular paper, "Ego Psychology and the Problem of Adaptation," (1956) first published in German in 1939, was widely known through its translation and accompanying adulatory praise in *Organization and Pathology of Thought* (Rapaport, 1951). However, between 1941 and 1951, psychoanalytic institutes established their primacy in medical schools and psychiatric training programs and built upon this base through their Board of Professional Standards that insured conformity or ostracism, so that by the end of the 1960s almost every chairman of every significant department of psychiatry in America was a psychoanalyst—even the director of the National Institute of Mental Health.

Anna Freud, Heinz Hartmann, and Ernst Kris as managing editors established and controlled a series of volumes, *The Psychoanalytic Study of the Child*, begun in the late 1940s and continuing to the present date. Hartmann extended the late work of Freud on the ego and psychic energy to develop a complete system of metapsychology referred to as ego psychology. Training analysts had to return for a second analysis—an ego analysis—to retain their prestige and authority. This theory postulated an autonomous ego with its own biological roots and a primary aggressive drive assimilated to notions of mastery and competitiveness popular in American mercantile culture; further, it generated a new technique of analysis, focusing more on the here-and-now aspects of interpersonal interaction most eloquently described by Ernst Kris.

In the latest deviation from the mainstream of orthodox Freudian psychoanalysis in America, the ego psychology of Hartmann, Kris, and Lowenstein has been supplemented by the object relations theory derived from Klein and Fairbairn in England, with an emphasis on exploring so-called narcissistic phenomena and with controversies over technique in the use of transference and countertransference. However, the object relations theorists comprise only one of many splinter groups, none of which dominate strongly at this time. This group itself has split into the strict object relations theorists, known as Kleinians, represented by Kernberg (1978); the followers of a particular approach to the self, represented by Kohut (1977); the semiotic group, initiated by Victor Rosen and Theodore Shapiro (1977); and the residual of the ego psychology group, represented by the Hempstead students of Anna Freud, who have come to America in increasing numbers.

PSYCHOANALYSIS, POLITICS, AND POP CULTURE

The post-World War II period, after Freud died and many psychoanalysts came from Austria and Germany to America, started an entirely new phase in psychoanalysis here, politically and in pop culture.

During the war, while the leaders of American psychiatry were taken up with the war effort, the recent Freudian immigrants who had begun to establish themselves in the late 1930s and in the war years took increasingly aggressive initiative in teaching psychiatry in the medical schools. By the postwar time, they had consolidated their powerful institutes, were increasingly dominating departments of psychiatry in medical schools, and had begun 2 decades of rule in American psychiatry in the 1950s and 1960s. A political base in pop culture—movies, newspapers, magazines, radio, etc.—was necessary to generate popular support both for the prestige of psychoanalysis in psychiatry and for the fees its practitioners earned, since psychoanalysis was never able to earn much scientific support in the academic community (see Bakan, Chapter 7). Psychoanalysts became administrators, in charge of disbursing grants in foundation and government positions. Many, like Lawrence Kubie, appeared on radio and television frequently; Kubie strongly influenced Yale (where Ernst Kris also taught), which is one of the last remaining bastions of Freudian psychoanalysis among medical schools today.

Literary personalities also contributed to the popularity of Freud at this time. David Riesman and Lionel Trilling (1955) each had a profound and wide-ranging influence in popular intellectual culture. Riesman was especially penetrating in his comments on Freud's popularity among religious intellectuals and theologians for his moral pessimism. However, Riesman also attacked Freud for failing to take religion seriously and for contributing to a new kind of neorealistic happening. In spite of his dismissal of Freud's thought, he still helped spread Freud's ideas by talking about them so eloquently. The radical Freudians, such as the Marxist writers Paul Goodman, Herbert Marcuse, Norman Brown, and the incredulous Wilhelm Reich, who intended to embrace orthodox Freudian ideas, saw Freud as a fellow radical against the Establishment. Of course, in Freud's case he was against the university–judicial Establishment and not the capitalist middle-class enterprise itself. He was opposed to the acceptance of overt Marxist analysts by the International Psychoanalytic Association.

CURRENT MARXIST PSYCHOANALYSIS IN EUROPE AND AMERICA

Lacan in France

Jaques Lacan, in psychoanalytic literature, does much the same as the artists influenced by psychoanalysis do in their work: That is, he rejects the objective for the symbolism of the subconscious.

There is an apparent feud going on between those who stress consciousness as the essence of the human organism and therefore advocate the analysis of its integrated states in its various forms; including the ego psychology psychoanalysis of America; the cognitive psychology groups, such as those of Jerome Bruner and Jean Piaget; as well as the neuropsychology movement exemplified by such individuals as Karl Pribram (1971), and Michael Gazzaniga (1978) and those who stress unconscious as fragmented and corrupting of authentic communication. Lacan in France uses a semiotic approach, engaging in polemics against American and British psychology and psychoanalysis while asserting the primacy of the subject and its totally subjective nature. More than anyone, he has flipped the lid off the Freudian id, flooding the subject with a nonobjectifiable nature—he makes man unavailable to discursive rational processes, rendering him nothing more than what myths are made of. The dialectical materialism of Karl Marx is connected with the work of Jacques Lacan by the shared notion that the subject is in the social process and cannot be abstracted from it. The only access to the subject is the signifier through language, namely, the word-in-context and the scientific study of symbols. Coward and Ellis (1977) state

> Lacan asserts that the discoveries of Freud open onto the mobility of which revolutions are made. They point to the "missing area" in human sciences, that of the process of meaning in language and ideology, the process of the "I" in history, an area which would operate in the same space as dialectical materialism itself (Kristenon, *Tel Quel* no. 48).

Freud and the Psychohistorians

Like many other popular movements, the Freudian movement in America followed the vacuum left by the abandonment of religion and church. However, as can be seen from the preceding material, popular Protestant religious values and thought were not abandoned but served as the groundswell for psychoanalysis. As psychoanalysis became accepted, Americanized, and institutionalized, it followed the pattern of Protestantism, with its internal feuds, charismatic personality cults, and division into numerous sects.

There were also many offshoots of "healing" groups and organizations—the encounter groups movement, bioenergetics (stemming from Freud's pupil, Wilhelm Reich), psychosynthesis, gestalt therapy, logotherapy, Silvan mind control, transactional analysis, EST, Rolfing (an offshoot of bioenergetics), Arica (a blend of Eastern religious thought with bioenergetics), Esalen and Esalen East, and others too numerous to mention.

The "psychohysterians" such as Lasch view these developments along with other developments as nothing more than substitutes for religion, with psychiatrists taking the part of high priests. Although his views have some validity, the psychiatrists and other therapists hardly constitute a priesthood in any strict sense of that term. (See Chapter 6 of this book.)

Defending Freud's libido theory and biological determinism, Lasch accuses all other schools of thought in sociology, anthropology, and psychology and especially the non-Freudian analysts (Horney, Adler, Thompson, Sullivan, and Fromm) as well as the Freudians who deviated somewhat from strict orthodoxy (such as Ernest Jones and Gregory Zilboorg) of contributing to and rationalizing the rejection of romantic love, the encouragement of promiscuity, the rejection of parental and ethnic values by youth, and the subservience of all to a cancerous political and economic tyranny.

Lasch's polemical style and passionate, witty, and extravagant manner tend to blind the reader to the uncritical dogmatism of his orthodox Freudian beliefs and reactionary Marxism. Like Stalin in 1930s Russia, Lasch today in America would have us do away with easy divorces and trial marriages, with abortions for all who need it, and with equal rights between the sexes. He would advocate the puritanical, patriarchal, and authoritarian Victorian family (of the small segment of the population making up the upper middle class in the nineteenth century) throughout all strata and ethnic groups of the United States—catering to the nostalgia for Victoriana and sentimentality that decorates bars, advertising, restaurants, and even the cartons merchandise is sold in.

Russell Jacoby (1975) (in *Social Amnesia*) takes a position similar to Lacan and Lasch in rejecting the American version of psychoanalysis. He too asserts a Marxist critique of contemporary bourgeois decadence, and he attempts to integrate Freud's original emphasis on instinctual drives, and the war between the instinctual man and the society that violates his privacy, with a neo-Marxist interpretation of the current historical process. The prose of all three is noteworthy for its polemical obscurantism and extravagant metaphor.

The Marxist–Freudians give their own personal interpretation to Freudian psychoanalysis, so that Freud's own rejection of socialism, his own capitalistic life-style, and his admiration for the military capitalism of pre-Hitler Germany are utterly ignored, while avowed socialists, such as Alfred Adler and Erich Fromm, who made important contributions to understanding and improving the plight of the poor, are contemptuously dismissed as foolish liberal ego psychologists and mere tools of the capitalist system.

It is a curious situation that although psychoanalysis has now declined, lost its power in medical schools throughout the country and much of its support from government and private foundations, it is seeking new images and banners in such figures as Chomsky. For instance, Wollheim (1974) in the preface of his book on Freud promises that Marshall (1974), writing a chapter in that book, would provide a historical background of Freud's view of language and show the similarities between Freud's views and Chomsky's views on language. Although Marshall's ideas have some very remote possible connections to the Chomsky view of language and mind, Marshall never brings any explicit parallels nor reference to Chomsky's work. Marshall basically deals with Freud's early work on aphasia and neurolinguistics and shows how they lay the foundation for his later work on the interpretation of dreams. The only direct connections between Freud and Chomsky were made by Victor Rosen and Theodore Shapiro (1977) and at Yale by Marshall Edelson (1975).

In 1976 Chomsky was invited to give the Edith Lecture at the Forum on Psychiatry and the Humanities at the Washington School of Psychiatry. (This lecture, entitled *Psychoanalysis and Language*, was published in Smith, 1978.) In November of that same year, he was invited to give the principal address to the American Psychoanalytic Association annual meeting in New York. Theodore Shapiro also organized a seminar on that occasion to bring together interested psychoanalysts to discuss with Chomsky possible common ground and appreciation for each others' work. The final outcome of this effort remains to be seen; but it is our view, having attended this seminar, that something of future importance will emerge, even though as far as we can tell, Chomsky himself offers no clear idea yet of what can be done with the merging of the psychoanalytic and linguistic approaches. As a further development of the current status of psychoanalysis, Marxists as we stated earlier have suddenly embraced Freud whom they once condemned as a champion of bourgeois conformity. Now that Freud is being abandoned by the Establishment, he can be hailed as a radical revolutionary leader. Is this new interpretation of Freud an insight or a mere political device?

THE NEW PSYCHOANALYSIS AND BIOLOGICAL PSYCHIATRY

As described in the preceding discussion, with the saturation of the marketplace with psychological healers and with the proliferation of ever more orthodox Freudian institutes outside of the medical psychiatric organizations (American Psychoanalytic Association and American Academy of Psychoanalysis), the psychoanalysts themselves began to lose their influence and credibility in the public eye and their powerful positions in medical schools, foundations, and governmental bodies. (This is exemplified in a polemic by Martin Gross, 1978.)

There are a number of factors related to this decline of psychoanalysis. First of all, its spokesmen were unable to produce what they promised, arousing doubts whether such results would ever be forthcoming. Second, there was increasing reluctance in government to spend money on research, education, and training in mental health. Third, the overproliferation of mental health professionals blurred the boundaries and definitions of the various disciplines, with consequent divisiveness undermining confidence in their professional expertise. Fourth, a shrinking economy produced competitive, less expensive services that threatened the expensive 45-minute hour as a paradigm. Fifth, the discovery and widespread use of pharmacologic treatment as an effective agent gave enormous prestige to biological research and treatment. Millions of chronically ill patients were transferred from expensive inhuman warehouse-type institutions to much less expensive and somewhat more human outpatient and intermediate-care facilities in the community. Such revolutionary biological discoveries as DNA, RNA, neurotransmitters, and new endocrine agents acted as catalysts for the emergence of a new Zeitgeist, especially in medicine and the behavioral sciences (see Galen 1974). The decline of the influence of behaviorism, as well as of psychoanalysis, is another manifestation of the biological development.

The sixth and last reason is that many psychoanalytically oriented psychiatrists and psychologists (e.g., Erich Fromm) became increasingly interested in radical and political movements. This development helped to alienate both the politicians and the public in terms of support of the psychoanalytic movement.

Conclusion

Both behaviorism and psychoanalysis are so deeply rooted now in America that the groups associated with these movements will attempt to reformulate and reconstruct their positions to be a more viable force in this period of transition. At this time, there is no one prevailing school of thought in psychology. Behaviorism and psychoanalysis were at one time the prevalent ideologies; their loss of this position (beginning in the late 1960s) has opened the field to the possibility of a new leader. The present contender for this position in psychiatry seems to be only biological psychiatry. There is no serious contender in medicine. However, there are small groups dissenting from the mainstream, such as the nutritional psychiatry group, exemplified by Linus Pauling; the radical psychiatry groups of, for example, Szasz and Laing; and the radical Marxist groups. In psychology, the major contenders are the new cognitive psychology, with developmentalists and cognitivists appearing slightly more active and popular at present than the others (Flavell, 1977; Neisser, 1976); the new neuropsychology (Pribram, 1971; Gazzanigga, 1978); and the humanistic group, which had its impetus in the late 1960s but has subsequently lost its power through splintering.

In conclusion, whatever the future may bring to both psychiatry and psychology, this transition period is very crucial. The foundations, or genetic code as it were, for what is going to be is being laid down now. Let us hope the dangers of reductionism are avoided. It is fallacious to see the mind as simply a by-product of brain mechanisms and biochemistry (neomaterialism). It is equally erroneous to reduce the mind to pure subjectivity that dismisses the body's physiology and chemistry as irrelevant (neoidealism). The real challenge is to achieve a comprehensive unified approach that sees mind within body in reciprocal relationships within the common humanity of interpersonal relations in a sound social value system that facilitates the survival of life as well as the survival of the life of the mind.

References

Adler, A. *Study of organ inferiority and its psychical compensation; A contribution to clinical medicine.* New York: Nervous and Mental Diseases Publishing Co., 1917.

Ansbacher, H. L., & Ansbacher, R. R. (Eds.). *The individual psychology of Alfred Adler.* London: George Allen & Unwin, 1958.

Bakan, D. *Sigmund Freud and the Jewish mystical tradition.* Boston: Beacon Press, 1975.

Bakan, D. Psychoanalysis in North America. *Modernist Studies,* 1977, *213,* 29–36.

Bottome, P. *Alfred Adler: A portrait from life.* New York: Vangard, 1957.

Breuer, J., & Freud, S. *Studien uber Hysterie.* Wein: Deuticke, 1895 [*Studies in hysteria* (J. Strachey, Ed. and Trans. in collaboration with A. Freud). New York: Basic Books.]

Chomsky, Noam. Language and unconscious knowledge. In J. H. Smith (Ed.), *Psychoanalysis and language.* New Haven: Yale University Press, 1978.

Coriat, I. H. *What Is Psychoanalysis?* New York: Moffat, Yard & Co., 1917.

Coward, R., & Ellis, J. *Language and materialism.* London: Routledge & Kegan Paul, 1977.

Dostoyevsky, Fyodr. *The double* (G. Bird, Trans.). Bloomington: Indiana University Press, 1958. (Originally published, 1850.)

Edelson, M. *Language and interpretation in psychoanalysis.* New Haven: Yale University Press, 1975.

Evans, Rev. W. R. *The mental cure.* Boston: Carter, 1869.

Evans, Rev. W. R. *Mental medicine.* Boston: Carter, 1872.

Evans, Rev. W. R. *Soul and body.* Boston: Carter, 1876.

Evans, Rev. W. R. *The primitive mind-cure: The nature of power of faith or elementary lessons in Christian philosophy and transcendental medicine.* Boston: Carter, 1885.

Flavell, John H. *Cognitive development.* Englewood Cliffs, N. J.: Prentice Hall, 1977.

Freud, S. *Collected papers* (Vols. 1, 2 & 3). (A. & J. Strachey, Trans.). London: Hogarth Press, 1946.

Freud, S. *Leonardo da Vinci; A study in psychosexuality* (A. A. Brill, Trans.). New York: Random House, 1947.

Freud, S. *An Outline of psychoanalysis* (J. Strachey, Trans.). New York: W. W. Norton & Co., 1949a.

Freud S. *The interpretation of dreams* (J. Strachey, Trans.). New York: Basic Books, 1955a.

Galen, D. Implications for psychiatry of left and right cerebral specialization. *Archives of General Psychiatry,* 1974, *31,* 572–573.

Gazzaniga, Michael S. and LeDoux, Joseph E. The integrated mind. Plenum, N.Y., 1978.

Gross, M. *The psychological society.* New York: Random House, 1978.

Hale, N. G. *Freud and the Americans.* New York: Oxford University Press, 1971.

Hallowell, A. I. Culture Personality and Society. In S. Tax (Ed.), *Anthropology today.* Chicago: University of Chicago Press, 1962.

Hilgard, E. Human motives and the concept of the self. *American Psychologist,* 1949, *4,* 374–375.

Hilgard, E. Freud and experimental psychology. *Behavioral Science,* 1957, *2,* 74–79.

Jacoby, R. *Social Amnesia.* Boston: Beacon Press, 1975.

James, W. *The letters of William James.* (H. James, Ed.). Boston: Atlantic Monthly Press, 1920.

Jastrow, J. *The house that Freud built.* New York: Greenberg, 1932.

Jung, C. *Two lectures on analytical psychology* (H. G. Bayse and C. F. Bayse, Trans.). London: Balliére and New York: Dodd Mead, 1928.

Kernberg, O. *Clinical psychoanalysis and object relations theory.* New York: Aronson, 1978.

Kohut, H. *The restoration of the self.* New York: International University Press, 1977.

Krafft-Ebing, R. Von. *Psychopathia sexualis*. New York: G. P. Putnam, 1969. (Originally published, 1886.)

LeVine, R. *Culture, behavior and personality*. Chicago: Aldine, 1973.

Marshall, J. Freud's psychology of language. In R. Wollheim (Ed.), *Freud*. New York: Doubleday, 1974.

McDougall, W. *Outline of abnormal psychology*. New York: Scribners, 1926.

Meyer, A. *The commonsense psychiatry of Dr. Adolf Meyer*. (A. Lief, Ed., with biographical narrative). New York: McGraw-Hill, 1948.

Morel, B. A. *Traité des dégénérescences physiques, intellectuelles et morales de l'espèce humaine*. Paris: Bailliere, 1853.

Neisser, U. *Cognition and reality*. San Francisco: W. H. Freeman, 1976.

Perry, R. B. *The thought and character of William James*. New York: George Braziller, 1954.

Pribram, K. *Languages of the brain*. Englewood Cliffs, N.J.: Prentice Hall, 1971.

Prince, M. *Psychotherapeutics*. Boston: Badger, 1909.

Prince, M. (Ed.), *Subconscious phenomena*. Boston: Badger, 1910.

Rapaport, D. *Organization and Pathology of Thought*. New York: Columbia University Press, 1951.

Rioch, J. Transference phenomena in psychiatry. *Psychiatry*, 1943, *6*, 147–157.

Schachtel, E. G. *Metamorphosis*. New York: Basic Books, 1959.

Schneider, I. Images of the mind Am v. Psychiatry, 1977, *134*:(6), 613–620.

Shapiro, T. Language and ego function of young psychotic children. In E. J. Anthony (Ed.), *Explorations in child psychiatry*. New York: Plenum, 1977.

Sidis, B. *The psychology of suggestion*. New York: Appleton, 1898.

Sidis, B. cited in *Psychopathological researches: Studies in mental dissociation*. New York: Stechert, 1902.

Smith, J. H. *Psychoanalysis and language*. New Haven: Yale University Press, 1978.

Sullivan, H. S. Erogenous maturation. *Psychoanalytic Review*, 1926, *13*, 1–15.

Sullivan, H. S. Affective experience in early schizophrenia. *American Journal of psychiatry*, 1927, *6*, 468–483.

Trilling, L. *Freud and the crisis of our culture*. New York: Doubleday, 1955.

Veblen, T. *Theory of the leisure class*. New York: Macmillan, 1899.

White, W. A. *Mental hygiene of childhood*. Boston: Little Brown, 1919.

Whiting, J. W. M., & Child, I. L. *Child training and personality*. New Haven: Yale University Press, 1953.

Wollheim, R. (Ed.). *Freud. A collection of critical essays*. New York: Doubleday, 1974.

Worcester, E. *Religion and medicine*. New York: Moffat, Yard & Co., 1908.

Recommended Readings

Bakan, D., Psychoanalysis in North America. *Modernist Studies*, 1977, *213*, 29–36.

Burnham, J. C. Psychoanalysis and American medicine, 1894–1918: Medicine, science, and culture. *Psychological Issues*, 1967, *5*(4). (Monograph 20.)

Hale, N. G., *Freud and the Americans*. New York: Oxford University Press, 1971.

Jacoby, R., *Social amnesia*. Boston: Beacon Press, 1975.

Jastrow, J., *The House that Freud Built*. New York: Greenberg, 1932.

Oberndorf, C. P. *A history of psychoanalysis in America*. New York: Harper & Row, 1953.

Shakow, D., & Rapaport, D. The influence of Freud on American psychology. *Psychological Issues*, 1964, *4*(1). (Monograph 13.)

GILBERT VOYAT **13**

In Tribute to Piaget:
A Look at His Scientific Impact
in the United States[1]

[1] A French version of this chapter was adapted for the *Bulletin de Psychologie de L'Universite de Paris, 30,* 1976–1977, special issue in honor of Jean Piaget.

PSYCHOLOGY:
THEORETICAL–HISTORICAL PERSPECTIVES

ISBN 0–12–588265–3

Although it is not an easy task in such a small compass, I want to try to convey here some idea of Jean Piaget's remarkably rich and prolific contribution and something of the vitality of the International Center for Genetic Epistemology in Geneva; to draw attention to the extensive and wide-ranging work of the Faculty of Psychology and Educational Sciences; to mention, if only summarily, the essential research carried out by Piaget's close collaborators, notably Bärbel Inhelder; and, above all, to offer some account of the influence of the thinking and writing of the Geneva school upon present-day American psychology.

In the first place, it must be borne in mind that aside from the spread of the influence of the Geneva school, the mainstream of American experimental psychology is still largely circumscribed by a behaviorist ideology. This ideology continues to offer stout and often sophisticated resistance to any theoretical approach based on an interactionist epistemology, and indeed to any theory at all that puts the emphasis on the idea of structure.

Secondly, we must remember the interesting fact that this dominant orientation of American psychology is more susceptible to the constraints imposed by a pragmatic and quasi-utilitarian conception of psychology and pedagogy than is psychology as taught in the majority of European universities.

In fact, the "American" approach, founded on the notion of transcendence and governed by the perspective of constant and rapid individual improvements, still colors the main concerns of most researchers and educational theorists—a fact that never ceases to amuse Piaget himself. By the same token, meanwhile, many American psychologists and educators treat the Piagetian idea of a dynamic synthesis, sustained thanks to an equilibrium among horizontal extensions of thinking within the framework of progressive restructurings as part of the "Genevan enigma."

The problem is not, however, that the concept of equilibration has failed to find articulate proponents in the United States. It is not—even less so, in fact—that this concept has not been accorded recognition as a basic notion of operational theory on a par with the concepts of assimilation, accommodation, schema, operation, and internalization. Operational theory is both easily accessible and intensively studied in North America. Twelve years after the publication of *Piaget Rediscovered* (Duckworth, 1964), an event that marked a rebirth of interest in the Geneva school in the United States, there is scarcely a manual of child psychology that does not offer an extensive account of the

Piagetian approach. There is not one volume of the journal *Child Development*, to take a case in point, that does not contain recapitulations, extensions, or refinements of the Genevan experiments.

In short, it is not a dearth of publicity from which the Geneva school suffers. The truth is that the school constitutes a manifest problem of accommodation for the behaviorist tendency—a fact of which the consequences are of the utmost importance if we wish to understand the impact of Piaget's school on American psychology as a whole. The influence exerted by Piagetian notions is best viewed as affected by two main factors. The first is an educational practice that—though no doubt open to the lessons of a wide spectrum of experience—remains captive to an approach of which the prime concern is the acceleration of development. The second factor is a theoretical psychological frame of reference of which the true goal is to further at all costs the pedagogical approach just described.

In confronting these limiting factors the Piagetians are not alone; psychoanalysis and its offshoots have to battle similar constraints. Behavior modification techniques—behavior modification therapy, for instance—find more grace in the eyes of Americans, because of their immediate results, than approaches calling for reflexive abstractions or introspection from subjects in whom insight may take as many years to acquire—perhaps even more—than the construction and mastery of concrete or formal thinking. Thus, many people cannot conceive of the time taken for a child to construct an operational universe without thinking in terms of those sacred cows of American educationalists, the "three R's" of reading, writing, and arithmetic.

Ideologically speaking, both psychoanalysis and operational theory have an important standing in the United States, yet they exist in parallel with each other and remain, in a peculiar sense, outside the behaviorist stream, which appears to furnish the most apt response to what are perceived as the immediate needs of education.

So far as the Geneva school is concerned, one of the reasons for this state of affairs is the stress Piaget lays on the individual's autonomous activity and on the essential role of the factors of assimilation in cognitive development. The contradiction that Piaget's thesis enshrines in the view of most American psychologists and educationalists resides in the very assumptions on which his argument is based. For Piaget sets out to discover, analyze, and explain the way in which the child *constructs reality*, whereas the American "common sense" approach persists in thinking that this development can be precipitated and directed by the appropriate external manipulation, by correct "programming."

It is within this context of cross purposes that we should approach the question of the influence of the Geneva school in America. For despite the contradiction between the two perspectives, the bald assertion that the mainstream of American psychology has undergone no far-reaching changes as a result of Piaget's ideas is far from the mark.

Operational Theory and the Mainstream of American Experimental Psychology

Among the many and various products of this first kind of interaction we may conveniently start by considering those that fall under the head of a systematic operationalization of the concepts and experimental method of the Geneva school. This kind of interaction often boils down to an American attempt to integrate Piaget's thinking into the behaviorist approach. This may be observed principally in two spheres. The first is the conceptual and theoretical sphere epitomized by Berlyne's book (1965), and by the work of Beilin (1969). Ironically enough, Berlyne sees Piaget as a neobehaviorist, whereas Beilin calls him a neomaturationist. This confusion is a typical expression of the difficulty Americans have in understanding not only the idea of interaction but also, and most importantly, the concept of new constructions as the outcome of internal regulations.

The second area in which this type of interaction may be seen is experimental and empirical; here the work of the Geneva school is operationalized, reproduced, or modified within the framework of an experimental approach in which conceptual advance is governed more by statistical considerations than by the findings produced by observation of the child's thought process.

Aside from misunderstandings of a semantic kind and those produced by the need for experimental adaptation, this first type of interaction brings out a real contradiction in the way in which the object of experimental psychology is conceived of by the Genevans on the one hand and by the Americans on the other. Even though behaviorism and operational theory may not necessarily be incompatible, and even though the discovery of a good deal of common ground between them has given rise to much useful and productive work, a great difficulty is related to the very foundation of Piaget's thesis and not to problems of methodological or conceptual adaptation.

The dialectical opposition that we run into here arises in part from the presence of two distinct methodological conceptions. Piaget, who in this respect follows in the footsteps of Binet, always takes care to adapt his conceptual and experimental strategy to the requirements of the problems that he has set himself. Behaviorism, however, adapts its problems to the methods it has at its disposition. According to Piaget's conception, the method to be followed is a function of the question being asked; according to the behaviorist approach, the methodological framework defines the hypothesis put forward and the problems to be solved.

In addition, it is hard to find any common measure between, say, the data produced by administering a 5-minute questionnaire to 100 children and that obtained by conducting a 100-minute experiment with just 5 children. Yet the differences between the results sought by the clinical or genetic method on the one hand and the classical behaviorist approach on the other are precisely of this order.

A second type of interaction between the Geneva school and the dominant tendency of American psychology is constituted by attempts to standardize the Genevan concepts and experimental methods. Piaget has concentrated most of his efforts on the study of the development of the "epistemic" subject, and in consequence, he has set out to give an account of the genesis of operational structures unaffected by sex, social class, or cultural differences (structural invariants in his view being more important than individual variations of this kind). For many Americans, however, such variables are of prime importance and must not be relegated to the status of secondary determinants in this way. These opponents of the Piagetian outlook consider the notion of an invariant development of operational structures to be highly abstract, arguing that it evokes an abstract mechanism for which norms and functional differences should be established.

Such considerations aside, there is no disputing the usefulness of quantitative studies of intellectual operations, or of the collection of psychometric data after the fashion of authors such as Pinard and Laurendeau (1962) and Beth Stephens *et al.* (1974)—to mention only two examples. Such data may not necessarily be indispensable to operational theory, but their implications are important because in this context "the constraints imposed by the empirical method invariably predominate over the properly clinical method of research [Piaget, in press]." The establishment of behavioral norms as typical for specific age groups calls de facto for the use of experimental techniques in which the systematic control of variables is indispensable. Also relevant in this connection are the very solid results generated by cross-cultural studies. Like the work just mentioned, this kind of research helps to clarify the problem of the relationship between given ages and given acquisitional stages and to verify the criteria governing the integration of successive structures.

Generally speaking, efforts of this type often end up by identifying the idea of operational evaluation with that of psychological testing (a favorite American pastime!), or even by substituting one for the other.

The dialectic involved in this second type of interaction embodies a subtle but real reversal of Piaget's intentions, which were never to treat intelligence as a progressive accretion of specific reactions, but rather to analyze it as an overall structure.

Where there is no basic incompatibility between operational theory on the one hand and psychometry, standardization, or empirical verification on the other, these interactions raise valuable problems whose resolution opens up many new areas. What is more, they allow us to see clearly that operational

theory has shown itself well able to endure the confrontation with behaviorism, benefiting greatly from the behaviorists' empirical contributions
and adapting itself readily to their findings.

Operational Theory, Clinical Psychology, and Education

There are two other areas of interaction, still within the psychological field,
that are worth our looking at. The first is interaction between the Geneva
school and clinical psychology, and the second is interaction between the
Geneva school and American education.

First of all, it should be pointed out that clinical psychology, just like
developmental psychology, occupies a rather special position in the United
States. Classical experimental psychologists, though ready to grant both of
these fields the status of disciplines and viable forms of knowledge in their
own right, remain skeptical as to their meeting the criteria of scientific rigor.
So far as operational theory is concerned, this attitude attests to a misunderstanding—perhaps even a total incomprehension—with regard not only to the
empirical nature of the data gathered by the Piagetian approach, but also to
the operational method of dealing with these data.

The problem becomes very clear if we compare the methodology of a Skinnerian with that of a Chomsky. On the one hand, both Skinner and Chomsky
assert that their theses are verifiable, Skinner's by empirical means, Chomsky's
by deductive reasoning. On the other hand, Skinner needs a horde of subjects,
whereas Chomsky needs none at all. Operational theory may be said to occupy a middle position between the two poles of Skinner and Chomsky. It
must rely on the deductive procedure in the formalization of structures, yet
the fact is that this procedure is every bit as scientific as the experiments
whose results it is designed to deal with.

Apart from this methodological affinity, the interplay between American
clinical psychology and operational theory has produced a plethora of results
that may best be divided up under two main headings. The first of these
covers theoretical contributions, for example, comparative studies of psychoanalysis and operational theory, like those of Wolff (1960). The second
category takes in experimental contributions in this area, and here a variety of
syndromes and a large group of psychopathological data have been clearly
defined, thanks to the use of operational tasks (see especially the work of
Escalona, 1968, and of Anthony, 1956).

In fact, this area of interaction has been very fruitful indeed, and it is worth
noting that one reason for this is that both operational theory and clinical
psychology lay much stress on the idea of process and on the modalities of
cognitive and/or affective organization. On the other hand, the dialectic that
develops here is also important, because once again it depends on a sort of

subtle distortion of Piaget's original aims. Operational theory seeks to explain the normal development of cognitive structures. Basically, it takes normality as its starting point and constructs its conception of cognitive development on this foundation. By contrast, clinical psychology sets out from the opposite pole, drawing inferences from its observation of the abnormal and sometimes—as in the case of Freud—developing a theory on this basis. It is quite clear, however, that operational theory constitutes an indispensable tool, and this not only methodologically speaking. As a matter of fact, it is the concept of structure that has elevated clinical psychology to its present essential position, because it is this concept that makes it possible to analyze the link and the transitional process between normal and abnormal thought. To take just one illustration of this, Rapaport's (1967) attempt to work out a psychoanalytic theory of thinking relies heavily on the notion of structure.

In sum, clinical psychology has taken very much into account the concepts developed by operational theory, recognizing their importance and the vital need for them in any thorough interpretation of personality development.

Interaction between the Geneva school and American pedagogy, affected as it is by the factors already mentioned, has been going through a very interesting development. One reason for this, no doubt, is that education and educational theory are intimately bound up with questions of social class and socioeconomic level. In the United States, as elsewhere, education is also a *political* reality. And it is precisely in this aspect that it is a sensitive issue.

The present situation of Piaget's influence on education in the United States is characterized by the publication of an ever-increasing flood of popular works like the one by Mary Ann Pulaski (1971) by a number of books and articles intended to encourage an experimental teaching genuinely based on operational theory, an example here being the collection *Piaget in the Classroom* (Schwebel & Raph, 1973); and, perhaps most strikingly, by a vast movement of educationalists broadly favoring the Piagetian approach.

The intensity and breadth of the interest aroused in America by the findings of the Geneva school are truly remarkable. A host of individual teachers and the many "new schools" (sometimes called "Piaget schools") all claim to base their educational epistemology on operational theory. One might well ask how such enthusiasm is possible when the mainstream of American pedagogy is still in thrall to a militant and vigilant behaviorism. Part of the answer to this question is that the demands that American education has to meet on the pragmatic level tend to maintain the system in a state of permanent instability. Another point worth mentioning is the complementarity and resemblance between Piaget's approach and Dewey's, which continues to underpin a dissenting tradition in educational thinking in America.

There is another reason, too, why American pedagogy has opened its doors to operational theory, and this is quite simply that an increasing number of educationalists find in this theory exactly what they are looking for, namely, a theoretical framework and the knowledge needed for the organization of their projected applications. In this connection, the following anecdote may be of interest. In 1975 Piaget paid a return visit to our teaching project in Harlem (the Children's Art Carnival), where every cognitive intervention is based on observations by psychoeducational teams (Voyat, 1975). His way of gauging the results of these attempts to apply psychopedagogical lessons was to look for changes in the behavior of the teachers he had first seen at work 3 years earlier; what he noticed was a new pedagogical understanding indicating that the teachers had assimilated the essential concepts of cognitive development.

Thus, it is not inconceivable that a teaching practice based on an appropriate application of operational theory will one day make its contribution to the reorganization in the United States of numerous pilot projects whose organizers explicitly cite Piaget's theory as their basic frame of reference. The American Jean Piaget Society has as many educators as psychologists among its members, while another association, Piaget Theory and the Helping Profession, held its sixth annual symposium in California. All this testifies to an overwhelming effervescence in this area, accompanied, as is inevitable, by all the problems of the rapid popularization and hurried application of a theory as complex as Piaget's.

It is clear also that this type of interaction has no true internal dynamic of its own. No unifying tendency is visible here save for the explicit invocation of Piaget's thought, and what we see is actually a large number of distinct trends with no predominant orientation emerging for the time being.

Operational Theory and Epistemology

Of all the areas of knowledge that Piaget has affected in the United States, that of genetic epistemology occupies the clearest, the best differentiated, and, in a sense, the most important position.

For one thing, structuralism as a method of analysis has undergone a thoroughgoing renovation, thanks to Piaget's influence, while at the same time the epistemology underpinning this method has enlisted the support of a select group of proponents in the United States.

Aside from Piaget's own efforts to disseminate genetic epistemolgy in North America, notably by delivering the Woodbridge Lectures at Columbia University (Piaget, 1970), which he devoted entirely to this area, and aside too from work dealing with the epistemology of operational theory itself (Gruber & Voneche, 1977), genetic epistemology has given rise to two kinds of interaction. The first occurs on a theoretical plane and is exemplified by the anthology *Cognitive Development and Epistemology* (Mischel, 1971), 7 of whose 15 contributors belong to philosophy departments. The second type is a result of the profound kinship between operational theory and cybernetics. As Papert and Voyat (1968) note, "It is people concerned with the resolution of specific problems arising from the operation of cybernetic machines who are the most urgently in need of a theory of knowledge [p. 92]." In this context we should note that work on artificial intelligence bears the deep imprint of Piaget's influence and has borrowed whatever it needed from both genetic epistemology and operational theory. Actually, the conceptual link with cybernetics was also established thanks to the concepts of regulation and self-regulation—that is, the intrinsic conceptual components of the notion of structure.

Theory of Knowledge and Biology

In the last reckoning, it is perhaps the interaction between the theory of knowledge and biology that best reveals both the problems and the achievements of Piaget's influence in the United States. It is worth our looking at some of the reasons for this, because it will help us form an overall view of the enormous impact of the Geneva school in America.

Taken in conjunction with the suspicion of "disguised Lamarckism" that it tends to arouse in its biological context, the notion that "one of the most general processes in the development of cognitive structures consists in the replacement of exogenous knowledge by endogenous reconstructions [Piaget, 1975, 193]," causes problems for many students, biologists included.

Though such ideas are far removed from the traditional framework of classical American psychology, there is some willingness to accept the conception of manipulation of the physical environment. And structuralism, equilibration, and the idea of contradictions are not completely unacceptable, either. But when it comes to the thesis that exogenous knowledge is liable to be superseded by endogenous reconstructions, the defenders of the classical approach tend to run out of patience.

Apart from his questioning of Darwinian assumptions, Piaget's hypothesis regarding the generality of the process of phenocopy (Piaget, 1974) is also very troublesome for many. And it must be admitted that the mechanisms of regulations are more difficult to grasp in a psychobiological context than in the more circumscribed sphere of cognitive development considered alone.

This brings us to what would seem to be a fundamental obstacle for operational theory in its interaction with the various tendencies of American psychology and pedagogy. The fact is that the concept of interaction is the one that remains the most mysterious to the American way of thinking. It is paradoxical to discover that this most vital element in operational theory, in tandem with the notion of equilibration as an essential mechanism in cognitive development, remains the most alien of concepts for those schooled in the classical tradition of American psychology.

The problem arises neither because of the overall structures that Piaget evokes to account for modes of organization; nor because of his interpretations of the notions of equilibration, creativity, or opening on to the possible; nor yet because of the type of misunderstanding to which his analytical approach sometimes gives rise. Rather, the difficulty is due to the intrinsic complexity of the development of knowledge itself.

   This complexity leaves its mark on every form of interaction between the
Geneva school and the different trends in American research, and it will
doubtless continue to do so. Since its "rediscovery" in 1964, Piaget's theory,
while certainly remaining true to itself, has undergone modification as a result
of both internal revisionism and outside pressures. But it is also true that
Piaget's ideas have contributed to the profound modification of the dominant
conceptual paradigm of American educational psychology. Although this
modification does not as yet amount to a qualitative or structural transformation of the paradigm, it is no longer inconceivable that the Genevan influence
may one day precipitate such a radical change.
   This prospect confirms our belief in the fecundity and originality of the
Piagetian approach and strengthens our conviction that its influence is destined to increase in the future.

References

Anthony, E. J. The significance of Jean Piaget for child psychiatry. *British Journal of Medical
   Psychology*, 1956, *29*, 20–34.
Beilin, H. Stimulus and cognitive transformation in conservation. In D. Elkind & J. H. Flavell
   (Eds.), *Studies in cognitive development: Essays in honor of Jean Piaget*. 409–437. New York:
   Oxford University Press, 1969.
Berlyne, D. E. *Structure and direction in thinking*. New York: John Wiley and Sons, 1965.
Duckworth, E. Piaget rediscovered. In R. E. Ripple & V. N. Rockcastle (Eds.), *Piaget rediscovered*
   (a report of the Conference on Cognitive Studies and Curriculum Development). Ithaca, N.Y.:
   Cornell University School of Education, 1964.
Escalona, S. *The roots of individuality*. Chicago: Aldine, 1968.
Gruber, H., & Voneche, J. *The essential Piaget*. New York: Basic Books, in press.
Mischel, T. (Ed.). *Cognitive development and epistemology*. New York: Academic Press, 1971.
Papert, S., & Voyat, G. A propos du perception: qui a besoin de l'epistemologie. *Etudes
   d'epistemologie genetique* (Vol. 22). Paris: Presses Universitaries de France, 1968.
Piaget, J. *Genetic epistemology* (E. Duckworth, Trans.). Woodbridge Lectures No. 9, New
   York: Columbia University Press. 1970.
Piaget, J. *Adaptation vitale et psychologie de l'intelligence. Selection organique et phenocopie.*
   Paris: Hermann, 1974.
Piaget, J. From noise to order: The psychological development of knowledge and phenocopy in
   biology. *Urban Review*, 1975, *8*(3), 209–218.
Piaget, J. Foreword. In G. Voyat, *Piaget systematized*. New Jersey: Erlbaum, in press.
Pinard, A., & Laurendeau, M. *Causal thinking in the child*. Montreal: International University
   Press, 1962.
Pulaski, M. A. *Understanding Piaget*. New York: Harper and Row, 1971.
Rapaport, D. Psychoanalysis as a developmental psychology. In M. Gill (Ed.), *The collected
   papers of David Rapaport*. New York: Basic Books, 1967.
Schwebel, M., & Raph, J. (Eds.). *Piaget in the classroom*. New York: Basic Books, 1973.
Stephens, B., *et al.* Symposium: Developmental gains in reasoning, moral judgement, and moral
   conduct of retarded and nonretarded persons. *American Journal of Mental Deficiency*, 1974,
   79, 113–161.
Voyat, G. Open education and the embodiment of thinking, reading and writing. *ADE Bulletin*
   (Special Carnegie Sponsored issue) (6).
Wolff, P. *The developmental psychologies of Jean Piaget and psychoanalysis*. New York: Interna-
   tional Universities Press, 1960.

Genetic Epistemology and Developmental Psychology

The Diagnosis
of Reasoning in the
Mentally Retarded

Bärbel Inhelder

Université de Genève

Prefaces by JEAN PIAGET

Translated from the French
by Will Beth Stephens and Others

CHANDLER PUBLISHING COMPANY
An *Intext* Publisher
NEW YORK • LONDON

PSYCHOLOGY:
THEORETICAL–HISTORICAL PERSPECTIVES

ISBN 0-12-588265-3

The genesis of knowledge, the productivity of the human mind, and its ceaseless inventions and discoveries have always been the central theme of Piaget's theoretical and experimental work in epistemology and psychology. His conceptual approach to these great problems has led to a highly consistent system, which nevertheless is in constant evolution. Growth in the biological sense, with both conservation and transformation of structures, is also the main characteristic of the human mind and figures prominently in Piaget's theory. Piaget himself seems to have wanted to make this perfectly clear: The subject he chose for this year's research at the International Center for Genetic Epistemology is how the child comes to envisage an ever-wider range of possibilities while simultaneously building up a concept of what is logically necessary.

Although Piaget's publications are widely disseminated, many psychologists find his work difficult to understand. This is partly due, I believe, to the interdisciplinary character of most of Piaget's research; he sets out to solve epistemological problems experimentally by combining the developmental approach with critical studies of the history of science and by using models based on logic, mathematics, and biological cybernetics. This multidimensional approach leads to a remarkably broad perspective of the laws and mechanisms of cognitive development; yet psychology proper has for Piaget always been a by-product of his genetic epistemology, as was stressed by the American Psychological Association when its annual award went to Jean Piaget.

Early Works and Influences

Since this book is concerned with the historical background of contemporary psychology, I should like first of all to sketch the initial steps that gradually led Piaget forward; he himself, by the way, maintains that he has never tried to build up a system, but has merely attempted to coordinate the results and interpretations of his many pieces of research, to explain certain key notions, to discern their epistemological signifcance, and to open up new directions for research.

Piaget took a Ph.D. in zoology and, as he is wont to remark, his only degrees in psychology are honorary. His first steps in psychology and epistemology were undoubtedly influenced by Immanuel Kant and, more directly, by Leon Brunschvicg, James Marc Baldwin, and Pierre Janet, who, like Freud, was a pupil of Charcot. "The children studied by Piaget are young Immanuel Kants and Piaget himself is a young Immanuel Kant grown old," as the Swiss philosopher Jean-Claude Piguet remarked. Writing many volumes on the development of the categories of space, time, and causality, and on number and logic, Piaget chose his problems outside the traditional fields of experimental psychology. He does not use an a priori interpretative framework: In line with the biological methods and concepts of his malacological studies, he reaches a kind of dynamic, one might say biological, Kantism and sees the mechanisms by which knowledge is constructed in an epigenetic perspective; the structures inherent in the subject are considered to be the result of progressive constructions due to the interaction of endogenous regulatory mechanisms and the impact of variations in the environment.

Brunschvicg's influence on Piaget was exerted principally through the former's critical relativism and his historicocritical method of analysis of the laws of evolution and revolution that characterize the progress of mathematics and physics. Since every scientist is first a child who has to discover once more the fundamental concepts of reason, Piaget studied the origins of knowledge in children. Yet, his aim was not to establish a direct parallel between cognitive development and the course of scientific thought, but to look for common mechanisms. Despite the structural differences between the elementary stages of child thought and the higher levels of human reason, many common functional mechanisms have been brought to light.

A number of Piaget's ideas and interests have sprung from Baldwin's work. Baldwin's theoretical project of founding a "genetic logic" has, in a sense, found experimental actualization in Piaget's research. Moreover, Baldwin's insistence on the social factor in the construction of reason is reflected in Piaget's early work, where the notion of progressive decentraliztion starting from a lack of differentiation between the young child's own point of view and that of others is elaborated, and in which the role of cooperation with their peers in the constitution of logical norms and autonomous morality is stressed. Even in his recent botanical work, in which he is concerned with organic selection, Piaget's findings are once again in agreement with the "Baldwin effect."

The constructivist hypothesis that is gradually refined and enriched in many of Piaget's work finds its clearest expression in the notion of stages in cognitive development. The concept of stages can be traced back to Janet's influence. Janet, while studying what he called "illness of belief" (hysteria and psychasthenia), which he considered to be a disintegration of the synthesis of mental energy, conceived a system of hierarchical stages in mental development. His frequent discussions with his friend Baldwin may well have roused Janet's interest in the development of intelligence in children, the origins of which he placed before the beginning of language.

At first, the concept of stages was used by Piaget as a useful heuristic with which to account for the successive, qualitatively different forms of a construction process; later, the developmental stages define equilibrium states in a continuous process of cognitive structurations whose formation is ordered so that each construction having attained a state of relative equilibrium opens up new possibilities, each step in the process being necessary for the subsequent one.

This conception of stages—which in essence is biological—paralleled embryological and epigenetic processes that have been variously accounted for by concepts such as competence, chreodes, hemeorhesis, and so on.

Sensorimotor Development

Piaget's (1952, 1954) studies on the sensorimotor origins of intelligence were a first example of a synthesis between epistemology and constructivist psychology with biological foundations. Some 30 years later, this first approach was further developed within the framework of modern biology in his work *Biology and Knowledge*. In 1974, Piaget published a new volume on the same subject, *Adaptation vitale et psychologie de l'intelligence* (Piaget, 1974) which aims to show the existence of a functional continuity between organic and psychological structures, the latter being considered as a special case of biological adaptation; psychological structures show the same kind of reciprocal relationship between assimilation and accommodation as organic structures do, but going further since they can generate new structures.

During the preverbal, sensorimotor period, a certain logic of actions, but without any extension, is built up and lays the foundations for later development of logic and of knowledge of reality. The infant who perceives and manipulates objects does not simply establish associations: Because the objects are integrated into his actions, the infant recognizes them and can generalize from one action situation to another. The fundamental psychological fact is, in this view, assimilation: assimilation between action schemes and objects, but also between different action schemes that become coordinated and thus prepare what later will be logical operations. The infant establishes correspondences: From the point of view of "putting into," a small box and a little ball are equivalent, since they can both be put into a large box, and he will repeatedly carry out this action, first with the small box, then with the little ball; the infant also notes differences in properties—the same little box and small ball are different, since he can put his finger inside the one but not inside the other, and he will repeatedly poke his finger into the ball and then put it inside the box. Primitive "intersections" are discovered: Certain objects (a ball, a round pencil) can be pushed so that they roll along by themselves, others (a small ruler, a spoon) can be stuck into a lump of clay; and, surprise, the pencil can be both an object to be rolled and an object to be stuck into something else.

Reciprocal assimilations of such nascent systems of action introduce a certain consistency into the immediate concrete universe of the child and lead to the more complex constructions that presage the culmination of the sensorimotor period, such as the capacity of spatial orientation (for the 1-year-old, within his immediate environment) according to a system that Poincare called the "group of displacements" and that, according to him, plays a part in all effective actions. Piaget has shown how this capacity is constructed during the first year or so of the baby's life, in close connection with the construction of the first cognitive invariant, object-permanency, and with the development of sensorimotor intelligence. Thus, the first fundamental forms of knowledge are constructed before the appearance of language and Piaget showed the important part played by the interaction between the infant and his environment. This research, which was published as early as 1936 and 1937, aroused great interest among Freudians such as David Rapaport, Peter Wolff, Thérèse Gouin Decarie, and Sybille Escalona.

From Sensorimotor Intelligence to the Operations of Thought

At some time during the second year of life, this first logic of actions with its principle of invariants and structures of movement in space is fully constructed and a new stage begins. The growth of the child's representational capacities—the symbolic function—makes for a restructuration of what has been acquired at the level of effective actions. Progressively, the child acquires concepts of conservation of numerical and physical quantities, and the development of these concepts goes together with that of concrete operations. Operations are defined as interiorized actions that are reversible, so that any transformation can be either cancelled by its inverse or compensated reciprocal transformation.

Following the sensorimotor period and before the first operator equilibrium is reached, the child's way of reasoning assumes a form that Piaget (1968) called "semilogical," or "half-logical," and whose one-way mappings will be transformed by reversibility. The one-way mappings conserve the directional property of the real actions out of which they grew; they are an important step toward concrete operations, but the inverse correspondences have to be established before the first level of equilibrium of thought can be attained. In the well-known problem of the quantity of clay[1] contained in a lump of play-dough before and after its shape has been altered, the younger child already has mentally established one correspondence: When one rolls out the dough, it becomes longer. He also establishes the inverse relation: When one compresses the dough and rolls it into a ball, it becomes shorter. However, these

---

[1] The conservation principle was first discussed by Piaget at the Tercentenary Celebration of Harvard University in 1936.

two correspondences (or functions, as Piaget calls them) remain at first separate; only later does each correspondence become completed by a covariance; when the dough is rolled into a sausage, it becomes thinner; when it is rolled back into a ball, it becomes fatter. As long as the child's thought remains unidirectional, conservation of quantity has no logical necessity. Once the operatory system is functioning, covariations become compensations, and conservation, instead of being only qualitative, becomes quantitative. Qualitative properties are, indeed, in a sense conserved much earlier; the child distinguishes between permanent and nonpermanent qualities of objects, but, though he asserts that "it's still the same play-dough," this does not mean that its quantity did not change.

At each level of organization, there is thus harmony between the various systems (action logic, semilogic, and operatory logic) and their invariant properties (object premanency, qualitative identity, and quantitative conservation). These systems have been formalized by Piaget, and such a structural analysis generates hypotheses about and suggests parallels between behavior patterns that at first might appear to be totally independent. The search on learning, for example, was based on such hypotheses and demonstrated reciprocal interaction between operatory systems by showing that training in conservation concepts greatly improved concepts of class inclusion and vice versa (Inhelder *et al.*, 1974).

Causality

The studies just mentioned are mainly concerned with the way the child constructs a certain consistency in his own thoughts, a development we may consider as being fundamentally logicomathematical. But simultaneously the child also constructs a coherence between what he thinks and what actually happens in reality, and this development provides the bases for his causal explanatory thought.

Piaget (1927/1930) devoted one of his early works to the child's concept of causality, and since then causality has been investigated in numerous experimental studies at the Center of Genetic Epistemology. A recurring theme of these studies is the child's understanding of mechanical links when movement is transmitted from one object to another. In general, the results of the experiments point to a parallelism between logicomathematical operations and the understanding of causal phenomena in that the subject "attributes" to the behavior of the objects the operations he elaborates in his logical thinking. Before the child understands transmission, he describes what he seems to observe in the following way: The marble that is rolling down hits the first marble, then skips in and out of the others and continues its trajectory. This is the only explanation he can find for the fact that three marbles remain motionless and only the first one is propelled. Such transmission of movement is understood at the same time that the concept of transitivity is reached in logicomathematical problems. This "attribution" (in mathematical terms) to the objects of the subject's own operations means that objects themselves become operators. From this point of view, the concept of causality, like the operations themselves, involves a compensatory relationship between transformations and conservations.

Nevertheless, the development of the capacity of causal explanation is not simply a repetition of what happens during the construction of logicomathematical operations: The latter are the result of free constructions by the subject, whereas the former depend on the properties of objects and their interactions. These object properties, and the fact that they may resist whatever the child wants to do with them, call for a very different mental effort, which is the main source of the child's discoveries about the physical world.

Other studies were concerned with the child's understanding of probability and chance (or randomness), time and space, measurement, and so on. The experimental situations were mostly chosen because of their epistemological meaning; in all of them it was possible to follow the way the child gradually builds up a coherent system of structures that permit him to deal with many problems of different kinds.

Reflective Abstraction and Constructive Generalization

How does the child build up these structures, and, especially, how, around the age of 11 or 12, does he attain a logical structure that goes beyond that of classes and relations, beyond the double-entry matrices of the concrete operations period? Piaget calls the mechanism by which this is achieved "reflexive abstraction." Such abstraction takes place when the subject derives from his actions and operations certain principles that lead to a new organization when he is confronted with a new problem. For example, at the level of concrete operations, the child is already capable of substituting one criterium for another (shifting) and of conserving the whole in whatever way it has been divided into parts (Inhelder & Piaget, 1959/1964). This is a manifestation of what has been called "vicariance." Subsequently, by reflexive abstraction, this concept leads to the idea of a division of one and the same totality into all its possible parts. Through this abstraction, which is accompanied by a constructive generalization, the subject reaches the logicomathematical concept of the set of all subsets. The different links between the parts form a combinatory system, one of the most fundamental structures of formal operations (Inhelder & Piaget, 1959/1964).

We have said that reflexive abstraction is always accompanied by constructive generalizations. Just as we have to distinguish two kinds of abstraction, empirical abstraction, bearing on objects and their properties, and reflexive abstraction, bearing on the actions of the subject, two kinds of generalizations have also to be distinguished; one simply extends an already existing concept and involves no more than a verification of the transition from some to all. Whereas the other can indeed be called constructive, since it introduces new combinations or operations on operations (such as combinatory systems and the set of all subsets).

At a lower level an example of constructive generalization is the following. The child is given 10 sticks of different lengths correctly seriated, and is asked: "How many sticks are there that are bigger than this tiny one?" The child easily shows the smallest stick and correctly counts the others. Then the experimenter shows the biggest stick and asks, "And how many are smaller than this one?" The 5–6-year old will then count the sticks again, whereas 1 or 2 years later he will laugh and immediately answer, "Nine also, of course." Such constructive generalization is the main mechanism of progress in mathematics, and it is striking that it should already be present in the child.

The relationship between reflexive abstraction and constructive generalization is necessarily a very close one; each abstraction leads sooner or later to constructive generalizations, and each generalization is based on reflexive abstractions.

Equilibration

Piaget's quest for a model to account for the continuity between biological and psychological adaptation goes back to his very first research, when he was still an adolescent, and may be thought of as the "red thread" that runs through his entire work, reappearing with particular clarity each time he discusses his equilibrium theory. His latest thoughts on equilibrium can be summed up as follows (Piaget, 1974a,b).

Three forms of equilibration can be distinguished. The simplest form, the first to appear during development, is that between assimilation and accommodation. Already in the sensorimotor period, an action scheme applied to new objects becomes differentiated as a function of the object's properties. An equilibrium is reached so that the action scheme is conserved and at the same time adapted to the object's properties. If these properties are unexpected and interesting, the equilibration can lead to the formation of a subscheme, or even of a new scheme, which in turn needs to be equilibrated. These functional mechanisms are at work at all levels.

A second form of equilibration takes place between the subsystems of the system of operations the subject is elaborating, for example, between numerical and spatial measurement systems in problems of quantification where both these subsystems play a part. Since such subsystems generally develop at different rates, conflicts may appear, and equilibration will necessitate a distinction between what is common to both subsystems on the one hand and their specific properties on the other. In one of the learning situations, for example, the children had to build what we called "roads" out of bits of wood, so that their "road" was of the same length as the experimenter's. The child was given bits of wood that were five-sevenths of the length of the bits the experimenter worked with, a fact that they could and did indeed observe in one of the situations where the experimenter put five bits into a straight line and the child was asked to construct his road directly underneath. This problem raises no difficulties. When, however, the experimenter built his road (of five bits of wood) in a zig zag and the children were asked to build theirs immediately below, they made the end points coincide with those of the experimenter's road, thus building a line that was far shorter than the model. When they were asked to build a road of equal length to the zig-zag model not directly below, but somewhere on the other side of the table, they no longer used the "not-going-beyond principle," but used a numerical equivalence idea; they counted the experimenter's bits of wood, five, and used five of their own bits. Going back to the proximity situation, in which four bits of wood constitute a line that does not go beyond the experimenter's, a conflict appears: Five is the answer based on numerical evaluation, four is the answer based on the topological correspondence (the "not-going-beyond principle"). The awareness of this conflict often led to curious compromise solutions, such as breaking one piece into two pieces without bypassing the endpoints of the configuration, and later on to correct solutions after a certain number of training sessions.

Piaget distinguishes further that a third form of equilibration is based on the second, but leads to the construction of a new total system; the process of differentiation of new subsystems demands a procedure that allows their integration into a new totality and thus constitutes a third form of equilibration.

Superficially, it would seem that equilibration implies a simple balance between opposing forces: the differentiation that threatens the unity of the whole and the integration that endangers the necessary distinctions. But more profoundly, the particularity of cognitive equilibrium is to ensure that the total structure is continuously enriched by the differentiations and that, reciprocally, these differentiations increase with the variations of the intrinsic properties of the total structure.

In other words, cognitive equilibration has the characteristic of being what Piaget calls "majorante," that is to say, augmentative; in other words, the various disequilibria do not lead to a simple reequilibration in the sense of a return to a former equilibrium state, but to a new and more powerful form of equilibrium that incorporates more numerous internal dependencies and logical implications. From this point of view, disequilibria acquire a functional importance, which is best examplified by Piaget's work on contradiction.

Contradiction

For Piaget, the periods of disequilibrium should not be explained by pointing to contradictions the subject feels in his logical reasoning; rather, the subject's inconsistencies and contradictions should point to a psychological source of such disequilibria. The problem of contradiction is closely related to another question: Why are there so many initial disequilibria, since it might have been expected that subjects at any level of development, however elementary, are capable, without contradictions, of mastering problems that do not go beyond an appropriate level of complexity? It turns out that the psychological source of many inconsistencies and contradictions is to be sought in a simple and general phenomenon: the difficulty of compensating affirmations (or positive factors) by negations (or negative factors). The young child is essentially focused on the effect he wants to achieve through his actions, and is likely to lose sight of the situation he started from. In number conservation situations, for example, the young child feels that something has somehow been added at the end of the transformation, but he does not understand that what has been added must in some way have been subtracted from the initial state (Inhelder *et al.*, 1975). In all mathematical and logical problems, the child "succumbs" to this primacy of positive factors over negative ones, which accounts for the lack of reversibility of thought in these areas. The same phenomenon appears also in different situations: For example, the young child understands quickly what it meant by a full glass, or an almost full or a half-full glass, but has much more difficulty with expressions such as half empty, almost empty, and so on. Very young children will not accept that a glass can at the same time be half full and half empty; for them, this is a contradictory statement. The fact is doubly instructive for the psychologist. On the one hand, it reaffirms the hypothesis of the primacy of positive factors over negative ones, and on the other hand it shows the importance of what for the adult are pseudocontradictions, such as are encountered in seriation tasks, where for children of a certain level, if *B* is bigger than *A*, *B* cannot at the same time be smaller than *C*.

Epistemology

Piaget's psychology cannot be separated from his epistemology. His epistemological theory may be called constructivist (and Piaget himself qualifies it thus) in the sense that knowledge is neither preformed in the object (empiricism) nor in the subject (nativism), but results from progressive construction. The two main considerations that lead to the rejection of empiricism are the following (Piaget, 1970, 1972).

1. Acts of knowledge are never simply based on associations, but always on assimilation, that is, on the integration of present data into already existing structures.

2. If the first point is conceded, development can no longer be an accumulation of pieces of learning, and learning must depend on the laws of development and the competence of the subject, according to his cognitive level, as has been shown in our research on learning and the development of cognition. In other words, knowledge is never a simple copy of reality, but always results from a restructuration of reality through the activities of the subject (on this point Piaget agrees with von Foerster's position concerning the cognitive relationships between subject and object).

To say that knowledge depends on the activities of the subject does not mean that knowledge is innate, since it is precisely the activities of the subject that constantly create new structures and new forms of organization. If knowledge were innate, logical necessity should be present before, rather than after, the subject masters certain construction. This appears not to be the case. The simplest example is that of the concept of transitivity ($A < C$ if $A < B$ and $B < C$), which is reached at the end of the operatory construction of seriation and is not understood at the level of empirical success in seriating sticks of different lengths.

T. Bower (1974) and others, it is true, have shown the existence of certain innate reactions, such as perceptive constancies. But between this early behavior and analogous behavior patterns that arise some months later, there is a necessary reconstruction and no direct continuity as would be supposed by a generalized nativism. Each new stage in cognitive development is characterized by new creations that, in turn, open up new possibilities. When the structure is comparatively weak, the new possibilities are comparatively few, but the more powerful the structure, the greater the number of new possibilities. This principle is illustrated not only by the child's cognitive development, but also by the history of mathematics and physics. Piaget *et al.* (1974, 1976) are working with the physicist and historian of science Rolando Garcia in order to elucidate the mechanisms that account for both the psychogenetic structuration of intelligence and the historical development of scientific thought.

The constructivist aspect of cognitive development is also manifest in the mechanisms of how subjects become aware of their own action or thought patterns. For most authors, and particularly for Freud, awareness does not go beyond the uncovering of realities that already existed in the subject's unconscious. According to Piaget, awareness always implies a conceptualization and therefore supposes a reconstruction that transforms whatever remained unconscious in action into new realities of a conceptual nature.

Piaget's work in genetic epistemology revealed a striking parallelism between the psychogenesis of concepts and the development of theories in mathematics and physics. The levels of abstraction as well as the types of concepts are obviously quite different among children and among scientists. Yet one finds surprising analogies between children's ways of explaining natural phenomena and the thinking about mechanics in Antiquity and the Middle Ages, especially when comparing the answers of children concerning the "explanations" with specific passages in Buridan or Oresme, the great masters of the fourteenth century. These analogies, however, may be considered as bearing on content of knowledge rather than on mechanisms of concept building. Parallels concerning mechanisms of progress are far more important. These mechanisms characterize not only the *stages* of development but furthermore—and this is perhaps more important—the transition from one stage to the next.

For example, in the history of geometry before our century, one may consider three stages characterized by (*a*) the geometry of the Greeks and its evolution up to the end of the eighteenth century; (*b*) the projective geometry (Poncelet, Chasles); (*c*) the "global" conception of geometry introduced by Klein. The development of descriptive geometry by Descartes and Fermat, and of calculus, provided the instruments for the transition from (*a*) to (*b*), and group theory for the transition from (*b*) to (*c*). Here one finds a similarity with the stages described by Piaget in children as "intrafigural," "interfigural," and "transfigural." The epistemological analysis of these differences shows profound reasons for this parallelism and has demonstrated, beyond expectation, the fertility of psychogenetic research for understanding the evolution of science.

This epistemological theory opened up many new directions in research. In Geneva, colleagues drew upon Piaget's work in pursuing studies in related fields—psycholinguistics, cybernetics, psychopathology of thought, and other fields—as well as in extending the scope of developmental psychology itself.

Until recently, studies in cognitive psychology were mainly concerned with the structural aspects of knowledge and the different modes of apprehending reality, and aimed at an analysis of the subject's cognitive potentialities at different periods of development. Research on learning led toward the study of the dynamic processes that make for the transition from one level of thought to the next. A better understanding of these processes drew attention to the important role played by the different strategies by which the subjects seek to generalize their newly acquired reasoning patterns. The latest research in Geneva (Inhelder *et al.*, 1976) is thus concerned with these processes of strategies in children: How does the child come to invent procedures that he thinks will help him to solve a problem, and what kind of relationship exists between his inventions and his "theories in action" or his implicit system of dealing with reality (Karmiloff and Inhelder, 1975)? These are among the fundamental questions we are dealing with at the moment.

For Piaget, psychology may be a mere by-product of his work in epistemology, especially of his constructivist theory of knowledge; but for his colleagues, collaborators, and admirers this by-product constitutes an extraordinarily rich source of inspiration.

Acknowledgment

I wish to express my gratitude to M. and H. Sinclair for their generous help in translating the manuscript.

References

Bower, T. *Development in infancy.* Freeman. San Francisco, 1974.

Inhelder, B., *et al.* Relations entre les conservations d'ensembles d'elements discrets et celles de quantites continues. *Annee Psychologique,* 1975, *75,* 23–60.

Inhelder, B., *et al.* Des structures cognitives aux procedures de decouverte. *Archives de Psychologie, 1976, 44,* (171), 57–72.

Inhelder, B., & Piaget, J. *The early growth of logic in the child (classification and seriation).* New York: Harper & Row, 1964. (Originally published, 1959.)

Karmiloff, A., & Inhelder, B. If you want to get ahead, get a theory. *Cognition, 3*(3), 1975, 195–212.

Moreno, L., Rayna, N., Sinclair, H., Stambak, M., & Verba, M. Les bebes et la logique. *Les Cahiers du CRESAS,* 1976, (14).

Piaget, J. The child's conception of physical causality. New York: Harcourt Brace, 1930. (Originally published, 1927.)

Piaget, J. *The origins of intelligence in children.* New York: International University Press, 1952.

Piaget, J. *The child's construction of reality.* New York: Basic Books, 1954. (Originally published, 1937.)

Piaget, J., *Adaptation vitale et psychologie de l'intelligence selection organique et phenocopie.* Paris: Hermann, 1968.

Piaget, J. *Genetic epistemology* (E. Duckworth, Trans.). Woodbridge Lectures No. 9, New York: Columbia University Press, 1970.

Piaget, J. *The principle of genetic epistemology.* London: Routledge and Kegan Paul, 1972.

Piaget, J. Recherches sur la contradiction. I. Les differentes formes de la contradiction. *Etudes d'epistemologie genetique* (Vol. 31). Paris: Presses Universitaires de France, 1974 (a).

Piaget, J. Recherches sur la contradicion. 2. Les relations entre affirmation et negations. *Etudes d'epistemologie genetique* (Vol. 32). Paris: Presses Universitaires de France, 1974 (b).

Piaget, J. L'equilibration des structures cognitives (probleme central du developpement). *Etudes d'epistemologie genetique* (Vol. 33). Paris: Presses Universitaires de France, 1975.

Piaget, J., *et al.* Epistemologie et psychologie de la fonction. *Etudes d'epistemologie genetique* (Vol. 23). Paris: Presses Universitaires de France, 1974.

Piaget, J., *et al. The grasp of consciousness.* Cambridge, Mass.: Harvard University Press, 1976. (Originally published, 1974.)

JEAN PIAGET **15**

Some Recent Research and Its Link with a New Theory of Groupings and Conservations Based on Commutability[1]

[1] Translated by Gilbert Voyat of The Graduate School and University Center of the City University of New York, in collaboration with Donald Nicholson-Smith. The French version will appear in the *Bulletin de Psychologie de l'Université de Paris*, special issue in honor of Paul Fraisse.

PSYCHOLOGY:
THEORETICAL–HISTORICAL PERSPECTIVES

ISBN 0-12-588265-3

Perhaps I may be permitted to add a few words concerning our current research before presenting a new theory of grouping and conservation. At the International Center for Genetic Epistemology in Geneva, we are at present dealing with what we call the opening up of new possibilities, that is to say, the way in which an action, an operation, or a structure acquired by the child generates new possibilities.

To give an example of our experiments, we place the child in the following types of situations. We give him, for instance, a piece of cardboard and three blocks, and he is asked to arrange these blocks in all possible ways without specification whether in regular, irregular, or random fashion. In another type of experiment, we give the child a square sheet of paper and ask him to cut it up in all possible ways. Will the child produce only diagonals or medians or will he find other ways? Or again, we show the child a half-hidden object and ask him to guess its complete shape or to suggest what possible ways he can think of to complete the visible portion.

There are, of course, many variations, and among young children from 4 to 6 years of age, we find little variation. They find 5–10 possibilities, then claim that nothing more can be done.

Between 7 and 11 we find a progressive increase of new possibilities and around 11–12 years of age the child, after two or three tries, immediately tells us that the number of possibilities is infinite and gives us justifications as to why. There is thus an increase with age of the number of possibilities perceived. Our fundamental thesis is that possibilities are not predetermined. It is in effect a contradiction in terms to talk of a totality of all possibilities. The concept of a totality of all possibilities is antinomic, because the whole is itself one possibility among others, and because every possibility generates new ones. There is something here which transcends all preformation. There is an authentic creativity which plays a fundamental role in my conception of equilibration: the "possible" is the moment of reequilibration between one form of equilibrium and the text.

Another avenue of research pursued at the Center for Epistemology, the result of which are still to be published, concerns what in mathematics are called correspondences or morphisms. Correspondences and morphisms had not been studied until recently. Previously, we had placed a great emphasis on operations as transformations of a given object, whereas correspondences and morphisms are essentially comparisons, comparisons that do not transform objects to be compared but that extract common forms from them or analogies between them.

As an example, we may take the case of family relationships. We confront the child with a series of identical dolls marked with arrows representing relations such as grandfather, uncle, nephew, cousin, brother, and so forth. Let us suppose that A is the grandfather of B. For A there exists a number of taxonomical relationships with all other members of the family, and the child will name them. A is the father of C, the cousin of D, and so on. Let us now take B, who is A's grandson. For B there is also a whole series of relationships with other family members. The child is asked to state the reciprocal relationships, taking into account the points of view of both A and B, that is, the grandfather and the son, where these two are to be taken together and compared with other members of the family such as a brother or a cousin. There is a system of correspondences here between two relational systems that the child is asked to establish. This is easy for the close relationships and becomes more and more complex and interesting to study when subjects reach 11–12 years of age.

This research on correspondences and morphisms has shown us, in regard to our previous research on operations and transformations, that the groundwork for any operation or transformation is laid by correspondences. One needs to understand the correspondence between an initial and a final state to understand what the transformation is that leads from one state to the next. Once the operations are completed, once the operational structures are built, correspondences become a function of the operational structures. They no longer prepare the operations but become their deductible consequences.

We have a number of completed studies that will soon be published, and here we can present only a small sample; these are only a few examples of the research presently under way in Geneva.

Inasmuch as this new research on possibilities had to be integrated with our earlier work on operations, we had to review its status on the basis of the results obtained. This enabled us to work out a new theory of groupings and conservations based on commutability. In addition, thanks to our new findings, it became possible to refine our grouping theory by introducing two kinds of fresh formalizations, one of them being logistic in character and the other categorical. Some account of this development follows.

New Formulations Regarding the Structure of Groupings and Conservations

In seeking to describe the earliest operational structures built by the child (classifications, seriations, etc.), we have used the term "grouping" to refer to a model that has generated little enthusiasm from logicians and mathematicians because of its unavoidable limitations (step-by-step composition, disjoint sets) and consequent "lack of elegance." Our defense, however, was that no matter how primitive its use is between the ages of 7 and 11 (and thus before the construction of "complete networks" or "integrated wholes"), "grouping" evoked a structure which from Linné to the present has provided an adequate basis for all zoological and botanical classifications (which are also never more than semilattices).

Just recently, however, two logicians and mathematicians have taken an interest in this problem and managed to give the concept of grouping a respectable status. One of them, H. Vermus (1973), has supplied a complete axiomatization. He bases himself on four very simple axioms: (a) The asymmetry of the binary predicate linking y to x as its "immediate successor," (b) the unicity of this successor; (c) the "contiguous junction" that gives rise to the immediate successor z from two contiguous elements x and y; and (d) the existence and the unicity of the (dichotomous) "subtraction" of one element from its successor.

The other mathematician, E. Whittman, taking the axiomatization produced by Vermus as his starting point, has shown that the "grouping" constitutes a special "category" in the sense in which this term is used by his mentor S. McLane. McLane inverted this notion of "categories" with Eilenberg, and he has endorsed Wittman's remarks. We have no need to recapitulate Wittman's account here, but since a "category" in this sense is a system of "morphisms" (i.e., correspondences in which the structure is conserved), it is worthwhile from the psychologist's point of view to isolate a few of these morphisms in order to see that the grouping is not just a system of operations (and hence transformations) but that it also embodies a set of correspondences (and hence of comparisons).

Classifications[2]

Piaget's formalization in the language of mathematics (See Piaget, 1977) concerns four basic logical structures: classifications, vicarious relationships, relationships of order, and conservations. The cognitive operations mentioned in the preceding discussion have a psychological counterpart, but Piaget treats them from an abstract frame of reference. The cognitive operations essentially correspond to similarities and differences in the every day cognitive life of an individual. As far as classifications are concerned, Piaget takes the example from zoological classifications, because it is basically concerned with taxonomical distinctions and has no nomenclature for relations between objects. The classifications consist of similarities between objects, persons, and events. One should also keep in mind that, taken as a system, classification constitutes a category in itself. A very important point here is Piaget's new interpretation of the phenomena of conservations, starting from the assumption that the subject arrives at a particular point when two conditions are met. The first is a change in the form of an object or collection of ob-

---

[2] This portion of the chapter is a summary of the section on classifications (Piaget, 1977) and was written by Gilbert Voyat.

jects. This is understood as being the result of surface changes in the position of the component of the objects. The second is that as any change in conservation that is added at the end has been removed from or substituted for the beginning. This leads to the operation of commutability, from which it follows that the categorical tools of conservation are also dependent upon. They are also dependent upon vicarious relationships, and commutability expresses the identity of a component even though movement takes place. Vicarious relationships express the consistency of the totality even though internal rearrangements have taken place. This provides the ability to combine rearrangements and movements to define "morphisms," by which Piaget means comparisons that basically leave intact the objects to be compared and slow the deductions or analogies between them. It can be concluded that conservations as well as the various groupings that are proposed do not consist solely in operational systems of transformations but also in correspondences, or morphisms. The originality of morphisms resides in the fact that this type of system paves the way for other operational systems. It should be noted, however, that the latter can also be derived from other operational systems. The reciprocal relationships that exist between correspondences and operational systems have to be organized into well regulated compositional structures to allow the reciprocal relationships to take place. Once these have taken place, a further elaboration of the possibility of formalized models is possible. (The details of these formalized models can be found in Piaget, 1977.)

References

Dieudonne, J. *Fondements de l'analyse moderne.* Paris: Gauthier-Villars, 1965.

Piaget, J. *Traite de logique. Essai de logistique operatorie.* Paris: Librarie Armand Colin, 1949.

Piaget, J. *Some recent research and its link to the new theory of groupings and conservations based on commutability.* In R. W. Rieber & K. Salzinger (Eds.), *The roots of American psychology: Historical influences and implications for the future,* New York: New York Academy of Sciences, Annal No. 291, 1977.

Piaget, J., *et al.* Relation entre les conservation d'ensembles d'elements discrets et celles de quantites continues. *Annee Psychologique,* 1975, 75, 23–60.

Vermus, H. Une axiomatisation des groupements, *Archives de Psychologie,* 1973, 42 (163).

Recommended Readings

Broughton, J. M., & Freemen-Moir, J. F. *The foundations of cognitive-developmental psychology: James Mark Baldwin's theory and its contemporary meaning.* New Zealand: Canterbury University, 1980.

Duckworth, E. Piaget rediscovered. In R. E. Ripple & V. N. Rockcastle (Eds.), *Piaget rediscovered (a report of the Conference on Cognitive Studies and Curriculum Development).* Ithaca, N.Y.: Cornell University School of Education, 1964.

Gruber, H. E. & Vonèche, J. J., (Eds.). *The essential Piaget.* New York: Basic Books, 1977.

Inhelder, B., *et al. Learning and the development of cognition.* Cambridge, Mass.: Harvard University Press, 1974.

Piaget, J. *Genetic epistemology.* New York: W. W. Norton & Co. 1970.

Riegel, K. F., *Psychology of development and history.* New York: Plenum Press, 1976.

Epilogue

Sitzfleisch, the Zeitgeist, and the Hindsightgeist

MACH SCHNELL

von

PROF. DR. WILHELM URPSYCHE

Nichtwahr Verlag
Schnellburg
1776

PSYCHOLOGY:
THEORETICAL–HISTORICAL PERSPECTIVES

ISBN 0–12–588265–3

Ambrose Bierce bitterly defined the historian as "a broad-gauge gossip," and many psychologists, taking his definition seriously, have taught the history of psychology in precisely this way. Suffice it to say that this volume has amply demonstrated how wrong that definition is. Unfortunately, my own background in the history of psychology comes from that time when history was viewed as a collection of hazy, unverifiable guesses about what in human behavior might have caused some particular experimental psychologist to have tried which particular experiment. In those days, we viewed history only as error from which we were, if smart enough, privileged to profit. To find the error of a previous scientist's ways was the highest kind of mental activity, even for the behaviorist.

In the course of my teaching career, I stumbled into a department of social sciences that includes among the subjects that it teaches both history and psychology, thus forcing me to learn some history just to communicate with my colleagues, and so I like to think that I am not altogether as ignorant of this subject matter as I used to be. Nevertheless, I cannot point to any publication directly bearing on the subject matter of the history of psychology in my vita. True enough, I did a few years ago introduce a daylong meeting on the history of psychology (Salzinger, 1976), and for that purpose, I did analyze somewhat the contents of some then recent issues of the *Journal of the History of the Behavioral Sciences*, but there are those who have not viewed that presentation entirely as a scholarly work of the first rank. Therefore, to overcome my inferiority complex in this area, I decided to use the occasion at last to prepare a scholarly piece of research in the history of psychology.

I have learned, by this time, that a true historian does not rely on mere published material to discover the contributions of, for example, some particular psychologist, but that he or she must make every effort to find in the personal effects of the significant figure being studied the unpublished, not to speak of the unpublishable, papers and, perhaps most important, to find those unpublished materials never meant to be seen by the public at all. [Since this chapter was orignally written during the United States bicentennial year I tried to find a person—unhappily, I must report I investigated the life of a man, not a woman, but that undoubtedly reflects those times rather than the capability of women in those days—living around two hundred years ago who might have been influenced by the writers of the Declaration of Independence, who was perhaps active in government, and, most important of all, who had not been studied by anyone else before. I am happy to report that I found a person having at least some of these qualifications.] Although I am not totally at liberty to divulge all of my sources, I can say that all were reliably checked by having at least two sources for every fact stated in this chapter. What's more, I expect to be able to write a book on the material that I found. The tentative title is *The First, Middle, and Final Days of Dr. Wilhelm Urpsyche.*

As you probably guessed from the name, our hero is of German extraction. The significance of that will come out of our discussion as we go on. I employed a recently discovered technique of using the impressions made on vases by the voices of the potters as they worked. Suffice it to say here that we replayed some of the vases that Dr. Urpsyche, an accomplished psycho-ceramicist, was known to have thrown, that is to say, to have made himself. The fidelity of these vases is not very good, but with the aid of some amplification equipment borrowed from the Haskins Laboratory, we have deduced a definite German accent in whatever the hell he could have been saying when he threw his pots. I hesitate to report what one observer has been insisting he heard, because this is the only instance of one source for a state-ment of fact. But it is interesting enough for us to speculate about, so I am in-cluding it here. The reported statement is: "Stop with the water already." The possible significance of this statement is such as to require no further com-ment.

But to return to the life of Dr. Wilhelm Urpsyche. As close as I could deter-mine, he was born in the year 1746. He was 30 years of age at the time of the signing of the Declaration of Independence. I wish I could say that his birth-day coincided with the day of the signing, but since I was unable to find his exact birthday, I am unable to do so. The only evidence I could find for any awareness of the fathers of our country was a statement by Urpsyche to the ef-fect that any man who invented as many things as Jefferson did had to be lazy.

Those of you who are interested in the methodology of obtaining original material might wish to hear how I came upon it. The tale of the finding of the records is actually quite brief. They were left on my doorstep in a carefully wrapped package measuring 4 feet wide, by 4 feet long, by 6 feet high. I de-cided to unwrap it, given the fact that it otherwise would have been impossi-ble for any of us in my family to get out the door. Now that I have told you how I acquired my data, I am not sure how I can advise you to make use of this method. As already indicated, I obtained confirmation of all the most ex-citing details of Dr. Urpsyche's life from at least one other source. Unfor-tunately, I am not at liberty to divulge the name of the medium. She insisted that we always work in the dark, a condition not unknown to some historians and which is what finally convinced me of her authenticity. She brought me into communication with the various compatriots of Dr. Urpsyche, and I shall have occasion to refer to those contacts later.

I might just point out to students how fortunate it is that I know German, since despite the fact that Dr. Urpsyche worked exclusively in the United

States, he wrote all his papers and books in German. After he wrote them, they had to be translated into English in order to be read by his colleagues. You must know languages, if you are going to do any significant work in the history of psychology.

The circumstance of Dr. Urpsyche's writing all of his work in German may well account for the fact that there is so little mention of him in our history of psychology books. It was one of the factors that held my work up very badly in communicating with the colleagues of Dr. Urpsyche through the medium: They all insisted that I translate long excerpts of Dr. Urpsyche's work for them; most of them had had only an inkling of his writings when they were all alive, having got to know his work based only on his infrequent lectures at a small college just outside Boston, called, they tell me, Saint Catastrophe. I have not, so far, been able to verify the name, although it does seem appropriate for an increasing number of schools. The school apparently did come to an untimely end sometime in the third quarter of the eighteenth century, according to my immaterial informants.

The informants were able to explain the existence of the large number of documents on this psychologist. According to them, he was always very conscious of what would happen after he died, and apparently he wanted to make sure that if ever there was a historian of psychology desirous of reconstructing his life and works, he, Dr. Urpsyche, would make it as easy as possible.

What makes the collection of notes and diaries from Dr. Urpsyche so valuable is that in his last few years he became obsessed with the idea of getting all of his thoughts down on paper. In order that he not lose anything, he refused to communicate with people at all unless they agreed to write down whatever they wanted of him and were willing to put up with having to wait for him to write down whatever he wanted to say in response.

As a result of his copious note keeping and the writing down of all of his conversations, I had quite a time separating the significant from the mundane. Just to give you one example, I cannot begin to tell you the number of times I came across the notation, "Please pass the salt," although I am having a graduate student get a precise count for me. On the basis of a preliminary analysis, I can say that the response of asking for salt clearly outnumbers the response of asking for molasses. In about three months, we should have precise figures on this matter.

The matter of asking for the salt to be passed as often as he did, by the way, may have some significance in that his colleagues described him to me as being a man who would take the then current theories of behavior with more than a grain of salt. He used to put it, one of my incorporeal informants reported, "Zu viel verstehen heisst zu viel verdrehen" (Too much understanding means too much confusing). The richness of information available on his behavior at home, so to say, provides us with a storehouse of insights into his behavior in the laboratory. The data we have on Dr. Urpsyche's private life might well bring within our reach the possibility of finally responding to the recent onslaught of psychohistories whose only validation is in the minds of their authors; we might look upon Dr. Urpsyche's historical analysis as a kind of Urpsychohistory.

Dr. Urpsyche's writings were legion, although, as already explained, his publications were rather slow in coming, since he wrote everything in German. Then, in characteristic fashion, having once finished a particular piece of work, he lost interest, refusing to return to it in order to translate it. The Hessian soldiers he employed to do the translation of his work at the time of the Revolution unfortunately did not live long enough to do the kind of thorough job he found acceptable, and in some cases, whole manuscripts were actually lost on the battlefield.

Of the book-length manuscripts that came to me in that large package of artifacts, I found first of all the book that apparently was instrumental in getting Dr. Urpsyche his first job at a university. The book was called *Mach Schnell;* it was the only book that was actually completely translated into English, but somehow it didn't get any publisher sufficiently interested to put it into print. Students apparently passed the book around from one to another, as can be gleaned from the various gratuitous remarks that are to be found on the margins of its pages. Suffice it to say that the student caliber of that day is quite comparable to that of today. The title, *Mach Schnell*, as you no doubt know, means Do It Quickly. It was Dr. Urpsyche's treatise on reaction time, was well liked among his colleagues, and apparently was also what got him elected to the status of Honorary Fellow in the International Society of Schnell Machen, so named after his book of similar title. He was just about putting the finishing touches on a second book, *Mach Schneller*, when he was elected president of that organization.

In his later years, when he completely disowned his earlier work and published his countertreatise, *Mach Langsam*, Do It Slowly, he was actually read out of that organization. We know how badly he felt about his colleagues' fair-weather friendship from the notes we see of conversations he had with his wife, Langsam. She kept asking, "Why is it important to do things quickly, Wilhelm?" and he kept retorting, "I know, I know, I will try to make it langsam, Langsam."[1] Once again, we see the importance of having available

---

[1] The remarkable coincidence of Dr. Urpsyche's wife's name, Langsam, and the meaning of the German word *langsam*—namely, slow—is in fact just that, a remarkable coincidence. The fact of the repeated occurrence of the word Mach in all the book titles so far treated, and the fact of Dr. Urpsyche's son's name being Ernst—as in Ernst Mach—are also, as far as I could determine from looking over the Mach papers, to be ascribed to coincidence. No historian can afford to read meaning into every observed coincidence of events, lest he or she commit the fallacy of misplaced literalism (Fischer, 1970). Ernst Mach never mentioned Urpsyche, which is not to say that he did not know of his existence, but certainly we have no proof that he did. Also, we have no evidence that Ernst Mach changed his name to Ernst Mach, which might be one way in which Urpsyche might have influenced Mach. Finally, although not directly pertinent to the point in question, Ernst Urpsyche (Dr. Urpsyche's son) died in an accident during a boat race (Mach Schnell?). His boat capsized, and his body was never found.

private conversations to shed light on the critical interactions that must take place in all scientists between their scientific and their private behaviors.

The last paper that I found written by Urpsyche was unfinished. It begins with the words, "Nun steh ich da, ich armer Tor" (Here I stand, poor fool I am). This is also the only paper in which he had a coauthor, a certain Dr. Faust. Dr. Faust left a note not to forget to thank Gretchen (no last name is given) for all her help in making this paper possible.

There are some other tidbits of Dr. Wilhelm Urpsyche's life that I have learned over the past few months in communication with my incorporeal informants. Dr. Urpsyche had a sense of humor. After particularly bad results on an examination that he gave his students, he was wont to say: "If God had really wanted people to think, he would have given them brains." This remark, oft repeated, eventually turned into, "Maybe God really didn't want people to think."

I have also looked a little into Dr. Urpsyche's childhood, his toilet-training regime, sleeping arrangements, opportunities to witness the primal scene, and such, but have so far found nothing of significance in that area beyond the fact that Dr. Urpsyche's family lived in one room, which contained one bed (quite large by reputation, although the exact dimensions were not available), and no toilet facilities. Apparently, all the toilet training was done at a neighbor's house some 2½ miles away. I am quite sure that none of these peculiar circumstances of early life have any bearing on Dr. Urpsyche's later—shall we say—unique sexual orientations. But I expect to continue to mine this large mound of information for a while longer and to report on these results on a later occasion.

Before I end my chapter, I should explain its title. The Zeitgeist hardly needs any explanation at all; it refers to the fact that the time has finally come when historians of psychology can freely talk about its history and do so in a professional way, my chapter notwithstanding. The Sitzfleisch concept refers to the fact that the bottom line of writing history is remaining in one place for a long time. Finally, the Hindsightgeist reminds us all to be modest in our historical analyses, for our wisdom comes from viewing things that have already taken place. To make even more significant contributions, we must try to spell out the lessons of foresight, namely how to do it better the next time around.

References

Fischer, D. H. *Historians' fallacies.* New York: Harper & Row, 1970.

Salzinger, K. What's in a title? *Annals of the New York Academy of Sciences,* 1976, *270,* 1–5.

Recommended Readings

Baker, R. A. (Ed.). *Psychology in the wry.* New York: D. Van Nostrand, 1963.

Bloch, A. *Murphy's law and other reasons why things go wrong.* Los Angeles: Prince, Stern, Sloan, 1977.

Borgatta, E. F. Sidesteps toward a nonspecial theory. *Psychological Review*, 1954, *61*, 343–352.

Salzinger, K. Pleasing linguists: A parable. *Journal of Verbal Learning and Verbal Behavior*, 1970, *9*, 725–727.

Salzinger, K. Psychology applied: A dream. In K. Salzinger & F. L. Denmark (Eds.). *Psychology: The state of the art. Annals of the New York Academy of Sciences*, 1978, *309*, 95–97.

Author Index

Numbers in italics refer to the pages on which the complete references are listed.

A

Abbagnano, N., *257*
Adler, A., 279, *303*
Adler, H. E., 19, *21*
Adorno, T. W., 87, 94, *96*
Alexander, P., 231, 233, *257*
Allegård, A., 156, *172*
Allport, G. W., 32, *40*, 67, 68, 69, 70, 71, 72, 73, 74, 75, 76, 77, *78*, 82, 91, 93, *96*
Ames, A., Jr., 239, *258*
Anderson, N. H., 19, *21*
Ansbacher, H. L., 279, 280, 281, 282, *303*
Ansbacher, R. R., 279, 280, 281, 282, *303*
Anthony, E. J., 310, *314*
Arnold, W. J., 207, *257*
Atkinson, R. C., 20, *22*
Aune, B., 236, *257*
Ayala, F. J., 152, *172*

B

Baird, J. C., 20, *21*
Bakan, D., 287, 293, *303*
Bakan, M., 83, *96*
Balance, W. D. G., 13, *21*, 26, *40*
Baldwin, J. M., 83, 88, 93, *96*, 152, *172*
Bandura, A., 206, *257*

Bateson, G., 92, *96*
Baum, W. M., 217, 227, 230, 234, *257*
Baxter, R., 105, *121*
Beattie, J., 108, *121*
Becker, C. L., 33, *40*
Begelman, D., 233, *258*
Beilin, H., 308, *314*
Bem, D. J., 206, *258*
Bennett, M. L., 211, 236, *258*
Bentley, M., 49, *53*, 54
Bergmann, G., 16, *21*
Berlyne, D. E., 308, *314*
Bernoulli, D., 18, *21*
Bernstein, D. J., 232, *258*
Bertocci, P. A., 71, *78*
Blackmore, J. T., 228, 229, 231, *258*
Blakey, R., 118, *121*
Blasi, A., 92, 94, *96*
Blough, D. S., 19, *21*, 23
Blumenthal, A. L., 26, 28, *40*
Boden, M. A., 207, 208, 211, 218, *258*
Boring, E. G., 12, 15, *21*, 26, *40*, *40*, 49, 50, *53*, 206, 209, 213, 215, 219, 221, 223, 225, 227, 228, 237, 238, 240, 241, 248, *258*
Bottome, P., 279, *303*
Bower, G. H., 250, 251, 252, 253, 254, *259*
Bower, T., 325, *327*
Bowers, K. S., 187, *189*
Bradley, J., 231, 233, *258*

345

Subject Index